D1616473

SIX-STRING STORIES

BY ERIC CLAPTON

THE CROSSROADS GUITARS

SIX-STRING STORIES

BY ERIC CLAPTON

THE CROSSROADS GUITARS

GENESIS PUBLICATIONS

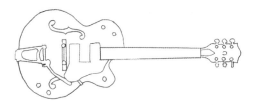

For all those who work, or have worked, at Crossroads Antigua
and to those who finally found the courage, through despair,
to take the first step of recovery through its doors – I dedicate this
book to you...

Whether you have found true sobriety, or just a moment's respite
from the hell of alcoholism, you are part of my life's dream...

Also to my friend David W, who has helped me to keep moving
for the last 20 years...
Thank you...

ERIC C

This edition first published in 2021
by Genesis Publications

Copyright © 2012, 2021 Genesis Publications Ltd

10 9 8 7 6 5 4 3 2 1

ISBN: 978-1-905662-68-5

Printed and bound in Italy by Grafiche Milani

This book first appeared as a limited edition
of 2,000 copies, signed by Eric Clapton

Genesis Publications Ltd
Genesis House, 2 Jenner Road
Guildford, England, GU1 3PL

Fine Books and Prints Since 1974
GENESIS–PUBLICATIONS.COM

www.genesis-publications.com

CONTENTS

Playlist: recordings
featuring the guitar
Gigs: performances
with the guitar
Highlights: significant
dates or tracks

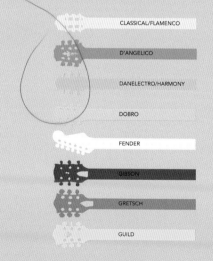

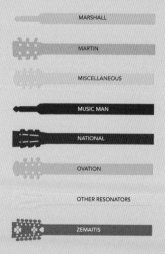

CLASSICAL/FLAMENCO

D'ANGELICO

DANELECTRO/HARMONY

DOBRO

FENDER

GIBSON

GRETSCH

GUILD

MARSHALL

MARTIN

MISCELLANEOUS

MUSIC MAN

NATIONAL

OVATION

OTHER RESONATORS

ZEMAITIS

ERIC Funnily enough there are
whole brands I didn't go anywhere
near as I'd never really developed
or instigated an interest in them.

AS AN AVID ROCK OR BLUES FAN I WOULD LOOK AT ALL THE PICTURES IN THIS BOOK. For example, you can see what Robert Johnson was playing because I finally ended up getting one of those guitars. I never really saw myself as a 'collector'. Otherwise there would have been a whole different atmosphere about these guitars. The collectors I've met have completely different philosophies about what they're doing and why they're doing it.

I've been pawn shop shopping all these years; all my life I've been going on the road and looking. When I go into a pawn shop there might be something that looks really good or fits a description of what I'm looking for, but if the guitar doesn't feel good when I pick it up, I put it down again. If it hasn't got something in it already, or it doesn't feel like it wants to go somewhere, I'm not interested. It's either there or it isn't. It isn't just the way it feels but the way it sounds too. Sometimes you might not know what you want from the sound of a guitar and then you'll play it and it's like you've never heard something like that before. That first sound is very inspiring; a lot of songs are born out of that.

MAKING THE TRANSITION FROM ONE GUITAR TO THE NEXT CAN COME FROM ANY DIRECTION. It can be triggered by a need to hear another sound. It might be that I've seen or heard somebody playing a guitar that I want to emulate. It might be that I'm listening to a song and think, 'I want one of them; I like the way it sounds on the record.' The musical side coupled with the image governs it. The image is always a big part of it, even if it's a period in time. It doesn't always mean that I'll stay there. Often I will start out with a really broad view of what I'm looking for and then narrow it down to the one that I think will be the most useful to me or the one that I'm most comfortable with.

These guitars have been really good tools; they're not just museum pieces. They all have a soul and they all come alive. They're playing instruments – they're to be played. What's clear is that these things don't really have a value. I don't know much about the auction business; it seems to be the nature of the game that they're quite conservative when it comes to putting the estimate in, but nevertheless, these things went through the roof.

IT COMES BACK TO THE CAUSE. If I had sold these guitars just to line my pockets, they wouldn't have even made the reserve prices. There were buyers who knew about recovery and knew that these auctions were a genuine attempt to do some good and then there was another level of buyer who just felt OK about putting money towards charity.

Crossroads is obviously very focused and specific and probably attracts a fairly specialised group of people, but nevertheless what seems to happen is it attracts a desire to do good, and we're very fortunate because of that. Last year many treatment centres closed in England because they couldn't afford to stay open. There's a lack of interest now whereas in the 1990s it was very popular to try and get sober. It seems to be a cycle – it may come round again. There are really low periods, but we're solvent and that's because of these auctions

I'm going to retire one day in the near distant future and it may not be possible to do this again. There isn't another auction planned as I'm actually working with a skeleton collection now. I bought a couple of guitars on eBay recently – actually very good buys, sight unseen. Fender and Gibson provide most of my guitars, like the reproduction models. So my guitars have really all gone.

Maybe people would like to have a regular Crossroads festival. The festival itself, like the treatment centre, could develop a life of its own. I would love that; that would be a proper legacy, something I could be proud of. The festivals look like a commercial venture but they're really driven by a very genuine intent. I think that's why the artists come too. A lot of them are either affected by alcoholism or addiction or have family that are and it means something to them, and I'm very proud of that.

ONE BY ONE THESE GUITARS WERE CHAPTERS OF MY LIFE. Some of the guitars were incredibly important, and they were the ones that probably did the best in the auctions because they had known provenance to fans and collectors. I had to be fairly conscientious about everything that went into the sales in terms of whether or not they were really viable parts of my history. Every one of them got played a little bit, but some were really vital.

The guitars did a tour before the first auction. I saw them in New York and there were celebrities there, people I had no idea would be interested in that kind of thing. As I was talking to them I was looking at these guitars that we were all talking about and thinking, 'I remember buying that for $60.' It was quite overwhelming to see them evolve into this collection, all together in one room. Each one of them had an important effect on my life and I was actually having to let go of not just one of them, but all of them at the same time. I'd be talking to people while part of me was beginning a mourning process.

I WATCHED THE 1999 CHRISTIE'S SALE FROM A REHEARSAL, LIVE ON SOMEONE'S LAPTOP, AND BROWNIE GOT A STANDING OVATION. It still chokes me up now. They did mean a lot and they still do. Overall it was quite a traumatic experience, though I would have played it down to anyone at the time. It's the cause that really makes the difference because I wouldn't have parted with Blackie and Brownie for anything else.

When I asked Brian Roylance at Genesis Publications to help me out with Crossroads, way back, he asked me, 'Are you willing to go to any lengths?' I said, 'Well yeah,' not even really realising what that meant. But then I found out! The philosophy was, 'I will go to any lengths to try and make this known and available,' and the other side of that coin was, 'If we get one person sober then it's all been worthwhile.' The Crossroads Centre is still going, so it all had some substance, and that made parting with my guitars OK.

The guitars are things of great beauty, but I remember learning something when I was a kid. I was always lusting after things and thinking, 'When I get this everything will be all right, when I get that things will be different.' Then, at some point in my late teens, I had a realisation. I said to myself, 'Well you know you'll probably never get one of them but you can still enjoy it.' Maybe it was a car or something... I looked at it and thought, 'It's still great; you can still love it without having to own it.' That was an early wake-up call for me and I've been applying that all my life.

THIS COLLECTION IS LIKE ART – IT'S VALUELESS UNTIL THERE'S AN INTEREST IN IT. I can sit and look at a painting for hours that someone else might not have any interest in. The value is sort of irrelevant. I bought Brownie for $100.

At the risk of being immodest I'd say I've got a pretty good eye for guitars. I naturally want to research things that I have a passion for, like painting or music. If I become interested in Gibson guitars I want to know everything I can find out about the peak of their production – in which period they were being made the best and what their philosophy was at that time. I get really absorbed by it all and then apply that to my choices, so I think that what you will find in this book is that a lot of these guitars are probably the zenith of that model or that maker.

It's a rock'n'roll and blues collection. It's not necessarily for jazz musicians or classical musicians, or even for folk musicians, but on the whole I've applied my passion to the way I've bought and collected these things, so I think that's quite resonant and something other people might find they have in common.

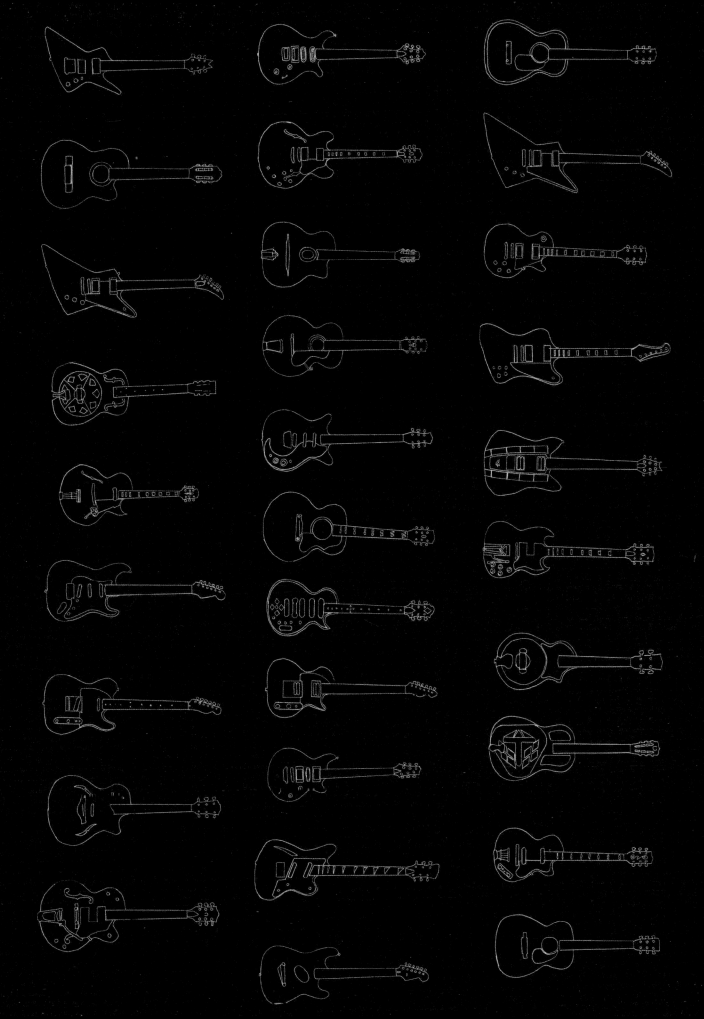

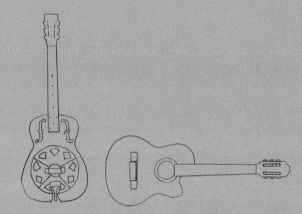

THE CROSSROADS GUITARS

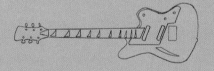

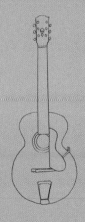

ERIC Every guitar is like an individual instrument. It's the same regardless of whether the guitar is a Gibson Les Paul, a Fender Strat or a Martin acoustic. Each individual instrument seems to have this character and in-built virtuosity of its own. If you're lucky enough to pick one up and play it and own it, it can take you another ten miles down the road. Once it stops taking you down the road it's time to move on to the next one. My career has been divided up with those instruments.

It's not about technique, it's not about what kind of instrument you play or how many strings it's got or how fast you can play or how loud or quiet it is; it's about how it feels and how it makes you feel when you play. Listen, listen, listen, and go back as far as you dare. That's what I still do today.

FIRST ACOUSTIC GUITAR – HOYER

Since most of the music I liked best was guitar music, I decided I would like to learn to play. The instrument I set my eyes on was a Hoyer, which was made in Germany and cost about £2. I was only 13 and I talked my grandparents into buying it for me. The guitar was very shiny and somehow virginal. It was like a piece of equipment from another universe – so glamorous – and as I tried to strum it, I felt like I was really crossing into grown-up territory. It was an odd instrument; it looked like a Spanish guitar, but instead of nylon, it had steel strings. I couldn't really get the hang of it. I tried and tried and tried but got nowhere with it. It was a very cheap guitar and most cheap guitars, as anyone will tell you who tries to play one, hurt to play. It sounded nice, but it was just such hard work I gave up. So I started when I was 13 and gave up when I was 13-and-a-half.

If you buy something cheap, it will actually inhibit your progress. It's probably best to go in at the deep end and buy something really good like a Fender or a Martin. You will find in their catalogue that there are lower-priced models that will still have the quality of workmanship, so you can make leaps and bounds in the earliest part of your trying. I think it's important to buy good, quality merchandise because it will enhance the playing and it will sound better.

SECOND ACOUSTIC GUITAR – WASHBURN

I tried playing with the Hoyer acoustic and I didn't get very far with that. The first guitar I ever had that had any real substance or value I bought in a market in Kingston, also for the amazing price of two quid. I remember I saw this very odd-looking guitar hanging up on one of the stalls and intuitively I knew it was good.

It was a George Washburn and it was what they call a 'parlour guitar'. Around the turn of the 20th century they were making these instruments for home entertainment. It was small, almost like a ukelele, but it was quite loud. They had copied the Martin neck – which was a V-shape at the back – and it had that narrow waist, so from then on that was the shape I always wanted. The 000-28 narrow body is what I would still name as being my favourite shape in an acoustic body. There was a painting of a naked woman stuck on the back of it which I had to peel off, but at last I had a proper guitar meant for folk music. Then I went through the whole thing of playing in pubs and everything with this guitar.

LOT 20 CHRISTIE'S 1999

Serial No: 376
Body: Laminated maple, hollow, spruce top, bound, single round cutaway, natural finish
Neck: Maple, 22 frets, bound ebony fingerboard with bow-tie inlays
Headstock: Inlaid floral motif
Bridge: Ebony with four saddle slots, nickel-plated brass trapeze tailpiece
Pickguard: Imitation tortoiseshell
Pickups: Two Hofner high-sensitivity black bar single-coil
Controls: Two volume
Switches: Two pickup on/off, rhythm/solo
Case: Black hardshell contour case with blue plush lining and handwritten adhesive paper label 'Hofner #376'

Imported American electric guitars were prohibitively expensive in England during the late 1950s, but instruments made in Europe by companies such as the German Hofner company provided a more affordable, high-quality alternative. George Harrison, John Lennon, and Paul McCartney all played Hofner Club 40 guitars early in their musical careers; Ritchie Blackmore's second guitar was a Club 50; and David Gilmour and Justin Hayward both bought the Club 60 – Hofner's top-of-the-line electric model – during the early 1960s.

Clapton's former manager Roger Forrester gave Eric this Hofner Club 60 as a Christmas present in the 1990s.

Hurtwood Edge
Surrey, UK

ERIC I remember seeing this model as the top-of-the-range guitar in the Hofner catalogue when I was 13 years old. When I was a little kid they were kind of big. They were rock and roll guitars; everyone wanted a Hofner.

ERIC Soul music was rare. The merest glimpse of Bo Diddley
or Chuck Berry would send me into frenzies of delight. At first
I played exactly like Chuck Berry for six or seven months. You
couldn't have told the difference when I was with The Yardbirds.
If you want to play rock and roll – or any upbeat number – and
you want to take a guitar ride, you end up playing like Chuck
because there is very little other choice. There's not a lot of other
ways to play rock and roll other than the way Chuck plays it;
he's really laid the law down.

When I listened to Bo Diddley or Chuck Berry, I'd hear slow songs that had intense
emotional appeal. And then I'd find out that they were cover songs that these guys had
done in tribute to people like Muddy Waters or other guys like that. I kind of became an
archivist. I started to research on my own and would go around record stores and look
for obscure blues records to educate myself on the history of music. All of it has influenced
me in time; all of it has taken part of my attention and contributed to what I feel I am as
a musician.

Fox Theater, St. Louis
Missouri, USA
Oct. 16, 1986

On stage with Chuck Berry
at Chuck Berry's 60th
birthday party.

LOT 83 CHRISTIE'S 1999

Serial No: A 23700
Factory Order No: V5305 2
Body: Flamed maple, bound thinline, single round Venetian cutaway, bound f-holes, natural finish
Neck: Maple, 22 frets, bound rosewood fingerboard with double parallelogram inlays
Headstock: Crown inlay
Bridge: Rosewood, gold-plated 'W-shaped' tubular trapeze tailpiece with pointed-end crossbar
Pickguard: Black five-ply (black/white/black/white/black)
Pickups: Two P-90 single-coil
Controls: Two volume, two tone
Switches: Three-position pickup selector
Case: Brown hardshell contour case with pink plush lining and handwritten swing label "56 E.S. 350.T # 23700' and adhesive paper label similarly inscribed

Although Chuck Berry is generally associated with the red Gibson ES-355 that he had played since the 1960s, he made rock and roll history with an ES-350TN similar to this guitar. Berry purchased his ES-350TN in 1956 from Ludwig's Music in St. Louis, Missouri, and used that guitar to record several of his biggest early singles, including 'Roll Over Beethoven', 'Too Much Monkey Business' and 'You Can't Catch Me'. Promotional photos of Berry playing his ES-350TN, dressed in a black tuxedo and performing his signature duck walk move, became iconic images of the birth of rock and roll.

Gibson introduced the ES-350T as a less costly alternative to the Byrdland with less elaborate binding, inlays and hardware but otherwise identical features, including the short 23½ inch scale. In 1957 the ES-350T was one of Gibson's first guitars equipped with their newly designed humbucking pickups (nicknamed PAFs).

Clapton bought this ES-350TN as a tribute to Berry, who is one of his musical influences and guitar heroes. He played this guitar onstage with Berry at one of Berry's 60th birthday concerts at the Fox Theater on October 16th, 1986, performing the songs 'Wee Wee Hours', and 'Rock and Roll Music', 'Hoochie Coochie Man' and 'School Days' with Etta James on vocals. The concert was filmed for *Hail! Hail! Rock'n'Roll*. Clapton says that he hoped to impress Berry by bringing a guitar like Chuck used to play on stage, but Chuck didn't even notice the guitar.

ERIC This guitar was like the Holy Grail for me. It's the fat-bodied guitar that Chuck Berry played in all the publicity photographs of him duck-walking: a Gibson ES-350. It's got those black P-90 pickups.

Playlist:
Hail! Hail! Rock'n'Roll, (film and album), 1987
Highlight:
Hail! Hail! Rock'n'Roll: Chuck Berry's 60th Birthday Celebration Fox Theater, St. Louis Missouri, USA Oct. 16, 1986

Serial No: 29482
Body: Ash, translucent blonde finish
Neck: Maple with skunk-stripe truss rod routing, 21 frets, maple fingerboard with dot inlays, neck date 8-58 written in pencil
Bridge: Gold-plated synchronised tremolo
Pickguard: White single-ply
Pickups: Three single-coil
Controls: Volume, two tone
Switches: Three-position pickup selector
Case: Tweed hardshell case with yellow plush lining and handwritten adhesive paper label 'Fender "Mary Kay" [sic] Strat #29482'

In 1956 Fender made a Stratocaster with gold-plated hardware and a white/beige blonde finish. The promotional photo for this model featured the 'First Lady of Rock and Roll', Mary Kaye of the Mary Kaye Trio, holding the guitar. This generated considerable demand for the model, which became known as the 'Mary Kaye Stratocaster'. In the February 1957 issue of *The Music Trades* magazine Fender announced a Strat with these features with a list price of $330, which was $55.50 more than a sunburst Strat cost. Ironically the guitar Mary Kaye was photographed with was just a prop, and she never owned a blonde Strat with gold hardware until Fender gave her a Mary Kaye reissue model in 2002.

Clapton sought a Mary Kaye Stratocaster for years before he finally found this 1958 example, which was used while recording his *Pilgrim* album.

Playlist:
Pilgrim, 1998
Gigs:
Royal Albert Hall
London, UK
Feb. 18-Mar. 3, 1996

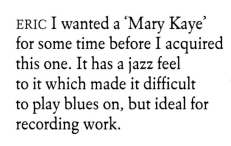

ERIC I wanted a 'Mary Kaye' for some time before I acquired this one. It has a jazz feel to it which made it difficult to play blues on, but ideal for recording work.

Opposite:
Palais des Sports
Paris, France
Sept. 22, 1970

Eric Clapton playing a similar Mary Kaye Strat with a rosewood fingerboard. This was a guest appearance with Buddy Guy and Junior Wells, supporting The Rolling Stones.

1994 FENDER STRATOCASTER ERIC CLAPTON SIGNATURE MODEL

EST: $6,000 - $8,000   PRICE: $50,000

LOT 13 CHRISTIE'S 1999

Serial No: VO66640
Body: Alder, Olympic White finish
Neck: Maple with skunk-stripe truss rod routing, 22 frets, maple fingerboard with dot inlays
Headstock: Back of headstock with printed transfer 'Custom Built Larry L.Brooks FENDER U.S.A.'
Bridge: Blocked synchronised tremolo
Pickguard: White single-ply
Pickups: Three Gold Fender Lace Sensors
Controls: Master volume, two tone, TBX active circuitry
Switches: Five-position pickup selector with white switch tip
Case: Tweed rectangular hardshell case with red plush lining and handwritten tie-on label 'White E.C. Strat V.O66640' and adhesive paper label similarly inscribed

Inspired by the 1962 Olympic White Fender Stratocaster that is one of Jimmie Vaughan's signature guitars, Clapton ordered this Strat and an identical spare from Fender's Custom Shop as a tribute to Vaughan. One of those two guitars was Clapton's main stage guitar from 1994 to 1996. He can be seen playing one of these Olympic White Strats in the *A Tribute to Stevie Ray Vaughan* concert DVD, which was filmed on May 11th and 12th, 1995, in Austin, Texas. This guitar and its companion were also used on various film scores, including *The Van*.

Playlist:
The Van, 1996
A Tribute to Stevie Ray Vaughan, 1995
Gigs:
World Tours 1994-1996
Highlights:
Stevie Ray Vaughan Tribute Concert
Austin Music Hall, Austin Texas, USA
May 12, 1995

Opposite:
Clapton playing one of these guitars at The Royal Albert Hall in 1996.

1994 FENDER STRATOCASTER ERIC CLAPTON SIGNATURE MODEL

EST: $6,000 - $8,000   PRICE: $50,000

LOT 35 CHRISTIE'S 1999

Serial No: V066445
Body: Alder, Olympic White finish
Neck: Maple with skunk-stripe truss rod routing, 22 frets, maple fingerboard with dot inlays
Headstock: Back of headstock with printed transfer 'Custom Built Larry L. Brooks FENDER U.S.A.'
Bridge: Blocked synchronised tremolo
Pickguard: White single-ply
Pickups: Three Gold Fender Lace Sensors
Controls: Master volume, two tone, TBX active circuitry
Switches: Five-position pickup selector with white switch tip
Case: Tweed rectangular hardshell case with red plush lining and handwritten adhesive paper label 'Fender Olympic White Strat #V066445 C.Shop. E.C. (L.EL)'

This guitar is a pair to the cream Strat (shown above).

Playlist:
The Van, 1996
A Tribute to Stevie Ray Vaughan, 1995
Gigs:
World Tours 1994-1996
Highlights:
Stevie Ray Vaughan Tribute Concert
Austin Music Hall, Austin Texas, USA
May 12, 1995

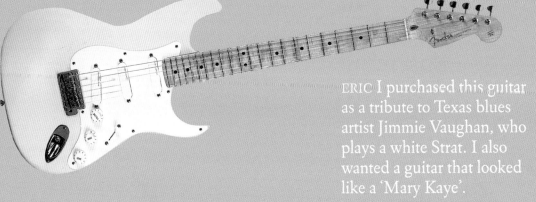

ERIC I purchased this guitar as a tribute to Texas blues artist Jimmie Vaughan, who plays a white Strat. I also wanted a guitar that looked like a 'Mary Kaye'.

ERIC I'd read things on the back of album covers like, 'rock and roll has its roots in blues', and stuff like that. And so I thought, what's all that about? I'll have to find out...

I was always mainly attracted by musicians from the Mississippi Delta – before I even knew they were from there. There was something about the quality and style that set them apart for me, from any other region. I was drawn to the Delta sound in whatever form it came – even when it got electric and those musicians moved up to Chicago, it was still them that I wanted to hear.

The music of Muddy Waters was the first that really got to me. He meant a great deal to me, and his music still does today, probably more than anybody else's. Whenever I've lost my way and want to know exactly what I should be doing, I always turn to Muddy Waters. I always find in him a great well of spiritual comfort – the man is strong. And that is where I belong.

In The Yardbirds we were doing songs by Snooky Pryor or Eddie Taylor, who were more the Chicago kind of sidemen. If we did a classic Freddie King, B.B. King or Buddy Guy song, we would seem to be paying homage. I wanted to be in Freddie King's band or Buddy Guy's band, that's the band I wanted to be in – the real thing. I didn't want to be in a white rock band, I didn't want to be in a black rock band, I wanted to be in a black blues band. But if we did a Snooky Pryor song or 'Wish You Would' by Billy Boy Arnold it sounded like The Yardbirds, because nobody knew who those guys were.

I used to think that I could make any kind of music, but the guitar playing would always be the blues. If I took a solo, I would always make sure that I could find some place to put the blues in. Then I would know, even if nobody else did, that I still had one foot on the path.

The blessing for me was that, early on in my career, I decided where my focus should be – and it is always to be true to the music, to think about what I can do to contribute to music as an art form, as a principle, as a tree of life. I think once that was established, it made everything else easy because my focus is always on, 'Is this good enough?' Not, 'Will it sell?' Always, 'Is this good enough? Is it good enough for me to live with and for the future of music? Does this serve the purpose of music?'

My purpose has always been to keep the blues tradition at the centre of whatever I do. That's always the core. To honour their memory and the beauty and tradition of their music. The most direct experience I have in music is listening to Little Walter, Muddy, Freddie King and B.B.

The blues is the thing I've turned to, the thing that has given me inspiration and relief. In all of the trials and tribulations of my life I've always had this incredible, secure place to go to with the blues.

LOT 30 CHRISTIE'S 1999

Serial No: 85566
Body: Maple back and sides, spruce top, f-holes, sunburst finish
Neck: Mahogany, 19 frets, bound ebony fingerboard with dot inlays
Bridge: Ebony, nickel-plated 'raised diamond' trapeze tailpiece
Case: Black hardshell contour case with green velvet lining and handwritten tie-on label 'Gibson L3 1928 #85566' and adhesive paper label similarly inscribed

Although the factory label inside of this guitar identifies it as an L-3 model, the L-3 typically featured either a round or oval soundhole and not f-holes like this example. Even more unusual is the fact that the label is a 'master model' label, which normally was used only on instruments designed by Lloyd Loar, such as F-5 mandolins and L-5 guitars made between 1922 and 1924. This guitar's f-holes, 'master model' label and 'Style spl L3' designation (with 'spl' meaning 'special') suggest that this instrument was a one-of-a-kind special order.

A mutual Mississippi blues fan gave this guitar to Eric as a gift.

LOT 31 CHRISTIE'S 1999

Body: Mahogany back and sides, spruce top, f-holes, sunburst finish
Neck: Mahogany, 19 frets, bound rosewood fingerboard with crown inlays
Bridge: Rosewood, nickel-plated trapeze tailpiece
Headstock: Metal truss rod cover
Case: Black hardshell contour case with pink plush lining and handwritten tie-on label 'Gibson L.50 S/Burst N.S.N.' and adhesive paper label similarly inscribed

This Gibson L-50 is far from stock. Its pickguard is missing; the trapeze tailpiece was replaced; and the metal truss rod cover is not original. The serial number and label are also missing, so it is difficult to pinpoint its exact production date. However, the guitar has the undeniable worn-in charm of a player's instrument that was used often because it sounded good.

Clapton purchased this L-50 because it reminded him of the Harmony archtop that Snooks Eaglin was pictured playing on the cover of his *New Orleans Street Singer* album.

ERIC 'Alberta' is an old Snooks Eaglin song. He was a great, great player and singer who recorded on the streets of New Orleans. The variety of his repertoire was absolutely amazing, but that song, 'Alberta', was accessible to me as a beginning guitar player because it consists of three chords and just strumming. It just lodged in my head as a very sentimental song, and part of my early influences. I bought this guitar because I wanted to sound like him.

1928 GIBSON L-3

Ocean Way Studios
Los Angeles
California, USA
Aug. 11, 2005

Clapton playing a late
1920s sunburst Gibson
L-5 acoustic archtop.

LOT 26 CHRISTIE'S 1999

Serial No: 96308
Factory Order No: 1157F
Body: Maple, arched spruce top, f-holes, sunburst finish
Neck: Maple, 20 frets, bound rosewood fingerboard with double parallelogram inlays
Headstock: Double-handled vase and curlicues inlay
Bridge: Rosewood, hinged nickel-plated 'raised diamond and arrowheads' trapeze tailpiece with pointed ends
Pickguard: Imitation tortoiseshell bound pickguard
Case: Black hardshell contour case with green felt lining and handwritten tie-on label 'Gibson L.7. '40. Sunburst. Ser #96308' and adhesive paper label similarly inscribed

The L-7 was one of Gibson's least-expensive large archtop models, but it still featured a variety of fancy appointments normally found on much pricier models, such as its double parallelogram fingerboard inlays and nickel-plated 'raised diamond and arrowheads' trapeze tailpiece with pointed ends. The double-handled vase and curlicues inlay on this L-7's headstock is particularly unusual, with the curlicues joined together to form a heart or vase shape instead of separated like they were on earlier examples.

Clapton admired sunburst guitars from a young age, and purchased this guitar as a collector's piece later in his career.

LOT 40 CHRISTIE'S 1999

Body: Maple back and sides, spruce top, f-holes, sunburst finish
Neck: Mahogany, 19 frets, rosewood fingerboard with dot inlays
Bridge: Rosewood, nickel-plated trapeze tailpiece
Pickguard: Imitation tortoiseshell
Pickups: Metal-covered single-coil with adjustable polepieces
Controls: One volume, one tone
Case: Tweed hardshell contour case with handwritten adhesive paper label 'Gibson E.S.100 one S.Burst'

Gibson developed their first budget electric model, the ES-100, in 1938, one year after the introduction of their first electric Spanish guitar model, the ES-150. Sometime during 1940 the placement of the ES-100 model's single-coil pickup was moved from the neck position to the bridge position. Gibson changed the model name to ES-125 during 1941, and production was suspended from 1942 to 1946 due to World War II. When production of the ES-125 resumed in 1946, the body size was increased to 16¼ inches and the pickup was moved back to a position near the neck.

LOT 3 CHRISTIE'S 1999

Serial No: A-9089
Factory Order No: 9111-34
Body: Maple back and sides, Sitka spruce top, sunburst finish, 16 inches wide
Neck: Mahogany, 19 frets, bound rosewood fingerboard with double parallelogram inlays
Headstock: Pearl script Gibson logo and pearl crown inlay
Bridge: Rosewood 'belly' pin bridge with pearl Maltese cross inlays
Pickguard: Imitation tortoiseshell
Case: Brown hardshell contour case with handwritten tie-on label ''50s J-185 Gibson' and adhesive paper label similarly inscribed

Gibson introduced the J-185 in 1951 and produced the model until 1959. A compact and more affordable alternative to Gibson's flashy J-200 model, the J-185 was a favourite of several blues guitarists, like Skip James. Eric bought this guitar primarily for collection purposes instead of for playing. Of the 77 J-185 guitars that Gibson made in 1951, 66 of them had sunburst finishes while the remainder had natural finishes.

ERIC I love the look of this guitar.

LOT 54 CHRISTIE'S 1999

Serial No: A10586
Factory Order No: 7613 2
Body: Maple back and sides, spruce top, round Venetian cutaway, bound f-holes, sunburst finish
Neck: Maple, 20 frets, bound ebony fingerboard with split-block pearl inlays
Headstock: Pearl Gibson script logo, split diamond inlay
Bridge: Rosewood, gold-plated Y-shaped trapeze tailpiece
Pickguard: Multi-bound imitation tortoiseshell
Additional: Printed set list 'Clapton/Cocker Set '93'
Case: Brown hardshell contour case with pink plush lining and handwritten tie-on label 'Gibson Super 400 c '52 Sunburst. Ser # A.10586' and paper adhesive label similarly inscribed

Introduced in 1934, the Super 400 was Gibson's top-of-the-line acoustic archtop model. While it remained Gibson's flagship instrument for many years, it underwent numerous changes and additions, including the introduction of the Super 400P 'Premier' cutaway model in 1939 (renamed the Super 400C in 1950) and the Super 400CES electric model in 1951. Production of the Super 400 was very limited. In 1952 Gibson made only 71 Super 400 guitars in various configurations, and only ten of those were Super 400C guitars like this example.

While Clapton loved the looks of this sunburst Super 400C, he found it too large to play comfortably.

ERIC I'm too small for that guitar.

ME & MY GUITAR

LOT 55 CHRISTIE'S 1999

Serial No: A25630
Factory Order No: V 7371 1
Body: Maple back and sides, spruce top, round Venetian cutaway, f-holes, sunburst finish
Neck: Maple, 20 frets, bound rosewood fingerboard with double parallelogram inlays
Headstock: Crown peghead inlay
Bridge: Rosewood, nickel-plated Y-shaped trapeze tailpiece
Pickguard: Multi-bound black
Case: Brown hardshell contour case with pink plush lining and handwritten tie-on label 'Gibson Super 300c '57 Sunburst AC Ser# A.25630' and paper adhesive label similarly inscribed

The Super 300 may have been designed as a plain version of Gibson's Super 400, but it is still a stunningly beautiful archtop guitar. Gibson introduced the Super 300 in 1948 at the same time as post-war production of the Super 400 resumed. The Super 300C model featuring a cutaway came along in 1954, and by the following year the Super 300C was the only variant of this model that Gibson produced.

Despite having the same large 18-inch body dimensions as the Super 400C, Clapton found this guitar more practical to play than his Super 400C.

LOT 36 CHRISTIE'S 1999

Factory Order No: S 613 13
Body: Laminated maple, bound thinline with single sharp Florentine cutaway, f-holes, sunburst finish
Neck: Mahogany, 20 frets, bound rosewood fingerboard with dot inlays
Bridge: Rosewood, nickel-plated trapeze tailpiece
Pickguard: Black five-ply (black/white/black/white/black)
Pickups: Two P-90 single-coil
Controls: Two volume, two tone
Switches: Three-position pickup selector
Case: Brown hardshell contour case lined in pink plush and handwritten paper adhesive label 'Gibson – 225 Sunburst #613 13'

Gibson's thinline guitars were originally designed as a compromise between the rich, resonant sounds of a hollowbody archtop guitar (without the bulky body depth) and the compact comfort of a solidbody guitar (without the extra weight). The concept was conceived by Gibson endorsees Hank Garland and Billy Byrd and incorporated in the Byrdland model they co-designed, introduced in 1955. Around the same time Gibson also produced the ES-225, with similar thinline dimensions but with modest appointments that kept the price more affordable. The ES-225 quickly became one of Gibson's most successful electric models during the mid to late 1950s.

The rosewood bridge and trapeze tailpiece on this guitar are not stock. The ES-225 originally featured a combination trapeze bridge/tailpiece designed by Les Paul, as found on Gibson's ES-295 and 1952 Les Paul models.

Factory Order No:
R 6784 5
Body: Maple, hollow
thinline, double cutaway,
f-holes, sunburst finish
Neck: Mahogany, 22 frets,
bound rosewood
fingerboard with dot inlays
Bridge: Nickel-plated
Tune-o-matic,
nickel-plated 'raised
diamond' trapeze tailpiece
Pickguard: Black five-ply
(black/white/black/
white/black)
Pickups: One P-90
single-coil
Controls: One volume,
one tone
Case: Brown imitation
alligator-skin contour case
with handwritten adhesive
paper label 'Gibson
330 – sunburst 1.P.90'

Although the single-pickup Gibson ES-330T initially outsold the double-pickup version (the ES-330TD) when it was introduced in 1959, demand for the double-pickup model increased significantly over subsequent years. As a result, production of the ES-330T decreased to 151 units in 1963 – the year that it was discontinued – while Gibson shipped 521 ES-330TD guitars in 1963 and 1,231 units in 1964. The unorthodox placement of its single P-90 pickup in the centre position is likely the cause of its decreased popularity.

ERIC I knew they had electric guitars in America; I'd seen them on record covers. But it wasn't until I saw Alexis Korner at the Marquee, when I was about 15, that I thought an electric guitar might be available to me.

I don't think anyone had seen a Gibson ES-335 in London, but Alexis had a Kay. Even in my addled consciousness at that time, I was aware that this was a cheap version of the ES-335. I was on the con to get one bought for me by my grandparents, so my grandmother came with me to Bell's in Surbiton – where one of these was in the window – and she bought it on the never-never.

Ricky Tick Club
Windsor, Berkshire, UK
1963

Eric Clapton, Robin Mason, Terry Brennan, Tom McGuinness, Ben Palmer. The Roosters played private parties and fewer than two dozen gigs, primarily in Greater London. Venues included the Carfax Ballroom in Oxford, the Ricky Tick Clubs in Kingston, Reading, West Wickham and Windsor, the Wooden Bridge Hotel in Guildford, the Jazz Cellar in Kingston, The Scene in Ham Yard, Soho and Uncle Bonnie's Chinese Jazz Club in Brighton.

FIRST ELECTRIC GUITAR – KAY JAZZ II

ERIC The Kay captured my heart, but there was always something kind of disappointing about it. It was never the real ticket. One thing that wasn't quite right with it was the colour. Though advertised as 'Sunburst', which would have been a golden orange going to dark red at the edges, it was more yellowy, going to a sort of pink, so as soon as I got it home I covered it with black Fablon. But trying to apply Fablon to a curved surface, man, it must have had ripples all over it. Can you imagine what it sounded like after that? Now, because a lot of the Chicago blues guys played Kays and Harmonys, they have a different provenance. At the time I just thought, 'I wish this was a Gibson so I'm going to try and make it look like one,' and the quick solution was to try and cover it.

It wasn't a very good guitar. It was very heavy and unbalanced and it didn't stand up too well. I think the neck bowed, and it didn't seem to me that you could do much about it. It had a truss rod, but it wasn't that effective, and the action ended up being incredibly high, which you couldn't lower without touching the fret bars. We hadn't bought an amplifier, so I could only play it acoustically and fantasise about what it would sound like.

It wasn't long after I got this guitar that I think I did a little show in Richmond, with just me and someone else. I met up with Tom McGuinness, who was going to get involved with a band, and I knew just about enough to be able to play and keep that end of it. So I got involved in The Roosters, and that was a good feeling.

We did 'Boom Boom' and a couple of other John Lee Hooker things, 'Hoochie Coochie Man' and some others by Muddy. We did whatever we could get on records, and some rock and roll things like 'Slow Down' by Larry Williams, because you had to have the odd rock and roll number in there.

The Roosters were a tiny outfit, with virtually no equipment. I had the Kay then and I did have the Gibson amp, but we started off all going through the one Selmer – guitar, vocals, keyboard all went through one amplifier.

We rehearsed more than we played – I remember the rehearsals being above a pub in Kingston. We did a gig every now and then, mostly in upstairs rooms of pubs. I think we played the Jazz Cellar in Kingston and maybe a couple of seaside places, but it was so, so chaotic and amateurish. I don't know how we got it together at all really. It was more about the excitement of meeting like-minded people. There was really nobody in Ripley that had any interest in blues.

Some of the band had day jobs that were more important to them than the band. Practical considerations brought the band down. But, by that time, I had no other interests at all. I practised a lot. After The Roosters, I got a job with Tom McGuinness in another band, Casey Jones and The Engineers. The best thing about playing with Casey Jones was the experience it gave me.

Gigs were so different then, because compared to today, the sound systems were so tiny. We would be playing through small amplifiers like Voxes or Gibsons and we'd have one each, so most groups would then be comprised of three amps plus the drum kit.

The repertoire of The Engineers consisted of some rock and roll but the majority of the material was heavily pop based, and I couldn't stand that for very long. I was too much of a purist, and after six weeks both Tom and I left.

LOT 41 CHRISTIE'S 2004

WORLD AUCTION RECORD FOR A GIBSON GUITAR AT TIME OF SALE
THIRD HIGHEST PRICE PAID FOR A GUITAR AT TIME OF SALE

Serial No: 67473
Body: Double cutaway thinline semi-hollow, maple, f-holes, maple centre block, cherry red finish
Neck: Mahogany, 22 frets, rosewood fingerboard with block inlays
Headstock: Pearl Gibson logo, crown inlay, black three-ply (black/white/black) truss cover engraved 'Custom'
Bridge: Nickel-plated Tune-o-matic with stop tailpiece
Pickguard: Black five-ply (black/white/black/white/black)
Pickups: Two humbucking with nickel-plated covers
Controls: Two volume, two tone
Switches: Three-position pickup selector
Label: 'Style ES-335 TDC/Gibson/Number 67473 is hereby/Guaranteed/against faulty workmanship and materials./Union Made/Gibson Inc/Kalamazoo Michigan,/U.S.A.'
Case: Original Lifton hardshell case, stencilled on the lid in white 'CREAM/DELICATE/HANDLE WITH CARE/DELICATE ELECTRONIC INSTRUMENT/HANDLE WITH CARE/EC G ES', with adhesive tape inscribed 'Auction (SADLY!)/Gibson Cherry Red-Cream/ '64-335-#67473'

Clapton purchased this Gibson ES-335TDC from a London music store in 1964.

He played it towards the end of his stint with The Yardbirds in 1964 and 1965. He may have used the ES-335 to record 'Good Morning Little Schoolgirl' as his guitar tone on the song is not as thin and twangy as it was on earlier studio recordings like 'Boom Boom' and 'A Certain Girl' where he played the Telecaster (pages 42-43). With the Bluesbreakers and Cream, Clapton favoured other Gibsons (pages 52-53), but in November 1968 the ES-335 resurfaced when he brought it to IBC Studios in London to record the songs 'Badge', 'Doing That Scrapyard Thing' and 'What A Bringdown' for Cream's *Goodbye* album. He also played it during Cream's farewell tour, including their final concert on November 26th, 1968, at the Royal Albert Hall.

During this period the ES-335 became Clapton's main guitar. He played it in an appearance with The Dirty Mac (featuring John Lennon, Keith Richards and Mitch Mitchell) on December 11th, 1968, that was filmed for The Rolling Stones' *Rock and Roll Circus*, and used it extensively in the studio and on tour with Blind Faith. Clapton switched to a Fender Stratocaster (page 72) shortly after Blind Faith dissolved, but he frequently brought this ES-335 on tour and to the studio over the next several decades. An inside cover photo of *No Reason To Cry* suggests that this guitar was present at the Shangri La Studio sessions in 1976, and it was also used on his rendition of Ray Charles' 'Hard Times' on *Journeyman* in 1989.

Clapton played this guitar often on his 1994-95 From The Cradle Tour, usually to perform the songs 'Have You Ever Loved A Woman', 'I'm Tore Down', and 'Someday After A While' in honour of one of his favourite blues guitar mentors, Freddie King. He also used the ES-335 to perform 'St. James Infirmary' with Dr. John during a show on May 9th, 1996, at New York's Roseland Ballroom that was filmed for VH1's *Duets* programme and at the Masters of Music for the Prince's Trust concert in London's Hyde Park on June 29th, 1996, for 'Have You Ever Loved A Woman' and 'I'm Tore Down'.

It sold for $847,500 at the 2004 Crossroads Guitar Auction at Christie's. Even though the guitar was 40 years old when Clapton sold it, it was in remarkably good shape and completely stock with the exception of its gold-plated Grover tuners that Clapton installed on the guitar very early on, the engraved 'Custom' truss rod cover, and black top hat control knobs that replaced the original 'metal cap' knobs. Even the Hare Krishna stamp that George Harrison affixed to the back of the headstock was still in good condition.

Below:
The Hare Krishna sticker on the back of the headstock was given to Eric by George Harrison during The Concert for Bangladesh, Aug. 1, 1971.

ERIC The second electric guitar I ever bought. The Kay got me into The Yardbirds, and then when we started making money, I found I had nothing else to spend it on but guitars. Though we weren't yet in the big-money league, we were making enough for me to buy my first really serious guitar, a cherry red Gibson ES-335, which was the instrument of my dreams, of which the Kay had been but a poor imitation.

Playlist:
Five Live Yardbirds, 1964
Goodbye, 1969
Blind Faith, 1969
No Reason To Cry, 1976
Another Ticket, 1981
Journeyman, 1989
From The Cradle, 1994
VH1 *Duets*, 1996 (TV)
Eric Clapton – Live in Hyde Park, 1996 (DVD)

Gigs:
Tours
1964-2004
Highlights:
Cream Farewell Concert
Royal Albert Hall
London, UK
Nov. 26, 1968
Rolling Stones' *Rock and Roll Circus* (TV)
Intertel Studios
Wembley, London, UK
Dec. 10-11, 1968

ERIC Maybe once a month throughout The Yardbirds I bought a guitar. The unfortunate thing was I didn't keep them. In those days, I was less of a collector. I didn't have the money or facilities. I wasn't really sure where I was living half the time, and it would have been cumbersome to have had more than two or three guitars. It wouldn't have occurred to me to think, 'Oh, for this song I'll use that' – I wouldn't have thought like that at all. I just was very focused on a guitar and would play that exclusively for a year, two years and then for some reason I'd go somewhere else. The only one I held on to was the ES-335; it was the oldest guitar in my collection. Well, not the oldest, but the one I had the longest.

Above:
The Black Cat Club
Woolwich, UK
Jan. 21, 1965

Clapton and his cherry Gibson guitar toured the UK with The Yardbirds until April 1965 when he left the band.

Opposite:
Cream Farewell Concert
Royal Albert Hall
London, UK
Nov. 26, 1968

Eric played his ES-335 during the evening performance of Cream's last shows.

ECHO THE BLUES

ERIC Throughout my life I chose a lot of my guitars because of the other people who played them, and this was like the one Freddie King played. In The Roosters, Tom McGuinness brought in 'Hideaway' by Freddie King, and the B-side was 'I Love The Woman', which is still one of the greatest. That's the first time I heard that electric-lead-guitar style, with the bent notes. I'd never heard anything like it, and it was what immediately made me want to carry on. I knew that was where I belonged, finally. That was serious, proper guitar playing, and I haven't changed my mind since. I still listen to his music in my car or when I'm at home and I get the same boost from it that I did then. There wasn't a great deal of footage or still photos or album covers that I could refer to that showed examples of this model, but I did see a Freddie King instrumental album and he was playing one of these.

I think the cherry Gibson ES-335 was really acceptable on every front. It was a rock guitar, a blues guitar – the real thing. Even in those days I may have had reservations about Fenders, in that they were solid, whereas this one was semi-acoustic. What I love about Fenders now I would probably have held in a little bit of contempt in those days, in that they didn't have any purfling down the side of the neck, and so on. This guitar had all the finish you would ever want and all the credibility a guitar needed at that time. The fact that Alexis Korner and I played those Kays was because you couldn't get these Gibsons in England – you didn't see them. You got copies, German guitars like Hagstroms, Hofners. I bought this brand new either from Denmark Street or Charing Cross Road.

Opposite:
Cream Farewell Concert
Royal Albert Hall
London, UK
Nov. 26, 1968

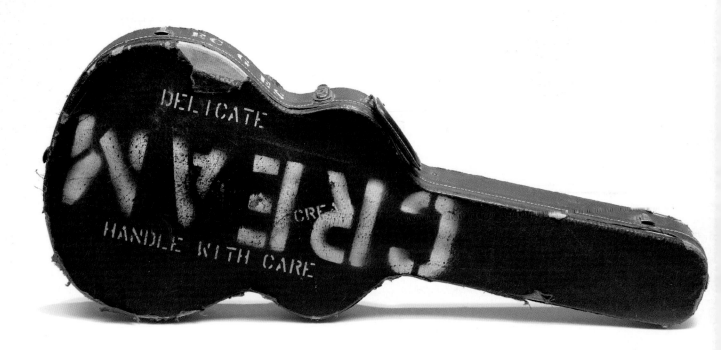

Left:
Clapton pictured on Blind
Faith's US tour between
July 12 and Aug. 24, 1969

Above:
Roseland Ballroom
New York, USA
May 9, 1996

Eric Clapton performing
with Dr. John on VH1's
Duets. This is one of the
last times the ES-335 was
used publicly.

ERIC The ES-335 is beautiful, and
I loved it. It was played regularly
over the years.

It got on albums, it never really changed.
It never got old, it never wore down. It never
lost anything. I'd play it now. Anything
that's been that long in my life and is still
functional – there aren't too many things
that can command that kind of respect. I've
had no cars that long for instance. There
are no other tools in my life that have been
as long-serving.

After I sold the red ES-335, I bought a
sunburst one. It's a great guitar and it's
so loud. I'd forgotten how loud they were.

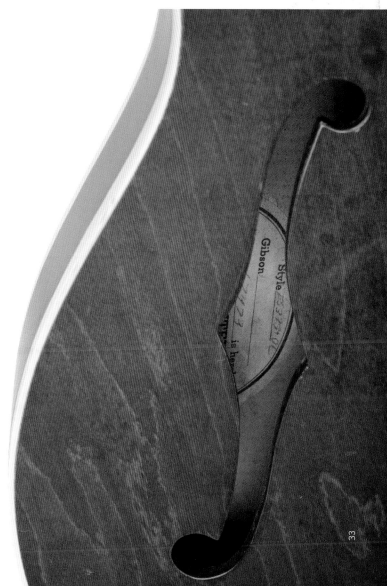

2005 GIBSON ERIC CLAPTON CROSSROADS ES-335 REPLICA PROTOTYPE EST: $15,000 - $20,000 PRICE: $25,000, $27,000

LOTS 116, 119 BONHAMS 2011

Serial No: Prototype 3,4
Body: Double cutaway thinline semi-hollow, maple, f-holes, maple centre block, cherry red finish
Neck: Mahogany, 22 frets, bound rosewood fingerboard with block inlays
Headstock: Pearl Gibson logo, crown inlay, black three-ply (black/white/black) truss cover engraved 'Custom', serial number '67473'. Hare Krishna stamp on back
Bridge: Nickel-plated Tune-o-matic with stop tailpiece
Pickguard: Black five-ply (black/white/black/white/black)
Pickups: Two humbucking with nickel-plated covers
Controls: Two volume, two tone
Switches: Three-position pickup selector
Label: Signed by Eric Clapton in black ballpoint pen
Case: Black Cream-era replica hardshell contour case stencilled on the lid in white 'CREAM/DELICATE/HANDLE WITH CARE', with gold plush lining, original cardboard box

Guitar Center generously cast a winning bid of $847,500 to purchase Clapton's 1964 Gibson ES-335 (page 26) from the Crossroads Guitar Auction. They have publicly shared it in Guitar Center's Legends collection since. They also secured Clapton's permission to commission the Gibson Custom Shop to build 250 accurate replicas of the guitar – scratches, dings and all. These sold out within three days of their release on August 1st, 2005, and Guitar Center donated a portion of the proceeds from the sale to the Crossroads Centre as well.

Gibson made five prototypes of Clapton's 1964 ES-335 replica, which they gave to Eric for his authorisation, approval and attention to detail that only a former owner of a guitar would notice. In addition to replicating the 40 years' worth of wear and tear that the guitar survived, Gibson's Custom Shop managed to duplicate the Hare Krishna stamp that George Harrison applied to the back of the guitar's headstock and the rips and stencilled graphics on the case.

A pair of these guitars were auctioned in the 2011 Crossroads auction, fetching a total of $52,000.

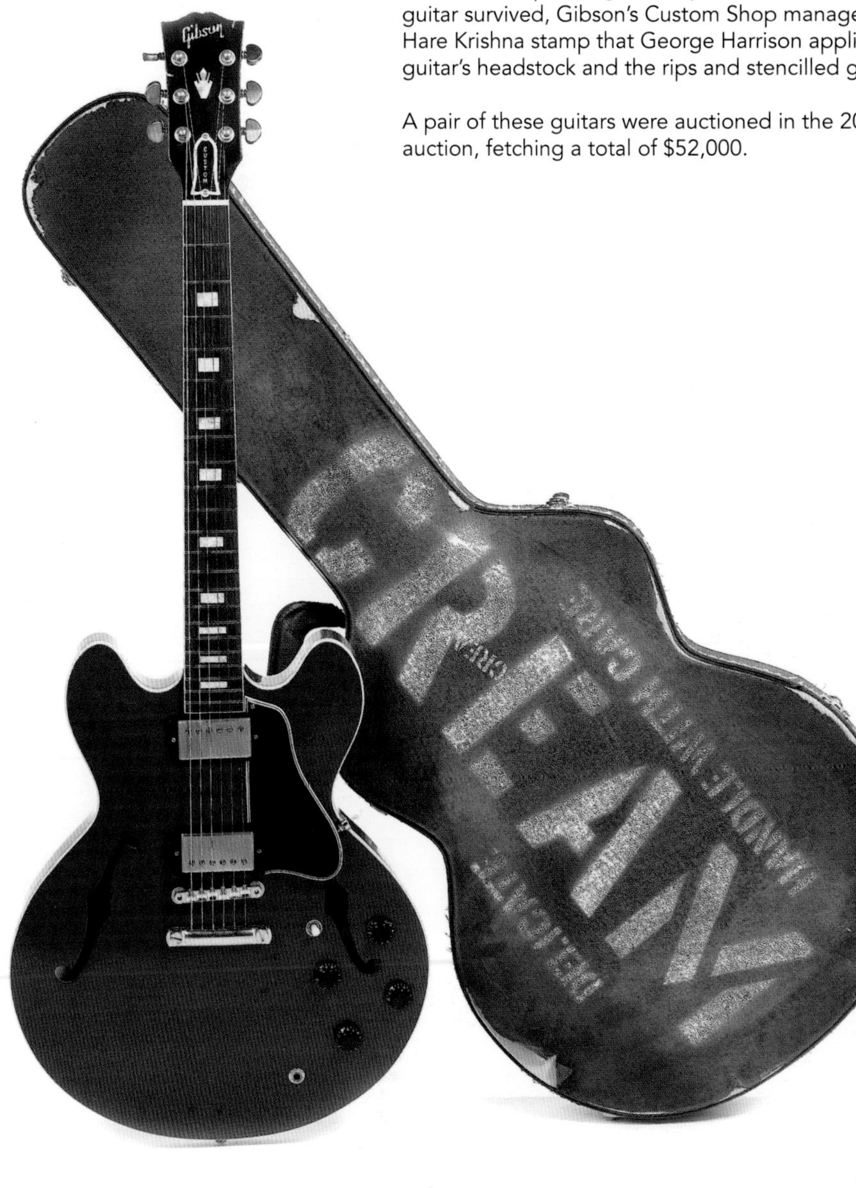

Opposite:
Royal Albert Hall
London, UK
May 5, 2005

A Crossroads ES-335 Replica case can be seen backstage at the Cream Reunion Concerts with Eric Clapton and Ginger Baker.

2001 GIBSON ES-335 EST: $12,000 - $15,000 PRICE: $28,000

LOT 51 BONHAMS 2011

Serial No: EC001
Body: Double cutaway thinline semi-hollow, maple, f-holes, maple centre block, cherry red finish
Neck: Mahogany, 22 frets, bound rosewood fingerboard with double parallelogram inlays
Headstock: Crown peghead inlay
Bridge: Nickel-plated Tune-o-matic with stop tailpiece
Pickguard: Black five-ply (black/white/black/white/black)
Pickups: Two humbucking
Controls: Two volume, two tone
Switches: Three-position pickup selector
Label: 'Style: ES335, Gibson: Guitar, Number: EC001, is hereby guaranteed against...'
Case: Brown Gibson hardshell contour case with plum plush lining, handwritten label inscribed 'Gibson/Cherry ES335 Ser E.C. 601' [sic]

The Gibson Custom Shop made this unique ES-335 for Clapton in 2001. The most unusual feature of this ES-335 is its double parallelogram fingerboard inlays, which are a distinguishing characteristic of Gibson's ES-345 model, although the remaining features all comply with standard ES-335 specifications. It's likely that Clapton asked Gibson to make him a guitar that visually resembled the ES-345 that Freddie King was photographed holding on the cover of his 1965 album *Freddy King Gives You a Bonanza of Instrumentals*, but with the less-complicated electronics of the 1964 ES-335 that was one of Eric's favourite guitars.

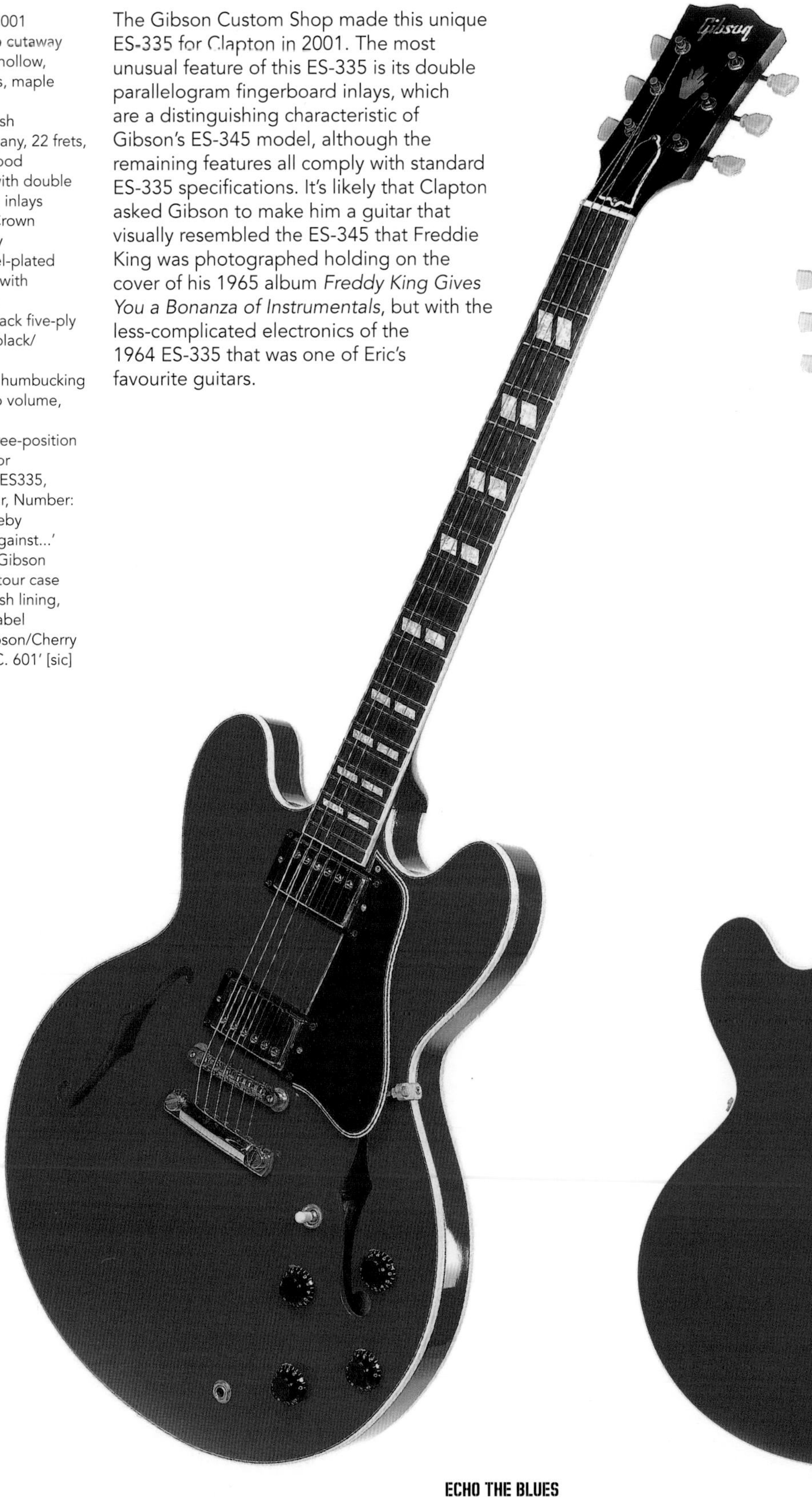

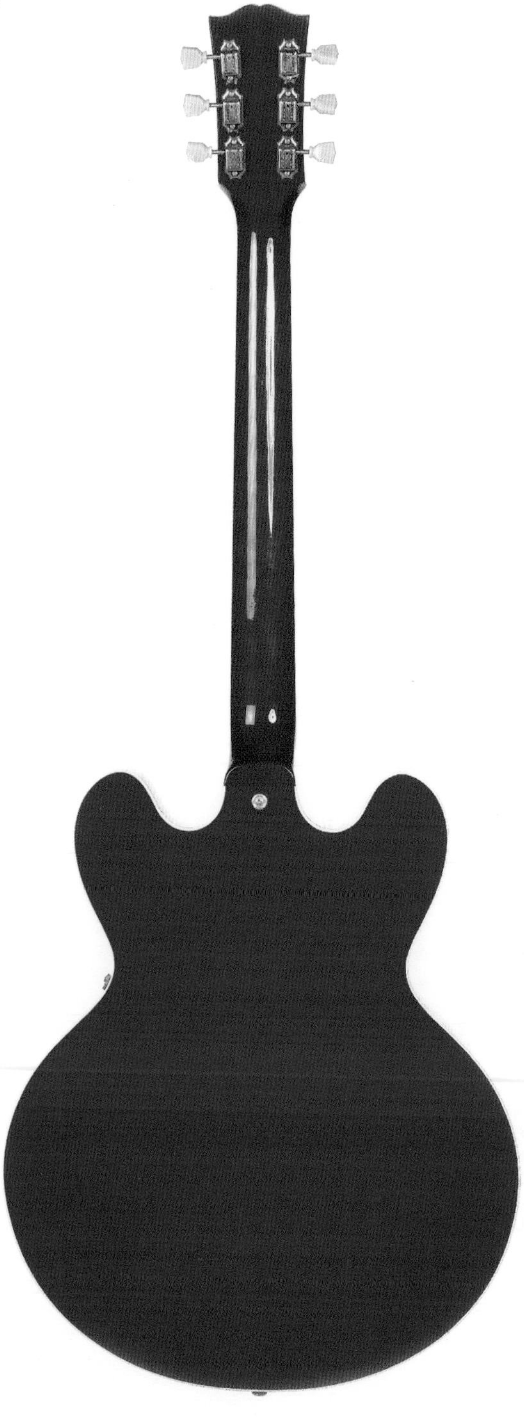

1996 GIBSON CUSTOM SHOP ES-336	EST: $2,000 - $3,000	PRICE: $8,365

LOT 43 CHRISTIE'S 2004

Serial No: 6 9830
Body: One-piece mahogany back, maple top, f-holes, sunburst finish
Neck: Mahogany, 22 frets, bound rosewood fingerboard with dot inlays
Headstock: Pearl Gibson logo, Gibson Custom Shop stamp on reverse
Bridge: Nickel-plated Tune-o-matic with stop tailpiece
Pickguard: Black five-ply (black/white/black/white/black)
Pickups: Two humbucking with nickel-plated covers
Controls: Two volume, two tone
Switches: Three-position pickup selector
Case: Original case with adhesive tape label inscribed 'Gibson 336/6-9830'

The ES-336 is essentially a small-body version of the ES-335 that Gibson introduced in 1996, although its construction is also different, featuring a carved, hollowed-out mahogany block for its body instead of a separate back and sides. The two upper bout cutaway horns are the same dimensions as those on a full-size ES-335, but the lower bout is narrower and shorter so the body shape is not as elegant as a 335's. The slim 'snakehead' headstock also deviates from the 'open book'-style headstock associated with most Gibson guitars. In 2001 Gibson modified this model's body shape so its proportions and curves more closely resembled those of an ES-335 while retaining the compact size and renamed it the CS-336.

Gibson gave this guitar to Clapton shortly after the model's development to get feedback from him concerning its design.

1996 GIBSON CUSTOM SHOP ES-336

2003 GIBSON CS-356	EST: $4,500 - $6,500	PRICE: $10,000

LOT 52 BONHAMS 2011

Serial No: CS30483
Body: One-piece mahogany back, carved figured maple top, multiple-layer binding, f-holes, cherry red finish
Neck: Mahogany, 22 frets, bound ebony fingerboard with block inlays
Headstock: Multiple-layer binding, pearl Gibson logo, split diamond inlay
Bridge: Gold-plated Tune-o-matic, stop tailpiece
Pickguard: Black five-ply (black/white/black/white/black)
Pickups: Two humbucking with gold-plated covers
Controls: Two volume, two tone
Switches: Three-position pickup selector
Case: Black Gibson hardshell contour case with claret plush lining, handwritten label inscribed with various details

Gibson greatly improved the 'compact ES-335' design of the ES-336 when they introduced the CS-336 in 2001, scaling down the size of the upper cutaway horns to make the body shape more aesthetically pleasing and incorporating a routed centre block and top bracing that improved the guitar's tone. Gibson also produced the CS-356 model, which featured a variety of upgrades, including gold-plated parts, a figured maple top, block fingerboard inlays, multi-layer body binding, and a split-diamond headstock inlay.

Judging by the generous wear and tear on this guitar's pickup covers and stop tailpiece, Clapton played this CS-356 often. He was photographed using this guitar to play 'After Midnight' during his November 15th, 2006, concert in Osaka, Japan, and he likely played it on several other occasions on that tour.

Gigs:
2006/2007 World Tour (Japan)
Nov. 11-Dec. 9, 2006
Highlight:
Osaka-Jo Hall
Osaka, Japan
Nov. 15, 2006

2003 GIBSON CS-356

41

LOT 75 CHRISTIE'S 2004

Serial No: 214861
Body: Ash, single cutaway, natural finish
Neck: Maple, 21 frets, maple fingerboard with dot inlays
Bridge: Stamped steel baseplate, three adjustable steel saddles
Pickguard: Black single-ply
Pickups: One single-coil (bridge), one humbucking (neck)
Controls: One volume, one tone
Switches: Three-position pickup selector
Case: Original hardshell case with adhesive label inscribed "67 I.H. Bucker I.S.C./Fender-Tele-Blonde #214861'

One of the first electric guitars that Eric Clapton ever bought was a Dakota Red early 1960s Telecaster with a rosewood fingerboard. That guitar was Clapton's main instrument when he played with The Yardbirds and inspired his 'Slowhand' nickname, but after Clapton left The Yardbirds he rarely performed with a Telecaster again. The whereabouts of Clapton's original Dakota Red Telecaster are unknown, as he sold or swapped the Telecaster long ago to replace it with another guitar.

Photographer Virginia Lohle (1957-2006) of Star File gave this 1967 Fender Telecaster to Eric as a gift. It was already modified with a non-stock humbucking neck pickup and jumbo frets when he received it.

Opposite:
The Dome
Brighton, UK
June 11, 1964

Eric Clapton with The Yardbirds, playing a Fender Telecaster similar to this model. The T-Bones, who were also signed to Giorgio Gomelsky, played that same night.

ERIC I've owned Telecasters and I've bought them. They are part of my history. I had a Telecaster in The Yardbirds from day one. So they are definitely part of my taste.

It would have been that guitar that earned me the nickname 'Slowhand' because it had those metal bridge pieces that would just saw through the strings.

I used light-gauge strings, with a very thin first string, which made it easier to bend the notes, and it was not uncommon, during the most frenetic bits of playing, for me to break at least one string. During the pause while I was changing my strings, the frenzied audience would often break into a slow handclap, inspiring Giorgio (Gomelsky, The Yardbirds' manager) to dream up the nickname of 'Slowhand' Clapton.

Serial No: 000
Body: Ash, bookmatched flamed maple top, single cutaway, bound, sunburst finish
Neck: Maple with skunk-stripe truss rod routing, 22 frets, maple fingerboard with dot inlays. Gold-plated neck plate engraved, '000 OF 300 CUSTOM MADE FOR ERIC CLAPTON 1992'
Bridge: Gold-plated flat baseplate, six adjustable saddles
Pickguard: Simulated ivory
Pickups: Two single-coil
Controls: One volume, one tone
Switches: Three-position pickup selector
Additional: Strap, Fender certificates and a lead
Case: Brown Tolex rectangular hardshell case lined with yellow plush and adhesive paper label 'Fender Custom Tele., S/Burst #000 of 300'

Between 1988 and 1990, Fender's Custom Shop produced a limited run of only 300 40th Anniversary Telecaster guitars. Fender had already sold out of all 300 of these guitars by the time Clapton took a fancy to the model and requested one from the company in 1992, but out of respect for Eric they built him the 301st 40th Anniversary Telecaster with a special '000' serial number and a specially engraved neck plate.

ERIC I played this from time to time.

Serial No: 0050
Body: Ash, single cutaway, 'butterscotch' blonde finish
Neck: Maple with skunk-stripe truss rod routing, 21 frets, maple fingerboard with dot inlays
Bridge: Vintage-style stamped steel baseplate, three adjustable brass saddles
Pickguard: Black single-ply
Pickups: Two single-coil
Controls: One volume, one tone
Switches: Three-position pickup selector
Additional: Guitar strap and 'ashtray' bridge baseplate cover
Case: Tweed contour case with brown plush lining and handwritten adhesive paper label 'J.Black-Relic-C.Shop Fender-Tele-Blonde #0050'

The Fender Custom Shop started producing its first Relic guitars in 1995, which involved a process of artificial ageing and distressing that duplicated the wear and tear of a well-played vintage instrument. Even though Relic guitars are brand new, they have the look and feel of a guitar that has survived more than 20 years of use and abuse.

The 1997 Fender Broadcaster Relic is an accurate reproduction of a 1950 Broadcaster guitar. Fender gave this guitar to Eric the same year that it was made.

ERIC I like the idea of making distressed instruments.

1992 FENDER 40TH ANNIVERSARY TELECASTER

1997 FENDER BROADCASTER RELIC

ERIC At the debut performance
of Blind Faith, I played a bound
Telecaster with a Strat neck.
I had probably two or three Strats,
and I never liked the Tele neck.
And I thought it would be unusual and
might have people guessing what kind
of guitar it was because of the head.

I think Blind Faith was over too soon; we
could have gone on maybe a couple more
years. We made one album, where we were
just beginning to scrape the surface of our
creativity and I was gone, off joining Delaney
and Bonnie. I always had in the back of my
mind that I would have to leave and pursue
my own personal journey.

Serial No: 28223
Body: Laminated maple, hollow archtop, bound, single round cutaway, f-holes, translucent red finish
Neck: Maple, 22 frets, ebony fingerboard with thumbprint inlays
Bridge: Single-saddle metal bar, Bigsby vibrato tailpiece
Pickguard: Black with Gretsch and Chet Atkins 'signpost' logos in white
Pickups: Single Filter'Tron humbucking
Controls: One volume
Switches: Three-position tone selector
Case: Black hardshell contour case with blue plush lining and handwritten tie-on label 'E.C. Gretch [sic] 6119 S/P.Up #28223' and adhesive paper label similarly inscribed

Although Clapton says that he didn't pursue the Gretsch Sound too much, he was photographed playing a double-cutaway, early 1960s Gretsch 6120 with The Yardbirds. This 1958 6119 Chet Atkins Tennessean is a stripped-down version of the late 1950s 6120 Chet Atkins model, featuring just one Filter'Tron humbucking pickup instead of two, an unbound fingerboard, and a pickguard made of black plastic instead of gold plastic.

ERIC I love Gretsch guitars in terms of their image and what they represent in rock culture. I love all those guitars that Diddley had made for him: square frame, red with black, beautiful things. There were a lot of people who endorsed them: Bo Diddley, Eddie Cochran, Chet Atkins.

I love their concept, look and design, but I have never pursued Gretsch too much. I can't get the hang of their wiring... I get lost. It's complicated. I think everything has to have a very healthy midrange; I'm very suspicious of too much top or too much bottom. I respect all the brands, but I always found it most difficult to get on with Gretsch because I'm not quite sure what they sound like. I could never really get them quite right. It's important that all the guitars I play have healthy attack.

Serial No: 961112060-1411
Body: Laminated maple back and sides, hollow archtop, bound, single round cutaway, f-holes, translucent orange finish
Neck: Maple, 22 frets plus zero fret at nut, ebony fingerboard with thumbprint inlays
Headstock: Inlaid Gretsch logo, horseshoe inlay
Bridge: Gold-plated Tune-o-matic-style on ebony base, aluminium Bigsby vibrato tailpiece
Pickguard: Clear single-ply with gold back painting and black Gretsch logo
Pickups: Two Filter'Tron humbucking with covers engraved 'U.S.PAT 2392371'
Controls: Master volume, neck pickup volume, bridge pickup volume
Switches: Three-position pickup selector, three-position tone colour
Label: 'Fred Gretsch Enterprises, Model No 6120-60, Serial...'
Case: Black Gretsch hardshell contour case with brown plush lining, handwritten label

After a nine-year hiatus, Gretsch guitars returned to the market in 1989 after Fred Gretsch III reacquired the rights to the Gretsch name when its former owners, Baldwin, went bankrupt. Although the initial plan was to develop new models, prices and demand for original 1950s Gretsch models soared during the 1980s so instead they focused on reissues of classic instruments from that era. Their reissue of the 6120, called the 'Nashville' since Gretsch no longer had the rights to use Chet Atkins' name, was their most popular model, and over the years they introduced several variations of the 6120 that reflected the features of different years of production. The 6120-60 was based on the 1960 Gretsch 6120 favoured by players like Brian Setzer of Stray Cats, an influential figure who inspired Gretsch's surge in popularity in the 1980s.

Clapton purchased this 1996 Gretsch 6120 reissue in October 2003 from Vintage Guitar Emporium on New King's Road in Fulham.

Associated-Rediffusion Studios
London, UK
Broadcast May 22, 1964

Eric playing an early 1960s Gretsch 6120 Chet Atkins on *Ready, Steady, Go!* with The Yardbirds.

47   1996 GRETSCH NASHVILLE 6120-60

Serial No: 46387
Body: Mahogany, burgundy sparkle Nitron top, bound
Neck: Mahogany, 21 frets, bound ebony fingerboard
Headstock: Bound
Bridge: Gold-plated 'space control' bridge, gold-plated Burns vibrato
Pickups: Two humbucking Filter'Tron with gold-plated covers
Controls: Three volume (master, neck pickup, bridge pickup)
Switches: Three-position pickup selector, three-position tone colour, two-position standby
Case: Original hardshell case with adhesive tape inscribed 'Auction #29 1962/Champagne Sparkle/Roc Jet #46387'

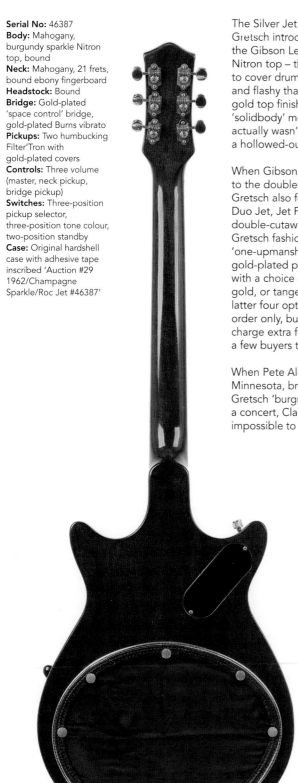

The Silver Jet was one of several models that Gretsch introduced in 1954 to compete with the Gibson Les Paul. With its sparkling silver Nitron top – the same material Gretsch used to cover drums – it is even more eye-catching and flashy than the Les Paul's early 1950s gold top finish. Like Gretsch's other 'solidbody' models of the day, the Silver Jet actually wasn't solid at all, but rather featured a hollowed-out mahogany body.

When Gibson switched the Les Paul's design to the double-cutaway 'SG' shape in 1961, Gretsch also followed suit by changing the Duo Jet, Jet Firebird and Silver Jet to double-cutaway models in 1962. In typical Gretsch fashion they took their 'one-upmanship' even further by using gold-plated parts and offering the Silver Jet with a choice of silver, burgundy, champagne, gold, or tangerine Nitron sparkle tops. The latter four options were available by custom order only, but even though Gretsch didn't charge extra for the optional colours only a few buyers took up their offer.

When Pete Alenov of Pete's Guitar in St. Paul, Minnesota, brought this stunning 1962 Gretsch 'burgundy' Jet backstage to a concert, Clapton found the guitar impossible to resist.

LOT 19 CHRISTIE'S 1999

Serial No: 167734
Body: Mahogany back and sides, mahogany top, natural finish
Neck: Mahogany, 20 frets, rosewood fingerboard with dot inlays
Bridge: Rosewood 'belly' pin
Pickguard: Imitation tortoiseshell
Case: Black hardshell contour case with brown plush lining and adhesive paper label 'Rosewood Martin 00-17 #167734'

With its mahogany back, sides and top, and plain styling, this modest Martin 00-17 was far removed from the considerably fancier Martins in Clapton's guitar collection.

ERIC I bought this guitar for nostalgic reasons. It reminded me of one I admired that Paul Samwell-Smith had in The Yardbirds.

1959 MARTIN 00-17

1948 MARTIN 00-17   EST: $2,500 - $3,500   PRICE: $20,315

LOT 7 CHRISTIE'S 2004

Body: Mahogany back and sides, mahogany top, natural finish
Neck: Mahogany, 20 frets, rosewood fingerboard with dot inlays
Bridge: Rosewood 'belly' pin bridge
Pickguard: Imitation tortoiseshell
Case: Hardshell case with adhesive tape inscribed ''48 Martin OO-17 Mahog./1948'

Like the 00-17 above, Clapton purchased this guitar as it reminded him of an acoustic guitar that Paul Samwell-Smith played while they were both in The Yardbirds. While touring the United States, Clapton often purchased duplicates of guitars he already owned in his extensive collection of Martin acoustics because he either forgot he already owned one or he found a better example.

ERIC I've always loved these little red Martins. I always wanted one.

ECHO THE BLUES

1948 MARTIN 00-17

Serial No: 32808
Body: Alder, sunburst finish
Neck: Maple, 21 frets, rosewood fingerboard with dot inlays, neck dated 12-58
Bridge: Six-saddle, separate vibrato unit
Pickguard: Anodised aluminium
Pickups: Two single-coil
Controls: One volume, one tone, rhythm volume roller, rhythm tone roller
Switches: Three-position pickup selector, rhythm circuit on/off
Case: Original hardshell tweed case with adhesive tape inscribed ''58 Sunburst/ Fender-Jazzmaster #32808'

When Fender introduced their Jazzmaster model guitar in 1958, they promoted it as an upgrade of the Stratocaster with a mellow tone that was suitable for jazz. Although jazz guitarists generally ignored the instrument, the Jazzmaster soon became a favourite of guitarists who played instrumental surf music during the early 1960s. Clapton also played a Jazzmaster for a brief spell with The Yardbirds in 1964-65.

The first Jazzmaster guitars that Fender produced from 1958 through the middle of 1959 have a distinctive golden-coloured metal anodised scratchplate, as seen on this example. In addition to looking very striking, the metal scratchplate also provided excellent shielding for the guitar's pickups and electronics. However, because the plating wore off easily, Fender switched to a celluloid imitation tortoiseshell pickguard, which was more durable cosmetically.

ERIC I had one of these in The Yardbirds, with a tortoiseshell-effect scratchplate. I had the Jazzmaster, the Tele, and also at one time I think a Silvertone that looked just like Jimmy Reed's.

This was a nostalgic buy; I got it for the look of the guitar as much as anything. Beautiful shaped body design, just pure. The Jazzmaster for me was a surf guitar.

This vintage Yardbirds postcard shows Chris Dreja holding what appears to be Eric Clapton's first Jazzmaster.

ECHO THE BLUES

Serial No: None
Body: Birch, hollowbody, sunburst finish
Neck: Maple, 20 frets, ebonised maple fingerboard with dot inlays
Bridge: Rosewood adjustable floating bridge, chrome-plated hinged trapeze tailpiece
Pickguard: White single-ply
Pickups: Two Rowe DeArmond single-coils
Controls: Two stacked concentric tone/volume
Switches: Three-position pickup selector
Case: Black softshell contour case with red plush lining and handwritten adhesive paper label 'Harmony Stratatone [sic] #N.S.N.'

Eric Clapton says that he bought this Harmony H46 Stratotone Mars because it reminded him of the early 1960s when The Yardbirds replaced The Rolling Stones in a residency at the Crawdaddy Club. Brian Jones played a Stratotone Mars almost identical to this one during the early days of The Rolling Stones, but his was a 1960 model while Clapton's was from either 1958 or 1959, identifiable by the long-tail 'Y' and the shape of the atomic symbol in the headstock graphics of Clapton's H46.

ERIC I bought this guitar because it reminded me of my Yardbird days and the Stones. The second time I went to see Alexis Korner play, Mick Jagger was there and we got talking. Brian Jones and Keith Richards were also there, and they'd all get up and play with Ginger Baker and Jack Bruce, or whoever was Alexis' rhythm section that particular night. After that, it was only a matter of time before I thought about trying to do it for myself.

The love affair, the obsession with the blues, was reinforced by the fact that it was so inaccessible. And having made a little inroad into it, I was one of the few who had not only the taste for it but the gift for it, too. I belonged to this incredibly exclusive club whose members included Keith Richards and people like that, who felt they had a mission.

When John Mayall called me up, about two weeks after I'd left The Yardbirds, it suited me fine because his was a blues band.

I suppose I seemed a musical drifter to most people but I always intended to do my own thing eventually – it's just that every time I got around to it something else cropped up. My life has really been my work – I tried not to do anything of which I wouldn't be a hundred percent proud. As a guitarist I was seeking refinement, which was the simplest and most effective way of saying the thing exactly as I wanted to.

The Station Hotel Richmond, London, UK 1963

Brian Jones is playing a similar Harmony Stratotone with The Rolling Stones.

LOT 122 BONHAMS 2011

Serial No: 01
Body: Mahogany, maple top, sunburst finish, single cutaway
Neck: Mahogany, 22 frets, bound rosewood fingerboard with crown inlays
Headstock: Pearl inlaid Gibson logo, 'Les Paul model' in gold paint, back of headstock signed by Eric Clapton in black felt pen and additionally inscribed in black felt pen with the number '1'
Bridge: Nickel-plated Tune-o-matic with stop tailpiece
Pickguard: Single-ply cream
Pickups: Two humbucking
Controls: Two volume, two tone
Switches: Three-position pickup selector
Label: Orange printed Gibson Custom label on back control cover inscribed 'Eric Clapton 01'
Additional: Black and yellow woven fabric strap, Gibson Custom Certificate of Authenticity in white leather folder with cover featuring Eric Clapton's machine-embroidered facsimile signature in pale blue thread, wooden presentation plaque with reproduction front cover of the *Beano* comic book, 7 May 1966 and engraved plate 'This issue of the iconic British comic - *The Beano* - was being read by EC on the album cover of John Mayall & The Bluesbreakers', and a recent vinyl pressing of the album *Blues Breakers With Eric Clapton*
Case: Black hardshell contour case with claret plush lining, the lid of the case with Clapton's facsimile signature and paper sticker inscribed in black felt pen '1'

The 1960 Gibson Les Paul that Eric Clapton used to record John Mayall's *Blues Breakers With Eric Clapton* album in 1966 caused the sunburst Les Paul to become one of the most sought-after and desirable solidbody electric guitars of all time.

Clapton purchased his 1960 Les Paul second hand from Lew Davis' music shop on Charing Cross Road in London in 1965 after he left The Yardbirds. Clapton bought the guitar because it resembled the goldtop 1954 Les Paul that Freddie King played, although King's guitar had single-coil P-90 'soapbar' pickups instead of a pair of humbucking pickups like the 1960 Les Paul. It didn't matter that Clapton's Les Paul was not an identical match for King's, as Clapton crafted a new sound with his 1960 Les Paul plugged into a Marshall 1962 combo amp that instantly redefined blues-rock guitar tone.

Unfortunately, Clapton's 1960 Les Paul guitar was stolen while Cream were rehearsing for their first tour in 1966, and the guitar has never resurfaced or been recovered since.

In 2010, the Gibson Custom Shop worked closely with Clapton to replicate every detail of Clapton's original 1960 Les Paul to the best of his recollection. Using the handful of photographs of Clapton's guitar from the Bluesbreakers as a starting reference point, Gibson consulted Clapton about the neck profile, weight, and overall feel of the instrument to duplicate it as closely as possible. Gibson even used Grover tuning machines like the ones that Clapton installed on the guitar himself shortly after he first bought it.

Gibson produced two different versions of the Eric Clapton 1960 Les Paul – a VOS (Vintage Original Specification) model and a hand-aged version. Production was limited to 350 VOS models and 150 hand-aged models. Clapton signed 55 of the hand-aged guitars, five of which Gibson gave to Clapton for his collaboration on the project, including this guitar featuring serial number 01.

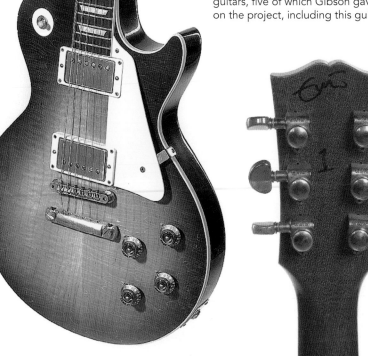

Opposite (above):
Pontiac Club
Putney, London, UK

Eric sitting on the stage with his original 'Beano' guitar during a gig with the Bluesbreakers in 1965.

Opposite (below):
The Twisted Wheel Club
Manchester, UK
July 30, 1966

This photograph was taken on the night before Cream's official launch at the 6th National Jazz & Blues Festival.

ERIC The best Les Paul I ever had was the one I had with John Mayall.

It was just a regular sunburst Les Paul that I bought in one of the shops in London right after I'd seen Freddie King's album cover of *Let's Hide Away And Dance Away*, where he's playing a gold-top. It had humbuckers and was almost brand new, with an original case with that lovely purple velvet lining. Just magnificent. It was stolen during rehearsals for Cream's first gig, and I never really found one as good as that. I do miss that one.

LOT 121 BONHAMS 2011

1969 GIBSON LP-2 POWER AMPLIFIER/SPEAKER CABINET

Serial No: 1013
Covering: Black Tolex, blue sparkle grille cloth
Speakers: four 12-inch, two treble horns
Switches: Power on/off
Inputs: Three
Label: 'Gibson Les Paul'

In 1968, Gibson collaborated with Les Paul on the design of two new guitars featuring low-impedance pickups: the Les Paul Professional and the Les Paul Personal. Both of these guitars were designed for use with a new LP-12 amplifier system, which consisted of the LP-1 preamp/effects head and the LP-2 speaker cabinet, which also featured a built-in solid-state power amplifier.

Gibson's first promo shot for the 2010 Gibson Les Paul Standard Eric Clapton 'Beano' Tribute Model also featured this amp.

LOT 28 BONHAMS 2011

CIRCA 1966-68 SUPRO S6698 SPORTSMAN AMPLIFIER

Serial No: 1-96500
Covering: Black Tolex with diamond-pattern centre strip
Switches: Power on/off, line reverse, standby
Controls: Standard volume, standard tone, reverb volume, reverb tone, tremolo speed, tremolo intensity, reverb intensity
Inputs: High Standard, Low Standard, High Reverb/Tremolo, Low Reverb/Tremolo
Outputs: One speaker
Footswitch inputs: Tremolo, Reverb

Chicago's Valco company produced Supro amps as well as several other brands of amplifiers, including Gretsch, Harmony, National, Oahu and many more, during the 1940s, 50s and 60s. The Supro S6698 Sportsman was one of several new amplifier models that Supro introduced in 1966 featuring distinctive chrome and turquoise blue control panels. The 35-watt Sportsman was the second biggest amp that Supro offered at the time, with only the 70-watt Statesman providing more output and features. Supro originally sold the Sportsman as a 'piggyback' package consisting of the S6698 Sportsman amp head and a speaker cabinet with two 12-inch Jensen speakers that was also sold with other Supro 'piggyback' amp packages. The Sportsman remained in Supro's product line until 1968, when Valco went bankrupt after merging with the Kay Musical Instrument Company.

Serial No: 1178
Covering: Varnished wood (Tolex removed)
Switches: Power on/off, standby
Details: Gold Plexiglas plate with Marshall in block letters
Controls: Presence, bass, middle, treble, high treble loudness 1, normal loudness 2
Inputs: Four
Outputs: Two speaker
Label: Sticker reading 'Repaired and serviced by Den Cornell TEL: (0702) 610964'
Case: Flight case

Playlist:
'Bernard Jenkins'
'I'm Your Witchdoctor'
'Telephone Blues'
Blues Breakers with Eric Clapton, 1966
Gigs:
John Mayall's Bluesbreakers – UK Club & Ballroom Circuit
Apr. 6-Aug. 29, 1965

The JTM 45 was based on the first amplifier circuit that Ken Bran constructed with Dudley Craven in Marshall's shop in 1962. Although the circuit was based on Fender's 5F6-A Bassman, the different transformer, tubes (valves), speakers and filtering gave the Marshall amp its own distinct personality. Marshall initially offered the 45-watt JTM 45 amplifier head along with a matching 4x12 speaker cabinet, and in 1965 added the JTM 45 MKII PA model amplifier head. This JTM 45 MKII is a 1985 (model number) PA model.

It features two GEC KT66 power amp tubes, three Mullard ECC83 (12AX7-equivalent) preamp tubes, and a Mullard GZ34 rectifier tube. Even though this model was sold as a PA head, it actually isn't much different than JTM 45 MKII lead and bass amps from this era. One of the ¼ inch output jacks on the back of the chassis is hand-marked 'D.I.', which suggests it may have been modified at some point. Marshall used the distinctive silver-face control knobs with black pointers found on this amp only for a brief period in 1965. These knobs were nicknamed 'Clapton knobs' after a photo of this amp, with a caption stating 'owned for some time now by Eric Clapton', appeared in Mike Doyle's book *The Sound of Rock: A History of Marshall Valve Guitar Amplifiers* (1982).

In 1965 Clapton played his 'Beano' Les Paul (pages 52-53) though a very similar amp to this one (with the original Tolex) on a 4x12 Marshall cabinet. This particular amp was purchased during the late seventies by Mike Doyle and gifted to Eric Clapton soon after.

The Falkoner Centret Copenhagen, Denmark Mar. 6, 1967

Clapton using a similar amplifier atop a Marshall stack during a soundcheck for Cream's performance that night.

LOT 28 CHRISTIE'S 1999

Serial No: 897024
Body: Mahogany, single cutaway, bound, walnut finish
Neck: Mahogany, 22 frets, bound rosewood fingerboard with block inlays
Headstock: Split diamond inlay, black three-ply (black/white/black) truss rod cover with 'Les Paul Recording'
Bridge: Chrome-plated large Tune-o-matic with stop tailpiece
Pickguard: Black five-ply (black/white/black/white/black), signed in felt pen 'To Eric my man! – '96, Les Paul'
Pickups: Two diagonally mounted low-impedance stacked humbucking
Controls: Volume, Decade, Treble, Bass
Switches: Tone selector, hi/low impedance, phase, three-position pickup selector
Additional: Gibson strap and two 4x6in. photos of Les Paul signing the guitar
Case: Black hardshell contour case, purple plush lining and handwritten label

The Gibson Les Paul Recording was Les Paul's favourite guitar design, featuring several uncommon innovations that Les developed for direct recording applications, including low-impedance pickups and an 11-position Decade control that provided various EQ settings. This model was his main performance and recording instrument from the 1970s to his death in 2009. Les gave this Les Paul Recording guitar, which was made between 1973 and 1975, to Eric in 1996.

LOT 16 CHRISTIE'S 1999

Serial No: 9 9272
Body: Mahogany with maple top, sunburst finish, single cutaway
Neck: Mahogany, 22 frets, bound rosewood fingerboard with crown inlays
Headstock: Pearl inlaid Gibson logo, 'Les Paul model' in gold paint
Bridge: Chrome-plated Tune-o-matic with stop tailpiece
Pickguard: Single-ply cream
Pickups: Two humbucking
Controls: Two volume, two tone
Switches: Three-position pickup selector
Case: Black hardshell contour case

Although the Les Paul Standard reissues that Gibson made in the late 1990s are not 100 percent accurate reproductions of the original late 1950s models, they are very good players' instruments with great looks and tone. Clapton probably acquired this 1959 reissue because it looked similar to the 1960 Les Paul Standard (pages 52-53) that he played on John Mayall's *Blues Breakers With Eric Clapton* album in 1966.

ERIC I never really replaced the Beano Les Paul, and I was constantly searching for something to come up to scratch.

1970s GIBSON LES PAUL RECORDING

1999 GIBSON LES PAUL STANDARD

LOT 7 CHRISTIE'S 1999

Serial No: 5 9476
Body: Mahogany, single cutaway, maple top with f-holes, sunburst finish
Neck: Mahogany, 22 frets, bound ebony fingerboard with block inlays
Headstock: Split diamond inlay, Gibson custom shop transfer on back
Bridge: Gold-plated Tune-o-matic with stop tailpiece
Pickups: Two single-coil Alnico V soapbar pickups
Controls: Two volume, two tone
Switches: Three-position pickup selector
Case: Brown hardshell contour case with pink plush lining and handwritten adhesive paper label 'Gibson F.Hole – Alnicos Les Paul #5.9476'

In 1995 Gibson's Custom Shop built a handful of Les Paul Custom guitars featuring hollowed-out mahogany bodies and f-holes cut into the maple tops. These guitars were given to several well-known guitarists, including Clapton, and the design later went into limited production as the Florentine model.

Eric's 1995 Gibson Les Paul Custom Florentine has similar features to the Les Paul Custom models Gibson produced during that time, including its split diamond headstock inlay and ebony fingerboard with block inlays. However, its rectangular-polepiece single-coil Alnico V soapbar pickups, which are unique to Eric's Florentine guitar, are based on the neck pickup found on the original 'Black Beauty' Les Paul Custom Gibson produced from 1953 through 1957.

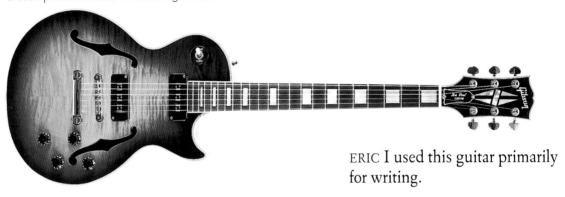

ERIC I used this guitar primarily for writing.

LOT 8 CHRISTIE'S 1999

Serial No: 4955H604
Body: Birch, sunburst finish
Neck: Black painted maple neck, 18 frets, ebonised maple fingerboard with dot inlays
Bridge: Ebonised maple pinless bridge
Pickguard: White pickguard signed and inscribed in black felt pen, 'To Eric without a Doubt a Great Player your friend Les Paul 10-3-94'
Additional: Case with two colour photographs of Les Paul, one signed on reverse, largest=10x8in. (25.4x20.3cm.); a Fat Tuesday's Hot Jazz Flash handbill, Oct.-Nov. 1994, signed and inscribed by Les Paul 'Hi Eric This Guitar is similar to the Guitar i'm [sic] made Electric in 1927/28, Les Paul', and a photocopy of Les Paul holding this guitar in the Fat Tuesday's club
Case: Beige softshell case with label 'Silvertone.AC. Signed Les Paul #4955H604'

Originally selling for less than $20, the Silvertone 604 was an inexpensive acoustic guitar made by Harmony from 1961 to 1967, although its predecessor, the 608 (produced 1959 to 1961), and successor, the 1204 (produced only for a few months in 1968), are essentially the same guitar. Sears, Roebuck and Co. sold thousands of these guitars to aspiring guitar players from its catalogue and retail stores during the 1960s. Harmony also produced the identical Stella H931 model, which was sold by retail music stores.

This Silvertone was a gift that Les Paul gave to Eric during one of Les's regular Monday night shows at the Manhattan nightclub Fat Tuesday's in 1994.

Olympic Studios
Barnes, London, UK
Nov./Dec. 1969

A 'loose jam' with
George Harrison, for
a proposed Ric Grech
solo album after the
Blind Faith split. Ric was
playing bass with Alan
White on drums. The
album never materialised.

Body: Mahogany, single cutaway, black finish
Neck: Mahogany, 22 frets, bound rosewood fingerboard with crown inlays
Headstock: Bound, painted Jay Turser logo
Bridge: Chrome-plated Tune-o-matic-style, stop tailpiece
Pickguard: Cream single-ply
Pickups: Two humbucking
Controls: Two volume, two tone
Switches: Three-position pickup selector
Label: Signed and inscribed in red felt pen 'To Eric, Keep Pickin! Les Paul'
Case: Cardboard shipping box

When Clapton and Steve Winwood performed a series of concerts at Manhattan's Madison Square Garden in February 2008, his old friend and mentor Les Paul came backstage at one of the shows and gave this autographed Les Paul-style Jay Turser JT-200 guitar to Eric as a gift. Les Paul passed away about a year and a half later at the age of 94 on August 13th, 2009.

Jay Turser is a budget brand owned by US Music Corporation that makes low-cost string instruments in China. Most of its electric solidbody models are based on popular designs like the Gibson Les Paul and SG and the Fender Stratocaster and Telecaster.

ERIC In terms of the neck shape and the fingerboard, I never got one that was anywhere near the original.

Falkoner Centret Copenhagen, Denmark Dec. 10, 1969

Clapton and Harrison are playing a concert in Copenhagen with Delaney and Bonnie. The model Clapton is playing served as inspiration for Jay Turser's guitar.

LOT 17 CHRISTIE'S 1999

Serial No: 47764
Body: Mahogany, cherry red finish, double cutaway
Neck: Mahogany, 22 frets, bound rosewood fingerboard with crown inlays
Headstock: Crown peghead inlay
Bridge: Tune-o-matic with 'sideways' Deluxe Gibson vibrato unit
Pickguard: Five-ply (black/white/black/white /black) pickguard
Pickups: Two humbucking
Controls: Two volume, two tone
Switches: Three-position pickup selector
Truss Rod Cover: Three-ply black/white/ black embossed with 'Les Paul'
Case: Black hardshell contour case with yellow plush lining and handwritten adhesive paper label 'Gibson S.G. Les Paul # 47764 Cherry Red – Trem'

Gibson radically redesigned the Les Paul Standard model in late 1960, replacing the maple top, single cutaway body with a thin, solid mahogany slab body with contoured edges and sharp, horn-shaped double cutaways that provide better fret access all the way up the neck.

This stock example is similar to the 1964 SG Standard that Clapton played in Cream, which later was given a psychedelic paint job by The Fool. The biggest difference is this guitar's much maligned 'sideways' Deluxe Gibson vibrato unit, which, unlike the Maestro Vibrola unit on Clapton's '64 SG, was better for knocking strings out of tune than producing usable vibrato effects.

ERIC I bought this guitar for nostalgic reasons. I wanted to recreate the same experience as the psychedelic guitar. It has an incredible design.

LOT 29 CHRISTIE'S 1999

Serial No: 72646
Body: Mahogany, cherry red finish, double cutaway
Neck: Mahogany, 22 frets, rosewood fingerboard with dot inlays
Headstock: 'Les Paul Junior' in gold paint
Bridge: Nickel-plated 'wraparound' compensated bridge/ stud tailpiece
Pickguard: Black three-ply (black/white/black)
Pickups: One P-90 single-coil
Controls: One volume, one tone
Case: Black softshell contour case with handwritten tie-on label ''62 Gibson S.G. Les Paul Jnr. #72646' and adhesive paper label similarly inscribed

With only one pickup, the SG/Les Paul Junior may not offer as much tonal variety as the SG/Les Paul Standard with its two humbuckers, but for many blues and rock guitarists the screaming, aggressive tone of its single-coil P-90 pickup is all they need. The deep double cutaways of the SG Junior also make it a favourite of slide players.

Clapton bought this guitar for collection purposes.

Opposite:
Cream in 1967 with their psychedelic guitars painted by The Fool.

1962 GIBSON SG/LES PAUL STANDARD

61

ERIC The Fool were two Dutch artists, Simon and Marijke, who had come over to London from Amsterdam in 1966 and set up a studio designing clothes, posters and album covers. They painted mystical themes in fantastic vibrant colours and had been taken up by The Beatles, for whom they had created a vast three-storey mural on the wall of their Apple Boutique in Baker Street. I asked them to decorate one of my guitars, a Gibson Les Paul, which they turned into a psychedelic fantasy, painting not just the front and back of the body, but the neck and fretboard too.

Opposite & above:
Palais des Sports
Paris, France
June 1, 1967

Clapton performing
with Cream at the 1st
International Festival
Of Pop Music.

I used the Fool guitar on *Disraeli Gears*, and from then on, really, a lot of the time. It came with the sideways tremolo on it, which I took apart, but I kept the bridge and the tailpiece. I never liked tremolos; I've never been able to stand the bloody things. Eventually I put a stop tailpiece on it.

LOT 14 CHRISTIE'S 1999

Serial No: 90441727
Body: Mahogany and
walnut neck-through-body
construction, mahogany
body wings, Cardinal
Red finish
Neck: Mahogany and
walnut, 22 frets, bound
rosewood fingerboard
with crown inlays
Headstock: Reverse
six-on-a-side with banjo
tuners, Gibson logo on
truss rod cover
Bridge: Nickel-plated
Tune-o-matic with
stop tailpiece
Pickguard: White/black/
white with red
Firebird motif
Pickups: Two mini
humbucking
Controls: Two volume,
two tone
Switches: Three-position
pickup selector
Case: Brown rectangular
hardshell case with pink
plush lining and
handwritten adhesive
paper label 'Gibson – Red
Firebird (Re-Issue)
#90441727'

Eric used this Cardinal Red Gibson Firebird V to play Eddie Boyd's
'Third Degree' and Lowell Fulson's 'Reconsider Baby' at the
Philadelphia Spectrum on September 13th, 1995, on his From the
Cradle Tour. The guitar was a gift from a fan, possibly chosen
due to Eric's association with the Firebird during Cream. Clapton
played this model on stage that night only hours after it was given
to him.

ERIC The SG became my
mainstay until I bought
a Gibson Firebird with one
pickup, and that for a time
became my most favourite
guitar. All during Cream
I'd play the ES-335 (page 26),
or the SG (page 61) or the
Firebird. I don't think I had
a Fender – I think it was only
Gibsons – but I may have
toyed with them.

In a trio I had to provide a lot more of the
sound. My technique altered quite a lot,
in that I started playing a lot more barre
chords and hitting open strings to provide
a kind of drone for my lead work.

Opposite:
New Haven Arena
Connecticut, USA
Oct. 11, 1968

Eric played a Gibson
Firebird, similar to this
one, on Cream's
Farewell Tour of the US.

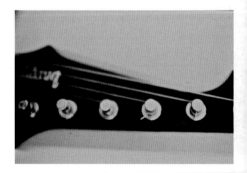

Gigs:
Spectrum, Philadelphia
Pennsylvania, USA
Sept. 13, 1995
Highlight:
'Third Degree'
'Reconsider Baby'

65

LOT 115 BONHAMS 2011

Serial No: N 08030228
Body: Mahogany back and sides, spruce top decorated with New York artist Louis Yanez's reproduction of the *Disraeli Gears* album cover
Neck: Mahogany, 20 frets, rosewood fingerboard with dot inlays
Bridge: Rosewood pin bridge
Case: Black hardshell contour case

For his day job, Louis Yanez of Queens, New York, works for the US Postal Service as a mail carrier. In his spare time, he paints acoustic guitars with highly detailed and incredibly precise reproductions of classic album covers and iconic images from the 1960s and 70s, applying very light layers of paint to preserve the guitar's tone. Yanez generously donated this Epiphone AJ-200EVS that he painted with a stunning reproduction of the cover of Cream's *Disraeli Gears* album to Bonhams March 9th, 2011 auction to benefit the Crossroads Centre.

LOT 95 CHRISTIE'S 1999

Serial No: 173299
Body: Rosewood back and sides, spruce top, bound, natural finish
Neck: Padauk, 20 frets, bound ebony fingerboard with indented triangular abalone insert block inlays
Headstock: Guild 'G-Shield' inlay, 'peaked' Guild logo, bound
Bridge: Ebony pin bridge
Pickguard: Black
Case: Black hardshell contour case with blue plush lining and handwritten tie-on label 'Guild D.55 #173299'

Long before Clapton became one of the most ardent ambassadors of Martin acoustic guitars, he endorsed Guild acoustics. In 1968, Clapton appeared on the cover of the Guild catalogue playing a maple-body Navarre F-50 jumbo acoustic. That was the same year that Guild introduced its new D-55 dreadnought model, which supplanted the F-50s status as Guild's top-of-the-line six-string flat-top acoustic and remained the company's flagship acoustic model through the early 1980s.

Clapton acquired this D-55 in 1978 and used it frequently for writing and recording. Although Clapton started to amass his impressive collection of Martin acoustics in 1970 (page 92), he has also owned and played various Guilds over the years.

ERIC When I went to America around this period I went to a guitar shop and was looking at Guilds. Then word went back to the company and we did a deal. They gave me this one for a sponsorship deal and I was pictured in magazines playing one.

Opposite:
Vognmandsmarken
Copenhagen, Denmark
Feb. 5-6, 1968

Eric filming in a market on the back of a flat-bed truck for the movie *Det Var En Lordag Aften (On A Saturday Night)*. The band mimed two songs, one which was set on a stage ('We're Going Wrong') and the second on a flat-bed lorry which was part of a parade ('World Of Pain'). This guitar was not part of the Crossroads guitar auction, but many Guilds Eric used throughout his career were included.

LOT 59 CHRISTIE'S 1999

Serial No: GF60014
Body: Rosewood back and sides, spruce top, bound, natural finish
Neck: Mahogany, 20 frets, bound ebony fingerboard with slotted diamond inlays. Neck block stamped with date 'JAN 22 1987'
Headstock: Guild 'G-Shield' inlay, 'peaked' Guild logo
Bridge: Ebony pin bridge
Pickguard: Imitation tortoiseshell
Sound Hole: Herringbone rosette decoration
Case: Black hardshell contour case with black plush lining and handwritten label 'Guild GF60 #GF60014 Blonde'

The Guild GF-60R has a similar jumbo body shape and dimensions to the Guild F-50 that Clapton played while he was in Cream. However, the GF-60R has a few different cosmetic features to Clapton's F-50, including its rosewood back and sides and slotted diamond fingerboard inlays. During the late 1980s Guild also offered the GF-60M with maple back and sides. Clapton endorsed Guild guitars around this time, appearing in a variety of Guild adverts in 1987 and 1988 with a GF-60R model.

ERIC The first Guild I saw was Duane Eddy's. He played one, so it was quite necessary to me to get one. Keith Richards had one for a little while too. Also Richie Havens was playing one when I first saw him and I loved the sound of it.

Clapton pictured with a similar model Guild in Surrey, 1993. This shot was used on the cover of the paperback edition of *Eric Clapton: The Autobiography*.

Serial Nos: GF600122, GF600128
Body: Rosewood back and sides, spruce top, bound, natural finish
Neck: Mahogany, 20 frets, bound ebony fingerboard with slotted diamond inlays. Neck block stamped with date 'MAY 10 1988'
Headstock: Guild 'G-Shield' inlay, 'peaked' Guild logo
Bridge: Ebony pin bridge
Pickguard: Imitation tortoiseshell
Sound Hole: Herringbone rosette
Case: Black hardshell contour case with black plush lining and handwritten tie-on label

Lots 65 and 66 in the 1999 Crossroads auction are virtually identical. They even have their necks stamped with the same date and serial numbers only six digits apart; however, it appears that Lot 66 was labelled incorrectly as a 1988 Guild F-61. Both guitars were bought for Clapton's collection.

ERIC I went through a whole period of using Guilds, a 12-string and a six-string. I still do quite like them. These were nice guitars.

1988 GUILD GF-60R

Serial No: KK000365
Body: One-piece routed mahogany, spruce top, multiple-layer binding, single cutaway, natural finish
Neck: Mahogany, 22 frets, rosewood fingerboard with dot inlays
Headstock: Guild 'Chesterfield' inlay, 'peaked' Guild logo
Bridge: Rosewood pin bridge
Pickguard: Imitation tortoiseshell
Soundhole: Round
Pickups: Fishman transducer
Controls: Volume, concentric treble/bass
Label: 'Songbird Amber KK000365'
Case: Black Guild hardshell contour case with black plush lining, handwritten label with various inscriptions including 'Guild Songbird Acoustic'

The Songbird was Guild's entry into a new category of guitar developed during the 1980s called the electric-acoustic. Unlike an acoustic-electric, which is essentially a standard acoustic guitar with a pickup and possibly a preamp system installed in it, an electric-acoustic resembles a solidbody or semi-hollow guitar but with special construction details and pickups designed to produce amplified acoustic guitar-like tones. Gibson's nylon-string Chet Atkins Standard/CE was one of the first electric-acoustic guitars on the market, and several companies developed steel-string models based on this concept.

Guild introduced the Songbird in 1988. The back and sides consist of a thin, hollowed-out slab of mahogany, while the top was made of thin spruce and braced similar to a standard flat-top steel-string acoustic. Unlike an acoustic-electric, the Songbird is more of an electric than an acoustic guitar as it does not offer full, rich acoustic tone when unamplified. However, when it is plugged in it is more resistant to feedback, which makes it ideal for use in loud bands along with drums and electric instruments.

1988 GUILD SONGBIRD AMBER

1989 GUILD F-46

LOT 60 CHRISTIE'S 1999

Serial No: KJ100096
Body: Rosewood back and sides, spruce top, bound, sunburst finish
Neck: Mahogany, 20 frets, bound ebony fingerboard with slotted diamond inlays. Neck block stamped with date 'FEB 17 1989'
Headstock: Guild 'G-Shield' inlay, 'peaked' Guild logo
Bridge: Ebony pin bridge
Pickguard: Imitation tortoiseshell
Case: Black hardshell contour case with black plush lining and handwritten tie-on label 'Guild F46 NT S/Burst # KJ100096' and adhesive paper label similarly inscribed

This is one of several Guild acoustics that Clapton acquired while he was endorsing Guild guitars during the late 1980s. The F-46 was originally part of a series of guitars designed with input from Nashville vintage guitar dealer/historian George Gruhn in 1984. After 1986, when Gruhn's collaboration with Guild ended, Guild renamed the F-46 as the GF-60 model, even though both models were essentially identical. Why this 1989 Guild is identified as an F-46 is unknown, although it's possible that due to a change of ownership that occurred around this time an old label that was still lying around was used. This is supported by the serial number on the label, which corresponds with the F-46 KJ letter code and that model's serial numbers from 1986.

The tie-on label affixed to the case identifies the guitar as a 'Guild F46 NT', but the 'NT' suffix is incorrect as that is Guild's designation for 'natural top'. The 1986 Guild price list includes F-46NT and F-46SB (sunburst) models, so it's likely that this guitar is actually a GF-60 with a sunburst finish and an old label that was supposed to go inside a 1986 F-46NT.

1992 GUILD SONGBIRD CUSTOM

LOT 105 BONHAMS 2011

Serial No: KK001422
Body: One-piece routed mahogany, spruce top, bound, abalone purfling, black finish
Neck: Mahogany, 22 frets, bound ebony fingerboard with mother-of-pearl block inlays with triangular abalone inserts
Headstock: Bound, Guild 'G-Shield' inlay, 'peaked' Guild logo
Bridge: Ebony pin bridge with abalone inlays
Pickguard: Black single-ply
Soundhole: Round, inlaid abalone rosette
Pickups: Fishman transducer
Controls: Volume, concentric treble/bass
Label: 'Guild, model Songbird Custom, Serial KK001422, Made in USA, Guild Music Corporation, Westerly, RI 02891'
Case: Brown Guild hardshell rectangular case with black plush lining, two handwritten labels

The Guild Songbird Custom was essentially identical to the Songbird with the exception of its gold-plated tuners, and selection of custom-colour finishes. This particular example is a custom variant, featuring much fancier inlays that include the fingerboard's mother-of-pearl block inlays with triangular inserts and multiple-layer strips placed near the inside edge of the lower and upper E strings normally found on Guild's flagship instruments, the abalone rosette ring and top purfling, and distinctive fern-like inlays on the ebony bridge.

Serial No: AA000124
Body: Flame maple back and sides, spruce top, bound f-holes, multiple-layer binding, round cutaway, natural finish
Neck: Laminated flame maple, 20 frets, bound ebony fingerboard with mother-of-pearl block inlays with triangle abalone inserts
Headstock: Multiple-layer binding, mother-of-pearl block inscribed Artist Award Model with abalone edges, peaked Guild logo, signed by Clapton
Bridge: Ebony, gold-plated 'harp' trapeze tailpiece with cut-out 'G'
Pickguard: Imitation tortoiseshell with multiple-layer binding
Pickups: One floating Kent Armstrong humbucking
Controls: One volume
Other: Gold-plated Grover Imperial tuners
Case: Black mock-crocodile hardshell contour case, green plush lining, handwritten label

Guild may be best known for its flat-top steel-string acoustic guitars, but the company also produced many outstanding archtop models that have a cult following in vintage guitar collector circles. Guild introduced its flagship archtop model, the Johnny Smith Award, in 1956. The model's name changed to the Artist Award in 1960 when Smith's contract with Guild expired and he signed a new endorsement agreement with Gibson. The specifications for the model remained the same, however, and the model has undergone only minor changes after nearly six decades of continuous production.

Fender Musical Instruments Corporation purchased Guild in 1995, and Guild continued to build guitars in its Westerly, Rhode Island factory (where Guild had produced instruments since 1967) until August 31st, 2001, when production moved to Fender's factory in Corona, California. Guild's most experienced craftsmen built only a few Artist Award guitars individually by hand each year using only the finest materials available, and each guitar took several months to complete.

1997 GUILD ARTIST AWARD

Serial No: AK700138
Body: Flame maple back and sides, book-matched spruce top, multiple-layer bound f-holes, multiple-layer binding, round cutaway, sunburst finish
Neck: Laminated flame maple, 20 frets, bound ebony fingerboard with mother-of-pearl block inlays with triangle abalone inserts
Headstock: Bound, Guild 'G-Shield' inlay, 'peaked' Guild logo, truss rod cover engraved 'X-700'
Bridge: Ebony, gold-plated 'harp' trapeze tailpiece with cut-out 'G'
Pickguard: Three-ply black (black/white/black) art deco stairstep
Pickups: Two humbucking with gold-plated covers
Controls: Master volume, two volume, two tone
Switches: Three-position pickup selector
Case: Dark brown Guild hardshell contour case with red plush lining, label with various inscriptions

Introduced in 1994, the Guild X-700 Stuart was Guild's top-of-the-line electric archtop model for a brief period through 1999 when it was discontinued. Guild produced these guitars in very limited numbers, making them highly desirable collector's items today. Featuring a body measuring 17 inches across the lower bout, the X-700 was Guild's equivalent of the Gibson L-5CES, and it is held in similar high regard by performing jazz guitarists who appreciate its refined tones and outstanding playability.

TIMEPIECES

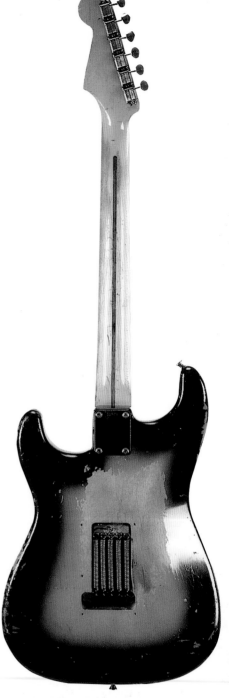

Serial No: 12073
Body: Alder, sunburst finish, dated 6-56
Neck: Maple with skunk-stripe truss rod routing, 21 frets, maple fingerboard with dot inlays. Neck date and initials XA-6-56 written in pencil
Bridge: Synchronised tremolo
Pickguard: White single-ply
Controls: One volume, two tone
Pickups: Three single-coil
Switches: Five-position pickup selector with white switch tip (replaced original three-position pickup selector sometime in the 1970s)
Additional: Red guitar strap
Case: Black rectangular hardshell case stencilled on both sides in yellow 'DEREK AND THE DOMINOS' and 'FRAGILE' and handwritten tie-on label inscribed '1956 Strat #12073 2TSB BR'

On May 7th, 1967, while he was playing with Cream, Eric Clapton purchased his first Fender Stratocaster – a used 1956 model – from London's Sound City music shop for £150. On June 24th, 1999, after Clapton made history with the guitar over the previous two decades, it sold for nearly $500,000 at the Eric Clapton Guitars in Aid of the Crossroads Centre auction held by Christie's in Manhattan.

Clapton made this sunburst Stratocaster, nicknamed 'Brownie', his main guitar in 1970. It first appeared on stage with Clapton when he was playing with Delaney and Bonnie, and he used the guitar to record several songs on the Derek and The Dominos album *Layla and Other Assorted Love Songs*, including the title track. Brownie also appeared in photographs inside *Layla*'s gatefold cover and on the cover of Eric's first solo album. From that point onwards it became one of his favourite guitars, used extensively in the studio and on stage over the years, although his black Stratocaster known as 'Blackie' (page 122) replaced Brownie's status as his main guitar in 1971.

* In succeeding years, Brownie's selling price was surpassed by electric guitars previously owned by Jimi Hendrix and Jerry Garcia (The Grateful Dead), respectively.

Playlist:
Eric Clapton, 1970
Layla And Other Assorted Love Songs, 1970
Gigs:
Delaney and Bonnie and Friends with Eric Clapton USA Tour Feb. 1970
Derek and The Dominos June-Dec. 1970
Highlight:
'Layla'

ERIC I don't think there's anything on the Stratocaster that doesn't come from pure logic. I would challenge anybody to come up with a better design for a guitar. The Stratocaster is as good as it gets, isn't it?

ERIC With Delaney and Bonnie I used my old Stratocaster, Brownie, which was really, really good – a great sound. It was just right for the kind of music I was playing with them.

ERIC I never met Leo Fender, but I wish I had. If I could go back and somehow talk to him about the Stratocaster, I'd say, 'You've created something that can't be bettered, really. How did you do that?' I know there were prototypes with the Telecaster and the Esquire, and some early experimental stages, but nevertheless, the fact that he got to this conclusion so quickly is remarkable. Leo Fender was so far in advance of anybody else, developing the Strat to the point where it just couldn't be bettered, even now. My hat's off to him.

I think Brownie dictated the way I played to a certain extent. Because the Strat has less sustain – it's harder to bend on and harder to hold the bends and apply vibrato – I play more notes. I didn't look at the change from Gibson to Fender as 'I'm done with that.' It was more a case of wanting to try something else.

In the early days I had predominantly played a Gibson Les Paul. The Les Paul had completely knocked the Strat out of the public eye back then. Everyone was playing Les Pauls (page 52) and 335s (page 26) and other guitars like that.

Fillmore East
New York, USA
Feb. 1970

Delaney and Bonnie and
friends with Eric Clapton.

ERIC I had a lot of influences when I took up the Strat. Everyone thought, 'What do you want with these? Nobody plays these any more,' but Buddy Guy was playing one, Steve Winwood was playing one, and Buddy Holly played one.

You could really hear the Strat on *Hoodoo Man Blues* by Junior Wells with Buddy Guy. It was so immediate. You heard the sound of the wood, and I wanted to pursue that sound. Buddy Holly played a sunburst Strat with a maple neck, and that became my Holy Grail. For me the whole thing went back to the cover of *The 'Chirping' Crickets*, the first album I ever bought. There was a picture of a Stratocaster on it, so it's been iconic for me from year one.

When I got my hands on one, I was surprised at how easy it was to play. One reason why I hadn't played Strats earlier in my career was that the necks always looked so narrow. I thought, 'I won't be able to bend any strings, no room,' but in fact I was wrong.

Picking up a Stratocaster makes me play a bit differently. I find that I play more with my fingers because of the way my hand sits on the guitar. I don't feel the need to use a pick quite so much as I would with any other guitar, where the bridge sits higher off the body. With the Strat the bridge is almost flush with the guitar, so my hand rests on the body, part of my heel rests on the bridge, and then my fingers rest on the scratchplate. It's really easy to play either way, but I've found more and more that I'm using just my fingers. It's got those famous lead tones, but it's so versatile you can use it in any kind of rhythmic sense as well – great big power chords, or that really light kind of Tamla/Motown chord sound with very little volume. Unlike most other electric guitars, it sounds almost better when the guitar's volume knob is on two or three, really under-amplified and quiet.

ERIC Brownie was the last guitar to be sold in the 1999 Crossroads auction and when it was brought out onto the revolving rostrum, they played 'Layla' over the PA and the whole audience stood up.

I had no idea what 'Layla' was going to be. It was just a ditty. When you get near to the end of it you know you've got something really powerful. I'm incredibly proud of 'Layla'. To have ownership of something that powerful is something I'll never be able to get used to. But the funny thing was that once I'd got 'Layla' out of my system I didn't want to do any more with the Dominos. I didn't want to play another note.

This shoot produced the album cover for Eric's first solo release, *Eric Clapton*, in 1970.

Body: Rosewood back and sides, cedar top, decorative back stripe with heart inlays, inlaid heart motif on top's lower bout, natural finish
Neck: Seven-ply laminated maple and walnut, 18 frets, bound ebony fingerboard with silver heart inlays, silver nut
Headstock: Three silver four-leaf clover inlays, silver heart-shaped truss rod cover engraved 'Eric Clapton'
Bridge: Ebony pin bridge with silver four-leaf clover inlays, silver engraved bridge pins and saddle
Soundhole: Heart-shaped with purple heart amaranth heart inlays, ebony edging
Label: 'Engraving D. O'Brien/Zemaitis/ Hand-Made Guitars/ Commissioned & Co. Designed/By/Eric Clapton esq/London/1969', signed and dated by maker 'Antonius Casimere Zemaitis 1969'. Label is heart-shaped and made from hand-illuminated parchment
Case: Anvil hardshell case with adhesive tape inscribed 'Auction #54/ Zemaitis 'Ivan' 12 St.'

Playlist:
Blind Faith, 1969
George Harrison:
'My Sweet Lord', 1970
Bobby Whitlock:
Bobby Whitlock, 1972
Highlight:
Derek and The Dominos' debut concert
Lyceum Ballroom
London, UK
June 14, 1970

Tony Zemaitis (1935-2002) first honed his woodworking skills as a cabinetmaker, but when he was unable to find a guitar to his liking in the 1950s he started building string instruments. By 1965 Zemaitis became a full-time luthier, working by himself in a workshop in London where he built acoustic guitars for many of Britain's top blues and folk guitarists, including Long John Baldry, Spencer Davis and Davey Graham. In 1968, Eric Clapton solicited Zemaitis to build a custom 12-string guitar for him.

Zemaitis completed the guitar that Clapton envisioned in 1969, and Clapton first played it while he was in Blind Faith. Clapton briefly loaned the guitar to George Harrison, who apparently used it on the recording of 'My Sweet Lord', released in 1970. Harrison later commissioned his own Zemaitis 12-string in 1974. Eric also loaned his guitar to Bobby Whitlock, who used it on his self-titled solo album in 1971, on which Eric guests. Dave Mason was photographed playing Eric's Zemaitis on stage when he sat in with the debut performance of Derek and The Dominos (page 89).

Shortly after that, Clapton's Zemaitis 12-string, which he had nicknamed 'Ivan the Terrible', met its initial demise, before being rebuilt by the maker years later.

ERIC There was a guy near London who made 12-string guitars on a massive scale, the likes of which no one had ever seen before.

ERIC I finally got to meet Tony Zemaitis in the mid-Sixties. I asked him to make a 12-string for me, bigger than he'd ever done before and inlaid with silver. I wanted it to be incredibly ornate. I wanted to explore everything we could. The heart shape and the four-leaf clover on the headstock were my ideas. So he made this guitar, it probably took about a year, and it was massive. It's reputed to be the biggest 12-string in the world. It's about the same dimensions as a mariachi bass. Tony really did a beautiful job. I used it with Blind Faith and I did some other material with it.

I was involved in a very, very stormy relationship at the time. During one of our big rows, I took the guitar and I demolished it. I took it by the neck and I banged it against the wall until there was nothing left. Then about five years later – I still had the neck – I took it back to Tony and said, 'I've got to tell you a terrible story, forgive me I can't bear to be without it,' and I apologised and made all the excuses I could think of. He was shocked, but he understood, so he built another body onto the neck. So this is Mark 2 – the first one was destroyed, but the neck is original.

Eric Clapton and his first Zemaitis photographed in Dec. 1969.

Notes written by Tony Zemaitis give an account of how his commission to make 'Ivan the Terrible' occurred. Apparently a previous client, who had just sold his giant 12-string Zemaitis to Clapton, rang one morning:

'He was a bit out of breath and said he and Eric plus minder were on the way over. To be honest I didn't realise just how big he was in the business. When he arrived he was charm itself and we almost immediately had a sheet of paper on the table to draw out his ideas. The resulting A/C 12 had 30 sec sustain, later cut to 26 secs, with added silver inlays to bridge plus solid silver bridge pins.

'It was my most adventurous and decorated guitar to that date and probably still is. It was so gigantic I had to re-think the internal struts into a double-kite shape to artificially reduce the front area. It sounded like an organ and was even taken for such when used on the *Blind Faith* album – then on "My Sweet Lord" when it was borrowed by George Harrison after a rebuild.

'The guitar was made in old S. American Rosewood with Cedar front and inlaid with ebony edged amaranthe [sic] hearts. Plus silver mounted F/Bound, inlays etc. It was loud and strong with a good tone and the phenomenal duration. Clapton asked me to raise the action as he double bent pairs of strings at a time. I cut the jig down by several inches to serve as a super giant A/C Bass – that's how big "Ivan the Terrible" was. It was also a showy "stage" guitar... a totally different instrument to a normal 12 sound.

'An American company tested the length of sustain and when they told me 26 seconds I couldn't believe it. I didn't set out with that purpose in mind when I built it. I thought it would sustain for maybe 17 seconds, which is still very good, but 26 seconds!' According to Zemaitis the sustain is all down to the string length, the standard he used was 25⅝ inches from nut to bridge.

An article in *Guitar Player*, October 1970 gives a full breakdown of how this unique Zemaitis guitar was made, confirming that it was co-designed by Eric and A.C. Zemaitis, with Eric concentrating on the inlays and general appearance and Zemaitis handling the technical and construction side. According to this article, Mark One took three months to make. The rosewood and cedar body of the jumbo 12-string had the following dimensions: 23 inches long, 20 inches wide and 6 inches deep. Heart inlays of purple-hued amaranth, edged in ebony, circle the heart-shaped soundhole and run down the back of the body. Special lacquering, which took approximately four weeks, has produced a loud and mellow voice that hints of organ and harpsichord tones. There are a few minor differences in the design detail of the rebuilt body; the neck however is the original and as such was made of amaranth, ebony and mahogany with an ebony fingerboard. All of the edging and heart-shaped inlays on the neck are of solid, hand-engraved silver. Nut, bridge saddle and engraved bridge pins are also in silver. Eric apparently requested a shorter neck than Zemaitis customarily built, with only 12 frets clear of the body, instead of 14 or 15. The head is similar to a 17th-century five-course guitar. 'Ivan The Terrible', which Bob Dylan apparently called the 'the love box', is significant for a number of reasons, not only because it was designed by and for Clapton, but also because few guitars are made, even on an individual basis, that include as much detailed work. Even the label on Eric's guitar is heart-shaped and made from hand-illuminated parchment.

LOT 49 BONHAMS 2011

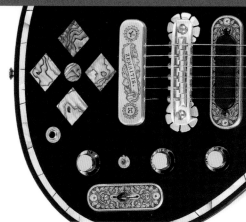

Serial No: A121904
Body: Mahogany, mother-of-pearl purfling, abalone diamond and dot inlays, single pointed cutaway, black finish
Neck: Mahogany, 22 frets, ebony fingerboard with diamond and dot inlays
Headstock: Two silver plaques – one engraved with a foliate motif, the other with Zemaitis 'Z' logo
Bridge: Duralumin Tune-o-matic-style, Duralumin stop tailpiece engraved with a foliate design and 'Zemaitis'
Pickups: Three DiMarzio single-coil
Controls: One volume, two tone
Switches: Three-position pickup selector, phase
Additional: Zemaitis tool kit
Case: Grey Zemaitis mock crocodile contour hardshell case with black plush lining, handwritten label with various inscriptions including 'ZEMAITIS SER E.CLAPTON /BLACK, ENGRAVED'

Shortly after Tony Zemaitis retired in 2000 he established a partnership with a Japanese company that he authorised to continue building Zemaitis models based on his original drawings and specifications. Although Zemaitis passed away before the first new Zemaitis models were completed, his wife (Ann) and son (Tony Zemaitis Jr.) continued to provide the support needed to faithfully reproduce his instruments. Engraver Danny O'Brien, who did the engraving work on the original Zemaitis guitars, also continued to create designs for the metal parts on the new Zemaitis guitars. The Greco guitar company also produces licensed Zemaitis guitar designs at more affordable prices.

ERIC I was introduced to the Zemaitis when I was about 13 years old. I saw this guy called Buck, who used to play on the streets in London, and I followed him around... there was a gang of bohemian characters and he was the Pied Piper.

LOT 14 BONHAMS 2011

Body: African blackwood back and sides, spruce top, asymmetrical twisted body shape, violin-style raised koa binding, gold leaf interior with three-dimensionally combined fan and X bracing, natural finish
Neck: Mahogany, 20 frets, ebony fingerboard
Headstock: Engraved aluminium 'Z' plaque with floral motif, engraved aluminium truss rod cover inscribed 'Eric Clapton'
Bridge: Ebony 'moustache' pin bridge
Soundhole: Heart-shaped with ebony-edged koa soundhole ring
Case: Black hardshell contour case with burgundy plush lining, handwritten label with various inscriptions including 'Made For EC'

In addition to producing a variety of solidbody instruments, today Zemaitis also makes several acoustic models based on or inspired by Tony Zemaitis' original designs. This 2005 Zemaitis custom acoustic features a unique, one-of-a-kind design that was developed especially for Clapton. The guitar has many unusual features, including an interior entirely covered in gold leaf, an unorthodox combination of fan and X bracing, and an asymmetrical pseudo-cutaway body shape that meets the neck at the 14th fret on the bass side and the 16th fret on the treble side. Danny O'Brien designed the 'Z' logo headstock plate and the floral motif truss rod cover engraved with Clapton's name. Only two were made and the model was never intended for production.

ERIC Buck would play all those songs by Jesse Fuller and Lead Belly, and he had a Zemaitis. It was huge, there was nothing on it and it was very primitive.

2005 ZEMAITIS S22BP 3S

2005 ZEMAITIS CUSTOM ACOUSTIC

TIMEPIECES

Serial No: 930682
Body: Rosewood back and sides, spruce top, abalone purfling, natural finish
Neck: Mahogany, 20 frets, bound ebony fingerboard with pearl snowflake inlays and mother-of-pearl 'Christian F Martin' signature inlay between the 18th and 19th frets
Headstock: Solid, bound, pearl vertical C.F. Martin inlay
Bridge: Ebony 'belly' pin bridge
Pickguard: Imitation tortoiseshell
Soundhole: Inlaid abalone rosette
Additional: Maker's warranty and various accessories
Case: Black hardshell contour case with green plush lining, handwritten label with various inscriptions including 'MARTIN D45V 'Dreadnought''

With the exception of some limited-edition instruments produced in recent years, the Martin D-45 is the fanciest dreadnought guitar model that Martin makes. Martin built its first D-45 in 1933 for Gene Autry and made another five in various configurations between 1934 and 1937. Regular production of the D-45 started in 1938 but lasted only a few years until production halted in 1942 due to World War II. Martin produced a total of 91 D-45 guitars during the pre-war period between 1933 and 1942. In 1968, Martin reissued the D-45 due to popular demand. The first 229 reissue D-45 guitars feature Brazilian rosewood construction, but in 1969 Martin switched to Indian rosewood due to restrictions on exports of Brazilian rosewood.

Clapton was seen playing a 1969 Martin D-45 during the late 1960s and early 1970s, including a 1969 German television appearance with Delaney and Bonnie and the debut performance of Derek and The Dominos at London's Lyceum Theatre. This 2003 Martin D-45V, which Martin gave to Clapton, is based on the earliest production version of the D-45 that Martin made during 1938 and early 1939, featuring a 14-fret neck and period-correct snowflake fingerboard inlays (Martin switched to large, hexagon-shaped fingerboard inlays later in 1939). This model features a reproduction of Christian F. Martin Sr.'s signature inlaid between the 18th and 19th frets, a feature initially introduced on the 1996 C.F. Martin Sr. Commemorative Edition D-45 models, but later also found on D-45V guitars produced from 1999 to 2005.

Lyceum Ballroom
London, UK
June 14, 1970

Clapton played a dreadnought at Derek and The Dominos' first concert. Dave Mason is playing Clapton's Zemaitis.

Body: Rosewood back and sides, spruce top, ebony binding with pearl purfling, natural finish
Neck: Mahogany, 20 frets, ebony fingerboard with pearl inlays, ebony binding with pearl purfling
Headstock: Solid, ebony binding with pearl purfling, pearl butterfly inlay
Bridge: Ebony 'belly' pin bridge with pointed extensions and pearl inlays
Soundhole: Pearl inlaid rosette
Pickguard: Black single-ply
Label: 'David Russell Young/Luthier' signed and dated 'David Russell Young/1978'
Case: Hardshell case with adhesive tape inscribed 'David Russell Young/6 String AC/1978'

David Russell Young's 1975 book *The Steel String Guitar – Construction and Repair* was one of a handful of resources that inspired aspiring independent acoustic guitar luthiers during the 1970s and 80s, establishing the foundation for today's steel-string acoustic guitar renaissance. This beautiful Martin D-45-inspired dreadnought that Young built in 1978 reveals the depth of his knowledge and his considerable craftsmanship. The level of detail in the butterfly inlay on the headstock is particularly stunning.

Clapton purchased this one-of-a-kind guitar from Fred Walecki of Westwood Music in Los Angeles, California.

ERIC It was the inlay that initially attracted me towards this guitar. It's a beautiful thing.

Serial No: 79081864
Body: Three-piece jacaranda and rosewood back with decorative wood strips, jacaranda sides, spruce top, multi-layer binding, natural finish
Neck: Mahogany, 20 frets, bound rosewood fingerboard with dot inlays
Headstock: Bound, rosewood veneer
Bridge: Ebony 'belly' pin bridge
Pickguard: Black single-ply
Controls: EQ, gain
Additional: Red, white and black machine-embroidered guitar strap
Case: Black hardshell contour case with yellow plush lining and handwritten label with various inscriptions including 'TAKAMINE... "D" SIZE ACOUSTIC'

The Japanese guitar manufacturing company Takamine caught the attention of guitarists in America and Europe during the 1970s thanks to their flat-top steel-string acoustic guitar models that offered an affordably priced alternative to Martin's most popular dreadnought models. However, the design and construction of Takamine guitars was a little too close to those of Martin guitars – even the 'Takamine & Co./Est. 1962' headstock logo closely resembled the Martin logo – so Martin sent Takamine a cease and desist letter in the early 1980s. The Takamine EF375S, which was based on the Martin D-35, was one of the models that motivated Martin to pursue legal action against Takamine.

One feature that Takamine guitars had that Martin weren't offering at the time was the palathetic pickup system featuring individual piezo transducers for each string mounted under the saddle and a built-in preamp with gain and EQ controls mounted on the guitar's side. This was one of the most successful early commercial systems for amplifying an acoustic guitar, which guitarists praised for its natural acoustic sound quality and resistance to feedback.

TIMEPIECES

Serial No: V25 583
Body: Maple/alder neck-through-body construction, hollow moulded composite shell wings with aluminium ribs, Ocean Pearl finish
Neck: Maple, 22 frets, rosewood fingerboard with abalone dot inlays
Headstock: White metal plaque engraved with 'Om' motif
Bridge: Strings-through-body nickel-plated bridge baseplate with six adjustable saddles
Pickguard: Composite with RKS logo
Pickups: Two humbucking
Controls: Internally mounted volume and tone
Switches: Internally mounted three-position pickup selector
Additional: Hexagonal keys, three picks
Case: Black rectangular hardshell case with black plush lining, handwritten label with various inscriptions including 'RKS "Dr Who Special" V25 583, Gift from Dave Mason, R.A.H. 05.'

American industrial designer Ravi K. Sawhney is the founder and CEO of RKS, a company known for its award-winning appliance, home electronics, kitchen utensil and medical equipment product designs and for its role in the development of the Panaflex Millennium XL camera system. Sawhney also helped develop touchscreen technology and the Teddy Ruxpin animatronic talking toy bear. In 2000 Sawhney conceived an innovative and unusual new guitar design, which inspired him to go into business as a guitar manufacturer.

Ravi's brother Ramesh introduced Ravi to his friend, guitarist/singer Dave Mason, who agreed to become a company partner and provide RKS Guitars with valuable constructive criticism about the guitar's design from his perspective as a professional musician. RKS developed a variety of solidbody and hollowbody models, all based upon a basic neck-through-body design with innovative wings that attached to the centre section with aluminium ribs that enhanced resonance. The guitar's distinctive body shape was allegedly based on the curvaceous hips of an unspecified famous singer/actress.

Although the design world, guitar magazines and a handful of players brave enough to stray from the comfort of traditional instruments praised Sawhney's visionary designs, RKS Guitars produced guitars only for a very brief period from 2003 through 2007. The biggest problem was the expensive price tag for their initial models. By the time RKS introduced their first affordable models it was too late as the company's profits were already experiencing a severe decline.

Mason, who toured with Clapton as a member of Delaney and Bonnie and Friends in 1969, personally gave this guitar to Clapton as a gift during the Cream reunion concerts at Royal Albert Hall in May 2005.

Serial No: 23399
Body: Rosewood back and sides, spruce top, rosewood back and top binding, natural finish
Neck: Mahogany, 20 frets, ebony fingerboard with dot inlays
Headstock: Slotted
Bridge: Ebony 'pyramid' pin bridge
Case: Later hardshell case with adhesive tape inscribed 'Martin 1925 #23399/O-Size'

The 0-21 was a slightly fancier version of Martin's 0-18, with the main differences being its bound back, herringbone rosette, and herringbone back strip. This 1925 example predates Martin's shift in 1927 to a steel-string version of this model. Production of the 0-21 was consistent until 1932, when Martin skipped a few years of making this model and offered it sporadically until 1948 when it was discontinued.

ERIC This guitar is beautiful. It was tough parting with this one. I used this guitar as a home guitar – for writing and playing at home.

Delaney was one of the first people to say to me, 'You can sing, you should sing.' Having got me to sing, Delaney started trying to get me to compose as well. So I was writing a lot. By the end of the tour with Delaney and Bonnie, I was ready to make my first solo album album and felt very sure of myself.

I thought of singing as the bit that went between the guitar playing – something I couldn't wait to get out of the way. It was originally like a chore that I didn't really enjoy. It wasn't until later in my career that all of the components became completely integrated, equally important and really dependent on one another.

Opposite:
Hurtwood Edge
Surrey, UK
1969

Eric Clapton pictured in his office with one of what he calls his 'home guitars'. This shoot accompanied an interview by *Melody Maker*'s Chris Welch.

LOT 1 CHRISTIE'S 2004

Serial No: 8324
Body: Rosewood back and sides, rosewood bound spruce top, natural finish
Neck: Cedar, 19 frets, ebony fingerboard with pearl dot inlays
Headstock: Slotted
Bridge: Ebony 'pyramid' pin bridge
Case: Later hardshell case with adhesive tape inscribed 'Martin O-Size 1898/(Has Guts On) #8324'

This Martin 0-18 is one of only 21 0-18 guitars that Martin made in 1898, the year that Martin introduced this model. The 0-18 model originally did not have any inlays on its fingerboard, so the pearl dot inlays seen here were likely installed later or the neck or fingerboard was replaced sometime during the guitar's history. Although today Martin is known primarily for its steel-string flat-top acoustic guitars, early Martin guitars like this one were designed for gut strings. Martin started producing its first traditional flat-top steel-string guitar models 24 years later in 1922, which were preceded by steel-string Hawaiian guitars that Martin started offering in 1917.

ERIC I've played this a lot. It was a home guitar. The gut strings get used a lot in my house because they're quiet... there's something about a gut string that makes it easier to be a solo instrument. Even with an acoustic guitar I feel like I should be in a band or at least have some other sideman or bass. But gut strings can play on their own really well.

1898 MARTIN 0-18

LOT 5 CHRISTIE'S 2004

Serial No: 12095
Body: Rosewood back and sides, spruce top, ivory back and top binding with multi-coloured purfling, natural finish
Neck: Cedar, 19 frets, ivory-bound ebony fingerboard with pearl inlays
Headstock: Slotted
Soundhole: Pearl inlaid rosette
Bridge: Ebony 'pyramid' pin bridge
Case: Later hardshell case with adhesive tape inscribed 'Auction #53/ O-30 1915'

Martin's Style 27 guitars do not conform to the company's designation system where the models become fancier as the style number increases. Martin didn't produce many Style 27 guitars – their production records list only 13 1-27 guitars and eight 2-27 guitars between 1898 and 1908 – so perhaps they decided that the amount made wasn't significant enough to confuse their customers by changing the style designation. Although Martin kept very detailed production records starting in 1898, no 0-27 guitar appears in their records so this 1915 0-27 could be a one-of-a-kind instrument. Details like its ivory binding, multi-coloured purfling, zig-zag back stripe, and fine-quality brass tuning machines give it a distinctive appearance unlike any other 0-size instruments from this era.

Eric Clapton kept this guitar at his country home for private use for a number of years, and played this guitar frequently in the years before it was sold.

ERIC This guitar had a lot of use.

1915 MARTIN 0-27

LOT 24 CHRISTIE'S 1999

Serial No: 13705
Body: Mahogany body, spruce top, natural finish
Neck: Mahogany, 19 frets, ebony fingerboard with dot inlays
Headstock: Slotted
Bridge: Ebony 'pyramid' pin bridge
Case: Black hardshell contour case with purple plush lining and handwritten tie-on label '1919 Martin Mod. 018 #13705' and adhesive paper label similarly inscribed

In 1919 when this guitar was built, the 0-18 was one of Martin's most popular six-string models, with only the 1-18 produced in greater numbers that year. Though designed for gut strings, the 0-18 features Martin's cross bracing that is strong enough to allow the guitar to be strung with light-gauge steel strings. When strung this way, these early Martins are renowned for their sweet, balanced tone.

This 0-18 was one of several guitars that Clapton kept around his house for songwriting purposes.

ERIC Sometimes I would have been on the road for maybe a month, and I'd see a guitar and forget that maybe I already had another one of that model at home and hadn't seen it for a couple of years. When we'd get home and tally it up I would find that I already had one. There are two or three instances where that's happened. Half the fun of going on the road, apart from playing music, especially in America, is what you do with your free time. You go and find a vintage guitar stall and look... you just might find the most spectacular version. You're always going to look.

1919 MARTIN 0-18

LOT 3 CHRISTIE'S 2004

Serial No: 179379
Body: Mahogany back and sides, spruce top, natural finish
Neck: Mahogany, 19 frets, rosewood fingerboard
Headstock: Slotted
Bridge: Rosewood straight pin bridge
Pickguard: Imitation tortoiseshell
Additional: Letter from The Martin Guitar Company, dated January 20th, 1989, signed by Mike Longworth
Case: Later hardshell case with adhesive tape inscribed 'Martin: 0-16 Auction #35/#179379'

Martin introduced the 0-16NY in 1961 to cater to the folk music boom that was thriving during that period in time. The 0-16NY could be strung either with nylon or light-gauge steel strings, and its 12-fret neck, natural satin finish, lack of fingerboard inlays and simple appearance were designed to evoke Martin's 19th-century instruments. The 0-16NY sold very well during the 1960s, but after sales decreased during the 1970s Martin offered it only on a special-order basis through the early 1990s when the model was discontinued.

When the guitar sold at Christie's 2004 Crossroads Guitar Auction, it was accompanied by a letter from Martin historian Mike Longworth dated January 20th, 1989.

ERIC I love this guitar. I love that concept in Martin, very plain and simple.

1961 MARTIN 0-16NY

Serial No: 73241
Body: Rosewood back and sides, spruce top, ivoroid binding with pearl purfling, natural finish
Neck: Mahogany, 20 frets, ivoroid bound ebony fingerboard with 'snowflake' inlays
Headstock: Solid
Bridge: Ebony 'belly' pin bridge
Soundhole: Pearl inlaid rosette
Pickguard: Imitation tortoiseshell
Case: Original hardshell case with adhesive tape inscribed 'Auction #52/1939 000-42 #2/Ser.#73241'

Although this 1939 Martin 000-42 is virtually identical to the 000-42 that Clapton played on *Unplugged* (page 230) and its serial number is only seven numbers apart, it sold in Christie's 2004 Crossroads Auction for ⅓ the price of the *Unplugged* guitar. Clapton may not have played this 000-42 as much or as publicly, but it still is a fine and rare guitar from the Golden Age of Martin flat-top steel-string acoustic guitars. The fact that it is in better condition reveals that it may not sound quite as sweet as the other 000-42, as players who are also collectors know that the best-sounding vintage instruments usually experience a lot of wear and tear while less attractive-sounding but better-looking instruments don't get played as much.

Clapton played this guitar at home, and also on recordings.

Eric Clapton playing his 000-42MEC Martin guitar based on this model at his home in 2007.

ERIC I bought this sight unseen from Gruhns. I had three guitars of that ilk, and had all of them on stands next to one another. I used to just sit and look at them, and play one after the other.

They were front-room guitars; they got played at home extensively, and on records. One was an OM, which I found better in the playing. The tone was different on all of them but I think it's the playability of the OM. It's so finite it's untrue. Nobody else but me would probably care, but I'm very picky because I'm lazy. The guitar has to do quite a lot of the work for me. OMs have a longer string length, which means they're going to be easier to bend and to project a little bit more. Shorter scale lengths are just harder to bend. I've found it actually feels like more tension, the shorter it gets. So I decided to sell two and keep the OM.

Cow Palace
San Francisco
California, USA
July 1974

Clapton playing his
OM-45 that he couldn't
bear to part with.

LOT 84 CHRISTIE'S 1999

Serial No: A32323
Factory Order No:
S 2734 1
Body: Maple back and
sides, spruce top,
sunburst finish
Neck: Maple, 20 frets,
bound rosewood
fingerboard with crest
'pineapple' inlays
Headstock: Crown inlay
Bridge: Rosewood
'moustache' pin bridge
with four semi-rectangular
pearl inlays and bridge
end cutouts
Pickguard: Imitation
tortoiseshell with moulded
floral motif
Case: Brown hardshell
contour case with pink
plush lining and
handwritten tie-on label
''60 Gibson J.200
S.Burst #A32323' and
paper adhesive label
similarly inscribed

One of Gibson's flashiest and most ornate acoustic flat-top guitars, the SJ-200 was originally designed for singing cowboy and country and western performers during the late 1930s. Gibson has produced the model continuously since then with the exception of 1941 through 1946, when production was temporarily halted. When post-war production resumed, Gibson shortened the model's name to J-200. Although it was initially designed for country musicians, the J-200 became a favourite of blues guitarists.

Clapton bought this vintage J-200 during the late 1970s.

ERIC The first acoustic Gibson that I liked was the J-200, which was like the Elvis guitar. I played this guitar frequently and kept it around at home for writing and so on.

LOT 36 CHRISTIE'S 2004

Factory Order No: 345 A
Body: Two-piece
mahogany back and sides,
spruce top, sunburst finish
Neck: Mahogany, 19 frets,
bound rosewood
fingerboard with dot inlays
Headstock: Pre-war script
Gibson logo, 'notched
diamond' inlay
Bridge: Rosewood,
nickel-plated 'raised
diamond' trapeze tailpiece
Pickguard: Bound
imitation tortoiseshell
Case: Original hardshell
case with adhesive tape
inscribed 'Gibson L.75.
#345A/A Top Ac.'

Gibson archtop guitars with round soundholes like the L-4 and L-50 transformed to f-hole designs in the mid 1930s, but the L-75 did the exact opposite, starting off as an f-hole archtop in 1932 and becoming a round-soundhole model in 1935. Clapton purchased this L-75 after selling his 1935 L-4 (page 99), which is quite similar to this guitar, at the 1999 Crossroads auction.

ERIC I bought this one to replace one that I sold and found hard to part with, so it was a gesture that had meaning. I didn't have this one for very long.

1966 DOBRO D12E COLUMBIA *(side margin)*

Serial No: 60557
Body: Mahogany, natural finish, single resonator, chrome-plated cover plate with four fan-shaped cutouts, two upper bout sound-hole grilles
Neck: Maple, 19 frets plus zero fret at nut, rosewood fingerboard with dot inlays
Headstock: Slotted
Bridge: Plastic, chrome-plated trapeze tailpiece
Pickups: One single-coil
Controls: One volume, one tone
Case: Black softshell contour case with green felt lining and handwritten tie-on label '12 String Dobro #60557?' and adhesive paper label similarly inscribed

Dobro was named after the Dopyera brothers John and Rudolph as well as the Czech word for 'good', and today is synonymous with the single-cone resonator guitar favoured by blues guitarists and slide players like Duane Allman. Dobros sold well from 1928, but after the war the growing popularity of the electric guitar made the resonator guitar obsolete. Emil Dopyera resurrected Dobro in 1959, opening a factory in Gardena, California. In 1966, Dopyera sold the company to Mosrite founder Semie Moseley, who designed new models built with original parts. This D12E Columbia 12-string electric resonator guitar was one of them. The model made a mark on music history when Pete Drake played one on George Harrison's 'My Sweet Lord'.

ERIC This is a wood body dobro with a Martin-type neck, reworked by Randy Wood. I got it at George Gruhn's shop in Nashville in the Sixties. This is one of the guitars I owned for the longest period of time, but I found it hard to play.

1935 NATIONAL DUOLIAN *(side margin)*

Serial No: 459
Body: Steel, nickel finish, upper bout f-holes, single resonator cone, nickel-plated cover plate with nine diamond-shaped cutouts and four raised ribs
Neck: Mahogany, 19 frets, ebonised maple fingerboard with dot inlays
Headstock: Slotted
Bridge: Maple 'biscuit' bridge, nickel-plated trapeze tailpiece
Case: Black hardshell contour case with blue plush lining and handwritten tie-on label 'Silver National Steel/Dobro #459' and adhesive paper label similarly inscribed

John Dopyera, who co-founded the National String Instrument Corporation in 1925 and founded the Dobro Manufacturing Company in 1928, conceived the design for the first resonator guitar. National and Dobro resonator guitars were very popular with blues musicians during the late 1920s and 1930s for several reasons, including their loud volume output, distinctive bright tone that is ideal for slide guitar playing and low cost – National and Dobro's entry-level models cost less than the equivalent of $500 in today's currency.

Between 1931 and 1938, National produced thousands of Duolian model steel-body resonator guitars, which were sold for only $32.50. The Duolian was made with a textured 'frosted Duco' finish in various shades, but a few Duolians with nickel-plated bodies like this example have emerged over the years, which were either made as custom orders (or possibly production anomalies) or later modified by owners who had them plated. Clapton acquired this Duolian sometime in the 1970s, and he used it often for playing slide at home and in the recording studio.

ERIC I used this National for playing slide both at home and in recording sessions for a long time – at least 20 years.

Serial No: 1098
Body: Maple back and sides, spruce top, bound f-holes, sunburst finish
Neck: Maple, 20 frets, bound ebony fingerboard with block inlays
Headstock: D'Angelico New York script logo, shield outline with 'Exel' [sic] inlay
Bridge: Ebony, gold-plated Grover De Luxe trapeze tailpiece
Pickguard: Bound imitation tortoiseshell
Pickups: Floating DeArmond pickup, control unit mounted on pickguard
Case: Imitation crocodile-skin hardshell contour case with blue velvet lining and handwritten tie-on label 'D'Angelico Exel [sic] #1098' and adhesive paper label similarly inscribed

Like the previous example, the serial number for this guitar does not appear in D'Angelico's record book, although an Excel model with serial number 1097 that was made for Ned Cosmo is listed. The construction features, low serial number and odd 'Exel' misspelling of the model's name on the headstock inlay suggest that this and Cosmo's guitar were the earliest – if not the first – Excel models that D'Angelico made in 1934. As on the previous example, the floating pickup was installed on the guitar years after it was made. Although the straight-cut f-holes are also unusual, D'Angelico made a few guitars with this feature throughout his career. John D'Angelico kept an Excel guitar with serial number 1108 and features virtually identical to this guitar – including the 'Exel' inlay and straight-cut f-holes – as his personal instrument.

ERIC This guitar is the first D'Angelico I got my hands on. I love these guitars.

LOT 101 CHRISTIE'S 1999

Serial No: 1076
Body: Maple back and sides, spruce top, bound, single sharp cutaway, f-holes, sunburst finish
Neck: Maple, 20 frets, bound ebony fingerboard with block inlays
Headstock: D'Angelico New York banner logo, floral inlay
Bridge: Ebony bridge, gold-plated Grover De Luxe trapeze tailpiece
Pickguard: Bound imitation tortoiseshell
Pickups: Floating DeArmond pickup, control unit mounted on pickguard
Case: Black hardshell contour case stencilled in yellow 'FRAGILE DEREK AND THE DOMINOS' on one side and 'FRAGILE' on the other, the case with green felt lining and handwritten 'D'Angelico S/C #1076' and adhesive paper label similarly inscribed

John D'Angelico, widely regarded as the premier archtop guitar craftsman of the 20th century, started building guitars in his own name in a small workshop on New York's Lower East Side in 1932. The design of his earliest guitars was inspired by Gibson's L-5; however, this early 1930s D'Angelico with its sharp 'Florentine'-style cutaway more closely resembles the Gibson ES-175 model, which Gibson introduced in 1949.

D'Angelico's meticulous, detailed record book oddly does not list this guitar's serial number, but its features – with the exception of the cutaway and floating DeArmond neck pickup – are consistent with those of instruments he made between 1933 and 1934. His record book also doesn't list any cutaway guitars until 1947, and the cutaways on D'Angelico guitars are typically rounded. What likely happened was that this guitar's owner brought it to D'Angelico for custom modifications sometime in the 1950s.

Clapton brought this D'Angelico on tour with Derek and The Dominos in 1970 and 1971, but there is no evidence that he ever played the guitar on stage.

ERIC The thing that interests me most right now is archtops – the jazz guitars of the 1930s and 40s. Gibson, D'Angelico and D'Aquisto made them. Their value's going up; you can get one now for £5,000 or £10,000. In a couple of years they'll be all gone.

Clapton playing a
D'Aquisto Ultra model
archtop guitar in his
drawing room in 1990
(pages 102, 257).

Serial No: T901
Body: Birch plywood, upper bout segmented f-holes, imitation tortoiseshell binding, stripped natural finish, single resonator cone, nickel-plated cover plate with 36 round holes
Neck: Mahogany, round with V-shaped profile, 19 frets, ebonised maple fingerboard with dot inlays
Headstock: Slotted
Bridge: Maple 'biscuit' bridge, nickel-plated trapeze tailpiece
Case: Original black hardshell contour case with red lining, handwritten label with various inscriptions including 'Dobro Stripped Body (For Slide) High Action.'

Although the first version of National's Triolian model introduced in 1928 had a wood body, National temporarily abandoned production of wood body instruments between 1929 and 1932. National offered the El Trovador model for a brief period during 1932 and 1933 before National replaced it with the much cheaper and less fancy Trojan, Estralita and Rosita models in 1934. The wood bodies and necks for these three new models were made for National by Harmony, and National simply installed their metal resonators in the guitars during final assembly.

This 1934 Trojan is far from original condition. The mahogany-colour finish was stripped to bare wood long ago, and the original raised-rib resonator cover was replaced with a cover that might have originally come from a late-1930s National/Supro Collegian student model instrument. The trapeze tailpiece is also from a later period. Clapton acquired this guitar in the 1990s and set it up for slide with a high action and an open G tuning.

Clapton probably purchased this guitar because the blonde-colour top reminded him of the much fancier Dobro Model 45 and Regal-made Dobros with spruce tops and rosewood back and sides that are his favourite vintage acoustic resonator guitars.

ERIC Derek and The Dominos was a quartet and I enjoyed that. It's the whole thing about having a Booker T. Jones-type feel. One guitar, keyboards, drums and bass. I had to work more, it's true, but what was appealing to me about that band was that they were journeymen too. If we were just left in a room we would play grooves 24 hours a day.

The *Layla* album had Duane Allman on it, but the life of the Dominos didn't have Duane in it. It was two bands. I did try and entice Duane and he stayed for a little while, but then we were back to me being the only guitar player.

Duane is the only person I consider a major dobro influence. He could play dobro any way, and in fact played it his way. The first dobro playing I heard that seemed to have a freedom of expression was definitely Duane's. I wasn't aware of that until we were doing the *Layla* sessions, and there were a couple of ballads where he decided to play straight dobro. It was the only time I heard dobro that wasn't strictly confined to being country dobro – meaning lap-style dobro, very regimented.

I don't have a developed style. If I were to play dobro unaccompanied I'd revert to playing like Bukka White, that kind of stuff where you're hitting the bass strings with your thumb. That's how I'd do it if I were playing a piece like 'Jitterbug Swing', one of those songs Bukka would do that had a set guitar pattern.

The first important dobro I bought was when I met Duane. His was the first one I ever saw and it came from GTR, so I went to GTR and they made a custom one for me. Since then, whenever I've seen a blonde wooden-top dobro that resembled my first one I buy it because they're very rare; very, very unusual. Usually they're very well made, and they sound good – so I've collected them. I've had a couple.

Serial No: 1587-91
Body: Black Lyrachord deep bowl with gold sparkles, unidirectional carbon-graphite top, textured 'binding', Reverse Blue Burst finish
Soundholes: 13-piece exotic wood inlays around 22 epaulette soundholes
Neck: Mahogany, 24 frets, resin-impregnated walnut fingerboard with maple triangular motif inlays
Headstock: Scrolled acanthus leaf motif
Bridge: Carved acanthus leaf design walnut bridge, Ovation high-output saddle pickup
Controls: One volume, one tone, stereo FET preamp
Outputs: Two
Label: 'CW Kaman II/1587-91/1687-8'
Additional: Photocopied sheet music for 'Streamline Woman' by McKinley Morganfield (Muddy Waters) and a guitar cable
Case: Brown Ovation hardshell contour case with brown plush lining and brown vinyl cover with zip fastening, handwritten label inscribed with various details including 'ADAMAS OVATION ....GRAPE SOUNDHOLE'

Ovation was an unusual offshoot of Kaman Corporation, which specialised in aerospace products such as composite missile nose cones and rotor blades for helicopters. Charles Kaman was also a guitarist and, when a slump in the aerospace industry inspired him to diversify, he realised that he might be able to make good acoustic guitars from the composite materials he used to build helicopter parts. His engineers developed a material called Lyrachord and a semi-parabolic bowl shape for the guitar's back and sides that were easy to manufacture and actually sounded quite good, and Ovation introduced its first guitars in 1966. Those weren't Ovation's only inspired ideas, as the company also developed one of the first commercially viable pickup systems for amplifying acoustic guitars, which made them instantly popular with performing professional guitarists.

Ovation's flagship Adamas guitars represented their most radical spirit of innovation. Adamas guitars offered numerous non-traditional features, including thin, responsive composite tops and unique upper bout soundholes. Models like the 1687 proved that an unorthodox acoustic guitar could still look attractive with its stylistic blend of composite materials and attractive woods used for the control knobs and epaulette sound holes.

ERIC I did a deal with Ovation guitars. I thought they were incredibly interesting in terms of evolution – they were the first successful acoustic electric guitars. I liked the idea a little, but on the whole the nature of the instrument was really too specific. It had to be used as an acoustic electric.

I found them quite hard to play. I had trouble with them because they had this curved moulded back, so if you were sitting down it just slid.

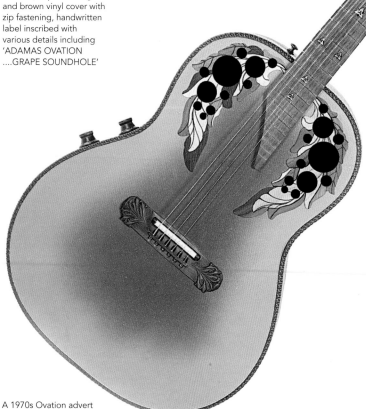

A 1970s Ovation advert featured Clapton.

LOT 100 BONHAMS 2011

Serial No: 310688
Body: Lyrachord deep bowl, spruce top, bound, abalone purfling, single round cutaway, black finish
Neck: Mahogany/maple laminate, 20 frets, bound ebony fingerboard with diamond and dot pattern inlays
Bridge: Ebony pinless with carved foliate decoration
Pickguard: Black single-ply
Soundhole: Mulite and abalone raised epaulette in a foliate motif
Controls: Concentric volume/tone
Outputs: Two
Case: Brown Ovation hardshell contour case with brown plush lining, handwritten label and strip of tape applied to lid inscribed 'Black, Ovation, Acoustic steel String, S.Cut. Gift From "Guitar Centre" To Go In 04 Auction, Didn't Make It, Mode [sic] 1669'

With features like deep cutaways and jet black finishes with ornate inlays, Ovation models like this 1669 Custom Legend guitar remain very popular with rock guitarists who find most traditional acoustic guitars too staid in appearance.

1985/86 OVATION MODEL 1669 CUSTOM LEGEND

LOT 101 BONHAMS 2011

Serial No: 307884
Body: Lyrachord deep bowl, cedar top, multiple-layer binding, single round cutaway, natural finish
Neck: Mahogany/maple laminate, 22 frets, ebony fingerboard
Headstock: Slotted, walnut veneer, back of headstock signed by Eric Clapton in black felt pen
Bridge: Walnut tie-block bridge
Soundhole: Mulite raised epaulette with foliate motif
Controls: Concentric volume/tone
Outputs: Two
Case: Black Ovation hardshell contour case with lilac plush lining, two handwritten labels with various inscriptions including OVATION "Nylon" Ser 307884 "Bowlback"

Ovation's first acoustic-electric guitar was a nylon-string model with a piezo pickup installed in the bridge that they made for Glen Campbell, who was one of Ovation's biggest endorsees, in 1970. Although Ovation's steel-string models with piezo pickups that the company perfected for its guitars sold in greater numbers than its nylon-string models, Ovation has continuously offered acoustic-electric nylon models since then.

1985/86 OVATION MODEL 1663 CLASSIC

Serial No: 2921
Body: Ash, single cutaway, natural finish
Neck: Maple with skunk-stripe truss rod routing, 21 frets, maple fingerboard with dot inlays. Neck date and initials 'TG 3-25-52' written in pencil
Bridge: Stamped steel baseplate, three adjustable brass saddles
Pickguard: Black single-ply
Pickups: Two single-coil
Controls: One volume, one tone
Switches: Three-position pickup selector
Case: Brown hardshell contour case with brown plush lining and handwritten tie-on label inscribed 'Natural Blonde Tele 52 #2921' and adhesive paper label similarly inscribed

Playlist:
Layla And Other Assorted Love Songs, 1970
Gigs:
Derek and The Dominos
June 14-Oct. 11, 1970
Throughout the 1970s
Highlights:
Crystal Palace Bowl
London, UK
July 31, 1976

Bass player Carl Radle worked with Clapton frequently for 10 years, starting in 1969 when both were members of Delaney and Bonnie and Friends. Radle was also a member of Derek and The Dominos, played on all of Eric's solo albums between 1970 and 1979, and performed in Eric's touring band from 1974 until 1979.

Radle gave Clapton this Telecaster while they were working together in Derek and The Dominos. Clapton used this guitar during the 1970s for recording and live performance.

ERIC In those early days, I was feeling biased towards a certain image and, for me, the Telecaster initially was more accessible. The image was one thing, but the guitar was quite difficult to play. With a Telecaster the feedback is not that easy to control. The pickups feed back, but they shriek. Humbucker pickups will feed back harmonically; you can control it according to where your finger is. So, playing-wise and in terms of being stage-friendly, the Strat is the most versatile guitar that Fender has made.

ERIC I used this guitar throughout the Dominos period.

KB Hallen
Copenhagen, Denmark
June 20, 1974

Clapton is pictured
here on his first tour
since disbanding the
Dominos four years
previously. He played
two shows in Scandinavia
before embarking on
a world tour.

Serial No: 34172
and 33583
Housing: Angled
(1960A)/straight (1960B)
closed-back cabinets
Covering: Dark green
Tolex, 'salt and pepper'
basket-weave speaker
cloth, 'Derek and The
Dominos' stencil on top
Speakers: 1960A with
three Celestion G12M
25-watt 12-inch speakers,
1960B with four Celestion
G12M 25-watt
12-inch speakers
Details: Large white
Marshall script logo
Handles: Metal

Clapton started using Marshall stacks while playing with Cream (page 55), placing a single 100-watt Marshall amplifier head on top of two stacked Marshall 4x12 cabinets (and often daisy-chaining the amp to a second Marshall stack for even more volume output). When he joined Delaney and Bonnie and Friends in 1969, he switched to 100-watt Fender Dual Showman Reverb heads with single 2x12 Fender cabinets.

Clapton was still using a Dual Showman Reverb rig during the early days of Derek and The Dominos when the band played a tour of clubs in the United Kingdom in 1970. When the band played a gig at Mothers in Birmingham on August 9th, 1970, a fan that apparently was used to the extreme, ear-splitting volume levels of Cream concerts heckled Clapton and complained that his guitar wasn't loud enough. After the show, Clapton sent out his road manager to buy him a Marshall stack, which Clapton used for a few select shows on the rest of the tour. These cabinets were part of the Marshall stack that Clapton's road manager bought.

These cabinets carry the same stencil applied to the guitar case of the 1956 Fender Stratocaster, Brownie (page 72).

ERIC I'd turn this amp and the guitar up all the way. It seems I'm known as a guitar player for that sustain sound – holding notes for a long time.

'Anything for Your Love', from the *Journeyman* album, has got Robert Cray playing on it. When I did the solo on that, I looked at him, and he was amazed that I had this one note – I just pushed it – at the end of a phrase.

Gigs:
Derek and The Dominos
– 1970 UK Club Tour
Aug. 1-Oct. 11, 1970

Opposite: 1970

Eric pictured with the
Dominos after switching
to a Marshall stack.

Serial No: 208511
Body: Rosewood back and sides, spruce top, ivoroid binding with pearl purfling, natural finish
Neck: Mahogany, 20 frets, bound ebony fingerboard with 'snowflake' inlays
Headstock: Ivoroid binding, vertical 'C.F. Martin' logo inlaid in pearl
Bridge: Ebony 'belly' pin bridge, dot inlays
Soundhole: Pearl inlaid rosette
Pickguard: Imitation tortoiseshell
Label: 'This instrument inlayed by Custom Pearl Inlay Service, 200 Hemphill Avenue, Chattanooga Tenn. 37411, work performed 000-28-45 No 67 April 11, 1966, Mike Longworth'
Case: Later hardshell case with adhesive tape inscribed 'Longworth/ Martin: 000-28-45 #208511'

Eric Clapton refers to this guitar as 'The Longworth', after the late Mike Longworth.

Martin Guitars initially hired Mike Longworth, a craftsman who specialised in custom inlays and a guitar collector with deep knowledge of Martin guitars, in 1968 to supervise the inlay work on Martin's reissue of the D-45. He stayed with the company long after that and became Martin's historian, writing *Martin Guitars: A History* in 1975, which is an incredible resource for Martin guitar collectors. Longworth retired from Martin in 1995 and passed away in 2003.

During the mid 1960s Longworth often converted new 000-28 and D-28 guitars into 000-45 and D-45 models, which Martin hadn't made since 1942, at his workshop in Chattanooga, Tennessee. He duplicated the appointments and inlay work of Martin's 45-style guitars in fine detail but distinguished his work by inlaying a small 'L' on the fingerboard below the 18th fret. This guitar is one of Longworth's 'conversion' 000-28/45 Martins from that period.

When Clapton was in Nashville to film an appearance on *The Johnny Cash Show* with Derek and The Dominos on November 5th, 1970, he purchased this guitar from GTR, a shop run by George Gruhn, Tut Taylor and Randy Wood. That same day he also bought several Stratocasters from Nashville's Sho-Bud guitar shop that he later used to assemble Blackie (page 122).

This Martin became one of Clapton's favourite acoustics shortly after he acquired it. He brought it with him in 1974 to Miami's Criteria Studios to record several tracks on *461 Ocean Boulevard* and is pictured playing the Martin on that album's back cover. He also brought it on tour that year, using it to perform 'Smile', 'Let It Grow' and 'Easy Now'. Clapton's 'Rodeo Man' Martin 000-28 (page 136) temporarily took its place as Clapton's main acoustic in 1976, but he brought out the 'Longworth' Martin again in 1983 during the ARMS (Action and Research for Multiple Sclerosis) Tour when he used it to perform 'Goodnight Irene' with Ronnie Lane.

Clapton began playing this guitar more frequently during the 1990s. Andy Fairweather Low played it during the filming of Clapton's MTV *Unplugged* session at Bray Studios in 1992, and Clapton used it for the acoustic section of his Royal Albert Hall concerts in 1993. It also was one of Clapton's main acoustic guitars on his From the Cradle Tour in 1994-5.

Playlist:
461 Ocean Boulevard
1974
Gigs:
1974 Tour
June 19-Dec. 5, 1974
1975 Tour
Apr. 11-Aug. 30, 1975
1975 Japan Tour
Oct. 22-Nov. 2, 1975
1993 Royal Albert Hall
Feb. 20-Mar. 7, 1993
1994-5 From The Cradle Tour
Oct. 3, 1994- Oct.13, 1995
Highlights:
The ARMS London Benefit Concert
Royal Albert Hall
London, UK
Sept. 20, 1983
Prince's Trust Concert
Royal Albert Hall
London, UK
Sept. 21, 1983
MTV *Unplugged* (TV)
Bray Film Studios
Windsor, Berkshire, UK
Jan. 16, 1992

Ryman Auditorium
Nashville, Tennessee, USA
Nov. 5, 1970

Carl Perkins, Johnny Cash and Eric Clapton performing 'Matchbox Blues' live on *The Johnny Cash Show*.

ERIC The Martin thing started with having seen pictures and footage of Big Bill Broonzy playing a 000-28 – the narrow-waisted acoustic guitar. When I started to hang out in London at the folk clubs all those guys wanted the big country guitar with the dreadnought body. I thought that shape was lovely but I was still drawn to the Big Bill Broonzy image and the sound he got too.

The Longworth is the first serious Martin that I ever bought. I got it from GTR when I was doing *The Johnny Cash Show* in 1970. It's a great guitar, a star guitar. It has all the Bakelite and mother-of-pearl inlays. After this guitar I was kind of easy game for anything vintage from Martin. But of course it would have to play well.

ERIC This guitar has a deep association for me. It's as important to me as the Rodeo Man guitar (page 136). In fact, much more so. I used this all through the Seventies on stage, from the time that I was doing *461 Ocean Boulevard* and taking that material on stage. It was incredibly well used.

After the Dominos, when I went on tour billed simply as Eric Clapton, I actually went onstage starting with an acoustic set. I did three or four songs with the Martin acoustic – and then got into some rock and roll and a few blues.

461 Ocean Boulevard
Golden Beach, Florida, USA
1974

A photo from this shoot was used as the front cover of Eric's 1974 album and this guitar is featured on the back cover.

Opposite:
Hyatt Hotel
West Hollywood
Los Angeles, USA
1976

Left:
Royal Albert Hall
London, UK
Sept. 20, 1983

Eric Clapton playing
'Goodnight Irene'
at the ARMS London
Benefit Concert.

Below:
Royal Albert Hall
London, UK
Feb. 3, 2001

He continued to use the
guitar on stage up to
three years before the
2004 auction.

TIMEPIECES

Serial No: 20036
Body: Alder, black finish
Neck: Maple, 21 frets,
maple fingerboard with
dot inlays
Bridge: Synchronised
tremolo
Pickguard: White
single-ply
Pickups: Three single-coil
Controls: One volume,
two tone
Switches: Three-position
pickup selector with white
switch tip
Case: Anvil case stencilled
in white with an image of
two cartoon duck heads
and lettering 'THE/DUCK
BROS./LONDON 01 486
8056' with adhesive tape
inscribed 'Auction
#15/BK/'56 '57
Black/Stratocaster'

Playlist:
461 Ocean Boulevard,
1974
*There's One In Every
Crowd,* 1975
E.C. Was Here, 1975
No Reason To Cry, 1976
Slowhand, 1977
Backless, 1978
Just One Night, 1980
Another Ticket, 1981
Money and Cigarettes,
1983
Behind The Sun, 1985
Gigs:
All Tours
1973-1985
1991 Royal Albert Hall
Feb. 5-Mar. 9, 1991
Highlights:
Eric Clapton's
Rainbow Concert
The Rainbow Theatre
London, UK
Jan. 13, 1973
The ARMS London Benefit
Concert
Royal Albert Hall
London, UK
Sept. 20, 1983
Live Aid
John F. Kennedy Stadium
Philadelphia
Pennsylvania, USA
July 13, 1985

Of all the various guitars that Clapton played during his career, none is more iconic and closely associated with him than this black 1950s Fender Stratocaster affectionately nicknamed 'Blackie'. The guitar prominently appears in photos used for numerous album covers, including *Slowhand, Backless, Just One Night* and *Time Pieces,* and it was his main guitar for a longer period than any other single instrument he has owned. Clapton played Blackie on stage continuously for 12 years from his debut appearance with it at the Rainbow Concert in London on January 13th, 1973, until his 1985 world tour, retiring it from action after the tour's completion.

Blackie is a composite of several Fender Stratocasters. In 1970 while he was on tour with Derek and The Dominos, Clapton visited the Sho-Bud guitar shop in Nashville, Tennessee, owned by steel guitar legend Buddy Emmons, in search of Stratocaster guitars. He compiled the best components from three or four guitars to make Blackie.

Most of Blackie's parts came from 1956 and 1957 Strats, although one of the single-coil pickups is dated 1970. The body is from 1956 and features a rare and original custom black finish. The neck was made in 1957 – the last year that Fender made necks with 'V'-shaped profiles before switching to rounded 'D'-shaped necks sometime in 1958.

After Clapton assembled Blackie in 1970, it became his constant companion in the studio and at concert performances. Clapton played Blackie at his most important concerts during this period, including The Band's Last Waltz concert on November 25th, 1976, at San Francisco's Winterland Ballroom; his performances alongside Freddie King in London and Dallas in 1976; his 1979 North American tour with Muddy Waters; the 1983 ARMS Charity concerts and tour; and the Live Aid concert at Philadelphia's JFK Stadium on July 13th, 1985.

Clapton decided to retire Blackie in 1985 because its neck had become worn down from incessant use. He brought Blackie out of retirement for a rare handful of occasions after that, including his 1991 Royal Albert Hall concerts and a 1990 Japanese television commercial for Honda, where he is seen in a New York recording studio playing a new guitar solo for 'Bad Love'.

When Blackie was sold at Christie's 2004 Crossroads Guitar Auction, it went for a record price of $959,500.

*In 2006, another Stratocaster, signed by a large group of celebrities including Clapton, was auctioned to benefit the victims of the 2004 Asian tsunami. Selling for $2.6 million, it surpassed Blackie's record.

ERIC The guitar I chose for my return to recording was one that I had built myself, a black Fender Stratocaster which I had nicknamed 'Blackie'.

It's probably a well-known story... I went into a shop in Nashville called Sho Bud which was owned by Buddy Emmons – the famous pedal steel player – and they had things like Rickenbackers in the front of the shop going for quite high prices. In the back they had this second-hand department and there was a row of Stratocasters, almost like clothes on pegs. I couldn't believe that Strats had sunk so low in public opinion. I felt like I'd stepped into a gold mine. Blonde, maple neck Stratocasters, all going for about $100-150 each, and I bought them all.

When I got home I gave one to Steve Winwood, one to Pete Townshend, another to George Harrison and kept the rest. Blackie was made out of three of these guitars – the body of one, the neck of another, the pickups of another. If I hadn't bought those guitars they probably would have been firewood and now the cost of 1950s Strats is ridiculous. They're things of great beauty.

Now the vintage Strats have all gone. That particular avenue has probably dried up unless someone finds one under their bed. They go into collections and they don't come out again. You'd have to be quite wealthy to even think of buying one.

FENDER 'BLACKIE' STRATOCASTER, 1956 AND 1957 COMPOSITE

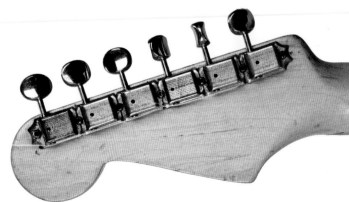

BY MY SIDE

The Rainbow Theatre
London, UK
Jan. 13, 1973

Eric Clapton made his first
performance with Blackie
at the Rainbow Theatre.

Something is just magical about that guitar. Maybe it's all the tender-loving care I've given it over the years. That's probably why I like buying second-hand guitars and old vintage guitars. This may sound superstitious, but you never know who owned a guitar before. That person may have been a master and he may have put something in there. The way the guitar was played and handled seems to stay with the guitar and you inherit that if you're lucky or aware enough to acknowledge it.

When I came back to recording, it was with a different point of view, a fresh enthusiasm and a kind of open-mindedness to learn about new music, because that's when I heard reggae. I was just like a kid in a sweet shop again. When we were recording *461 Ocean Boulevard*, we'd walk into the studio and jam, and then we'd listen to it back and write the song. We'd pick out a riff, or part of the jam that was good and then write a song with it. We really got it going in the end.

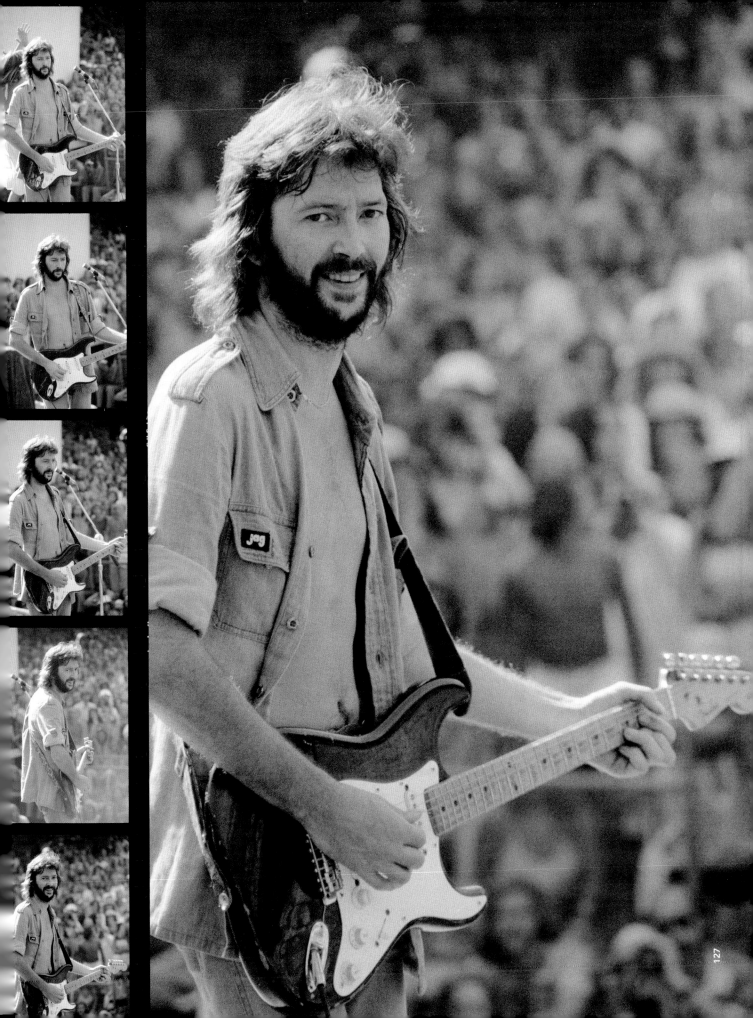

ERIC I get seriously attached to an instrument and I felt that Blackie had become part of me. A guitar like Blackie comes along maybe once in a lifetime. I played it for 12 years non-stop on the road.

Previous page (left):
Clapton on his 1978
US tour.

Previous page (right):
Stanford University
California, USA
Aug. 9, 1975

Opposite:
Eric Clapton performing
in LA in the 1970s.

Brownie (page 72) was a much more industrial guitar. Blackie was really refined, it was like the racer. The action was perfect even when the neck was quite worn down and narrow. All you had to do was pick it up and it played itself. I developed a lot of trust and security with that instrument. It's a remarkable guitar.

It was hard for me to part with Blackie but I had to put it into perspective. My working relationship with Blackie was exclusively and extensively through the Seventies and early Eighties and then after that it was removed from working life.

On tour with the Dominos, Blackie got some incredibly bad treatment. When I was playing with the guys from Tulsa – Jamie Oldaker, Carl Radle – I remember ending a song by falling face down on stage on top of Blackie. I cracked the nut and it just shattered. Apart from that the guitar was fine.

I think the old repair on Blackie's headstock was originally there when I got it. The reason I chose that neck was because it's got quite an extreme V. It's the most extreme V on a maple neck that I've found. It was a beautiful neck and had a lovely feel. I think even today that Blackie would be my ideal. If you asked me to pick the classic Fender, it's a black Strat with a maple neck.

BY MY SIDE

Serial No: YS434
Body: Alder, black finish, body signed and inscribed in silver felt pen 'Eric Clapton 2010'
Neck: Maple with skunk-stripe truss rod routing, 21 frets, maple fingerboard with dot inlays
Headstock: Back of headstock with printed transfer number YS434
Bridge: Synchronised tremolo
Pickguard: White single-ply
Pickups: Three single-coil
Controls: One volume, two tone
Switches: Five-position pickup selector with white switch tip
Additional: Fender Custom Shop certificate signed by master builder Yuriy Shishkov, Fender Custom Shop black leather wallet containing a further certificate and DVD, black leather Fender guitar strap, and an unopened plastic bag containing various items including a guitar cable, Fender cleaning cloth, extra three-position pickup selector switch, and Owner's Manual
Case: Anvil case with brown plush lining, the lid stencilled in black and white with the cartoon duck head logo and lettering 'THE DUCK BROS. LONDON 01 486 8056'

About a year after Guitar Center purchased Clapton's original Blackie Stratocaster (page 122), they received Clapton's permission to work with the Fender Custom Shop to create a detailed replica of the guitar. The Fender Custom Shop spent several months photographing, measuring and analysing every detail so they could duplicate the guitar with 100 percent accuracy. They reproduced the output of the pickups; the electronic components; the distinctive V-shaped neck profile and fretboard wear from years of playing; the cigarette burns on the headstock; the stencilled road case; and non-stock parts like the high E string's aged and worn gold-plated tuner, which replaced the original chrome-plated tuner years ago. Work on the project was divided up equally among the Fender Custom Shop's various master builders, who produced a total of 275 Blackie replicas. This Blackie replica is marked 'YS434', which reveals that it was made by master builder Yuriy Shishkov. All 275 guitars sold out within minutes after they went on sale, and buyer Nicolaus Springer kindly donated his instrument to Bonhams 2011 Crossroads benefit auction.

Mike Eldred of the Fender Custom Shop commented: 'It was really neat to dig in there and then try to figure out how to replicate details like the refinished neck. At some point the neck's finish had worn off from being played heavily, and sweat, grime and dirt had worn right into the wood. The neck wasn't sanded before it was refinished because that would change the shape of the neck, so all of that sweat, dirt and grime was underneath the new finish. We had to figure out how to duplicate that. The body was constructed from three pieces. Most of the bodies we make in the Custom Shop are either one-piece or two-piece, so we had to have custom three-piece spreads made. The pickups were also custom made because none of the pickups we make were similar enough to use in the Blackie replica.'

'When the first replica was finished, Mike Doyle and I took it to the Royal Albert Hall where Eric was playing with his band. Guitar Center was gracious and smart enough to allow us to take the original with us as well. Eric got to sit down with both guitars in a dressing room and look at, play and compare them side-by-side. He liked the replica so much he actually played it at that night's concert.'

ERIC It's exactly the same as Blackie. They duplicated the way Blackie felt, so I would have two or three Blackies, in effect. I think that anyone who buys one will be very happy with it. This is the most satisfying guitar for me to play.

Serial No: 44218
Body: Alder, black finish
Neck: Maple, 22 frets, rosewood fingerboard with dot inlays
Bridge: Blocked synchronised tremolo
Pickguard: White single-ply
Pickups: Three single-coil
Controls: One volume, two tone
Switches: Three-position pickup selector
Case: Re-issue tweed hardshell case with adhesive tape inscribed '59-'60 R.Wood/ Fender-Strat-Black #44218'

The Stratocasters that Clapton plays on stage almost always have maple fingerboards; however Clapton has owned a few made from rosewood.

Clapton's former guitar technician assembled this Stratocaster from parts from various guitars, in a similar fashion as Clapton himself did when he put together Blackie. The body is from a 1959 Strat but it was refinished in black, and the neck is from an early 1960s Strat. In May 1959 the rosewood fingerboard became a standard feature on the Stratocaster, replacing the previous maple configuration. This lasted until 1965, when Fender started to offer the Strat with a maple fingerboard option. Another reason why the neck on this guitar felt different to Clapton is its D-shaped, rather than V-shaped, profile.

ERIC I have an aversion to rosewood fingerboards, even though some of my earlier guitars had them. The rosewood neck does feel different. Maple's fine... maybe it's an illusion, but it feels softer. Rosewood's a hard wood.

LOT 15 CHRISTIE'S 1999

Serial No: 139653
Body: Mahogany with maple top, cherry red finish, single cutaway
Neck: Mahogany, 22 frets, bound ebony fingerboard with block inlays
Headstock: Split diamond inlay
Bridge: Gold-plated Tune-o-matic with stop tailpiece
Pickguard: Cream single-ply
Pickups: Two humbucking
Controls: Two volume, two tone
Switches: Three-position pickup selector
Truss Rod Cover: Three-ply black/white/black embossed with 'Les Paul Custom'
Case: Brown hardshell contour case with pink plush lining and handwritten adhesive paper label 'Gibson Cherry Flame Les Paul # 139653'

Opposite:
The Rainbow Theatre
London, UK
Jan. 13, 1973

The Rainbow Concert's organiser and star perform together on stage. Eric is playing a Les Paul Standard similar to the one sold in the Christie's 1999 auction. Pete Townshend chose to play his Gretsch guitar as it was the loudest he owned.

This guitar has a similar transparent cherry red finish to the refinished 1957 Les Paul Standard that Clapton played on 'While My Guitar Gently Weeps' and subsequently gave to George Harrison as a gift. Clapton later borrowed the guitar from George to play at his Rainbow Concert in 1973, organised by Pete Townshend to bring Eric back into the spotlight.

Gibson offered the cherry red finish as an option on the Les Paul Custom model starting in 1971. Gibson assigned 100000 series serial numbers at random and even assigned the same serial numbers to instruments several times during the early 1970s, so the date of this guitar's manufacture can only be narrowed down to some time between 1971 and 1975.

ERIC The plan was for me to join a band put together by Pete Townshend to play at a concert at the Rainbow Theatre in London as part of 'Fanfare for Europe', celebrating Britain's entry into the Common Market. Because it was Pete I went along with it, and I had a good time doing it.

All the while I had shut myself away I had been listening to music and playing the guitar, but to fully develop your craft you need to interact with other people, and what was missing was the fact that since the Concert for Bangladesh I hadn't actually played with any other musicians. When we got into rehearsals, which took place at Ronnie Wood's house, I made a real attempt to practise, play and compose, if on a limited level. Thank God that Steve Winwood was there to give me confidence, since it must have been clear to all the other players that there was something seriously lacking in my playing. Fortunately I knew in my head what I wanted to do, as well as what was required of me, it was just the problem of communicating that to my fingers.

The band, which we called the Palpitations, included Pete, Steve, Jim Karstein, Jim Capaldi and Ric Grech. We opened with 'Layla', and included songs like 'Badge', 'Bottle of Red Wine', 'Bell Bottom Blues' and 'Presence of the Lord', and having such a great band pushed me to the limits of my playing in the state that I was in. Though it wasn't bad, listening to the tapes later made me realise that my playing and singing were miles off course. It sounded just like the charity benefit it really was. I had a great time doing it and the welcome I was given by the audience was very moving.

BY MY SIDE

ERIC I liked the look of this guitar but found it very heavy to play.

Serial No: 353275
Body: Rosewood back and sides, spruce top, natural finish, large sticker on upper bout side with blue lettering 'SHE'S IN LOVE WITH A RODEO MAN'
Neck: Mahogany, 20 frets, ebony fingerboard with dot inlays
Bridge: Ebony 'belly' pin bridge with two floral inlays
Pickguard: Black
Pickups: Barcus-Berry piezo transducer
Output: Barcus-Berry mini jack strap button output
Additional: Red strap
Case: Grey hardshell contour case with white stencilled lettering 'ERIC CLAPTON GROUP TULSA, OKLA. DELICATE ELECTRONIC INSTRUMENT HANDLE WITH CARE', blue plush lining and handwritten tie-on label 'Martin 000-28 (Rodeo Man) #353275' and adhesive paper label similarly inscribed

Playlist:
Slowhand, 1977
Eric Clapton – The Man and his Music (TV), 1986
Gigs:
1977 Tour
Apr. 20-Oct. 10, 1977
1978 European Tour
Nov. 5-Dec. 7, 1978
Highlights:
Old Grey Whistle Test (TV)
BBC Television Theatre
London, UK
Apr. 26, 1977
Crystal Palace Bowl
London, UK
July 31, 1976

Clapton says that he used this Martin 000-28 to write several songs, including 'Wonderful Tonight', and that it was his main acoustic guitar for recording and performance during the mid and late 1970s. He was seen playing this Martin on 'Hello Old Friend', Bob Dylan's 'Sign Language' and 'Alberta' in an April 26th, 1977 performance filmed for the BBC's *Old Grey Whistle Test*. He also used the 'Rodeo Man' guitar to play a bluesy, Big Bill Broonzy-inspired arrangement of the jazz standard 'When Did You Leave Heaven' on a bus on his 1978 European tour, which was filmed for the unreleased documentary *Eric Clapton and his Rolling Hotel* (later released as part of the South Bank Show special *Eric Clapton – The Man and His Music*).

Viewers with sharp eyes may have noticed the presence of a large white bumper sticker on the guitar's upper bout side, which wasn't on the guitar during the *Old Grey Whistle Test* performance. Allegedly Don Williams gave Eric the sticker, which is printed with the title of Williams' single 'She's In Love With A Rodeo Man', when the two crossed paths in 1978. This may have been the same meeting when Williams' guitarist Danny Flowers showed Williams and Clapton a new song he wrote called 'Tulsa Time', which Clapton and Williams both recorded separately later in 1978. Williams was a big influence on Clapton's music during this period. Clapton often attended Williams' concerts, and he joined Williams on stage in London on September 18th, 1976 at the start of Williams' UK Tour. Clapton also recorded a cover of Williams' 'We're All the Way' for his *Slowhand* album and played 'She's In Love With A Rodeo Man' during his 1978 US tour.

ERIC I'm a friend and fan of Don Williams. He had a song called 'She's In Love With A Rodeo Man', and he gave me this sticker. It was like a bumper sticker really.

What a show Don Williams gives! He just taps his foot. When I saw him the first time, the lighting was unbelievable. At the end of a number the lights would go up. And then when the next one started, the lights would go down again – there was just a spotlight on him, and that was it. None of this purple all over the place. Just simplicity. It was great. I talked to him in the Seventies about being able to write a song where halfway through the listener will know the end and be able to sing along. I didn't want people to sit down and listen to my albums really hard 20 times to find out what I was saying. I wanted to make it as simple as possible.

Eric Clapton and his band in 1975.

BY MY SIDE

ERIC This was a touring hotel room guitar and I played it on stage during the 1970s. It was a working instrument and probably my best friend at the time. It is a 000-28, the basic model without any inlay. It very much suited my way of looking at the world at that point.

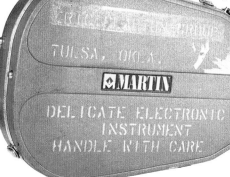

Crystal Palace Bowl
London, UK
July 31, 1976

Right:
Hammersmith Odeon
London, UK
Apr. 27, 1977

Serial No: 7431
Body: Alder, sunburst finish
Neck: Maple with skunk-stripe truss rod routing, 21 frets, maple fingerboard with dot inlays. Neck date and initials T-G-9-54 written in pencil
Tailpiece: Hardtail with six adjustable saddles and through-body stringing
Pickguard: White single-ply
Pickups: Three single-coil
Controls: One volume, two tone
Switches: Three-position pickup selector
Additional: Strap
Case: Tweed rectangular hardshell case with red plush lining and handwritten adhesive paper label ''54 S/Burst Fender Strat #7431'

Opposite:
Le Pavilion
Paris, France
Nov. 18, 1978

When Fender introduced the Stratocaster in 1954, they were so proud of their new synchronised tremolo that it was offered as a standard feature while Strats with 'hardtail' bridges like this example were only available by special order. But even though 1954 hardtail Strats are not as common as the tremolo model, collectors do not consider hardtail Strats as valuable.

Clapton set up this guitar for slide playing, using it often on stage and in the studio from the mid 1970s through the 1980s. This was his preferred instrument for performing 'Tulsa Time' from 1979 through 1985, including his performance with Jimmy Page, Bill Wyman and Jeff Beck at ARMS. He also played this guitar when he appeared on stage with Roger Waters' band for the 1984 Pros and Cons of Hitch-Hiking Tour.

ERIC This 1954 sunburst Stratocaster accompanied me on numerous tours up until the Behind the Sun Tour.

Playlist:
Just One Night, 1979
Gigs:
1979-1985
Highlights:
1979 Far East Tour
Nippon Budokan
Tokyo, Japan
Dec. 3-4, 1979
The ARMS London Benefit Concert
Royal Albert Hall
London, UK
Sept. 20, 1983
Roger Waters' Pros and Cons of Hitch-Hiking Tour
June 16-July 31, 1984
Prince's Trust Concert
Royal Albert Hall
London, UK
Sept. 21, 1983

Serial No: 13385
Body: Alder, sunburst finish. Body date 8-56 written in pencil
Neck: Maple with skunk-stripe truss rod routing, 21 frets, maple fingerboard with dot inlays. Neck date '9-56' written in pencil
Bridge: Synchronised tremolo
Pickguard: White single-ply
Pickups: Three single-coil
Controls: One volume, two tone
Switches: Three-position pickup selector
Case: Black rectangular hardshell case with black plush lining and handwritten tie-on label ''56 S/B Strat #13385' and adhesive pencil label similarly inscribed

Clapton said that he played this 1956 Strat, which has a raised nut set up for playing slide, frequently during live performances in the 1970s. He used it to record several albums, including the studio albums *Slowhand*, *Backless* and *Another Ticket* and the live album *Just One Night*. Clapton also used this Strat, which was tuned down a half step (E♭, A♭, D♭, G♭, B♭, E♭), to play the song 'Forever Man' during his 1985 Behind the Sun Tour.

Playlist:
Slowhand, 1977
Just One Night, 1980
Backless, 1978
Another Ticket, 1981
Gigs:
Throughout the 1970s
1985 Behind The Sun Tour
Feb. 27-Nov. 6, 1985

Opposite:
Festival Hall
Osaka, Japan
Sept. 26, 1977

Eric Clapton playing this or a similar sunburst Stratocaster on his 1977 Japan Tour.

1975 FENDER TELECASTER

EST: $6,000 – $8,000   PRICE: $42,000

Serial No: 635063
Body: Ash, blonde finish
Neck: Maple with skunk-stripe truss rod routing, 21 frets, maple fingerboard with dot inlays
Pickguard: White three-ply (white/black/white)
Pickups: Two single-coil
Controls: One volume, one tone
Switches: Three-position pickup selector
Bridge: Stamped steel baseplate, three adjustable steel saddles
Additional: Floral strap
Case: Black rectangular hardshell case with orange plush lining and handwritten tie-on label 'Tele - Cream - Blonde #635063' and adhesive paper label similarly inscribed

Although the Stratocaster is Clapton's preferred Fender electric model, he's played a Telecaster on a handful of occasions, like this mid 1970s Tele, which he used on stage during his 1975 Japan tour. In an interview that Eric conducted with Japan's *Music Life* magazine during the tour, he said that this Tele was a gift from a friend, who bought the guitar for Eric before the band's rehearsals in the Bahamas in preparation for the tour. After the tour the Tele lay dormant for nearly two decades until Clapton dusted it off in 1994 and played it in the studio while recording *From the Cradle*.

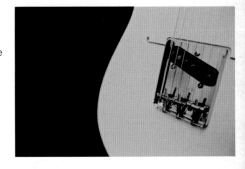

Playlist:
From the Cradle, 1994
Gigs:
1975 Japan Tour
Oct. 22–Nov. 2, 1975

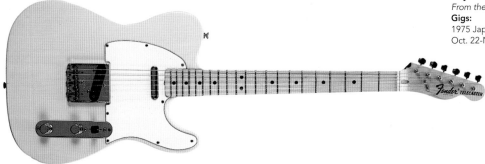

CIRCA 1974 PIGNOSE 7-100 AMPLIFIER

EST: $750 – $1,000   PRICE: $8,000

Serial No: 13489
Covering: Brown Tolex, black speaker cloth with blue and silver plastic Pignose logo
Speakers: One 5-inch
Controls: One 'Pignose' rotary volume knob/power switch
Inputs: One
Outputs: Preamp
Power: Battery-operated with 9V adaptor input

Richard Edlund and Wayne Kimbell started making Pignose amps in 1973 based on a battery-powered amp that Edlund designed with a 5-watt solid-state circuit housed in a wooden cologne box. Thanks to the amp's brown leatherette covering, distinctive volume knob/power switch shaped like a pig's nose, low price and battery-powered design that allowed guitarists to play anywhere, the amp was a huge success, selling more than 50,000 units in its first year. Guitarists particularly loved the Pignose amp's surprisingly raunchy overdrive, and many players used them in the studio. Eric also used this mini amp at home and was photographed playing his 1975 Telecaster through it in 1978.

Playlist:
461 Ocean Boulevard, 1974
Highlight:
'Motherless Children'

ERIC I recorded 'Motherless Children' with just a pignose mini amp.

ERIC I've never able to get a sound out of a Telecaster, but because I've never been able to do it I've often gone back to it, thinking I must have missed something the last time round and maybe if I just turn the tone down a little bit...

What baffles me is that a couple of people I know – for example Jeff Beck – use them and make them sound so wonderful I think I must be missing something. That's why I've gone back to them time and time again. I love the design too.

Nippon Budokan
Tokyo, Japan
Nov. 2, 1975

Eric playing this
Telecaster on the
final date of his
1975 Japan Tour.

LOT 6 BONHAMS 2011

Covering: Natural wood cabinet, black speaker cloth
Speakers: One 10-inch JBL 2110
Switches: Power on/off
Controls: Volume, tone
Inputs: One
Outputs: Line
Additional: Signed by Eric Clapton on the back in black felt pen

The Mitchell Speaker Company of Riverside, California, manufactured a variety of amplifiers during the late 1970s and early 1980s designed by Tom Mitchell. Most of Mitchell's products were based on popular amps made by Fender, Marshall and Mesa-Boogie. The Mighty Midget is a solid-state practice amp that Mitchell designed to compete with the Pignose 7-100. It features a similar battery-powered circuit and a hardwood cabinet inspired by Mesa-Boogie combo amps that were popular during that era.

LOT 31 BONHAMS 2011

Serial No: R00320
Covering: Black Tolex
Switches: Power on/off, standby
Controls: Volume, master, bass, middle, treble, presence
Inputs: High, low
Outputs: 4-ohm, 8-ohm, and 16-ohm speaker, line

During the late 1980s as the end of the Cold War became imminent, Mike Matthews (founder of stomp box effect company Electro-Harmonix) purchased a factory in Russia that manufactures vacuum tubes (valves), which he still sells today under the Sovtek brand name. In 1993, Sovtek started producing its first 50- and 100-watt tube amplifier heads, and by the mid 1990s Sovtek offered a full line of amp heads, including the diminutive-sized but full-powered 50-watt Tube Midget 50H model. Priced much lower than other tube amps available at that time, Sovtek amps were quite successful, and thousands were sold before the Russian factory stopped building amps in the late 1990s.

BY MY SIDE

Covering: Stained figured mahogany cabinet, oxblood basketweave front cloth
Switches: Three-position off/30-watt/60-watt switch, ground, standby
Controls: Volume/pull presence, treble/pull bright, bass
Inputs: Two
Outputs: Two speaker
Other: Fender transformer
Label: Black back panel stamped 'Designed & manufactured by Jim Kelley & Dale Fortune, Fortune Musical Instruments Tustin CA'

Acclaimed 'boutique' amp builder Jim Kelley got his start in the musical instrument industry in 1978 when he rented space in Tustin, California from luthier Dale Fortune and opened Active Guitar Electronics. At the 1979 NAMM (National Association of Music Merchants) convention Kelley introduced the first Fortune amplifier, which was named after his business partner. After the convention Kelley sent one of his first five prototypes to Eric Clapton, which is the amp seen here.

Kelley changed the brand name to 'Jim Kelley Amplification' in 1980 and produced about 600 amps before closing his shop in 1985. Unfortunately, Kelley's product and business model was a few years ahead of its time, as the 'boutique' amplifier phenomenon gained momentum in the early 1990s and is still going strong today. Jim Kelley amplifiers are quite collectible and are sought after by discriminating amp collectors and guitarists.

LOT 8 BONHAMS 2011

Serial No: 22
Body: Flame maple back and sides, spruce top, sunburst finish
Neck: Maple, 18 frets, ebony fingerboard with dot inlays
Headstock: Solid, bound, abalone purfling, inlaid Ferrington 'F' logo, rosewood veneer, back of headstock signed by Eric Clapton in black felt pen
Bridge: Ebony 'pyramid' pin bridge
Pickguard: Imitation tortoiseshell
Rosette: Abalone rosette inlay
Label: Inscribed 'Ferrington, Built for Eric Clapton, Nov. 8, 1979, #22, Nashville, Tennessee', signed by Danny Ferrington
Case: Black hardshell contour case with dark blue plush lining, Philippine Airlines First Class Cabin baggage label

Danny Ferrington started his career in 1975 as a guitar repair apprentice at Nashville's Old Time Pickin' Parlour music shop. In 1977 he built his first guitar for singer-songwriter Paul Craft, who proudly showed Ferrington's work to other musicians he knew. Word quickly spread about Ferrington's talents, and a few years later Eric Clapton approached Ferrington about building a few custom acoustic guitars.

This diminutive guitar, which measures a total of 17 inches from the tip of its headstock to the bottom of its lower bout, was the first instrument that Ferrington completed for Clapton and only the 22nd guitar he made overall. It's about the same size as a Spanish tiple, but it has six strings like a standard guitar. Ferrington commented: 'I call these guitars professional-quality toys. Eric said that he liked how it looked when he carried it around. He loved to play it when he travelled on airplanes.' Judging by the numerous pick scratches on the guitar's top, Clapton flew with the guitar often.

LOT 7 BONHAMS 2011

Serial No: 25
Body: Flame maple back and sides, spruce top, sunburst finish
Neck: Flame maple, 20 frets, bound rosewood fingerboard with dot inlays
Headstock: Solid, bound, abalone purfling, inlaid Ferrington 'F' logo, rosewood veneer, back of headstock signed by Eric Clapton in black felt pen
Bridge: Rosewood 'pyramid' pin bridge
Pickguard: Imitation tortoiseshell
Soundhole: Abalone rosette inlay
Label: Inscribed 'Ferrington, Built for Eric Clapton, Jan 28, 1980, #25, Nashville, Tennessee', signed by Danny Ferrington
Case: Black hardshell contour case with maroon lining, handwritten label inscribed with various details

This custom Danny Ferrington flat-top acoustic has a traditional body shape based on that of a Martin 000 guitar. Before completing this guitar, Ferrington had an extremely rare opportunity to play Clapton's Blackie Strat, and he based this guitar's V-shaped neck profile on Blackie's neck knowing that it was Eric's favourite guitar.

Ferrington moved his workshop to Santa Monica, California the same year that he completed this guitar. Since then he has built one-of-a-kind instruments for numerous well-known musicians, including J.J. Cale, Johnny Cash, Kurt Cobain, Ry Cooder, Elvis Costello and many others.

Serial No: BO10175
Covering: Black Tolex, silver speaker cloth
Plates: Music Man logo, '210-HD One thirty'
Speakers: Two 10-inch alnico
Switches: Bright/normal, deep/normal, hi/standby/lo, ground, power on/off, 4-ohm/8-ohm speaker impedance
Controls: Volume, treble, bass (channel 1), volume, treble, middle, bass (channel 2); reverb, intensity, speed, master
Inputs: Two (channel 1), two (channel 2)
Outputs: Speaker (two)
Footswitch inputs: Reverb, tremolo

The Music Man 210 HD-130 features the same amplifier chassis as the HD-130 Reverb housed in a combo configuration with a pair of 10-inch alnico speakers. Clapton used this amp (or another of the same model) at a Valentine's Day dance at Cranleigh Village Hall, Surrey, on February 14th, 1977. For this surprise small venue performance Clapton's band, featuring Ronnie Lane, was advertised under the pseudonym Eddie and The Earth Tremors. Clapton also recorded numerous tracks with this Music Man combo amp long after he stopped using Music Man amps on stage.

Cranleigh Village Hall
Surrey, UK
Feb. 14, 1977

Eddie and The Earth Tremors perform on Valentine's Day, fulfilling a plan Eric revealed to interviewer Barbara Charone in 1976:
'I'm actually gonna form a group called "The Hypocrites" with Ronnie Lane. We'll record on our own label called "Get Away With Murder Records". The first gig is at the Cranleigh Village Hall.'

Highlight:
Eddie and The Earth Tremors Charity Concert
Cranleigh Village Hall
Surrey, UK
Feb. 14, 1977

SLOWHAND RIFFS

Serial No: BO10815
Covering: Black Tolex, silver speaker cloth
Plates: Music Man logo, 'HD-130 Reverb'
Switches: Bright/normal, deep/normal, hi/standby/lo, ground, power on/off, 4-ohm/8-ohm speaker impedance
Controls: Volume, treble, bass (channel 1); volume, treble, middle, bass (channel 2); reverb, intensity, speed, master
Inputs: Two (channel 1), two (channel 2)
Outputs: Speaker (two)
Footswitch inputs: Reverb, tremolo

Two 1974 Music Man 212 HD-130 speaker cabinets
Housing: Straight open-back cabinets
Covering: Black Tolex, silver speaker cloth, top cabinet with 'E' and 'TOP' stencilled on the back, bottom cabinet with 'C' stencilled on the back
Plates: Music Man logo, '212-HD One Thirty' (each cabinet)
Speakers: Two 12-inch JBL blue label K120 alnico (each cabinet)
Case: Two blue flight cases with 'The Duck Bros' logo stencils

Gigs:
World Tours
1974-1984

In 1976 Music Man published adverts featuring a photo of Clapton, taken in 1974. He is standing in front of three HD-130 stacks and holding his 'truncated' late 1950s Gibson Explorer.

After Leo Fender sold Fender to CBS in 1965, he worked as a silent partner with former Fender employees Forrest White and Tom Walker to establish a new musical instrument company that they eventually called Music Man. Their first product, announced in early 1974, was an amplifier called the 'Sixty Five', which featured a hybrid solid-state preamp/tube power output design that became the basis for their entire amp line. Later that year, Music Man announced the 'One Thirty' available in various combo and head configurations like the HD-130 Reverb head seen here.

Rated at 130 watts RMS, the HD-130 is an extremely loud, powerful amp with considerable clean headroom. Featuring two channels, tremolo and reverb, it bears more than a passing resemblance to the Fender Twin Reverb, suggesting that Leo Fender was prepared to compete with his old company. When Leo Fender's non-competition clause expired in 1975, he made his intentions public knowledge when Music Man announced his new position as the company's president.

Clapton was the first well-known guitarist to use and endorse Music Man amps and was seen on stage during 1974 performing in front of HD-130 Reverb stacks with two 2x12 speaker cabinets. The open-back Music Man 212 HD-130 speaker cabinets with JBL 12-inch speakers were not stock production items and were likely custom made for Clapton by Music Man.

ERIC In the Seventies I switched to Music Man amps. My favourite was a Music Man HD-130 Reverb because they have dual volume controls. You can use them in the studio at low volume, and still get a fair amount of distortion – just as if it were a really big amp. I also liked their sound. They're just like Fenders – in fact I think Leo Fender had a big part in designing them.

No Reason To Cry was pretty live. I like to record a lot of tracks as live as possible, including voice. So if you've got a really loud amp, you're going to leak onto everyone else's track, and you won't be able to sing either.

Music Man discovers MUSIC MAN

1970s Music Man HD-130
Serial No: AO04231
Covering: Black Tolex,
silver speaker cloth
Plates: Music Man logo,
'HD One thirty'
Switches: Bright/normal
(two), deep/normal,
hi/standby/lo, ground,
power on/off, 4-ohm/8-
ohm speaker impedance
Controls: Volume, treble,
middle, bass (channel 1);
volume, treble, middle,
bass (channel 2); master
Inputs: Two (channel 1),
two (channel 2)
Outputs: Speaker (two)

1970s Music Man 412-GS
speaker cabinet
Housing: Straight
closed-back cabinet
Covering: Black Tolex,
silver speaker cloth, 'TOP'
stencilled on the back
Plates: Music Man
logo, '412-GS'
Speakers: Four 12-inch
Case: Blue flight case with
'The Duck Bros' logo
stencilled on either side
and '19' on top

1970s Music Man 212-RH
130 speaker cabinet
Housing: Closed-back
bass reflex port cabinet
Covering: Black Tolex,
silver speaker cloth,
'BOT'M' stencilled on
the back
Plates: Music Man logo,
'212-RH One thirty'
Speakers: Two
12-inch alnico

Overleaf:
Hammersmith Odeon
London, UK
May 15, 1980

Clapton using this or
a similar non-reverb
Music Man HD-130 amp.

The Music Man HD-130 amplifier head did away with the HD-130 Reverb's tremolo and reverb features and expanded channel 1 with a midrange EQ control and a bright/normal switch. The 212-RH 130 closed-back 2x12 speaker cabinet with a bass port at the bottom was Music Man's stock production 2x12 speaker cabinet. The silver dust caps visible through the 412-GS 4x12 speaker cabinet's grille suggest that Clapton may have had JBL K120 alnico speakers installed in this cabinet to match the speakers in his custom 212 HD-130 cabinets.

Albert Lee spoke to Guitar Center about the origin of the Duck Bros logo: 'When I joined Eric's band in 1979 I had this duck call and of course Eric was enchanted with it. I think during rehearsals one of the crew went to a hunting shop and came back with a couple of duck calls and some shoulder holsters. So Eric and I became the 'Fabulous Duck Brothers'. The next thing we had T-shirts made up with 'Fabulous Duck Brothers' on them and then Sterling Ball from Ernie Ball made up some picks with 'Fabulous Duck Brothers' on them as well. Eric was 'Peking' and I was 'Bombay'. It went on from there, and every once in a while we would pull out these duck calls and drive everybody mad with them.

'I remember being in Atlanta, Georgia after a gig – we got in this elevator with a newlywed couple and we serenaded them! I'm sure they had no idea who we were – no idea it was Eric! I guess it was a few months later we showed up for another tour and lo and behold all the flight cases had the 'Duck Bros' logo on them. I still see these cases everywhere and I still have some myself.'

Highlight:
Hammersmith Odeon
London, UK
May 15, 1980

Serial No: BO13153
Covering: Black Tolex, silver speaker cloth
Plates: Music Man logo, 'HD-150 Reverb'
Switches: Bright/normal, deep/normal (deep re-labelled 'mid shift'), hi/standby/lo, ground, power on/off, 4-ohm/8-ohm speaker impedance
Controls: Volume, treble, middle, bass (channel 1); volume, treble, middle, bass (channel 2); master
Inputs: Two (channel 1), two (channel 2)
Outputs: Speaker (two)
Footswitch inputs: Reverb, tremolo
Other: Effects loop (preamp line out, power amp line input)

1974 Music Man 212 HD-130 speaker cabinet
Housing: Straight open-back cabinet
Covering: Black Tolex, silver speaker cloth, 'E' stencilled on the back
Plates: Music Man logo, '212-HD One thirty'
Speakers: Two 12-inch JBL blue label K120 alnico
Case: Blue flight case with 'The Duck Bros' logo stencilled on one side and '14' on all sides

Music Man's 65- and 130-series amps remained mainstays of the company's amp line from 1974 until 1979, but by 1980 Music Man had completely revamped and expanded their line, which now consisted of the 65- and 100-series single-channel and 75- and 150-series dual-channel amps, all offered in various head and combo configurations. True to Leo Fender's goal, Music Man decreased CBS/Fender's market share significantly, and his old company struggled to keep up with his new innovations. By 1981 when Fender introduced a 135-watt version of the Twin Reverb (with boosted power output likely designed to compete with Music Man's HD-130 Reverb) Leo and Music Man were already one step ahead of them in the power wars with their mighty 150-watt HD-150 model.

Music Man's second series of amps are immediately identifiable by their 'reverse' logo and model plates, which previously were black on a silver background and now were silver on a black background. Clapton's HD-150 Reverb amp heads had several custom modifications (installed by Tom Walker at the Music Man factory), including a 'mid shift' switch and an effects loop. These extremely loud amps were ideal for arena and stadium shows, like the 1983 ARMS Benefit concerts where these HD-150 Reverb amps appeared in Clapton's back line. The 212 HD-130 2x12 cabinet seen here is one of Clapton's original Music Man cabinets from 1974.

Gigs:
The ARMS US Tour
Nov. 28-Dec. 9, 1983
Highlight:
Madison Square Garden
New York, USA
Dec. 9, 1983

Madison Square Garden
New York, USA
Dec. 9, 1983

Eric performing 'With a Little Help from My Friends' with Jimmy Page, Joe Cocker, Charlie Watts and Jeff Beck. He is playing Blackie through this half-stack.

LOT 87 CHRISTIE'S 1999

Serial No: 15
Body: Maple back and sides, spruce top, single round cutaway, natural finish
Neck: Maple neck, 21 frets, bound ebony fingerboard with art deco fan-shaped inlays
Headstock: 'SCGC' logo inlay
Bridge: Ebony pin bridge
Pickguard: Clear
Case: Black hardshell case with black plush lining and handwritten tie-on label 'Santa Cruz Blonde #FTC 15' and adhesive paper label similarly inscribed

Opposite:
Hurtwood Edge
Surrey, UK
Jan. 1981

Eric Clapton playing this guitar in his garden.

Introduced in 1978, Santa Cruz's FTC (Flat Top Cutaway) model was based on the body shape of a Gibson J-185 and designed to offer players exceptional versatility, with a dynamic voice equally suitable for fingerstyle, flat pick or rhythm players. The FTC model prototype (FTC-1) was prominently featured on the cover of the Santa Cruz catalogue as well as in their print ads. When Clapton saw a photo of the FTC model in *Guitar Player* magazine, he fell in love with the guitar's looks and called Santa Cruz Guitars to order one. That guitar was later damaged in the Bahamas, so Clapton custom ordered the FTC shown here as a replacement.

LOT 86 CHRISTIE'S 1999

Serial No: 13
Body: Maple back and sides, spruce top, bound, sunburst finish
Neck: Mahogany, 20 frets, bound ebony fingerboard with slotted diamond inlays
Headstock: 'SCGC' logo inlay
Bridge: Ebony 'belly' pin bridge
Pickguard: Imitation tortoiseshell
Case: Black hardshell contour case with black plush lining and handwritten tie-on label 'Santa Cruz Tob-S/Burst #F.13' and adhesive paper label similarly inscribed

When Santa Cruz Guitars replaced the FTC model's carved, arched back with a flat back, they also simplified the model name to F and made the cutaway an option. The F Model remains one of Santa Cruz's bestselling guitars today. Clapton's Santa Cruz F was built to his custom specifications, and he kept the guitar for many years to play around his home. He also temporarily loaned it to Albert Lee while Albert was playing in Eric's band.

ERIC I don't play the electric guitar much at home. In the Eighties, I usually played these acoustics that I got from the Santa Cruz Guitar Company because they had a nice sound.

LOT 21 CHRISTIE'S 2004

Serial No: 2/2063
Body: Rosewood back and sides, spruce top, sycamore binding, natural finish
Neck: Mahogany, 18 frets, ebony fingerboard
Headstock: Slotted
Bridge: Ebony, silver-plated copper trapeze tailpiece with silver-plated medallions engraved 'Awarded to Zogbaum & Fairchild. For the best guitarists. Tilton's Patent 1865. American Institute. New York. Lovett.'
Case: Period wood 'coffin' case labelled 'HART & SON/28 WARDOUR STREET/LONDON. W.', with adhesive tape inscribed '"LIGVODER"/ Auction #50/Tilton'

William B. Tilton was a guitar maker in New York City who invented two patented improvements for guitars, including a wooden tone bar mounted longitudinally inside the body with a metal disc attached to it, as seen inside this guitar's soundhole. The disc is engraved with 'Wm. B. Tilton's Improvement. New York. Patented March 4th, 1856. Zogbaum and Fairchild. New York.' Although Tilton & Company built guitars during the 1850s and 1860s, this guitar was likely manufactured by Boston's John C. Haynes Company, a manufacturing and distribution subsidiary of Oliver Ditson & Company formed in 1865 that also made Bay State and Excelsior guitars. Many guitars like this are identified as Tilton guitars, but usually they are Haynes-built instruments that were made with Tilton's improvements installed.

Specific details about these guitars remained a mystery for many years, so Clapton came up with his own story when people asked about this instrument, which he called the 'Ligvoder Strut'. He concocted an elaborate story that the Bavarian brothers Karl Heinz and Willy Von Ligvoder, who were early and influential innovators of the resonator guitar's concept, made this one-of-a-kind instrument.

ERIC This was a birthday or Christmas present from my first wife. For a long time I couldn't figure out what the hell it was and then it turned into a legend in its own right for other reasons – it became a story. I created a legend around it, which is completely fictitious.

People would always ask if it ever appeared anywhere and if I had it in the studio with the case open people would just walk into it like a baited trap.

LOT 71 CHRISTIE'S 1999

1982 FENDER VINTAGE '57 REISSUE STRATOCASTER

Serial No: V014299
Body: Alder,
sunburst finish
Neck: Maple with
skunk-stripe truss rod
routing, 21 frets, maple
fingerboard with dot inlays
Bridge: Blocked
synchronised tremolo
Pickguard: White
single-ply
Pickups: Three single-coil
Controls: One volume,
two tone
Additional: Strap, tags
and various parts including
a bridge cover plate and
tremolo arm
Case: Tweed rectangular
hardshell case with orange
plush lining and
handwritten tie-on label
'57 Re-Issue Strat "F"
#V.014299' and
adhesive paper label
similarly inscribed

During the 1970s many guitarists discovered that the tone and quality of Fender's guitars made prior to the company's sale to CBS in 1965 were much better than Fender's new guitars. Increased demand for pre-CBS Fenders helped lead to the development of the vintage guitar market. By 1982 Fender realised that most guitarists preferred vintage-style instruments to the ones with modern features that they were making, so the company introduced a new line of reissue models based on its classic guitars. Although the Vintage '57 Reissue Stratocaster that made its debut in 1982 was not an exact duplicate of an original 1957 Strat, players welcomed the development, which revealed Fender's respect for its history and dedication to improving its instruments after surviving a period that many collectors consider its darkest. In fact, Fender veteran engineer Freddie Tavares, who helped design the original Stratocaster in the 1950s, was so proud of the reissue that he personally presented this Vintage '57 Reissue Stratocaster as a gift to Eric after a concert in 1982.

LOT 85 CHRISTIE'S 1999

Serial No: 153677
Body: Double cutaway
thinline semi-hollow,
maple, f-holes, maple
centre block,
sunburst finish
Neck: Mahogany, 22 frets,
bound rosewood
fingerboard with double
parallelogram inlays
Headstock: Crown
peghead inlay, black
three-ply (black/white/
black) truss rod cover
embossed with 'Stereo'
Bridge: Gold-plated
Tune-o-matic,
stop tailpiece
Pickguard: Black five-ply
(black/white/black/
white/black)
Pickups: Two humbucking
with gold-plated covers,
stereo wiring
Controls: Two volume,
two tone
Switches: Three-position
pickup selector,
six-position Vari-Tone
Case: Black hardshell case
with purple plush lining,
and handwritten tie-on
label 'Gibson 345 Stereo
'64 Sunburst Ser. #153677'

In 1959 Gibson introduced its first electric guitar model with Stereo Vari-Tone circuitry – the ES-345TD. Gibson also offered the stereo circuit as an option on the ES-345's upscale cousin, the ES-355TD-SV. With the exception of its Vari-Tone circuit, gold-plated hardware, and double parallelogram fingerboard inlays, this model is essentially identical to the ES-335. Gibson produced the ES-345 until 1982.

Freddie King played an ES-345 during the mid 1960s before he switched to an ES-355. Clapton used this guitar often in the recording studio during the 1980s.

Playlist:
Recording work
in the early 1980s

SLOWHAND RIFFS

1982 FENDER VINTAGE '57 REISSUE STRATOCASTER

1964 GIBSON ES-345TD

EST: $5,000 - $7,000   PRICE: $35,000

Serial No: 000002
Body: Alder, 25th Anniversary Stratocaster Silver finish
Neck: Maple with skunk-stripe truss rod routing, 21 frets, maple fingerboard with dot inlays. Neck plate engraved with serial number and '1954 F 1979 25th Anniversary'
Bridge: Blocked synchronised tremolo
Pickguard: Black three-ply (black/white/black)
Pickups: Three single-coil
Controls: One volume, two tone
Switch: Five-position pickup selector with black switch tip
Additional: Bridge cover plate, tremolo arm
Case: Tweed rectangular hardshell case with orange plush lining and handwritten tie-on label "79 Silver Anniversary Strat #000002'

Fender has produced a variety of anniversary model guitars over the years, but the practice started in 1979 when Fender made the 25th Anniversary Stratocaster guitar to commemorate the introduction of the Strat in 1954. Although Fender promoted the model's production as 'limited', they actually allegedly made 10,000 25th Anniversary Strats, which is a larger amount than the average production run for most standard models. The first 500 had a new white finish that cracked severely shortly after the guitars were shipped, so Fender switched to a metallic silver finish.

Most 25th Anniversary Stratocasters have six-digit serial numbers that begin with 25, but Fender also made a truly limited run of these guitars with six-digit serial numbers beginning with 0000 that were presented to VIPs in recognition of their contributions to the Stratocaster's success over the years. For example, Fender presented a guitar with serial number 000009 to Buddy Holly's widow, Maria Elena, and guitars with serial numbers 000000 (the prototype) and 000001 to Bill Carson, a western swing guitarist who influenced many of the 1954 Strat's original features. Clapton was presented with 000002, showing that Fender obviously held his contributions to the Strat's success in very high regard. Clapton played this guitar occasionally onstage during the early 1980s.

Gigs:
Used on stage in the early 1980s

LOT 55 BONHAMS 2011

Serial No: 01012
Body: Alder, bound, single cutaway, black finish
Neck: Maple with skunk-stripe truss rod routing, 21 frets, maple fingerboard with dot inlays
Bridge: Strings-through-body gold-plated Gotoh baseplate with six adjustable saddles
Pickguard: White single-ply
Pickups: Two DiMarzio humbucking
Controls: One volume, one tone
Switches: Three-position pickup selector
Label: Two handwritten labels with various inscriptions, including 'Custom "Bluesmaster", Black, Memphis'
Case: Black rectangular hardshell case with blue plush lining containing Strings & Things Custom printed order form inscribed with various details, including 'Eric Clapton' and the date '2/19/83'

Henry W. Kiel
Municipal Auditorium
St. Louis, Missouri, USA
Feb. 18, 1983

Clapton playing this guitar, which he had borrowed that morning to try out in concert.

Gigs:
Henry W. Kiel
Municipal Auditorium
St. Louis, Missouri, USA
Feb. 18, 1983

In 1978, Tom Keckler helped Schecter Guitar Research to produce their own line of solidbody electric guitars. In 1983 Keckler returned to his old job as a repairman for the Strings & Things music store and soon convinced the founders of Strings & Things to produce their own line of guitars based on his designs.

The Bluesmaster was the first model Keckler developed for Strings & Things. The body shape was based on that of a Fender Esquire, shaved down so its curves more closely resembled those of a Les Paul. The original model was basically a Telecaster with Keckler's modified body shape and two full-size DiMarzio humbucking pickups.

When Clapton played a concert in Memphis at the Mid-South Coliseum on February 17th, 1983, Charles Lawing of Strings & Things brought a couple of its new guitars backstage to show to Clapton. Although Clapton was too busy before the show to see the guitars, he agreed to come to the store at 8am the next morning. As Clapton arrived at the store, he immediately noticed this black Bluesmaster and asked if he could borrow it for his show in St. Louis, Missouri, that night. Clapton promised that if he liked the guitar, he would return to Memphis to purchase it. True to his word, he returned the next day and purchased this black Bluesmaster guitar along with another Bluesmaster guitar that later became the basis for the St. Blues Bluesmaster II model.

By 1984, Strings & Things started marketing their guitars under the St. Blues brand name and produced instruments until 1989. In 2005 Keckler and his new business partner Bryan Eagle revived the St. Blues brand and started producing guitars again.

Serial No: 01412
Body: Ash, bound, single cutaway, sunburst finish
Neck: Maple with skunk-stripe truss rod routing, 21 frets, maple fingerboard with dot inlays, neckplate engraved 'Strings & Things Ser. 01412, Custom Made for Eric Clapton'
Bridge: Strings-through-body gold-plated Gotoh baseplate with six adjustable saddles
Pickguard: Cream single-ply
Pickups: Two 'Slant Six' single-coil
Controls: One volume/pull tap, one tone/pull tap
Switches: Three-position pickup selector
Case: Black rectangular hardshell case with blue plush lining, handwritten label

When Clapton returned to Memphis on February 19th, 1983, to purchase two Bluesmaster guitars from Strings & Things, Keckler and Lawing asked Eric if he would be interested in collaborating with them on the design of an Eric Clapton model guitar. Clapton agreed, and he left behind this guitar so it could be modified to his specifications. Clapton asked for single-coil pickups, and the company developed its own 'Slant Six' pickups with coil taps to provide a wider variety of tones than those of standard single-coil pickups. Somewhat ironically, the guitar Clapton specified moved away from the Les Paul/Telecaster hybrid that distinguished the original Bluesmaster model and reverted back to a classic Telecaster-style design. After the guitar was modified, a custom neckplate engraved with Eric's name was affixed to the guitar.

Unfortunately, Strings & Things jumped the gun and announced its new Eric Clapton model in an advertisement that was published without Clapton's prior approval, which caused Clapton to withdraw his endorsement. When Strings & Things adopted the St. Blues brand name for its guitars in 1984, they offered a model similar to this guitar called the Bluesmaster II.

St. Blues Guitar Workshop, Memphis Tennessee, USA Feb. 19, 1983

ERIC Strings & Things from Memphis tried to get me interested in a fairly revolutionary-looking guitar, the St. Blues. I tried it, and I liked it, and then I played it on stage and liked it a lot. But, while I was doing that, I was thinking, 'Well, Blackie's back there. If I get into this new guitar too deeply, it's tricky, because then I won't be able to go back to Blackie. And what will happen to that?' This all happens in my head while I'm actually playing. I can be miles away thinking about this stuff, and suddenly I shut down and say, 'This is enough. No more. Nice new guitar. Sorry. You're very nice, but...'

LOT 92 CHRISTIE'S 1999

Serial No: 8 4541
Body: Korina, natural finish
Neck: Korina, 22 frets, rosewood fingerboard with dot inlays
Headstock: 'Scimitar' shape, pearl Gibson logo inlay
Bridge: Gold-plated Tune-o-matic, gold-plated stop tailpiece
Pickguard: White three-ply (white/ black/white)
Pickups: Two humbucking with gold-plated covers
Controls: One volume, two tone
Switches: Three-position pickup selector
Additional: Set of single-stripe Kluson Deluxe gold-plated tuners and strap
Case: Black rectangular hardshell case with brown plush lining and handwritten tie-on label ''58 Gibson Explorer 84541' and adhesive paper label similarly inscribed

With only 22 examples made during 1958 and 1959, the original Gibson Explorer is one of the most collectible and coveted Gibson solidbody guitars ever made. Clapton was fortunate to own two late 1950s Gibson Explorers, including the example shown here. His other late 1950s Explorer (page 147) was heavily modified by a previous owner, who cut off a significant portion of the lower bass bout and rounded off its distinctive asymmetrical angular body shape, allegedly in an attempt to make the guitar more comfortable to play. Clapton used the modified Explorer frequently during the mid 1970s, playing it on his *461 Ocean Boulevard* and *E.C. Was Here* albums and appearing in a 1976 advert for Music Man amplifiers with the guitar.

Clapton says that he bought this Explorer in February 1983 from a fan in Austin, Texas. Later that year he played it on stage at London's Royal Albert Hall during the ARMS Benefit Concert on September 20th and 21st, performing the songs 'Rita Mae', 'Rambling On My Mind', 'Have You Ever Loved a Woman' and 'Cocaine'. He also brought the Explorer to the United States for the nine ARMS Benefit concerts in Dallas, San Francisco, Los Angeles and New York.

ERIC This 1958 Gibson Explorer was used on the ARMS Tour.

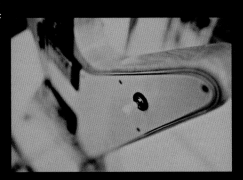

The ARMS London Benefit Concert Royal Albert Hall London, UK Sept. 20, 1983

Eric Clapton is playing his Gibson Explorer on stage alongside Bill Wyman.

Playlist:
The ARMS Benefit London Concert, 1983
Gigs:
The ARMS US Tour Nov. 28-Dec. 9, 1983
Highlight:
The ARMS London Benefit Concert Royal Albert Hall London, UK Sept. 20, 1983

ERIC Obviously the ARMS Benefit was
a concert I very much wanted to do both
on behalf of Ronnie, and on behalf of the
Action and Research for Multiple Sclerosis
fund. But that didn't mean I wasn't nervous.
Far from it – I was petrified when we had
the first rehearsals. But it rapidly became
great fun. It was a delight to work with such
a competent bunch of musicians. Originally
the idea was for everyone to just loosely jam
together, but subsequently it was quite
rightly decided that everyone involved
should do their own little regular sets, with
the rest of the band providing the backing.
We were all playing together for the first
time, and because we were doing it for
Ronnie rather than for money, we left our
egos at the door and it was great.

LOT 10 CHRISTIE'S 1999

Serial No: 94056324
Body: Mahogany, black finish
Neck: Mahogany, 22 frets, rosewood fingerboard with dot inlays
Bridge: Chrome-plated Tune-o-matic with stop tailpiece
Pickguard: White
Pickups: Two uncovered humbucking
Controls: Two volume, master tone
Switches: Three-position pickup selector
Case: Brown rectangular hardshell case with pink plush lining and handwritten adhesive paper label 'Gibson - Black Explorer /?94056324'

It's estimated that Gibson produced fewer than 40 of their original Explorer model guitars. When they reissued the model in 1975 a few changes were made, most notably the use of mahogany for the body instead of the korina wood that the original was made from. In 1990, Gibson reissued the 1970s version of the Explorer, which they officially named the Explorer '76 in 1991. Clapton bought this guitar at a Stevie Ray Vaughan benefit auction in the late 1990s.

LOT 47 BONHAMS 2011

Serial No: 15100
Body: Mahogany, black finish, signed and inscribed on the body in silver felt pen 'Eric Clapton 2010'
Neck: Mahogany, 24 frets, bound rosewood fingerboard with dot inlays
Bridge: Kahler double-locking tremolo
Pickups: Two humbucking
Controls: One volume, one tone
Switches: Three-position pickup selector
Case: Black rectangular hardshell case with black plush lining, two handwritten labels with various inscriptions including 'Dean "Mini Explorer" Ser 15100'

Dean Guitars introduced their first Baby models in 1982, which featured scaled-down bodies based on their angular-shaped V, Z and ML models but with full-size necks to improve playing comfort. During the first few years of production, Dean Baby guitars were made in the USA, but around 1985 production shifted to Japan, to the same factory that produced ESP guitars. This example is a Japanese-made Baby Z, featuring a 24-fret neck, Kahler double-locking tremolo, and the distinctive 'shrimp fork' headstock shape that Dean first introduced on their Baby models before the design migrated to other Dean guitars.

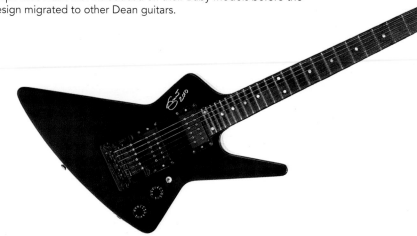

SLOWHAND RIFFS

Body: Alder, Ice Blue metallic finish
Neck: Maple with skunk-stripe truss rod routing, 21 frets, maple fingerboard with dot inlays
Bridge: Blocked synchronised tremolo
Pickguard: White single-ply
Pickups: Three single-coil
Controls: One volume, two tone
Switches: Five-position pickup selector with white switch tip
Case: Black rectangular hardshell case with black plush lining and handwritten tie-on label 'R. Giffin Custom Blue Strat N.S.N.' and adhesive paper label similarly inscribed

From the late 1960s until 1988, Roger Giffin built guitars in a small London workshop. His clientele consisted of several members of Britain's rock royalty, including David Gilmour, George Harrison, Mark Knopfler, Paul McCartney, Jimmy Page and Pete Townshend. Giffin temporarily closed shop and moved to the United States to work for the Gibson Custom Shop, but in the mid 1990s he started making his own guitars again. Today he builds guitars in his workshop in Portland, Oregon.

During the 1980s, Giffin made a pair of guitars for Clapton that were exact duplicates (other than the colour) of Eric's beloved Blackie Strat (page 122). Giffin built this blue Blackie copy in 1983, which Eric set up for slide playing. Clapton played this guitar on 'Everybody Ought to Make a Change' at the Royal Albert Hall ARMS Benefit Concert on September 20th, 1983, and he also used it to play songs like 'Motherless Children' and 'Tulsa Time' on his 1985 Behind the Sun Tour.

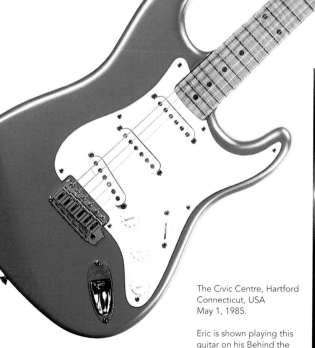

Playlist:
The ARMS Benefit London Concert, 1983
Eric Clapton – Live 1985 (TV), 1985
Gigs:
1985 Behind The Sun Tour
Feb. 27-Nov. 6, 1985
Highlight:
The ARMS London Benefit Concert
London, UK
Sept. 20, 1983
Prince's Trust Concert
Royal Albert Hall
London, UK
Sept. 21, 1983

The Civic Centre, Hartford Connecticut, USA
May 1, 1985.

Eric is shown playing this guitar on his Behind the Sun Tour. This concert was filmed and released on video by Channel 5 as *Eric Clapton – Live 1985*.

LOT 84 BONHAMS 2011

Serial No: BO12944
Covering: Black Tolex, silver speaker cloth
Plates: Music Man logo, 'HD-150 Reverb'
Switches: Bright/normal, deep/normal (deep re-labelled 'mid shift'), hi/standby/lo, ground, power on/off, 4-ohm/8-ohm speaker impedance
Controls: Volume, treble, middle, bass (channel 1); volume, treble, middle, bass (channel 2); master
Inputs: Two (channel 1), two (channel 2)
Outputs: Speaker (two)
Footswitch inputs: Reverb, tremolo
Other: Effects loop (preamp line out, power amp line input)

1981 Music Man 412-GS speaker cabinet
Housing: Straight closed-back cabinet
Covering: Black Tolex, silver speaker cloth
Plates: Music Man logo, '412-GS'
Speakers: Four 12-inch
Case: Blue flight case with 'The Duck Bros' logo stencilled on either side, '15' on the top and sides, various stickers

Clapton's use of Music Man amps as his main stage amps lasted about as long as the product line did, from 1974 until late 1983. Some of the last shows where he performed with Music Man amps as a regular fixture of his back line were the 1983 ARMS Benefit concerts in the United States.

In early 1984, the Music Man company was sold to Ernie Ball, which discontinued the amplifier line and maintained production only of the Music Man StingRay bass guitar. Shortly after Music Man stopped making amps, Clapton switched to the elaborate Bob Bradshaw-designed custom rack-mounted amp and effects systems (page 175) that started to become immensely popular with professional guitarists during this time.

Gigs:
The ARMS US Tour
Nov. 28-Dec. 9, 1983
Highlight:
Madison Square Garden
New York, USA
Dec. 9, 1983

ERIC We enjoyed ourselves so much that we decided that if everyone would agree, we should take the show on the road to try to make a lot of money for ARMS. The result was a successful tour of America, playing 20,000-seat arenas in Dallas, San Francisco, LA and New York, and thoroughly enjoying ourselves.

SLOWHAND RIFFS

Madison Square Garden
New York, USA
Dec. 9, 1983

Clapton is pictured
playing Blackie through
the Music Man pictured,
or a similar half-stack.
Ronnie Lane appeared
at the New York concert
but was unable to attend
the other USA shows.

LOT 87 BONHAMS 2011

1984 Marshall JCM 800 1987 50-watt Lead MKII (two), 1984 Marshall JCM 800 1959 100-watt Super Lead MK II (two)
Serial Nos: S03314 and S03293 (1987 50-watt); S15384 and S15385 (1959 100-watt)
Covering: Black Tolex, dark grey front panel cloth, back panels missing on 50-watt amps
Details: Large white Marshall script logo
Switches: Power on/off, standby, 4-/8-/16-ohm impedance selector, 120V/220V/240V mains selector
Controls: Presence, bass, middle, treble, volume I, volume II
Inputs: Four, D.I. (100-watt 1959 model only)
Outputs: Loudspeaker (two)
Case: Black flight case for all four heads with 'The Duck Bros' logo stencilled on lid and '5' on side, various stickers

1980s Marshall JCM 800 1960A/B speaker cabinets
Serial Nos: 15816 (1960A), 9387 (1960B)
Housing: Angled closed-back (1960A), straight closed-back (1960B)
Covering: Black Tolex, black speaker cloth
Speakers: none
Details: White Marshall script logo, gold plate with 'JCM 800 Lead Series'
Handles: Plastic
Other: XLR cannon plug inputs on back

Opposite:
Bray Film Studios
Windsor, Berkshire, UK
Apr. 14, 2005

One of the JCM-800 amps in this lot, or one similar, is seen behind Clapton at rehearsals for the Cream reunion concerts.

After spending most of the 1970s and early 80s using Fender or Music Man amplifiers, Clapton returned to Marshall again in 1984 prior to going on the road with Roger Waters' The Pros and Cons of Hitch-Hiking Tour in 1984. Former Director of Marshall Amplification Mike Hill recalls that he delivered several 50- and 100-watt JCM 800 amplifier heads and 1960 4x12 speaker cabinets to Clapton during rehearsals for the tour and that Clapton purchased two of each on the spot. In 1985 these amps were regularly rotated into Clapton's Bob Bradshaw-designed rig (page 175), either replacing or paired with the Dean Markley amp heads that he also liked to use during the mid 1980s until 1987 when he switched to Fender Dual Showman amps.

Clapton also used one of these JCM 800 heads on stage during the early 2000s to drive a Leslie rotating speaker cabinet. The empty 1960 4x12 speaker cabinets are a bit of a mystery. A plausible explanation is that the speakers were removed either so they could be used with another cabinet or combo amp or they were taken out so they could be replaced with other speakers that never were installed in the cabinets.

ERIC I like to have the time where I can get away from being in the lead. It's like having a little holiday in a way. It gives you a sense of reality.

Gigs:
Roger Waters' Pros and Cons of Hitch-Hiking Tour June 16-July 31, 1984
Highlight:
Live Aid
John F. Kennedy Stadium
Philadelphia
Pennsylvania, USA
July 13, 1985

ERIC The first Music Man amps were really great, but then I started blowing them up a lot, and they started sounding really thin. So I went back to Marshall in around 1985.

EST: $600 - $900   PRICE: $7,500

LOT 9 BONHAMS 2011

Body: Rosewood back and sides, spruce top, wood binding with herringbone purfling, natural finish
Neck: Mahogany, 20 frets, ebony fingerboard
Headstock: Solid, inlaid 'S.K.' logo, rosewood veneer, back of headstock signed by Eric Clapton in black felt pen
Bridge: Ebony 'belly' pin bridge
Pickguard: Black single-ply
Soundhole: Herringbone rosette
Label: 'Stephen Kearney Guitars, Nungurner Jetty, Victoria 3909'
Case: Black hardshell contour case with blue plush lining, two handwritten labels inscribed with various details including 'Made In "Oz"'

Stephen Kearney is a New Zealand-born musician who is best known for the fine, handcrafted guitars he built for musicians like Clapton, Neil Finn and Mark Knopfler in a workshop located in a remote southern Australian town east of Melbourne called Nungurner Jetty. Clapton purchased this Stephen Kearney guitar while on tour in Australia in November 1984. Kearney stopped making guitars in the mid 1990s when he was diagnosed with psoriatic arthropathy (an inflammatory arthritis) and resumed his career as a musician, working with various projects, including his band Spike.

EST: $900 - $1,200   PRICE: $8,500

LOT 57 BONHAMS 2011

Serial No: 1004
Body: Alder, sunburst finish
Neck: Maple with skunk-stripe truss rod routing, 22 frets, rosewood fingerboard with dot inlays, black neckplate engraved 'Made for Eric Clapton 10/84 by Steve Ripley ser 1004'
Headstock: Back of headstock signed by Eric Clapton in black felt pen
Bridge: Blocked Floyd Rose tremolo
Pickups: Three Bartolini multi-channel
Controls: One volume, one tone, six small rotary stereo pan
Switches: Three-position pickup selector, power on/off, two mini toggles with unknown functions
Additional: Signal splitter box, guitar cable, two handwritten labels
Case: Black rectangular hardshell case with black plush lining

Steve Ripley started his music industry career as a guitarist who played in various bands based in Tulsa, Oklahoma. He also worked as an engineer on J.J. Cale's *Shades* and a guitarist on Bob Dylan's *Shot of Love*, both released in 1981. In 1982 he started building guitars, which he sold under the Ripley brand name. One of his models was an innovative stereo guitar that featured individual pickups and panning controls for each string to allow guitarists to pan each string to its own location in a stereo mix. Ripley Stereo Guitars ended up in the hands of numerous players like Ry Cooder, Eddie Van Halen and Dweezil Zappa, who used them in the recording studio. In 1985 Kramer Music Products hired Ripley to design guitars for them.

1988 FENDER STRATOCASTER XII

EST: $6,000 - $8,000   PRICE: $42,000

LOT 76 CHRISTIE'S 1999

Serial No: E804764
Body: Alder, sunburst finish
Neck: Maple, 22 frets, rosewood fingerboard with dot inlays
Bridge: 12-saddle through-body tailblock
Pickguard: White single-ply
Pickups: Three single-coil
Controls: One volume, two tone
Switches: Five-position pickup selector
Case: Tweed rectangular hardshell case with orange plush lining and handwritten adhesive paper label 'Fender 12 String Strat. E804764'

Although the mid 1960s Fender Electric XII model was not as popular as Rickenbacker's 12-string electric guitar introduced around the same time, it was a favourite of players like Pete Townshend, Jimmy Page and Tim Buckley. Clapton also used a Fender Electric XII with Cream in 1967 to record 'Dance the Night Away'. When Fender decided to make a second attempt at producing an electric 12-string model in the late 1980s, they reconceived it as a 12-string version of the Strat. Clapton loved the rich, ringing tones of this Stratocaster XII guitar, and he used it a few times to record rhythm guitar tracks in the studio.

ERIC This guitar is fabulous, a valued piece. I used it for recording.

1985/86 FENDER SHORT SCALE STRATOCASTER

EST: $300 - $500   PRICE: $12,000

LOT 109 BONHAMS 2011

Serial No: A007037
Body: Alder, sunburst finish
Neck: Maple with skunk-stripe truss rod routing, 21 frets, rosewood fingerboard with dot inlays
Headstock: Back of headstock signed by Eric Clapton in black felt pen
Bridge: Blocked synchronised tremolo
Pickguard: White single-ply
Pickups: Three single-coil
Controls: One volume, two tone
Switches: Five-position pickup selector
Additional: Various accessories
Case: Black Fender rectangular hardshell case with black plush lining

At a casual glance, this guitar looks like a regular Stratocaster, but closer examination reveals that the pickups appear more closely spaced and the control knobs and output jack appear larger than normal. This guitar is actually a Short Scale Stratocaster model that Fender Japan produced especially for the Japanese market starting in 1989, featuring a 24-inch scale and proportionally downsized body and synchronised tremolo.

This Short Scale Stratocaster differs slightly from the models that Fender Japan produced. Most Japanese Short Scale Strats have a 22-fret neck, but this one has a 21-fret neck. The serial number on the neck plate is also consistent with serial numbers for Fender Japan guitars built in 1985 or 1986. Either this guitar is an early experimental model that was built in the mid 1980s or it simply has a leftover serial number plate from an earlier year.

Serial No: K824044
Body: Alder, double cutaways, candy apple red metallic finish
Neck: Maple with skunk-stripe truss rod routing, 21 frets, maple fingerboard with dot inlays
Bridge: Tremolo
Pickguard: White three-ply (white/black/white)
Pickups: Three single-coil, hexaphonic synth pickup
Controls: Master volume, guitar tone, balance, cut-off frequency, resonance, LFO depth
Switches: Three-position mode, five-position pickup selector
Case: Black contour hardshell case with black plush lining and handwritten adhesive paper label 'Roland Synth GTR C. Apple #K 824044'

Serial No: 400401
Body: Metallic grey finish
Controls: Memory, string select, dynamics controls
Switches: 11 footswitches
Display: LED
Inputs/Outputs: Multiple inputs/outputs
Additional: PG 200 unit with multiple controls, flight case

Serial No: 314451
Body: Blue finish
Controls: Eight rotary controls
Switches: Ten switches and five footswitches
Inputs: Six inputs and guitar input
Additional: Original packaging

Roland was not the first company to develop a guitar synthesiser, but their GR-500 system, introduced in 1977, was the first commercially viable product offering this technology. In 1980 when Roland introduced its second-generation guitar synthesiser, the GR-100, they also offered a selection of three guitar synth controllers – the G-202, G-303 and G-505, which is the guitar pictured here. These controllers were also compatible with subsequent guitar synthesiser systems, including the blue GR-300 and grey GR-700 floor units shown with this guitar. Roland's guitar synth controllers were actually manufactured by Japan's Fujigen Gakki Company, which also made guitars for Ibanez.

Clapton used his Roland guitar synth system while he was writing and recording the score to the British television series *Edge of Darkness*. He also says that the guitar synth inspired him while he was writing songs for *Behind the Sun*. Clapton played the guitar synth on several of that album's tracks as well as on his 1985 tour in support of the album.

Playlist:
Behind the Sun, 1985
Edge of Darkness, 1985
Gigs:
First leg of the US 1985 Behind The Sun Tour April 9-May 3, 1985
Highlight:
'Never Make You Cry'

ERIC If I am stuck it helps to pick up a new instrument. Usually it happens with an acoustic guitar or a gut string or, as was the case with *Behind the Sun*, the Roland. It inspired me, just picking it up and playing a chord.

Phil Collins and I made *Behind the Sun*, finished it, mixed it and sent it off, and thought no more about it. I should say that we made the record on Phil's wish and my wish too. We wanted the record to be the first album to be a true portrayal of what I could do in all the areas that I play in. There was a little reggae, a little acoustic blues, and a lot more of me playing that Roland guitar synthesiser, sounding like a saxophone, a harmonica and so forth. We were very satisfied with it as a concept album, showing the different sides of me.

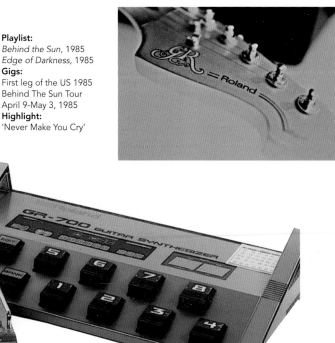

Serial No: 257
Body: String instrument-shaped carved mahogany casing, brass front control plate/speaker grille engraved 'Sonica TM' and 'By Frank Eventoff', natural finish
Headstock: Heart-shaped brass 'headstock' plate engraved 257
Controls: Key, volume/power switch
Pressure pads: Half step, tone, slider
Speaker: Three-inch
Output jack: ⅛ inch mini
Label: Brass back plate engraved 'Sound Instruments Los Angeles, California, Sonica TM, Patent No D249.280 Other Pats. Pend.'

The Sound Instruments Sonica is a brilliantly designed alternative electronic synthesiser instrument that combines space-age ingenuity with styling reminiscent of a miniature Turkish cura saz. The Sonica features a diatonic-tuned two-octave touch-sensitive membrane 'fingerboard' that allows players to trigger notes with the left hand while the right hand triggers three touch-sensitive pads for 'slider' (vibrato), half-step (raises pitch by a half step to facilitate playing chromatically) and tone functions. The Sonica's sound can best be described as a combination of a theremin's electronic character, a sitar's drone and a violin's legato.

Frank Eventoff designed the Sonica, which features a simple analogue oscillator circuit designed by Serge Tcherepnin (of Serge Modular fame). Battery operation and a built-in speaker allow users to play it anywhere, and an ⅛ inch output jack was provided for plugging the Sonica into effects processors and external amplification. Eventoff's neighbour hand-carved each Sonica body out of mahogany and produced 24 units at a time. Sound Instruments made a total of 650 Sonicas in 1979 before production ceased that same year.

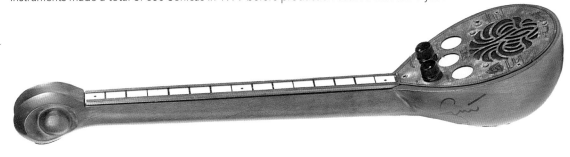

1979 SOUND INSTRUMENTS SONICA

Serial No: T00093
Body: Alder, black finish
Neck: Maple, 22 frets, ebony fingerboard with dot inlays
Headstock: Back of headstock signed by Eric Clapton in black felt pen
Bridge: Floyd Rose-licensed locking tremolo
Pickguard: Matt black single-ply
Pickups: Two single-coil, one humbucking, one hexaphonic
Controls: One guitar volume, one synth volume, one tone/pull coil split
Switches: Five-position pickup selector, eight programme, octave up, octave down, tuner, card
Other: Two-digit LED, MIDI out connector, guitar output jack, synth output jack, RAM/ROM card slot
Case: Black rectangular hardshell case with tangerine plush lining, two labels inscribed 'E.C. Black Casio Synth Guitar'

Featuring a built-in polyphonic Casio VZ synthesiser module with 64 preset tones, the Casio PG-380 could operate as a standalone guitar synthesiser in addition to controlling external synthesisers via MIDI. By placing the synth module in a high-quality guitar built at Japan's Fujigen Gakki factory, which also manufactured guitars for Ibanez and Fender Japan in the 1980s, Casio's PG-380 made guitar synth technology accessible, easy to use, and enjoyable to play.

Clapton occasionally used guitar synthesisers as a songwriting tool during the 1980s, finding the wide palette of sounds inspirational. His good friend J.J. Cale also used a Casio PG-380 on stage as his main guitar.

ERIC I wrote most of the songs for the *Behind the Sun* album on synthesisers. I'd run out of ideas on the guitar. Synths sounded so great, writing was easier.

SYNTHS & SIGNATURES

1987 CASIO PG-380 MIDI GUITAR

Serial No: EN01603
Covering: Black Tolex, silver speaker cloth
Plates: Music Man logo, '112 RD Fifty'
Speakers: One Music Man 12-inch
Switches: Bright/normal, limiter/clean, power on/off, ground
Controls: Volume, treble, bass (channel 1), volume, treble, bass, gain (channel 2), reverb
Inputs: One
Outputs: 8-ohm speaker, 8-ohm external speaker, line
Footswitch inputs: Reverb, distort

Considering that Music Man seemed engaged in a conquest to develop the loudest and most powerful amps available, it's somewhat ironic that the last amp model the company introduced (in 1982) was also its smallest – the 50-watt RD-50 combo, available with either a 10-inch speaker (110 RD-50) or 12-inch speaker (112 RD-50). The RD-50's circuit differed from previous Music Man models, featuring a 12AX7-driven limiter/distortion circuit. Although the RD-50 is often described as a 'single-channel' amp (perhaps because it has only one input jack instead of separate input jacks for each channel) it actually has separate clean and limiter/distortion channels – each with their own EQ and volume controls – that can be switched with the front panel toggle or a footswitch controller. Despite its compact size, the RD-50 is an impressively loud amp that produces sufficient volume output for playing live gigs.

This amp made a cameo appearance in Clapton's first-ever music video, 'Forever Man', directed by Kevin Godley and Lol Creme, the former members of 10cc who became known for their innovative music videos in the early 1980s. The amp can be seen directly behind Clapton in a handful of shots. It was also used when Clapton played an informal gig with Stan Webb's Chicken Shack at Finchley Cricket Club on August 15th, 1986.

ERIC Making the 'Forever Man' video was fun, but it went against the grain for me.

Playlist:
Pilgrim, 1998
Gigs:
Bunbury Cricket Club Charity Match Jam Session Finchley Cricket Club London, UK Aug. 15, 1986
Highlight:
'Forever Man' video, 1985

A photograph of Blackie and this amplifier was used on *The Cream of Eric Clapton* compilation CD, released in 1987.

During the recording sessions for *Behind the Sun*, session guitarist Steve Lukather turned Clapton on to the work of Bob Bradshaw, who built sophisticated amp and effects switching systems that made it easy for performing guitarists to control and access a wide variety of sounds from equipment that was normally used in the recording studio. Clapton started using a custom Bradshaw system during his 1985 world tour, and over the years he experimented with different amp heads, rack effects processors and stomp box pedals that came and went as Clapton explored the new world of sounds that lay accessible at his feet. This was quite a radical departure from Clapton's 1970s stage rig, where he used no effects at all.

From 1985 until 1987, Clapton frequently switched between Marshall JCM 800 and Dean Markley Signature Series 120 amps. Driven by four 6L6GC power tubes and three 12AX7 preamp tubes, the Signature Series 120 amps are an ideal foundation for the multitude of distortion and effects textures produced by the Bradshaw system's various pedals and processors.

Pair of 1980s Dean Markley Signature Series 120 amps
Serial Nos: T120R-003 (top), T120RM-181 (bottom)
Switches: Ground, standby, power on/off, +15dB input, voicing
Controls: Preamp, master, bass, midrange, treble, presence
Inputs: One
Outputs: 4-ohm speaker (two), 8-ohm speaker (two), 16-ohm speaker (two)
Footswitch input: Reverb
Other: Effects loop (line out, power amp in)
Case: Grey Packhorse flight rack case with stickers

Bob Bradshaw switching system
Housing: Carpet-covered 9U rack case with drawer
Master unit (in rack): Pad/stock switch, input, outputs (two), external loop (send and return), multi-pin connector
Foot controller: 12 footswitches with individual red LEDs labelled RATE, SPR-1, SPR-2, 3000, TSC, HARM, COMP, HM-2, PS-1, PS-2, PS-3 and PS-4

1980s Marshall JCM 800 1960A speaker cabinet
Serial No: 25331
Housing: Angled closed-back cabinet
Covering: Black Tolex, black speaker cloth
Speakers: Four 12-inch Celestion G12M70
Details: White Marshall script logo, gold plate with 'JCM 800 Lead-1960'
Handles: Plastic
Case: Black flight case with 'The Duck Bros' stencilled logo on top, '7' on one end

1980s Marshall JCM 800 1960B speaker cabinet
Serial No: 13066
Housing: Straight closed-back cabinet
Covering: Black Tolex, black speaker cloth
Speakers: Four 12-inch Celestion G12M70
Details: White Marshall script logo, gold plate with 'JCM 800 Lead-1960'
Handles: Plastic
Case: CP flight case

Gigs:
1985 Behind The Sun Tour Feb. 27-Nov. 6, 1985
The Prince's Trust 10th Birthday Party Wembley Arena London, UK June 20, 1986
Royal Albert Hall 1985-87
25th Anniversary Japan Tour Oct. 31-Nov. 5, 1988
Highlights:
Live Aid John F. Kennedy Stadium Philadelphia Pennsylvania, USA July 13, 1985
Nelson Mandela 70th Birthday Tribute Concert Wembley Stadium London, UK June 11, 1988

Body: Alder, Arctic White finish
Neck: Maple with skunk-stripe truss rod routing, 21 frets, maple fingerboard with dot inlays
Bridge: Chrome-plated six-saddle bridge/tailpiece
Pickguard: White three-ply (white/black/white)
Pickups: Three Fender Elite Alnico II active single-coil
Controls: One volume, two tone
Switches: Five-position pickup selector with white switch tip
Other: Side-mounted output jack
Case: Tweed rectangular hardshell case with red plush lining and handwritten adhesive paper label 'Fender "Elite" Strat. White, # None'

Designed by a team that included John Page, Dan Smith, Chip Todd, and the designer of the original 1954 Stratocaster, Freddie Tavares, the Fender Elite Stratocaster model introduced 16 new features, enhancements and innovations to the Strat. The most notable innovations were its active TBX treble/bass expander and MDX midrange boost circuits, which later were incorporated on the Eric Clapton Signature Model Stratocaster.

This Elite Stratocaster has no serial number and several features that differ from the version that was introduced to the public in 1983, including its 1950s-style neck, standard control knobs (instead of the Elite's knobs with serrated rubber inserts), and a traditional five-position pickup selector switch (instead of the Elite's trio of pushbuttons), which suggests it may have been a prototype.

ERIC **I messed around with this guitar.**

Gigs:
1985 Behind The Sun Tour
Feb. 27-Nov. 6, 1985

1983 FENDER ELITE STRATOCASTER

EST: $5,000 - $7,000   PRICE: $26,000

LOT 91 CHRISTIE'S 1999

Body: Alder, black finish
Neck: Maple with skunk-stripe truss rod routing, 21 frets, maple fingerboard with dot inlays
Tailblock: Chrome-plated six-saddle bridge/tailpiece
Pickguard: White three-ply (white/black/white)
Pickups: Three Fender Elite Alnico II active single-coil
Controls: One volume, two tone, TBX/MDX active circuitry
Switches: Three pickup on/off
Other: Side-mounted output jack
Case: Black rectangular hardshell case with black plush lining and handwritten tie-on label 'Fender Elite Black N.S.N.'

This Fender Elite Stratocaster also has no serial number and could be another prototype, but its features are more consistent with those of the final production model. Although Clapton says that he didn't use these Elite Strats very much, he did compliment the guitars' fretwork in an interview with *Guitar Player* magazine. He was also impressed with the Elite's TBX and MDX active circuitry, which he requested for his signature model Strat a few years later.

ERIC All of them need to be about ⅛ inch in the action, and I like it to be constant all the way down. I like frets to be generally somewhere between a Strat and a Les Paul. Les Pauls are too thick and Fenders are sometimes too thin. The Fender Elite is very nice because it's a blend.

Serial No: 1-14258
Body: Moulded Res-o-glas (fibreglass), single cutaway, black finish
Neck: Black painted wood, 20 frets, rosewood fingerboard with dot inlays
Bridge: Height-adjustable rosewood, chrome-plated trapeze tailpiece
Pickguard: White single-ply
Pickups: One single-coil
Controls: One volume, one tone
Additional: Three pages of mimeographed typescript lyrics entitled '*Water*: Front Credits Song', 'Song For Freedom' (June 29, 1984) and 'All As One' (June 6, 1984)
Case: Beige softshell contour case with red plush lining inscribed 'National F/Glass Black. S.#1-14258'

In 1962, long before guitar manufacturers became concerned about dwindling sources of natural tone woods and started building instruments from alternative materials, the Valco company of Chicago, Illinois introduced National and Supro brand guitars made from Res-o-glas, which was actually moulded fibreglass. The National Studio 66, which was renamed the Varsity 66 in 1964, was Valco's most modest Res-o-glas guitar model, featuring a body shape that resembled a Les Paul instead of the more elaborate 'map' shapes of its National-brand brethren.

Clapton used this National Varsity 66 to record several songs for the soundtrack to the political farce *Water*, which was produced by George Harrison's Handmade Films. He can also been seen playing this guitar in a cameo appearance as himself near the end of the film, performing as a member of the Singing Rebels' Band.

Playlist:
Water, 1985

Right:
Three pages of mimeographed typescript lyrics entitled, '*Water*: Front Credits Song', 'Song For Freedom' (June 29, 1984) and 'All As One' (June 6, 1984).

Opposite:
This photograph was taken during the filming of *Water*, the 1985 film produced by George Harrison. Eric Clapton and this guitar joined George Harrison, Ringo Starr, Jon Lord and Billy Connolly, to perform the song 'Freedom'.

ERIC Dick Clement and Ian Le Frenais, or someone in that outfit, wanted me to write the song for *Water*. I wrote the song and then we did a sort of video for it, with Billy Connolly and George and Ringo and everyone playing. That might have been this guitar's only outing.

1986 FENDER STRATOCASTER ERIC CLAPTON SIGNATURE MODEL

EST: $10,000 - $15,000   PRICE: $95,000

LOT 62 CHRISTIE'S 1999

Serial No: V000009
Body: Alder, Pewter finish
Neck: Birdseye maple with skunk-stripe truss rod routing, 22 frets, maple fingerboard with dot inlays. Dated 2/23/88
Bridge: Blocked synchronised tremolo
Pickguard: White single-ply
Pickups: Three Gold Fender Lace Sensors
Controls: Master volume, two tone, TBX active circuitry
Switches: Five-position pickup selector with white switch tip
Case: Black rectangular hardshell case with black plush lining and handwritten tie-on label 'E.C. E.C. Grey Strat V000009' and adhesive paper label inscribed 'Fender – Pewter Strat # V000009 (Mike Stevens #2) Pewt. Grey C. Shop E.C.'

Playlist:
August, 1986
Journeyman, 1989
Gigs:
World Tours
1986-1990
1989 Royal Albert Hall
Jan. 20-Feb. 3, 1989
1991 Royal Albert Hall
Feb. 5-Mar. 9, 1991

Royal Albert Hall
London, UK
1991

This signature model photographed from backstage at rehearsals for Eric's 1991 Royal Albert Hall season.

Clapton played a major role in the Fender Stratocaster's popularity during the 1970s and its resurgence during the 1980s. In recognition of Eric's contributions to the Stratocaster's success, Fender introduced the Eric Clapton Signature Model Stratocaster in 1988, which was Fender's first signature model Strat.

Fender approached Clapton with a proposal to produce the Eric Clapton Signature Model Stratocaster in 1985. After Clapton accepted, George Blanda built three prototypes based on Eric's input and feedback in 1986 with serial numbers V000007, V000008 and V000009. One of the prototypes had a Torino Red finish (page 190) while the other two had a Pewter finish as seen on this guitar. The Pewter finish was inspired by the colour of a Mercedes-Benz that Clapton owned when the guitar was built. This guitar originally had a 21-fret neck, but in 1988 Clapton replaced it with a 22-fret birdseye maple neck made by Michael Stevens of Fender's newly founded Custom Shop.

This Strat was Clapton's main stage guitar during his 1989 concerts at the Royal Albert Hall, and he also played it frequently on stage and in the studio during the late 1980s.

ERIC I used the Eric Clapton Signature model on every song on *Journeyman* apart from 'Hard Times', where I used the ES-335 to get a kind of an old studio sound, a more acoustic blues guitar tone.

Whenever I make a record my life seems to change yet again. The nature of that depends as much on the influence of the people involved as it does upon the music. It's as if, like a sponge, I absorb the general vibe and the change slowly starts to take place, new patterns of thought, new forms of language, new musical directions, new things to laugh at, then suddenly it's all over and we have to say goodbye until the next time.

Shoreline Amphitheater
Mountainview
California, USA
May 5, 1990

ERIC Blackie (page 122) was simply worn out. The problem was in the neck. The rest of the guitar was okay, but the neck was worn out. The frets were almost down to the wood and it had already been refretted once; it couldn't take another refret. I'd played it so much that even the sides of the neck – running along the length of the fingerboard – were wearing down; the neck was actually getting thinner. It wasn't even wide enough to support the six strings, so I simply had to go with something else.

I was worried that if something happened to Blackie I'd be out on a limb. It has a great character – the guitar itself is really a character – and it worried me, taking it on the road. It just seemed to be unfair. It's like taking a very old man and expecting him to do the impossible every night.

Dan Smith, who was head of Fender at the time, wanted to have a meeting with all the guitar players and he got all the people together in this country and introduced himself, which was a pretty revolutionary thing to do in a way. He came to me especially and said that he'd be very interested in putting a guitar out with my name on it, and would I specify the way I would want it.

I said Blackie was my favourite guitar, so if they could make copies of that, especially the neck shape, I wouldn't want any changes. In actual fact, it could have been anything. If it had been someone else it probably would not have been a Stratocaster, it would have been a new shape. I just asked them to make a running list of guitars like Blackie, except I wanted one little thing – to fatten the sound up. To have an optional sound, so you'd have the Stratocaster sound throughout but then you could fatten it up with just a tone knob. You've got one volume and two tones, and the second tone is this compression sound. The more you turn it clockwise, the fatter the sound gets. It's quite an individualistic sound that I like.

The colours I asked for were Ferrari Red (page 190), 7-Up Green (page 192) and charcoal grey.

Opposite:
Eric playing this guitar with a Versace guitar strap on the 1990 Journeyman Tour.

Serial Nos: CN402429, CN504689
Body: Alder with custom Emerald Black metallic finish
Neck: Maple with skunk-stripe truss rod routing, 22 frets, maple fingerboard with dot inlays, Custom Shop neckplate
Bridge: Blocked synchronised tremolo
Pickguard: White single-ply
Pickups: Three Gold Fender Lace Sensors
Controls: Master volume, two tone, TBX active circuitry
Switches: Five-position pickup selector with white switch tip
Case: Black hardshell contour cases with black plush lining and handwritten adhesive paper labels 'M.Kendrick – Black Green Fender-Strat – #C.N.40242, Merc – C.36 and #C.N.504689 Merc. C.36'

Although Fender made many guitars with colourful non-standard finishes during the 1950s, they first officially announced guitars made with standardised 'custom DuPont Duco finishes' in 1957. DuPont Duco paint is a nitrocellulose-based lacquer that was marketed specifically to the car industry and developed with assistance from General Motors engineers. Custom colour Fenders are highly collectible thanks to the rarity of certain colours and their bold appearance.

Eric Clapton added a new chapter to Fender's automotive-inspired custom colour finishes when he asked the Fender Custom Shop to make him a variety of Stratocasters painted to match his favourite European sports cars. These two examples were finished with Mercedes-Benz Emerald Black metallic paint to match the colour of a Mercedes-Benz C36 AMG that he owned at the time.

ERIC I used this guitar on stage in the mid Nineties and on the *Pilgrim* album.

Blackie is the template for all of these signature guitars.

You just pick one up, and it's exactly right. For me, it's exactly the way I would want a guitar to be. I'm very, very happy with it. And someone else that I know, who's very into guitars, came along and gave me an objective point of view. He said it was the best guitar he'd ever played, all round. I mean, it's hard for me to say that – about my guitar that I've kind of put my name to – but for someone else to say it, I was very impressed.

Opposite:
Masters Of Music Concert for The Prince's Trust Hyde Park, London, UK June 29, 1996

Eric Clapton playing this guitar or its partner in lot 39. Clapton played a set that mixed various blues numbers with his popular hits, typical of the period. It was the first time that Clapton played at Hyde Park since June 1969 when he appeared there with Blind Faith. The concert was filmed and released as a video, *Eric Clapton at Hyde Park*.

Playlist:
Eric Clapton at Hyde Park (Film), 1997
Pilgrim, 1998
Gigs:
Used on stage in the mid 1990s
Highlight:
Masters of Music Concert for The Prince's Trust Hyde Park, London, UK June 29, 1996
Giorgio Armani Gala Lexington Armory New York, USA Sept. 12, 1996

Serial No: CN404005
Body: Alder with custom Midnight Blue metallic finish
Neck: Maple with skunk-stripe truss rod routing, 22 frets, maple fingerboard with dot inlays, Custom Shop neckplate
Bridge: Blocked synchronised tremolo
Pickguard: White single-ply
Pickups: Three Gold Fender Lace Sensors
Controls: Master volume, two tone, TBX active circuitry
Switches: Five-position pickup selector with white switch tip
Case: Black hardshell contour case with black plush lining and handwritten adhesive paper label 'Midnight Blue Met., Fender-Strat #CN404005'

Clapton commissioned this guitar's Midnight Blue finish, which was done with the same paint and colour used for Mercedes-Benz cars. Eric likes to have many of his guitars finished to match cars he owns, although in this case the blue Strat preceded his ownership of a blue Mercedes.

ERIC Painting my guitars to match my cars was someone else's idea. I think my first reaction was 'corny', but then I thought, 'Why not?' The car paints were getting better and guitar colours weren't, so it seemed like a logical conclusion that if you had a nice car you'd paint the guitar to match, just because it was a great colour.

Playlist:
Pavarotti & Friends for War Child Foundation 1996
Highlight:
Pavarotti & Friends for War Child Foundation
Parco Novi Sad
Modena, Italy
June 20, 1996

Opposite:
Pavarotti and Friends
Parco Novi Sad
Modena, Italy
June 20, 1996

The concert, organised by Pavarotti, was held in aid of the charity War Child to benefit the children of Bosnia. Clapton and Pavarotti sang a duet of 'Holy Mother'. Clapton also played 'Third Degree' and provided backing for Sheryl Crow and the popular Italian artist Zucchero. Elton John and John McLaughlin also performed on that occasion and the concert was televised in Italy in the style of Live Aid. Decca subsequently released the soundtrack, which features a shot of Clapton playing this guitar on stage on the CD insert.

LOT 63 CHRISTIE'S 1999

Serial No: SE803563
Body: Alder, Torino Red finish
Neck: Maple with skunk-stripe truss rod routing, 22 frets, maple fingerboard with dot inlays
Bridge: Blocked synchronised tremolo
Pickguard: White single-ply
Pickups: Three Gold Fender Lace Sensors
Controls: Master volume, two tone, TBX active circuitry
Switches: Five-position pickup selector with white switch tip
Additional: Black strap with locking plastic plates
Case: Tweed rectangular hardshell case with red plush lining and handwritten tie-on label 'Red E.C. Strat "Slide" #SE803563' and adhesive paper label similarly inscribed

Even the most casual motor enthusiast will recognise the colour of these Strats as *rossa corsa* ('racing red'), the brilliant red hue associated with Ferrari sports cars. Although Fender called this colour 'Torino Red', perhaps in reference to the red Ford Gran Torino driven by Starsky and Hutch, the red finish on Clapton's signature model guitars was inspired by his request of having a guitar that matched the colour of a Ferrari he owned when his first signature model guitars were made.

The standard nut on this guitar was replaced with a higher-profile nut to raise the strings for playing slide. 'D tune' and 'G tune' labels affixed to the back of the headstock also reveal its use as a slide guitar, since Clapton often plays slide in open D (D, A, D, F#, A, D) or open G (D, G, D, G, B, D) tunings. Clapton played this guitar on the *Journeyman* album and on stage during the late 1980s.

Playlist:
Journeyman, 1989
Gigs:
Used on stage in the late 1980s
Rock Legends: George Harrison with Eric Clapton 1991 Japan Tour Dec. 1-17, 1991
Highlight:
Alpine Valley Music Theatre, East Troy Wisconsin, USA Aug. 26, 1990

LOT 67 CHRISTIE'S 1999

Serial No: SE900427
Body: Alder, Torino Red finish
Neck: Maple with skunk-stripe truss rod routing, 22 frets, maple fingerboard with dot inlays
Bridge: Blocked synchronised tremolo
Pickguard: White single-ply
Pickups: Three Gold Fender Lace Sensors
Controls: Master volume, two tone, TBX active circuitry
Switches: Five-position pickup selector with white switch tip
Case: Tweed rectangular hardshell case with orange plush lining and handwritten tie-on label 'Red E C. Strat #SE900427' and adhesive paper label similarly inscribed

This guitar is similar to the Strat above, but it features a standard nut instead of a raised nut.

ERIC I chose the colour of these guitars to match the red Ferrari I had at the time.

Gigs:
Used as a rehearsal guitar and spare in the late 1980s
Rock Legends: George Harrison with Eric Clapton 1991 Japan Tour Dec. 1-17, 1991

Opposite:
Clapton playing this guitar or its partner in 1987.

LOTS 64, 78 CHRISTIE'S 1999

Serial Nos: V025609, V025603
Body: Alder, custom Candy Green metallic finish
Neck: Maple with skunk-stripe truss rod routing, 22 frets, maple fingerboard with dot inlays
Bridge: Blocked synchronised tremolo
Pickguard: White single-ply
Pickups: Three Gold Fender Lace Sensors
Controls: Master volume, two tone, TBX active circuitry
Switches: Five-position pickup selector with white switch tip, additional active/passive switch on lot 78
Case: Tweed rectangular hardshell case and handwritten tie-on labels

Car paint jobs were not the only inspiration for the colours of Clapton's signature model Stratocasters. Shortly after receiving his first Torino Red and Pewter prototypes, Eric asked Fender to make him a guitar in the same shade of metallic green as found on a 7-Up can. Fender called this finish 'Candy Green' to avoid any trademark conflicts with 7-Up. Clapton's '7-Up Green' Strats were some of his favourite stage instruments during the late 1980s. Lots 64 and 78 in the 1999 Crossroads Auction were identical with the exception of the additional active/passive switch on lot 78, which was installed on a handful of Clapton's earliest signature model guitars and prototypes. Eric was photographed for the cover of *Rolling Stone* magazine with one of these 7-Up guitars in 1988.

A 7-Up guitar being restrung backstage in Japan, 1991.

Gigs: Touring in the late 1980s
Rock Legends: George Harrison with Eric Clapton 1991 Japan Tour Dec. 1-17, 1991

ERIC **This colour is great.**

LOT 75 CHRISTIE'S 1999

Serial No: BL100177
Body: Mahogany, curly maple top, bound, single sharp cutaway, green metallic finish
Neck: Mahogany, 22 frets, ebony fingerboard with slotted diamond inlays
Headstock: Guild 'G-Shield' inlay, 'peaked' Guild logo
Bridge: Gold-plated Tune-o-matic-style, stop tailpiece
Pickguard: Imitation bound tortoiseshell
Pickups: Two EMG humbucking
Controls: One volume, one tone
Switches: Three-position pickup selector
Additional: Black strap
Case: Brown rectangular hardshell case with black plush lining and handwritten adhesive paper label 'Guild - Nightbird #BL 100177 7-Up Green'

The Nightbird was one of several guitar models that Nashville vintage guitar dealer/historian George Gruhn helped Guild develop during the mid 1980s. Luthier Kim Walker, who ran the repair shop at Gruhn Guitars, also helped design this model. Clapton allegedly acquired this Nightbird because he wanted a guitar similar to the Guild Bluesbird that Buddy Guy was playing during this period, although the Bluesbird had hollowed-out body chambers instead of a solid body like the Nightbird. Clapton commissioned this '7-Up' green finish from Guild around the same time he requested a similar finish from Fender for his signature model Strats.

Clapton played this guitar on stage in the 1980s.

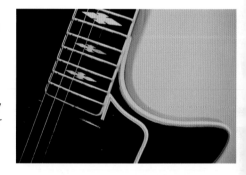

Gigs: Touring in the 1980s

Rolling Stone

ERIC CLAPTON
The Rolling Stone Interview

ROBERT DE NIRO
A Rare Talk with the Star of 'Midnight Run'

WHERE ARE THEY NOW?
Cat Stevens, the Box Tops, Billy J. Kramer and more

FALL FASHION
The Rolling Stone Collection

34790

Body: Alder, black finish
Neck: Maple with skunk-stripe truss rod routing, 22 frets, maple fingerboard with dot inlays, neck end inscribed 'R&D #1 CS 2/23/88'
Bridge: Blocked synchronised tremolo
Pickguard: White single-ply
Pickups: Three Gold Fender Lace Sensors
Controls: Master volume, two tone, TBX/MDX active circuitry
Switches: Five-position pickup selector with white switch tip
Case: Re-issue hardshell tweed case with adhesive tape inscribed 'Auction #13/Blk. EC Strat. N.S.N./ Mike Stevens'

Playlist:
Pilgrim, 1998
Gigs:
1990 Journeyman Tour
Mar. 28-Dec. 13, 1990
1991 Royal Albert Hall
Feb. 5-Mar. 9, 1991
Rock Legends: George Harrison with Eric Clapton
1991 Japan Tour
Dec. 1-17, 1991
World Tours
1992-3
Highlights:
Columbia Records Celebrates the Music of Bob Dylan
Madison Square Garden
New York, USA
Oct. 16, 1992
Rock and Roll Hall of Fame 8th Annual Induction Ceremony
Century Plaza Hotel
Los Angeles, USA
Jan. 12, 1993

In 1988, soon after the first red (page 190), green (page 192) and pewter (page 181) Eric Clapton Signature Model Strats hit the market, Clapton decided to have one made with a black finish similar to his recently retired Blackie Stratocaster (page 122). The black version of the Eric Clapton Signature Strat became an instant hit both with devoted Clapton fanatics and guitarists who preferred more traditional styling. Michael Stevens, who established the Fender Custom Shop with John Page in the mid 1980s, built this black Stratocaster Eric Clapton Signature Model prototype for Eric.

This guitar was Clapton's main stage instrument from the summer 1990 leg of his Journeyman Tour through his February and March 1993 concerts at London's Royal Albert Hall. This period included Clapton's 1991 Royal Albert Hall performances, the 1991 Tour of Japan with George Harrison, the 1992 World Tour, and his appearance at the Bob Dylan 30th Anniversary Concert Celebration at New York's Madison Square Garden on October 16th, 1992, where he performed Dylan's 'Don't Think Twice, It's Alright'.

Perhaps the guitar's most important appearance during this period was when Clapton played it onstage with Jack Bruce and Ginger Baker during Cream's reunion performance at the Rock and Roll Hall of Fame's 1993 Induction Ceremony on January 12th, 1993, at the Century Plaza Hotel in Los Angeles, California. Cream's first performance together in more than two decades consisted of the songs 'Sunshine of Your Love', 'Born Under a Bad Sign' (dedicated to Albert King, who passed away a few weeks earlier), and 'Crossroads'. Clapton played this black Strat for the entire set.

This guitar's headstock is scarred with cigarette burns that resulted from Clapton using the section of strings between the tuners and nut as a cigarette holder while he played. Clapton quit smoking about the same time that he stopped playing this guitar, so it is one of the last of his guitars with this distinguishing characteristic.

Opposite:
Royal Albert Hall
London, UK
1991

Serial No: 0195
Body: Alder, black finish
Neck: Maple with skunk-stripe truss rod routing, 22 frets, maple fingerboard with dot inlays
Headstock: Two printed transfers on back: serial number and 'CUSTOM-BUILT J.W.Black FENDER U.S.A.'
Bridge: Gold-plated blocked synchronised tremolo
Pickguard: White single-ply
Pickups: Three Gold Fender Lace Sensors
Controls: Master volume, two tone, TBX/MDX active circuitry
Switches: Five-position pickup selector with white switch tip
Case: Tweed rectangular hardshell case with red plush lining and handwritten tie-on label inscribed 'E C Blackie Gold Hdw Slide 0195' and adhesive paper label inscribed 'Black & Gold Custom Fender-Strat. #0195'

With its raised nut set up for slide playing and gold-plated tuners, tremolo bridge and output jack, this black Strat differs from other Blackie-inspired Strats that Clapton has owned and played. Eric played this guitar on tour during the early 1990s.

Gigs:
Used on tour in the 1990s

Opposite:
MGM Grand
Garden Arena
Las Vegas, Nevada, USA
May 30, 1998

MINIMAX MINI STRATOCASTER COPY

EST: $700 - $1,000   PRICE: $9,500

LOT 111 BONHAMS 2011

Body: Alder, sunburst finish
Neck: Short scale maple neck, 22 frets, rosewood fingerboard with white dot inlays
Headstock: Back of headstock signed by Eric Clapton in black felt pen
Bridge: Synchronised tremolo
Pickguard: White single-ply
Pickups: Three single-coil
Controls: One volume, two tone
Switches: Five-position pickup selector
Case: Black vinyl softshell case with handwritten label

Production of miniature solidbody electric guitars proliferated during the 1980s. From mass-produced models like the Chiquita travel guitar and Guild Ashbory bass to custom-built instruments made by Phil Kubicki and Dave Petschulat, mini guitars suddenly became widely available. The origins of this MiniMax guitar are unknown, although it seems likely that it was manufactured in Asia in the 1980s. In addition to this miniature Stratocaster-style model, MiniMax also made mini Les Paul-style guitars. Clapton recalls receiving this MiniMax Strat as a gift from Barry Gibb of the Bee Gees during the late 1980s or early 1990s.

1982 PHIL KUBICKI EXPRESS

EST: $450 - $650   PRICE: $9,000

LOT 110 BONHAMS 2011

Body: Maple neck-through-body construction with mahogany wings, natural finish, signed by Eric Clapton in black felt pen
Neck: Maple, 22 frets plus zero fret at nut, rosewood fingerboard with dot inlays
Headstock: Headstock signed and inscribed in black ink 'Best Wishes Eric – Phil Kubicki'
Bridge: Strings-though-body nickel-plated bridge plate with six adjustable brass saddles
Pickups: Seymour Duncan Quarter Pound Strat single-coil
Controls: One volume, one tone
Switches: One coil tap
Case: Green padded softshell case with handwritten label

Philip Kubicki worked for Fender from 1964 until 1973 as an assistant to Roger Rossmeisl, who was the head of Fender's research and development department. Some of the guitars that Kubicki personally helped design include the Telecaster Thinline, the Rosewood Telecaster (Kubicki gave the first one to George Harrison in 1969, which Harrison can be seen playing in 'Let It Be') and the Rosewood Stratocaster – a one-of-a-kind guitar completed for Jimi Hendrix in April 1970 but never delivered to him.

After Kubicki left Fender he built guitars as an independent luthier, focusing mainly on acoustic instruments although he also made custom instruments and Fender-style necks and bodies sold as aftermarket parts. Since 1985 Kubicki has focused primarily on production of his Factor bass, which he briefly licensed to Fender from 1988 through 1991.

In 1982 Kubicki started producing a pair of ⅞ size electric solidbody model guitars called the Arrow and the Express. Both models were essentially identical with the exception of the Arrow's Flying V-inspired shape and the Express's single-cutaway Les Paul-style shape.

SYNTHS & SIGNATURES

MINIMAX MINI STRATOCASTER COPY

1982 PHIL KUBICKI EXPRESS

198

1986 SCHON NS6

LOT 46 BONHAMS 2011

Serial No: NS60120
Body: Maple
neck-through-body
construction, alder body
wings, white finish
Neck: Maple, 24 frets,
ebony fingerboard with
double parallelogram
inlays at 12th fret
Headstock: Back of
headstock signed by Eric
Clapton in black felt pen
Bridge: Nickel-plated
Tune-o-matic,
string-through-body
nickel-plated 'Ferrari
Tails' tailpiece
Pickguard: White
three-ply (white/
black/white)
Pickups: Two humbucking
Controls: One volume,
one tone
Switches: Five-position
pickup selector
Additional: Ernie Ball
white cloth guitar strap
Case: Black hardshell
contour case, two
handwritten labels with
inscriptions including
'Neal Schon Model'

When Duane Allman turned down Clapton's offer to become a member of Derek and The Dominos, Clapton hired 16-year-old guitarist Neal Schon in early 1971 to fill the role. Later, after playing with Santana for a few years, Schon formed the band Journey.

In 1986, Schon collaborated with luthier Grover Jackson (of Jackson Guitars) on a line of solidbody electric guitars sold under the Schon brand name. Schon conceived most of the various models' designs, including the distinctive 'Ferrari Tails' tailpiece, which was inspired by the body intake vents on the mid 1980s Ferrari Testarossa. The Jackson factory was barely able to keep up with demand for its own products, so made only about 200 Schon guitars before Canada's Larrivée guitar company took over production. Larrivée made a few changes to the basic design, including a longer scale length, 22-fret neck (instead of 24 frets) and different pickups. They built about 500 Schon guitars before production ceased in 1991.

Schon gave this early Jackson-made NS6 guitar to Clapton in 1986.

1986 SCHON NS6

1988 PENSA-SUHR MK

LOT 73 CHRISTIE'S 1999

Body: Mahogany, quilted
maple top, double
cutaways, honey/
amber finish
Neck: Maple with
skunk-stripe truss rod
routing, 21 frets,
rosewood fingerboard
with dot inlays
Tailpiece: Bridge plate
with adjustable saddles
Pickups: Two EMG
single-coil and one EMG
humbucking
Controls: One volume,
one tone
Switches: Five-position
pickup selector with
black switch tip
Case: Black rectangular
hardshell case with red
plush lining and
handwritten tie-on label
'Pensa – Suhr Custom
Strat N.S.N.' and
adhesive paper label
similarly inscribed

In 1980, Dire Straits' guitarist Mark Knopfler had his friends Rudy Pensa (the owner of Rudy's Music Stop in Manhattan) and John Suhr (who was the shop's repairman) build a custom solidbody guitar for him, which later became known as the MK model. Knopfler was so pleased with the instrument that he encouraged Pensa and Suhr to go into business building electric guitars. The first Pensa-Suhr guitars were introduced in 1984. Suhr left the company in 1990 to work as a Senior Master Builder at the Fender Custom Shop. When Mark Knopfler was a member of Clapton's band in the late 1980s, he gave him this Pensa-Suhr MK as a gift.

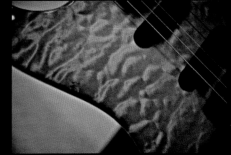

1988 PENSA-SUHR MK

Serial Nos: LO-80632 and LO-80610
Covering: Black Tolex, silver front panel cloth
Switches: Hi/med/lo damping, hi/lo output, standby, power on/off, loop level lo/mid/hi (rear panel), 4/8/16 ohms (rear panel)
Controls: Volume, treble/pull boost, mid/pull cut, bass (channel 1); gain, treble/pull boost, mid/pull boost, bass/pull boost, presence/pull notch, volume/pull channel select
Inputs: Two (channel 1), two (channel 2)
Outputs: XLR line, external speaker series, main speaker, external speaker parallel
Footswitch input: One
Other: Fender logo, effects loop (preamp out, power amp in, power amp thru), two rear panel bias/balance adjustment controls
Case: Grey Packhorse flight case designed to transport the two amplifiers together, various stickers

1987 Fender 4x12 'The Wedge' speaker cabinets
Serial Nos: LO79423 and LO79264
Housing: Straight closed-back cabinets
Covering: Black Tolex, silver speaker cloth
Speakers: Four 12-inch
Details: Fender logo
Case: Grey Packhorse flight case

Gigs:
Used on stage between 1987 and 1988
Highlight:
Nelson Mandela 70th Birthday Tribute Concert Wembley Stadium London, UK June 11, 1988

Clapton spent most of the period between his 1986 *August* album and his 1989 *Journeyman* album on tour. Sometime in mid-1987 he replaced the Dean Markley and Marshall amps in his Bob Bradshaw-designed stage rig (page 175) with a pair of new Fender Dual Showman amps. The post-CBS Dual Showman featured an entirely new 100-watt circuit driven by four 6L6GC power amp tubes, four 12AX7 preamp tubes, and a 12AT7 for the effects loop section.

Clapton's Dual Showman amps were used at the Nelson Mandela 70th Birthday Tribute at Wembley Stadium on June 11th, 1988, where Clapton shared the stage with Dire Straits for a seven-song set. That concert (or perhaps Clapton's July 2nd, 1988 performance with Band Du Lac) may have been the last time that the Dual Showmans appeared on stage with Clapton, as Eric became quite enamoured with the tone that Dire Straits guitarist Mark Knopfler was getting from his Soldano amps during rehearsals for the Mandela tribute. Clapton brought these Dual Showman amps back into the studio while he was recording *Journeyman*.

ERIC **With Delaney and Bonnie, I used a Dual Showman – a big Fender amp.**

But I hardly ever jacked it right up. I wasn't getting the sustain or hold-over sound I used to get. It was still there a bit, but that's the Stratocaster. When I used the Stratocaster and the Dual Showman, I had the pickup switch set between the first and middle pickups – which is a very bright sound, but not completely trebly. I took a little of the treble off, and I put on all the bass and the middle. And I set the volume at about half.

I'LL PLAY FOR YOU

Wembley Stadium
London, UK
June 11, 1988

Mark Knopfler and Eric
Clapton performing on
stage at the Nelson
Mandela 70th Birthday
Tribute Concert. These
amps can be seen stage
left of Clapton.

1989 FENDER PRINCETON CHORUS

EST: $450 - $650   PRICE: $1,000

LOT 38 BONHAMS 2011

Serial No: LO-71545
Covering: Black Tolex, grey speaker cloth
Plate: Princeton Chorus
Speakers: Two 10-inch
Switches: Mid boost, overdrive select, chorus select, power on/off
Controls: Volume, treble, mid, bass, reverb, gain, limiter, presence, overdrive volume, rate, depth
Inputs: Two
Outputs: Headphone
Footswitch input: One
Other: Stereo/mono effects loop (two sends, two returns)

The Princeton Chorus model amplifier that Fender introduced in 1989 was a radical departure from the beloved Princeton and Princeton Reverb models that Fender previously produced. Unlike the earlier Princetons, all of which (including the early 1980s Paul Rivera-designed Princeton Reverb II) featured tube circuits, the Princeton Chorus was solid-state, offered a built-in chorus effect, and came with a pair of 10-inch speakers (instead of one 10-inch like earlier Princeton and Princeton Reverb models or one 12-inch like the Princeton Reverb II). Despite these rather dramatic departures from prior Princeton models, the Princeton was one of Fender's most successful amps during the 1990s, and it remained in Fender's amp line until 1999 when the Princeton Chorus DSP model replaced it.

1989 FENDER PRINCETON CHORUS

EST: $450 - $650   PRICE: $1,000

LOT 37 BONHAMS 2011

Serial No: LO-023467
Covering: Black Tolex, grey speaker cloth
Plate: Princeton Chorus
Speakers: Two 10-inch
Switches: Mid boost, overdrive select, chorus select, power on/off
Controls: Volume, treble, mid, bass, reverb, gain, limiter, presence, overdrive volume, rate, depth
Inputs: Two
Outputs: Headphone
Footswitch input: One
Other: Mono/stereo effects loops (two sends, two returns)

I'LL PLAY FOR YOU

Serial No: LO-55091
Covering: Black Tolex, grey speaker cloth
Plate: The Twin
Speakers: Two 12-inch Electro-Voice EVM12L
Switches: Reverb select (ch. 1/both/ch. 2), output hi/lo, standby, power on/off, loop level (rear panel), 4/8/16 ohms (rear panel)
Controls: Volume, treble/pull boost, mid/pull cut, bass (channel 1); gain, treble/pull boost, mid/pull boost, bass/pull boost, presence/pull notch, volume/pull channel select (channel 2); reverb
Inputs: Two (channel 1), two (channel 2)
Outputs: XLR line, external speaker series, main speaker, external speaker parallel
Footswitch input: One
Other: Effects loop (in, out, thru jacks), two rear panel bias/balance adjustment controls

Fender's Twin and Twin Reverb models remained mainstays for professional guitarists ever since 1952 when Fender introduced the first Twin model. However, between 1985 and 1987 Fender offered no Twin model at all, as Fender's new ownership discontinued the Twin Reverb II in 1985 in favour of designing an entirely new model. Simply called 'The Twin', this model was the first product offered by Fender's new amp design division, and it continued the power reduction trend started by the Twin Reverb II, going from the 135-watt 1981 Twin Reverb to the 105-watt Twin Reverb II to the 100-watt The Twin.

1987 FENDER THE TWIN

Serial No: L070580
Covering: Black Tolex, grey speaker cloth
Plate: The Twin
Speakers: Two 12-inch CTS ceramic
Switches: Reverb select (ch. 1/both/ch. 2), output hi/lo, standby, power on/off, loop level (rear panel), 4/8/16 ohms (rear panel)
Controls: Volume, treble/pull boost, mid/pull cut, bass (channel 1); gain, treble/pull boost, mid/pull boost, bass/pull boost, presence/pull notch, volume/pull channel select (channel 2); reverb
Inputs: Two (channel 1), two (channel 2)
Outputs: XLR line, external speaker series, main speaker, external speaker parallel
Footswitch input: One
Other: Effects loop (in, out, thru jacks), two rear panel bias/balance adjustment controls

Whereas the Twin Reverb II mainly added channel switching and an effects loop to the classic Twin design, The Twin was a radical redesign characterised by its numerous tone-shaping and gain boost pull-out control knobs. Fender hoped to make a bold statement with its amp's new red knobs, but traditionalists spurned the new cosmetics as much as they disliked the aggressive overdrive textures and dramatic changes to the beloved Twin's clean character. Fender toned down the cosmetics a few years later, but by then the damage had already been done, and The Twin was discontinued in 1994 after a moderately successful seven-year run.

1987 FENDER THE TWIN

1982 GIBSON CHET ATKINS STANDARD

PRE-SALE EST: $5,000 - $7,000 PRICE: $35,000

LOT 61 CHRISTIE'S 1999

Serial No: A064
Body: Chambered mahogany, spruce top, single round cutaway, round soundhole, natural finish
Neck: Mahogany, 19 frets, rosewood fingerboard
Headstock: Slotted
Bridge: Rosewood tie-block bridge
Pickups: Gibson hex piezo bridge transducer
Controls: Volume and tone roller controls on upper bout
Case: Rectangular brown hardshell case with green plush lining and handwritten tie-on label 'E.C. Chet Atkins Gutstring # A064' and adhesive paper label similarly inscribed

During the early 1980s, Chet Atkins showed Gibson a prototype for a solidbody nylon-string guitar he developed that featured hollowed-out body chambers and a bridge-mounted piezo pickup that produced an amplified sound similar to an acoustic classical guitar. Gibson introduced a model based on this prototype – the Chet Atkins Standard – in 1982, and later changed the model's name to the Chet Atkins CE. This guitar was very popular with performing guitarists who wanted the warm, rich sounds of an acoustic classical guitar without the feedback hassles of amplifying those instruments. This guitar appears in a photo amongst wardrobe cases and other guitars in Clapton's 1989 Journeyman Tour programme.

Gigs:
1990 Journeyman Tour
Jan. 14-Dec. 13, 1990
Highlight:
'Can't Find My Way Home'

1990 GIBSON CHET ATKINS CE

EST: $5,000 - $7,000 PRICE: $35,000

LOT 79 CHRISTIE'S 1999

Serial No: 90810523
Body: Chambered mahogany, spruce top, single round cutaway, round soundhole, black finish
Neck: Mahogany, 19 frets, rosewood fingerboard
Headstock: Slotted
Bridge: Rosewood tie-block bridge
Pickups: Gibson hex piezo bridge transducer
Controls: Volume and tone roller controls on upper bout
Case: Brown hardshell contour case with pink plush lining and handwritten tie-on label 'Gibson Chet Atkins Black Elec. Gutstring Ser.#90810523' and adhesive paper label similarly inscribed

During the early 1990s Clapton played these two Chet Atkins guitars frequently on stage, usually to perform Blind Faith's 'Can't Find My Way Home', which was sung by his bassist Nathan East.

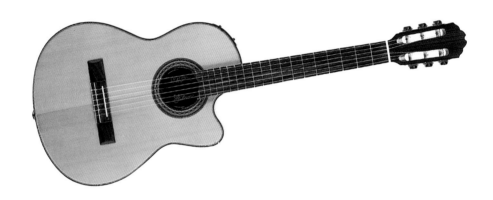

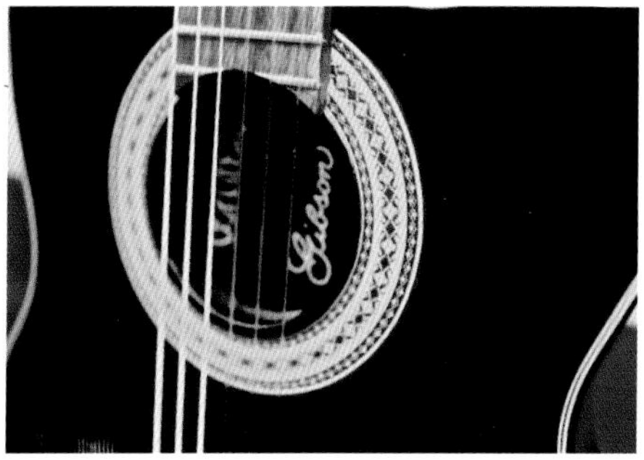

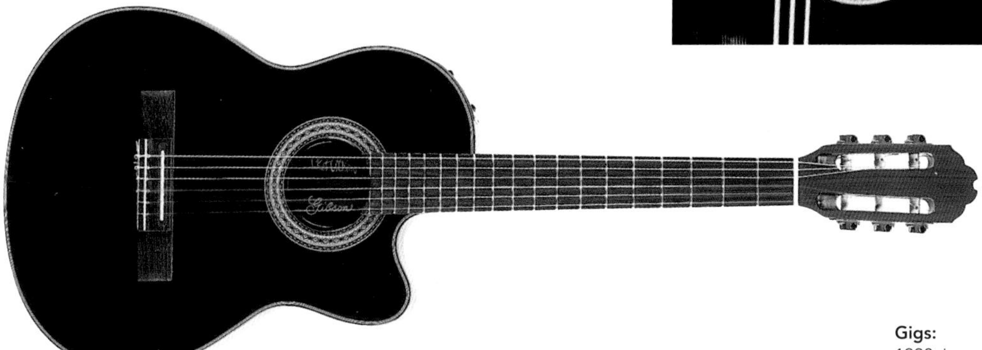

Gigs:
1990 Journeyman Tour
Jan. 14-Dec. 13, 1990
Highlight:
'Can't Find My Way Home'

Left:
Miami Arena
Florida, USA
July 1990

Below:
Royal Albert Hall
London, UK
1991

ERIC The Chet Atkins is the only guitar you can use on stage that will sound like it's truly acoustic and we've tried lots of others.

With normal acoustic guitars – Martins for instance – we still end up using part of a DI direct signal and part microphone, but the problem with microphones is that they pick up so much ambient stuff. If you've got drums, or other instruments, they leak in. This guitar has got a direct signal but it sounds absolutely perfectly acoustic, so I love them. They also have a classical acoustic neck – a Spanish neck, quite wide – and so you're really playing a gutstring guitar. They're absolutely perfect; they're still unbeatable for playing onstage.

LOT 49 CHRISTIE'S 2004

Serial No: 93348472
Body: Chambered
mahogany, spruce top,
single round cutaway,
round soundhole,
natural finish
Neck: Mahogany, 19 frets,
rosewood fingerboard
Headstock: Slotted
Bridge: Rosewood
tie-block bridge
Pickups: Gibson hex piezo
bridge transducer
Controls: Volume and
tone roller controls on
upper bout
Case: Original hardshell
case with adhesive label
inscribed 'Gibson Chet
Atkins/Solid Gut
#93348472'

After selling his black 1990 Gibson Chet Atkins CE (page 204) in the
1999 Crossroads auction, Clapton acquired this 1998 Chet Atkins CE
as a replacement. He used it in November and December 2003
while on tour in Japan to perform 'Can't Find My Way Home'.

Gigs:
2003 'Just For You'
Japan Tour
Nov. 15-Dec. 13, 2003

I'LL PLAY FOR YOU

ERIC Fabulous guitars... this is
an incredible guitar. I used this
one on the 2003 Japanese Tour.

Serial No: R5 280 89D
Body: Mahogany,
chrome-plated cover plate
with nine diamond-shaped
cutouts and handrest, two
upper bout f-holes, brown
finish with stencilled
Hawaiian motif
Neck: Mahogany, round,
19 frets, rosewood
fingerboard with dot inlays
Headstock: Slotted
Bridge: Maple 'biscuit'
bridge, chrome-plated
trapeze tailpiece
Case: Hardshell case with
adhesive tape inscribed
'Duolian Dobro/'Hawaiian'
Style #R.528089D'

In 1970, Semie Moseley transferred the rights to the Dobro name
back to Emil Dopyera after producing Dobro instruments for only
a few years. Dopyera's Original Musical Instrument Company, Inc.,
better known as OMI, which he established in 1967 after selling
Dobro to Moseley, manufactured resonator guitars under the Dobro
name until 1993 when Gibson purchased the company.

Clapton purchased this Dobro while on tour during the early 1990s.
Allegedly he and guitarist Phil Palmer both bought similar Dobros
with Hawaiian motifs at the same shop together. Although Clapton
has brought the guitar into the recording studio for several sessions,
he generally prefers the tone of his vintage Dobro and National
resonator guitars.

I'LL PLAY FOR YOU

Serial No: 380538
Body: Semi-hollow mahogany with single 'cat's eye' soundhole, bound figured maple top, sunburst 'Transparent Star Glo' finish
Neck: Maple, 24 frets, bound rosewood fingerboard with 'shark tooth' inlays
Headstock: Figured maple veneer with sunburst finish, back of headstock signed by Eric Clapton in black felt pen
Bridge: Strings-through-body nickel-plated bridge baseplate with six adjustable saddles
Pickguard: Pearloid
Pickups: Two 'lipstick tube' cylindrical-shaped single-coil
Controls. One volume, one tone/pull phase
Switches: Three-position pickup selector
Case: Gray hardshell contour case with black plush lining, two handwritten labels inscribed with various details including 'E.C. S.burst, Charvel Custom non-Trem Surfcaster'

Charvel/Jackson made a variety of hot rodded superstrat-style guitars, popular with heavy metal guitarists during the 1980s, but when alternative rock and grunge began to surpass the popularity of heavy metal in the early 1990s sales of Charvel's superstrats declined as well. However, Charvel noticed guitarists' increased interest in vintage instruments, particularly Rickenbackers and inexpensive 'oddball' guitars made by Danelectro, and the company had already begun developing the Surfcaster model in 1989. Although Charvel originally conceived the Surfcaster as an instrument for country and blues guitarists, the model's debut in 1991 was perfectly timed to coincide with the shift in popular music tastes.

The Surfcaster's design was inspired by several different vintage guitars, with 'shark fin' fingerboard inlays and a 'cat's eye' soundhole reminiscent of Rickenbacker guitars, an offset body shape similar to a Fender Jazzmaster, and a pair of 'lipstick tube' pickups similar to those used on Danelectro guitars. The Surfcaster pictured here is an unusual anomaly, featuring a Strat-style strings-through-body hardtail design. Most hardtail Surfcasters have a Tune-o-matic-style bridge and Gretsch-style cutout 'C' trapeze tailpiece that anchors the strings above the body.

Clapton purchased this guitar while on tour in the 1990s.

I'LL PLAY FOR YOU

Serial No: 156
Body: Mahogany, bound, upper bout f-holes, sunburst finish, single resonator cone, nickel-plated cover plate with nine diamond-shaped cutouts, handrest
Neck: Mahogany, 19 frets, bound ebony fingerboard with dot inlays
Headstock: Imitation mother-of-pearl overlay
Bridge: Maple 'biscuit' bridge, nickel-plated trapeze tailpiece
Case: Black hardshell contour case with burgundy plush lining and handwritten tie-on label 'National Resophonic Sunburst #156' and adhesive paper label similarly inscribed

In 1989 Don Young and McGregor Gaines revived the National name by forming the National Reso-Phonic Guitar company and producing reproductions of original National resonator instruments in their garage. The following year, National moved into a factory in San Luis Obispo, California, and started offering a variety of models, including the M-1, which was based on the wood body single-resonator instruments National made during the 1920s and 1930s.

Clapton purchased this National M-1 from Westwood Music in Westwood, California, while he was working on the score to the film *Rush*. He used this guitar to record the film's soundtrack and to play Robert Johnson's 'Terraplane Blues' and 'Come On In My Kitchen' during his performances at London's Royal Albert Hall between February 20th and March 6th, 1994.

Playlist:
Rush, 1991
Gigs:
1994 Royal Albert Hall
Feb. 20-Mar. 6, 1994

Opposite:
Royal Albert Hall
London, UK
1994

Eric Clapton playing one of the two opening Robert Johnson numbers, 'Terraplane Blues' or 'Come On In My Kitchen', on this guitar.

I'LL PLAY FOR YOU

Serial No: 12580
Body: Rosewood back and sides, spruce top with abalone purfling, single sharp cutaway, natural finish
Neck: Mahogany, 20 frets, ebony fingerboard with 900 Series inlays and the initials E.C. inlaid at 17th fret
Headstock: 900 Series inlay, oval brass plate fixed to back of headstock engraved 'To E.C. From Richie'
Tuners: Gold-plated, ebony buttons
Bridge: Ebony 'belly' pin bridge
Rosette: Single-ring, abalone
Label: Internal white paper label printed 'Specially Made For Winter NAMM January 1991, Taylor Guitars, Made in U.S.A.' and signed 'Robert D. Taylor'
Case: Brown hardshell contour case with wine-coloured plush lining and handwritten adhesive paper label 'Taylor 12 String #12580 955C-Custom-S/C.A.- Sambora'

In 1991 Clapton made a guest appearance on Bon Jovi guitarist Richie Sambora's first solo album, *Stranger In This Town*, playing a solo on 'Mr. Bluesman'. In appreciation of Clapton's participation, Sambora gave Eric this custom-made 1991 Taylor 955-C 12-string acoustic during the session.

Playlist:
Richie Sambora:
Stranger In This Town 1991

ERIC I got a very sweet, dedicated letter from Richie Sambora and I was deeply touched; my ego was pumped up. I thought, of course I have to do this.

I never really listened to the song. Then Richie came to London with the tape, and I showed up at the studio, and he gave me a gift, this massive 12-string Taylor guitar with my name on it – it was magnificent. Then he put the tape on, and I realised instantly that I was completely out of my depth. The song wasn't what I expected it to be, and I had to sit down and go to the bottom of my socks and pull up whatever I had to make it work. It took hours; it was the kind of thing you would like to go and do in private.

I'LL PLAY FOR YOU

LOT 45 CHRISTIE'S 1999

Serial No: 5263
Body: Mahogany back and sides, spruce top, f-holes, sunburst finish
Neck: Mahogany, 19 frets, rosewood fingerboard with dot inlays
Bridge: Rosewood, nickel-plated trapeze tailpiece
Case: Black softshell contour case with handwritten adhesive paper label 'Gibson Kalamazoo F. Hole Ac.' and another additionally inscribed '... Low 'F's...# None'

Introduced in 1938, the Kalamazoo KG-21 was the 'entry level' archtop model of Gibson's Kalamazoo budget brand. The only difference between the KG-21 and KG-16 model, introduced a year later, was that the KG-21's had a bound back while the KG-16 had no back binding. The pickguard on this KG-21 was removed long ago, which is a common occurrence.

Clapton purchased this guitar in Memphis along with the fancier Kalamazoo KG-32 that he used on the *Pilgrim* album (page 276).

ERIC This is a hotel room guitar.

1990s VICENTE SANCHIS FLAMENCO MODEL 41

EST: $3,000 - $5,000   PRICE:$26,000

LOT 22 CHRISTIE'S 1999

Body: Cypress back and sides with rosewood backstripe, spruce top
Neck: Cedar, 19 frets, ebony fingerboard
Headstock: Slotted
Bridge: Rosewood tie bridge
Pickguard: Transparent protective golpeador plate
Rosette: Multi-coloured floral marquetry
Label: Signed 'V. Sanchis'
Case: Black hardshell contour case with red plush lining and tie-on label 'Sanchis – Flamenco (Model 41) #19' and adhesive paper label similarly inscribed

Vicente Sanchis made flamenco and classical guitars in a small artisan workshop in the Spanish town of Masanasa, south of Valencia, until 2000, when he retired and his son and business partner took over the shop. The Model 41 is one of his higher-quality flamenco guitars, noted for its crisp, loud tone and authentic 'gypsy' character.

This Vicente Sanchis guitar is one of several nylon-string flamenco/classical guitars that Clapton used in the recording studio during the 1990s.

Playlist:
Used for recording in the 1990s

Body: Rosewood back and sides, cedar top, natural finish
Neck: Mahogany, 19 frets, ebony fingerboard
Headstock: Slotted
Bridge: Rosewood tie bridge
Rosette: Multi-coloured marquetry
Label: 'Constructor/Juan Alvarez/año 1977/Calle San Pedro, 7/Madrid-14 España,' signed 'J Alvarez'
Additional: Top signed and inscribed in black felt pen, 'For Giorgio and everyone at 'El Gadir' – my love Eric C. 96', additionally annotated with a heart motif, additionally inscribed by Clapton adjacent to the fingerboard 'no more tears in heaven' and inscribed by Giorgio Armani in black felt pen 'Giorgio 2.3.01'
Case: Hardshell case

Juan Álvarez Gil (1935-2001) established a guitar workshop in Madrid in 1952, where he built classical and flamenco instruments entirely by hand using traditional methods taught to him by his mentor, Marcelo Barbero, who also trained José Ramírez III. Juan Miguel Álvarez continued to make Juan Álvarez guitars in the traditional 'Madrid School' style after his father's death in 2001.

Clapton first used this guitar in the studio to record several songs for the *Rush* soundtrack, including 'Tears In Heaven' and he played it in the promotional video for that song. Clapton also played the guitar during his 1992 MTV *Unplugged* performance of the songs 'Signe', 'Tears In Heaven', and 'Lonely Stranger'. During his 1992 UK Tour, he used the Álvarez to perform those same three songs. In 1996, Clapton gave the guitar as a gift to his good friend, fashion designer Giorgio Armani, who in turn donated it to the 2004 Crossroads auction where it set a record price for a classical guitar.

Playlist:
Rush, 1991
Gigs:
MTV *Unplugged* (TV)
Bray Film Studios
Windsor, Berkshire, UK
Jan. 16, 1992
1992 UK Tour
Feb. 1-Mar. 3, 1992
Highlight:
'Tears In Heaven'

Bray Film Studios
Windsor, Berkshire, UK
Jan. 16, 1992

Eric Clapton playing 'Tears In Heaven' on this guitar.

I'LL PLAY FOR YOU

ERIC I used this guitar on the *Rush* soundtrack and *Unplugged*. I wrote most of those songs on this guitar. I had it in my hands all day until I went to sleep. And I composed. 'My Father's Eyes' and 'Tears In Heaven' came out of that; the songs just grew out of me. I played them over and over again. It healed me.

This guitar has got a full-length story. There was a tour with me and Ronnie Lane in 1977, which was fairly bizarre: it was a tour of Europe on boats. We sailed around the Mediterranean, and we'd pull into different ports like Ibiza and St. Tropez. Most of the playing was done on the quayside for tourists, although we had official venues to play as well. We had one boat for the road managers and one boat for the acts, and we'd play cards and have fun. When we got to Barcelona, John Porter (who was in Ronnie's band), Ronnie and I were walking through the Ramblas, and we found this guitar stall and we bought three of these guitars. They were identical, all made by the same man, Álvarez. They were beautiful, all made of this beautiful dark wood.

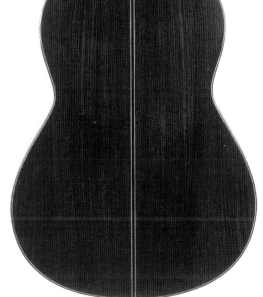

Body: Rosewood back and sides, cedar top, natural finish
Neck: Mahogany, 19 frets, ebony fingerboard
Headstock: Slotted
Bridge: Rosewood tie bridge
Rosette: Multi-coloured marquetry
Label: 'Robert S. Ruck/Middleton, Wisconsin 53562/1975', signed by maker 'R.S. Ruck'
Case: Hardshell case with adhesive tape inscribed 'Ruck Gut String/Robert Ruck/Auction #48/ Ruck Guitar'

Robert Ruck started building classical guitars in the United States during the 1960s. He quickly achieved a reputation as a builder of fine classical instruments, eventually attracting the attention of classical virtuoso Manuel Barrueco, who has played Ruck guitars on most of his recordings. Ruck built more than 800 guitars over the course of his career.

Serial No: 000-255
Body: Sycamore back and sides, spruce top, rosewood binding, natural finish
Neck: Cedar, 19 frets, ebony fingerboard
Headstock: Slotted
Bridge: Rosewood tie bridge
Rosette: Multi-coloured marquetry
Label: 'Alhambra/Muro del Alcoy-Spain/Mod.7 Fs No.000255', stamped 'Guitarras Alhambra/Muro del Alcoy'
Case: Case with adhesive tape inscribed 'Alhambra Gut String/Flamenco #000-255'

In 1965, José Botella drove a friend who wanted to buy a Spanish guitar to a workshop in Muro del Alcoy. When Botella arrived, he was told that he arrived just in time as the company was closing in a week. Botella went home, organised a group of investors, and purchased the company, which he renamed Manufacturas Alhambra, S.A. Today Guitarras Alhambra offers a wide variety of high-quality classical and flamenco guitars, from student models to professional instruments played by guitarists like Cesar Rosas (of Los Lobos), Fareed Haque and Flavio Rodrigues.

Clapton installed a microphone in this guitar in an early attempt to perform with an acoustic nylon-string guitar on stage. He used it occasionally during rehearsals in the 1990s.

ERIC This was probably the first proper flamenco guitar that I ever bought. Love of music and love of flamenco led me to start using this guitar. Also the way that gut string guitars had sounded in jazz with Charlie Byrd and people like that. The idea of bringing that sound or playing blues on a gut string guitar is quite an interesting experiment.

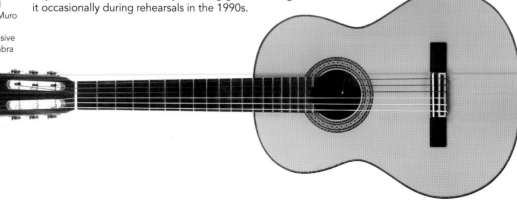

I'LL PLAY FOR YOU

Body: Rosewood back and sides, spruce top, natural finish
Neck: Mahogany, 18 frets, ebony fingerboard
Headstock: Slotted, centre-stripe inlay
Bridge: Rosewood tie-block bridge with inlays
Rosette/purfling: Ornate chevron-pattern mother-of-pearl inlays
Label: 'Fabrica de Guitarras de Salvador Ibáñez, Bajada Sn. Francisco 23, Valencia'
Case: Black hardshell contour case with green plush lining and handwritten tie-on label 'Salvadore Ibanez [sic] Gutstring (Pearl Inlays) #23' and adhesive paper label similarly inscribed

In 1870 Salvador Ibáñez established his own guitar workshop in Valencia, Spain, where he built classical guitars until his death in 1920. His sons resumed making guitars in his name, but sadly the workshop was destroyed during the Spanish Civil War in the late 1930s. Hoshino Gakki, which was Japan's importer of Ibáñez guitars, purchased the Ibáñez trademark after the workshop closed and started producing their own Ibáñez brand guitars. Today Ibáñez is one of the world's most successful guitar brands.

Although this 19th-century classical guitar is about as far removed from the blues as a guitar could be, it was one of Clapton's favourite instruments for warming up before shows. It was often seen backstage with him before his concerts at the Royal Albert Hall in the 1990s.

ERIC This guitar had a great sound. I kept it as a dressing room guitar. Normally, my guitar technician will leave me an acoustic and an electric in the dressing room in case I want to warm up.

Strap (#38): Black webbing and leather strap decorated with rhinestones, red, yellow, green, lilac and blue sequins and imitation jewels in a pattern of flower heads and stylised musical notes

Strap (#43): Black webbing and leather strap decorated with a pattern of red, blue, fuchsia, green, white and gold sequins and bugle beads

Strap (#80): Black webbing and leather strap lavishly decorated with a pattern of pink, yellow, blue, fuchsia, lilac, yellow and black sequins, bugle beads and imitation jewels

Versace made these one-of-a-kind guitar straps for Eric, which feature intricately woven patterns of colourful sequins, beads and imitation jewels. Although Eric wore Versace guitar straps during his 1990 Journeyman Tour and at the series of 1991 shows at the Royal Albert Hall that were recorded for the *24 Nights* live album, he never wore these particular straps on stage.

ERIC I am a Gianni Versace fanatic. His approach to design and his sensitivity to colour appeal to the dormant artist in me and somehow I feel that his clothes bridge the gap between the fire of rock and roll and the purity of classical tailoring.

Royal Albert Hall
London, UK
1991

Versace guitar straps photographed backstage at the Royal Albert Hall and drawn by Sir Peter Blake in his limited edition book, *24 Nights* (Genesis Publications, 1991).

FENDER/VERSACE GUITAR STRAPS

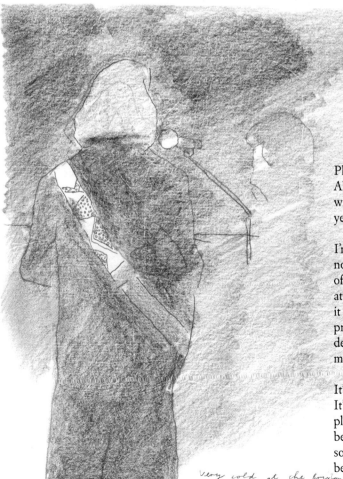

Playing successive nights at the Royal Albert Hall in London became a tradition, with the number of gigs increasing each year until they would peak in 1991 with 24.

I'm a very habitual person, and I like nothing more in my life than to have a kind of routine, even if it's only a yearly project at the Albert Hall. I don't see any reason for it to end. To me it's like setting up a new proms. Because, yes, I do tend towards delusions of grandeur. It's a failing of most musicians I find.

It's a selfish thrill to play with an orchestra. It's a very hit-or-miss process, because they play in a different time scale: they play behind the beat. I play right on the beat or sometimes in front of it: I like pushing the beat. It was a challenge to get it right.

Very cold at the Brixton Academy. Eric wearing a long black coat

Brixton Academy. Eric & Jerry Portnoy. Feb 21st   *Peter Blake*

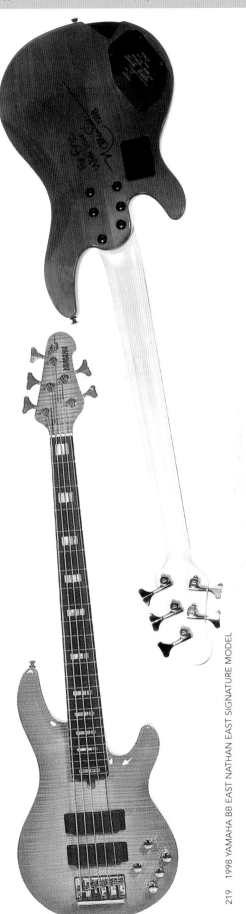

Body: Alder, figured maple cap, Amber Burst finish, back of body signed and inscribed in black felt pen 'For Eric With Love Nathan East 1998'
Neck: Maple, 24 frets, ebony fingerboard with segmented block inlays, low block at 24th fret engraved 'ERIC CLAPTON'
Headstock: Figured maple veneer, black painted Yamaha logo and Nathan East signature
Bridge: Gold-plated brass with five adjustable saddles
Pickups: Two single-coil with dummy coil
Controls: Volume, pickup pan, treble boost/cut, user definable midrange, bass boost/cut
Additional: Various accessories including owner's manual and cable
Case: Black Yamaha rectangular hardshell case with black plush lining, handwritten label with various inscriptions including 'Honeyburst 5 string from Nate'

Clapton first hired Los Angeles session ace Nathan East in 1984 to play bass on his *Behind the Sun* album. East later went on tour as Clapton's bassist during Clapton's 1986 European Jazz Festival Tour and performed at his July 15th, 1986, concert at Birmingham's National Exhibition Centre that was filmed for the *Eric Clapton and Friends* video. East remained a fixture of Clapton's studio and touring bands through 2004, playing bass on *August, Journeyman, 24 Nights, Unplugged, Pilgrim, Riding With The King, Reptile, One More Car, One More Rider, Me and Mr. Johnson* and *Back Home* as well as the *Homeboy* and *Rush* soundtracks.

East collaborated with Yamaha on the design of his first signature model bass, the Yamaha BB East Nathan East Signature Model, which was introduced in 1994 and produced until 2002 when Yamaha replaced this model with several new Nathan East signature basses. East had Yamaha build this custom five-string BB East bass, which features Eric's name engraved in the 24th fret inlay, as a gift that he gave to Eric in 1998.

ERIC I met Nathan East and Greg Phillinganes in the studio when we were recording *Behind the Sun*. They'd been hired to play on the songs by the president of Warner Brothers, Lenny Waronker. I thought they were great.

Clapton with one of Nathan East's basses during the 1991 Legends Tour of Japan.

I'LL PLAY FOR YOU

Serial No: 0091
Body: Alder, black finish
Neck: Maple with skunk-stripe truss rod routing, 22 frets, maple fingerboard with dot inlays
Headstock: Customised cigarette holder, printed transfer 'CUSTOM-BUILT J.W. Black FENDER U.S.A.' on reverse
Bridge: Blocked synchronised tremolo
Pickguard: White single-ply
Pickups: Three Gold Fender Lace Sensors
Controls: Master volume, two tone, TBX active circuitry
Switches: Five-position pickup selector with white switch tip
Case: White hardshell rectangular case with black plush lining and two handwritten swing labels 'E.C. # 'Smoker's Neck' E.C. Black Strat. #0091'

Fender supplied this guitar to Eric Clapton in 1991.

During rehearsals for the Eric Clapton/George Harrison Japan Tour at Bray Studios in October 1991, Clapton and Harrison discussed this guitar while being interviewed by Subarashiki Nakama-tachi for Japan's TBS television network. Harrison asked Clapton to 'get the one with the ashtray on it', and picked up one of Clapton's black signature model Strats. Showing the headstock to the camera, Harrison said, 'This bit here is burned because this naughty boy smokes cigarettes. Fender have made him one with a little hole here [showing a hole on the Strat's headstock near the nut] so he can put his cigarette in there. I have one that has a cupboard in the back with my sandwiches and tea.'

Clapton then explained his 'smoker's model' and placed a burning cigarette in the cigarette-holder hole. Although he joked that these guitars were available in shops in Japan and told viewers to ask for the smoking or non-smoking version, the 'smoker's model' never actually went into production.

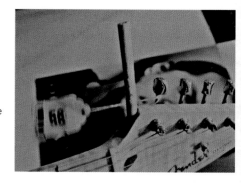

ERIC The guitar that made me give up smoking!

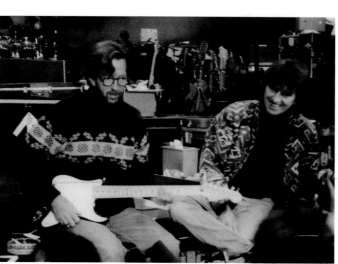

Playlist:
Live in Japan, 1992
Gigs:
Rock Legends: George Harrison with Eric Clapton 1991 Japan Tour Dec. 1-17, 1991

Far left:
This photograph shows where the cigarette could be placed in the headstock.

Left:
Bray Film Studios Windsor, Berkshire, UK Oct. 1991

Eric Clapton and George Harrison demonstrating the 'smoker's model' during their TV interview.

Opposite:
Clapton pictured putting this model to good use during his 1991 Legends Tour of Japan.

I'LL PLAY FOR YOU

ERIC I put it to George that he come out to Japan with us. All he had to do essentially was walk out on the stage and strum an acoustic guitar. He was delighted and scared at the same time because it had been a long time, 15 years or so, since his last American tour.

1988 Soldano SLO-100 Super Lead Overdrive amp heads
Serial Nos: 88043EC and 88044EC (with stickers Nos. 1 and 2 respectively)
Covering: Grey Tolex, black metal grille with Soldano logo
Switches: Crunch/clean, bright/normal, standby, power on/off, 4-/8-/16-ohm speaker impedance
Controls: Preamp normal, preamp overdrive, bass, middle, treble, master normal, master overdrive, presence, slave level
Inputs: One
Outputs: Speaker (two), slave
Footswitch input: One
Other: Effects loop (send and return)
Label: No.1 signed 'Michael Soldano', no. 2 inscribed on the top with black marker pen 'Eric Thank you very much. Keep playing those same old blues. Michael Soldano'

Pete Cornish rack system
Housing: 25U Packhorse steel frame, shock mount rack flight case
Rack units (top to bottom):
-Furman PL-8 power conditioner
-Samson UR-5D UHF wireless receiver
-Samson BR-3 VHF wireless receiver
-Cornish custom guitar/effects routing units (38 rotary controls, eight illuminated push switches, 10x10 matrix patch bay, four toggle switches, two level meters, 24 pilot lights, multi-voltage)
-Drawmer 1960 tube compressor
-Yamaha SPX90 multi-effects processor
-Dyno-My-Piano CS-5 Tri-Stereo Chorus
-TC Electronic 2290 Dynamic Digital Delay
-Dynacord CLS 222 Leslie simulator
-Yamaha GEP50 guitar effect processor
-Roland SDE-3000 digital delay
-TC Electronic 1210 Spatial Expander

Pete Cornish Custom Remote Control Footswitch Unit
Switches: Nine footswitches

Pilot lights: Ten, marked A to I
LEDs: 21, marked MT=MUTE AUDIO, LD=LEAD MODE, COMP, PRE1 LD, PRE2 LD, PRE1 MT, PRE2 MT, VOLUME, WAH-WAH, SPARE BR4, SPX-90, TRI-STRO, TC2290, DYNA222, SPARE SR9, DRY L MT, DRY R MT, GEP-50, SDE-3000, STRO EQ, BOOST
Other: Grey metallic remote control unit with pilot light marked J

Pete Cornish Custom Mains Power Distribution Unit
Housing: 20U Packhorse steel frame, shock mount rack flight case
Switches: Six
VU meters: Seven
Indicator lights: Nine
AC plugs: Five
Other: Multi-voltage with a selection of power cables

Marshall JCM 900 1960B speaker cabinets
Serial No: 09283 and 25352 (with yellow stickers Nos. 1 and 2, respectively)
Housing: Straight closed-back cabinet
Covering: Black Tolex, black speaker cloth
Speakers: Four 12-inch Electro Voice EVM12L (each cabinet)
Details: White Marshall script logo (M damaged on No. 1), gold plate with 'JCM 900 Lead-1960'
Handles: Plastic
Other: XLR cannon plug inputs on back
Case: Black flight cases with 'The Duck Bros' logo stencil, one with various stickers and '8' stencilled at one end

Accessory/cable road case
Case: Grey Packhorse flight case covered in various stickers
Accessories/cables: Two Cry Baby wah-wah pedals (No. 4, Serial No: CB487671; No. 5, Serial No: CB206667), two Ernie Ball volume pedals, Tupperware container with spare parts, a quantity of multi-pin cables, guitar cables, stage boxes, and UHF and VHF wireless transmitters in carrying cases, spare UHF receiver in a cardboard box

It's hard to believe that over the short span of five years Clapton went from a relatively simple stage rig consisting of a guitar, a cable and a few Music Man stack amps to this mammoth rack-based system. During the late 1980s guitarists determined that the only way to get the studio sounds that they loved on stage was by bringing virtually the entire studio with them (sans the tape machine and mixing console). Technicians like Bob Bradshaw and Pete Cornish built ever-expanding systems for guitarists who spared no expense or excess to achieve the most pristine sounds imaginable on the concert stage.

This period was also the beginning of the golden age of the 'boutique' amplifier. During the 1980s many amplifier technicians spent more time modifying existing amplifiers with high-gain circuits, effects loops, line outputs and other improvements than they did repairing or restoring amps. Eventually several of those techs, like Michael Soldano, went into business building new amp models to satisfy the needs of modern guitarists (and stop the destruction of classic amps that fell into the hands of less skilled technicians). Soldano Custom Amplification's SLO-100 100-watt Super Lead Overdrive amp head, introduced in 1986, was an instant hit with guitarists who loved its smooth, singing high-gain distortion.

When Clapton plugged into Mark Knopfler's Soldano SLO-100 amps during rehearsals for the Nelson Mandela 70th Birthday Tribute, he immediately fell in love with its warm, round tone and responsive dynamics and placed an order with Soldano for his own SLO-100 heads. Soldano placed Clapton at the front of his rather lengthy waiting list, but it still took him two months to complete the order because he built his amps entirely by hand.

In early 1989, a few months after the Soldano amps arrived, Clapton commissioned British electronics wizard Pete Cornish to build him an entirely new rack system based around his Soldano heads. With Clapton's input, Cornish made this sophisticated 'everything but the kitchen sink' rig that featured a custom signal routing unit, a custom footswitch controller, a sophisticated power distribution unit, UHF and VHF wireless receivers, and studio-quality effects processors by Drawmer, Roland, TC Electronic, and Yamaha. The system was programmed to provide instant access to any variety of complex signal paths while maintaining pristine sound quality with minimal noise or interference. Everything was mounted in road cases so it could be packed up and loaded within minutes after a show.

This Soldano/Pete Cornish system remained Clapton's main stage rig for concert performances through 1994 when he simplified his rig dramatically for the 1994-95 From the Cradle Tour.

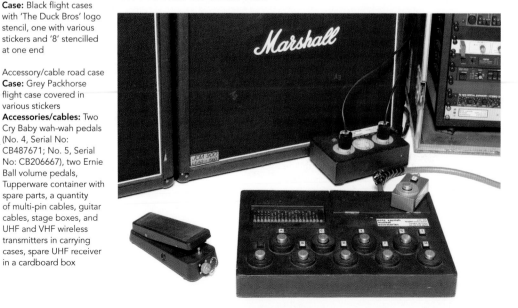

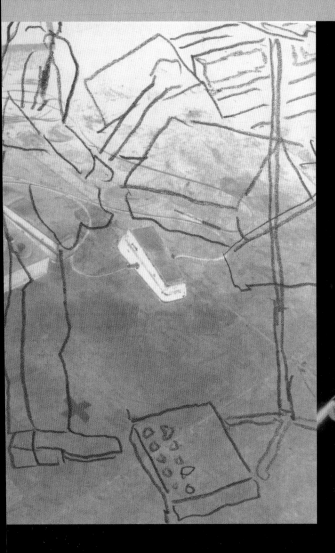

ERIC I had been using Fender Dual Showman amps when I heard Mark Knopfler at rehearsals and was impressed by his sound. I realised it was Knopfler's amp rather than the guitar that was responsible for the sound character. I tried Knopfler's amp and, liking its warm and round sound, immediately placed an order with Michael Soldano.

Playlist:
24 Nights, 1991
Live in Japan, 1992
Gigs:
1991 Royal Albert Hall
Feb. 5-Mar. 9, 1991
Rock Legends: George
Harrison with Eric
Clapton 1991 Japan Tour
Dec. 1-17, 1991
World Tours
1990-1994

Above:
Sir Peter Blake's sketch
shows the footswitch
controller during
Clapton's 24 Nights at
the Royal Albert Hall
in 1991.

Right:
Eric Clapton is shown
using this system on his
1991 tour of Japan.

EST: $7,500 - $10,000   PRICE: $32,000

Serial No: A-00752
Covering: Tweed, 'oxblood' brown speaker cloth
Plate: Fender Twin amp
Speakers: Two 12-inch 1973 blue Fender ceramic speakers with annotations 'TM 9-30-95', 'TM 9-29-95', 'TM 9-30-95' and 'TM 10-8-95'
Switches: Custom voltage selector, power on/off, standby
Controls: Presence, bass, treble, bright volume, normal volume
Inputs: Four
Label: Tape label inside the chassis inscribed 'Cesar Diaz [sic] 10-10-1986'
Case: Aluminium flight case

During the 1980s, Clapton bought this tweed 1957 Fender Twin amp from Pete Alenov of Pete's Guitar in Minnesota. César Díaz worked on amps for a variety of famous guitarists, including Keith Richards, Stevie Ray Vaughan and Neil Young, and he also built his own line of guitar amps and effects pedals. Díaz made numerous modifications to this 1957 Twin's original 5E8-A circuit to improve its reliability, roadworthiness, output, and sound. Díaz told *Tonequest Report* in 2000: 'I changed the transformer to a Fender export transformer. It's the same power transformer that went into the Showman for its first two years of production. I also took the two tube rectifiers [5U4GA] out and replaced them with a silicon diode, then I installed two more 6L6 tubes like you'd see in a later model Twin.'

Díaz also replaced the 12AY7 preamp and phase inverter tubes with 12AX7 tubes and installed a voltage selector switch so the amp could be used in any country without a voltage converter. Clapton started to use this Twin amp at a select handful of shows in 1991, including the blues nights during his 24-show concert series at Royal Albert Hall that year. It later became a full-time component of Clapton's stage rig, playing a prominent role on his 1994-5 From The Cradle Tour as well during the recording of the album.

Playlist:
24 Nights, 1991
Live in Japan, 1992
From the Cradle, 1994
Gigs:
1991 Royal Albert Hall Feb. 5-Mar. 9, 1991
Rock Legends: George Harrison with Eric Clapton 1991 Japan Tour Dec. 1-17, 1991
1994-5 From The Cradle Tour Oct. 3, 1994-Oct. 13, 1995
World Tours 1990-1997
Highlights:
Columbia Records Celebrates the Music of Bob Dylan Madison Square Garden New York, USA Oct. 16, 1992
Masters Of Music Concert for The Prince's Trust Hyde Park, London, UK June 29, 1996

ERIC The old tweed Fender Twin was my number-one amp in the studio. I found it at Pete's Guitars in Minneapolis, St. Paul. It was rewired several times because it heated up. Every time I used it, it blew up! When it sounded really good, that was the time to watch out! César Díaz came in and insulated everything with this extra-strong cable, because it would melt after you played it for a while.

Royal Albert Hall
London, UK
Feb. 1991

I'LL PLAY FOR YOU

1988 SOLDANO SLO-100 AMPS, 1989 PETE CORNISH GUITAR ROUTING SYSTEM, MARSHALL JCM 900 1960B SPEAKER CABINETS

1994 FENDER '59 BASSMAN

LOT 42 BONHAMS 2011

EST: $750 - $1,000

PRICE: $2,000

Serial No: AA07104, EH date code on tube chart
Covering: Tweed, brown speaker cloth
Plate: Fender Bassman
Speakers: Four 10-inch blue alnico
Switches: Ground, power on/off, standby
Controls: Presence, middle, bass, treble, volume bright, volume normal
Inputs: Four

Demand for original tweed-covered 4x10 Bassman combo amps that Fender produced in the late 1950s increased dramatically during the 1980s as many blues and rock players rediscovered that these vintage amps deliver the warm, classic tones they loved and were loud enough to play on stage with a full band. However, original 1950s amps weren't reliable enough for most players and soaring prices for Bassman amps on the vintage market made many players hesitant to bring their Bassmans on the road.

When Fender's '59 Bassman reissue made its debut in 1990, the timing was perfect as the new model cost less than a vintage Bassman and it was much easier to maintain and replace than an original model. The reissue's circuit was based on the 5F6-A circuit found on Bassman combos that Fender made from 1958 through 1960. Although the reissue isn't an exact reproduction – the reissue uses a printed circuit board instead of point-to-point wiring, the speakers are different, the cabinet is birch plywood instead of solid pine, etc. – guitarists found that it does an excellent job of producing classic tweed Bassman tones.

Clapton and George Harrison used '59 Bassman reissue amps similar to this one on their 1991 Tour of Japan.

Clapton and Harrison's amps seen from the back during their 1991 Tour of Japan.

Playlist:
Live in Japan, 1992
Gigs:
Rock Legends: George Harrison with Eric Clapton 1991 Japan Tour
Dec. 1-17, 1991

Serial No: F309847, F312558
Covering: Black Tolex, silver speaker cloth
Speakers: One Fender/Electro-Voice 12F 12-inch
Switches: Power on/off, ground (rear panel)
Controls: Volume/pull lead, treble/pull bright, mid/pull boost, bass, reverb, lead level, master, presence, hum balance (rear panel)
Inputs: One
Outputs: Speaker, line/recording
Other: Reverb/lead footswitch, two pedal inputs, reverb input, reverb output

By the early 1980s, Fender's amp sales had dwindled to an insignificant number due to competitors like Marshall and Mesa-Boogie that progressively and successfully chipped away at Fender's market share during the 1970s. In 1981 Fender hired engineer Paul Rivera to completely redesign its amp line, which hadn't changed much since CBS took over the company in the mid 1960s. Rivera developed seven tube amp models that produced classic Fender clean tones as well as high-gain tones and versatile midrange tone shaping features similar to Mesa-Boogie amps. Rivera-designed models like the 20-watt Princeton Reverb II combo, which featured 'blackface' control panels inspired by Fender's mid 1960s amps, helped Fender regain its reputation as a builder of quality guitar amps.

When CBS decided to sell Fender in 1985, Rivera made an unsuccessful bid to purchase the company. Fender's new owners ousted Rivera, and all of the Rivera-designed amp models were discontinued later that year.

1993 PARK G10 AMPLIFIER

Serial No: 930300915
Covering: Black Tolex, black speaker cloth
Speakers: One 10-inch
Switches: Power on/off
Controls: Gain 1, gain 2, treble, middle, bass, master volume
Inputs: One
Outputs: Headphone
Additional: Signed by Eric Clapton on the back in black felt pen

Park amplifiers initially were a second brand of amplifiers that Marshall sold through its old distribution network after Marshall signed an exclusive distribution deal with Rose-Morris. Marshall produced Park amps from 1965 until 1982, and in 1992 Marshall revived the Park brand when they introduced a new line of inexpensive solid-state amps made in Asia.

Clapton often used small amps like this Park G10 to warm up backstage before concert appearances.

I'LL PLAY FOR YOU

LATE 1980S FENDER 15 AMPLIFIER

EST: $300 - $400   PRICE:$2,200

Serial No: M-26139
Covering: Black Tolex, silver speaker cloth
Speakers: One 8-inch
Switches: Power on/off
Controls: Volume, gain, master, treble, middle, bass
Inputs: One
Outputs: Headphone
Additional: Signed by Eric Clapton on the back in silver felt pen

Playlist:
Live in Japan, 1992
Gigs:
Rock Legends: George Harrison with Eric Clapton 1991 Japan Tour Dec. 1-17, 1991

While musicians generally accepted the guitars and basses that Fender produced during its early post-CBS ownership era in the 1980s with open arms, Fender's amp designs during that time were not as warmly welcomed. Part of the problem was simply cosmetic – although many of the guitars they produced closely resembled the classic instruments Fender made during the 1950s and 1960s, most of their new amp designs suffered from garish cosmetics, such as the red knobs featured on the new line of products they introduced in 1988.

The Fender 15 is a small 15-watt solid-state combo amp that Fender produced during this period. This amp was photographed on the workbench of Clapton's guitar tech during Eric's 1991 Tour of Japan with George Harrison. Clapton's tech likely used this amp to assist with the tuning of Eric's guitars.

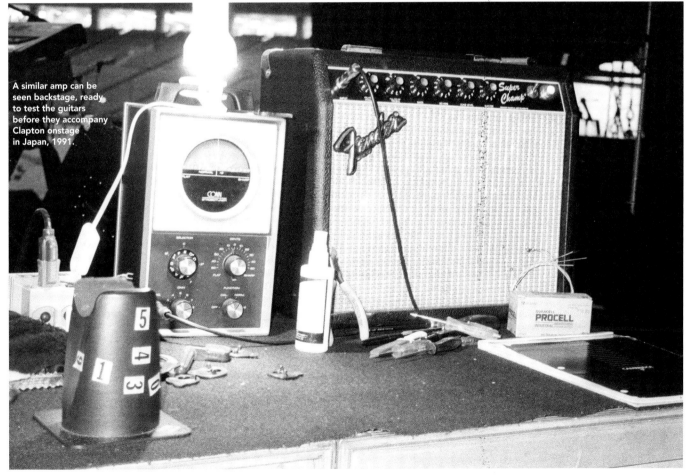

A similar amp can be seen backstage, ready to test the guitars before they accompany Clapton onstage in Japan, 1991.

I'LL PLAY FOR YOU

Serial No: 73234
Body: Rosewood back and sides, spruce top, ivoroid binding with pearl purfling, natural finish
Neck: Mahogany, 20 frets, ivoroid bound ebony fingerboard with 'snowflake' inlays
Headstock: Solid
Bridge: Ebony 'belly' pin bridge
Soundhole: Pearl inlaid rosette
Pickguard: Imitation tortoiseshell
Case: Leather-covered hardshell case with adhesive tape inscribed 'Auction/Boo-Hoo/Auction #30/M. 000-42 # 73234'

Eric Clapton's performance on MTV *Unplugged*, filmed at Bray Studios on January 16th, 1992, was a landmark event that elevated Clapton's career to new heights of success and significantly boosted interest in and demand for acoustic guitars, particularly small-body flat-tops like the ones Clapton played during the show. Martin noted a dramatic increase in its guitars' sales figures, and independent acoustic guitar builders experienced a spike in sales that ushered in a new renaissance for acoustic guitar design and innovation.

Although Clapton played four different guitars during the performance, including a Juan Álvarez classical (page 214), a Martin D12-20 12-string and a Dobro, this Martin 000-42 is the instrument that most guitarists noticed and sought after the performance was broadcast. During the *Unplugged* performance he played it on 'Before You Accuse Me', 'Hey Hey', 'Nobody Knows You When You're Down and Out', 'Layla', 'Malted Milk' and 'Old Love', and a photo of Clapton playing the guitar also appeared on the cover of his *Unplugged* CD. Guitarists who wanted an instrument like Eric's soon discovered that original Martin 000-42 guitars are extremely rare. Martin made only 127 000-42 guitars from 1918 until production of the model halted in 1943, with most of these guitars being built between 1938 and 1943.

After *Unplugged*, Clapton frequently played this guitar on stage, starting with his series of performances at the Royal Albert Hall in February and March 1993. It remained his main acoustic guitar for live performance until the first leg of his 1998 Pilgrim Tour in the USA. He also played it in the studio on all of his albums from *From the Cradle* to *Me and Mr. Johnson*.

> ERIC I started my career playing the Washburn acoustic guitar (page 10) in a pub by myself, and this is how simple it can be, and how enjoyable it is on that level. That's what *Unplugged* was about for me.

Bray Film Studios
Windsor, Berkshire, UK
Jan. 16, 1992

Eric's MTV *Unplugged* session was filmed at Bray Studios in front of a small audience. A similar photograph was used on the cover of the *Unplugged* album released later that year.

Playlist:
Unplugged, 1992
From the Cradle, 1994
Pilgrim, 1998
Riding with the King, 2000
Reptile, 2001
One More Car, One More Rider, 2002
Me and Mr. Johnson, 2004
Gigs:
1993 Royal Albert Hall
Feb. 20-Mar. 7, 1993
1994-5 From The Cradle Tour
Oct. 3, 1994-Oct. 13, 1995
1997 Far East Tour
Oct. 9-31, 1997
1998 Pilgrim North American Tour
Mar. 30-June 6, 1998
Highlight:
MTV *Unplugged* (TV)
Bray Film Studios
Windsor, Berkshire, UK
Jan. 16, 1992

ERIC This is an incredible guitar. I would never have been able to part with it if I didn't have one as good, which I kept (an OM, page 97). It was the *Unplugged* guitar and got played throughout that whole period on stage. It was the finest Martin I had, although I think I had the guitar that Andy played for longer. Both the *Unplugged* guitar and the Longworth (page 114) were incredible playing instruments.

Serial No: 745944
Body: Brazilian rosewood back and sides, spruce top, ivoroid binding with pearl purfling, natural finish
Neck: Mahogany, 20 frets, ivoroid bound ebony fretboard with 'snowflake' inlays, 'Eric Clapton' signature inlay between 19th and 20th frets
Headstock: Ivoroid binding, pearl 'fern' inlay
Bridge: Ebony 'belly' pin bridge, 'snowflake' inlays
Soundhole: Pearl inlaid rosette
Pickguard: Imitation tortoiseshell
Label: 'CF Martin & Co./000-42ECB/Eric Clapton/Signature Edition/1 of 200/The Martin Guitar Company/Nazareth, Pennsylvania USA' Signed 'Eric Clapton' and 'C.F. Martin IV'
Case: Original hardshell case with adhesive tape inscribed 'Auction #41/EC 000-42 #1 of 200'

Inspired by the 000-42 used as Clapton's main guitar for his MTV *Unplugged* performance, Martin introduced the 000-42EC limited-edition acoustic guitar in 1995. All 461 of these guitars sold out immediately.

In 2000, Martin announced their second limited-edition Eric Clapton model, the 000-42ECB, which was the first time in Martin's history that they had produced two signature limited-edition guitars for a single artist. This version was even fancier than its predecessor and production was limited to only 200 instruments. Only the finest materials were used to build these guitars, including rare Brazilian rosewood, Engelmann spruce and gold-plated Waverly tuning machines. The 'fern'-style headstock inlay was based on a design found on only four 00-45 guitars that Martin made in 1902.

Clapton used this guitar, which is number 1 of the 200 000-42ECB guitars Martin made, to record several tracks on his *Reptile* album.

ERIC This guitar is definitely on *Reptile*. I think Martin were very, very pleased that I'd done so much to boost their image, by using Martins on stage and in *Unplugged*... obviously I'm a staunch admirer. So they offered me a chance to put together a guitar with my wish list and make it.

It's the same kind of thing with the Strat — you get an offer like that from a company that's already kind of evolved to the point where it can go no further. All I wanted was a 000-28 or a 000-45, just with different kinds of wood. The main thing that I wanted was to get it to look like it was old, although it was brand-new. The first time they submitted a prototype, I said, 'It's just too white; it looks like it was made today. I want one that looks like it's 50 years old,' and they did it. All we did was choose some different kinds of inlay and so on. Then they offered me some different variations, simpler models, a 28 or a Brazilian rosewood model, which has been fantastic. We made a black one that's been fairly successful. It works for studio or on stage as well, because it's got a built-in mic. That's what I like about Martin; they're keen to try anything.

Playlist:
Reptile, 2001

Opposite:
Jan. 8, 2001

Clapton with another of his signature Martins, the 000-28EC model, during rehearsals for his Reptile Tour.

Serial No: 60929
Body: Rosewood back and sides, spruce top (replaced), ivoroid binding with herringbone purfling, natural finish
Neck: Mahogany, 20 frets, bound ebony fingerboard with hexagonal pearl inlays
Headstock: Vertical 'C.F. Martin' logo inlaid in pearl
Bridge: Ebony 'belly' pin bridge
Soundhole: Pearl inlaid rosette
Pickguard: Imitation tortoiseshell
Label: Internal stamp 'C.F. Martin & Co/Nazareth, PA/F-7 60929', label 'Matt Umanov/Guitars/35 Bedford St, N.Y.C.' with signature 'Top made for Matt Umanov Guitars, Jeff Levin 2/2/73'
Case: Original hardshell case with adhesive tape inscribed 'Auction #33/Martin F.7./#60929'

From 1931 until 1942, Martin produced a variety of archtop steel-string acoustic guitar models, including the F-7. Martin offered this guitar from 1935 until 1942, in which time they produced just 187. The materials and dimensions of Martin's archtop guitars were similar to those of many Martin flat-top models, so over the years many of these instruments have been converted to flat-top guitars. The Martin F-7 archtop is a particularly desirable foundation for a conversion because it has an ornate neck with the same vertical C.F. Martin headstock inlay and bound ebony fingerboard with hexagonal inlays as a D-45, and beautiful Brazilian rosewood back and sides with a Style 45 back stripe. Most F-7 conversions result in a hybrid of a 000-size guitar and a D-45, although the F-7's body dimensions generally fall between that of a 000- and D-size guitar, with the exception of its lower body bout, which is a ⅜ inch wider than a D-size guitar.

Matt Umanov of Manhattan's Matt Umanov Guitars started converting Martin archtops in the late 1960s when David Bromberg brought in his F-7 and asked the shop to convert it to a flat top. Bromberg's converted F-7 became the inspiration for the Martin M-38, which Martin introduced in 1977. Other guitarists followed suit, and Umanov's shop performed many similar conversions for guitarists over the years. Umanov's shop installed a spruce top with Style 28 ivoroid binding and herringbone purfling on this example.

Clapton bought this guitar for Andy Fairweather Low, who played it on stage with Clapton from 1993 until 1998.

Right & opposite:
The Royal Albert Hall, London, UK
Feb. 1993

Andy Fairweather Low playing 'The Andy Guitar' during an unplugged session with Clapton at the Royal Albert Hall.

Gigs:
Used by Andy Fairweather Low on stage with Clapton 1993-1998

I'LL PLAY FOR YOU

ERIC 'The Andy Guitar' –
he played this on stage with
me for many years. I've played
it too but it's not my first choice
of acoustic, it was his. I got
it around the time I was doing
Unplugged on stage. Andy
loved it because of the volume.
It's a great rhythm guitar.

Serial No: A 1852
Body: Maple back and sides, spruce top, ivoroid binding, single round Venetian cutaway, natural finish
Neck: Maple with mahogany centre strip, 20 frets, multi-bound rosewood fingerboard with block inlays
Headstock: Multi-bound, pre-war script Gibson logo, flowerpot inlay
Bridge: Rosewood, gold-plated L-5 trapeze tailpiece with silver insert, Allen wrench tension adjustment hole, and engraved 'L5'
Pickguard: Multi-bound marbled imitation tortoiseshell
Label: 'Style L-5-P/ Gibson Guitar/Number A-1852'
Case: Earlier hardshell tweed case with adhesive tape inscribed '948 Alan Reuss [sic]/ Gibson-L.5. Blonde./ '48 #1582'

This guitar is one of the earliest post-World War II L-5 models, which can be distinguished by the 'P' designation (for 'Premier', which was Gibson's pre-war designation for a cutaway model L-5) that appears on its label. Later in 1948 Gibson changed this designation to 'C' for 'cutaway'. As their supply of ebony was depleted shortly after the war, Gibson substituted rosewood for the fingerboards of guitars that normally were made with ebony fingerboards for a short period in the late 1940s. This L-5 Premier allegedly previously belonged to Allan Reuss, who played with various elite big bands and appeared in Gibson ads for the L-5 guitar. Clapton purchased the guitar in the early 1990s, and brought it to recording sessions over the years. Andy Fairweather Low took an immediate interest in the guitar, and he played it on several tracks on Clapton's blues-based albums.

Playlist:
From the Cradle, 1994
Riding with the King 2000
Me and Mr. Johnson 2004

1985 MARTIN SHENANDOAH 000-2832   EST: $3,000 - $5,000   PRICE: $21,000

LOT 12 CHRISTIE'S 1999

Serial No: 454899
Body: Laminated rosewood veneer back and sides, spruce top, natural finish
Neck: Mahogany, 20 frets, ebonised rosewood fingerboard with dot inlays
Headstock: Flowerpot inlay
Bridge: Ebonised rosewood 'belly' pin bridge
Pickguard: Imitation tortoiseshell
Electronics: Fishman soundhole pickup, input jack
Case: Black hardshell contour case with green plush lining and handwritten tie-on label (torn) and adhesive paper label inscribed '(Jap.) AE. Martin 000-28/32 #454899' and another tie-on label inscribed 'Eric's'

Martin produced the Shenandoah series guitars between 1983 and 1996 to compete with the growing number of low-cost acoustic instruments produced in Asia. Although the back headstock of some Martin Shenandoah guitars are stamped 'Made in the USA', the guitars were actually only assembled and finished in the USA, while the body and neck were manufactured in Japan. From 1994 Shenandoah guitars were produced in full in Japan.

Clapton replaced the 000-2832's stock under-saddle 332 Thinline piezo pickup with a Fishman soundhole pickup. Andy Fairweather Low often played this guitar on stage with Clapton's band.

I'LL PLAY FOR YOU

LOT 51 CHRISTIE'S 1999

Serial No: 77643
Body: Mahogany back and sides, spruce top, natural finish
Neck: Mahogany, 19 frets, rosewood fingerboard
Headstock: Slotted
Bridge: Rosewood tie bridge
Case: Black softshell contour case with purple plush lining and handwritten tie-on label 'Martin 00-18G '41 Natural Classical Ser #77643' and adhesive paper label inscribed 'Martin Gutstring 1941 '41 00-18G #77643'

Although Martin guitars made prior to 1928 were designed for gut strings, they had cross bracing that was different to the fan bracing used to make traditional classical guitars and therefore sounded quite different. Martin's G series guitars, which were built with fan bracing and other classical guitar construction features, were the company's first attempt to build classical guitars that would appeal to Spanish guitar players. Introduced in 1936, the 00-18G along with the fancier 00-28G were Martin's first classical guitar models.

LOT 2 CHRISTIE'S 2004

Serial No: 87485
Body: Mahogany back and sides, spruce top, natural finish
Neck: Mahogany, 20 frets, rosewood fingerboard with dot inlays
Headstock: Solid
Bridge: Rosewood 'belly' pin bridge
Pickguard: Imitation tortoiseshell
Case: Original 'chipboard' case with adhesive tape inscribed 'Martin O-18 Model/1944 #87485'

Most musical instrument companies cut back or suspended production of guitars during World War II, or made guitars from reduced-quality materials; however Martin generally maintained the quality of their products and even increased the production of a few models like the 0-18 during this period. In fact, Martin halted production only of their fancy Style 40, 42, and 45 models with abalone-shell trim. Many collectors refer to the desirability of 'pre-war' Martins, but actually many guitars that Martin made during the war until 1944 – when they temporarily stopped scalloping the internal top braces – are comparable to their pre-war counterparts. This 1944 0-18 predates that internal bracing change, which started on a guitar with serial number 89926.

ERIC Not only playing, but also succeeding at playing with the guitar that I used on *Unplugged*, I became very, very absorbed in the history of Martin. I thought, 'I love this style; I wonder if I could find another one that plays as well.'

It was almost a fruitless search. I kept finding one online or in a store and I'd buy it, and I'd play it, and I had to accept in the end that what I was trying to compare them to was impossible to get anything close to. It's like a car: you get one occasionally that is absolutely spotless, perfect.

I'LL PLAY FOR YOU

Serial No: 12077
Body: Rosewood back and sides, spruce top, ivory back and top binding with pearl purfling, natural finish
Neck: Mahogany, 19 frets, ivory-bound ebony fingerboard with 'snowflake' inlays
Headstock: Solid, 'torch' inlay, ivory binding
Soundhole: Pearl inlaid rosette
Bridge: Ivory 'pyramid' pin bridge
Case: Circa 1890s C.F. Martin 'coffin' case with adhesive tape inscribed 'Auction #34/Martin "O"'

Martin first started listing Style 45 guitars in their catalogue in 1904, but they made a few 00-42 guitars with special inlays that were considered the prototypes to the Style 45 guitar in 1902. Martin's Style 45 guitars are true top-of-the-line instruments, built using only the finest available materials by the company's best craftsmen. This exquisite 1915 Martin 0-45 is one of only two of these models built by Martin that year.

ERIC I was searching really for something older that would have the same playability as the *Unplugged* guitar, and I don't think that I ever found it.

I remember buying this guitar because of the ivory bridge. It stood in a corner of a room in my house in Chelsea, and I'd often pick it up and play it. It has a lovely, delicate, light sound because it has a small body, but it can be very hard on the left hand when you play it. Apart from my OM-45, this was the highest price I've ever paid for a guitar.

Serial No: 38471
Body: Rosewood back and sides, spruce top, ivoroid back and top binding with pearl purfling, natural finish
Neck: Mahogany, 20 frets, ivoroid-bound ebony fingerboard with 'snowflake' inlays
Headstock: Slotted, 'torch' inlay, ivoroid binding
Soundhole: Pearl inlaid rosette
Bridge: Ebony 'belly' pin bridge
Pickguard: Black single-ply
Case: Original 'chipboard' case

The Style 45 guitars that Martin produced during the 1920s and 1930s are stunning artistic achievements from both design and performance perspectives, with sound that is as beautiful as the guitars' appearance. Clapton bought this 1929 00-45 for his Martin collection from Gruhn Guitars in Nashville, Tennessee, while he was on tour during the late 1990s. Although the pickguard and bridge on this guitar are not original, 00-45 guitars from this era are so rare and desirable that those modifications do not significantly detract from its value. Martin did not offer a pickguard for the 00-45 until 1932, and this guitar's original 'pyramid' bridge was replaced with a 'belly' bridge with a slanted saddle, which Martin did not use on this model until 1930. Martin made only 10 00-45 guitars in 1929, which originally sold for $160 (about $2,150 in today's currency – still quite a bargain for the craftsmanship and materials involved in the construction).

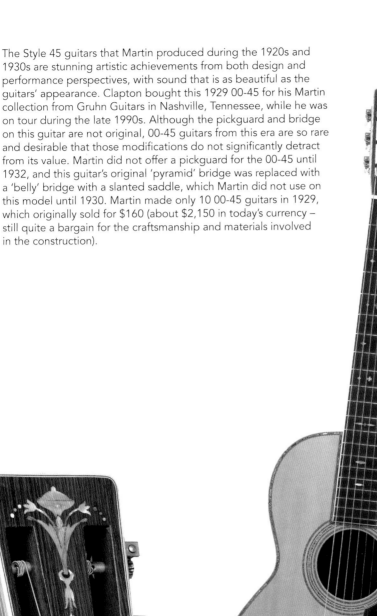

I'LL PLAY FOR YOU

Serial No: EC006
Body: Routed semi-hollow one-piece mahogany, spruce top, multiple-layer binding, black finish
Neck: Mahogany, 22 frets, pau ferro fingerboard
Headstock: Fender Custom Shop transfer and serial number EC006 on back of headstock
Bridge: Asymmetrical pau ferro/ebony sandwich strings-through-body bridge
Soundhole: Angled elliptical
Pickups: Fishman bridge saddle transducer
Controls: Volume, treble, bass sliders
Additional: Unopened bag of accessories including Fender webbing guitar strap, cable, and Fender cleaning cloth
Case: Black rectangular hardshell case with grey plush lining, two handwritten labels with various inscriptions including 'Fender Teleacoustic E.C.006 Blk. Custom Shop'

When John Page was manager of the Fender Custom Shop, he designed this Telecaster-style electric-acoustic called the Telecoustic during the early 1990s. Page and Mark Kendrick built the first set of four prototypes in 1992. Page kept one and the others were sent to Clapton, Bob Dylan and Jon Bon Jovi for constructive criticism. The Fender Custom Shop built a limited production run of the Telecoustic, making about 20 guitars. Fender later offered standard production Telecoustic models (Standard, Custom and Deluxe) that were made in Japan from 1993 through 1995. These models were based on the Custom Shop Telecoustic and shared similar styling and features – such as set neck construction, a distinctive elliptical soundhole and asymmetrical bridge – but lacked the fancy materials and meticulous attention to detail of the hand-built Custom Shop guitars. When Fender resumed production of the Telecoustic in 2000, it was a completely different instrument, featuring a bolt-on neck, fibreglass body, block-shaped pin bridge, and numerous other differences.

Thanks to the popularity of Clapton's *Unplugged* album, sales of acoustic guitars soared during the early 1990s. Page hoped to capitalise on this by producing a full line of Fender Custom Shop acoustics. The Telecoustic was his first attempt to develop this line.

I'LL PLAY FOR YOU

1993 FENDER STRATOCASTER

LOT 78 CHRISTIE'S 2004

Serial No: EC 07
Body: Cast aluminium with polished 'mirror' finish
Neck: Maple with skunk-stripe truss rod routing, 22 frets, maple fingerboard with dot inlays
Headstock: Back of headstock inscribed 'EC 07/Custom Built/J.W. Black/Fender USA.'
Bridge: Blocked synchronised tremolo with metal 'block' saddles
Pickguard: Black single-ply
Pickups: Three Gold Fender Lace Sensors
Controls: Master volume, two tone, TBX/MDX active circuitry
Switches: Five-position pickup selector with black switch tip
Additional: Fender Custom Shop Certificate Of Authenticity
Case: Original hardshell case, tape inscribed 'Chrome EC Strat'

Master builder J.W. Black of the Fender Custom Shop built this unusual aluminium-body Stratocaster prototype and gave it to Eric for evaluation purposes. The body is made of two separate slabs of aluminium with hollowed-out chambers to reduce weight and provide resonant tone. Although the guitar is quite attractive, ultimately its construction was too expensive for Fender to consider offering it as a production model.

1993 FENDER STRATOCASTER

1993 FENDER STRATOCASTER ERIC CLAPTON SIGNATURE MODEL

LOT 47 CHRISTIE'S 1999

Serial No: V065024
Body: Alder with Olympic White finish
Neck: Maple with skunk-stripe truss rod routing, 22 frets, maple fingerboard with dot inlays
Bridge: Blocked synchronised tremolo
Pickguard: White single-ply
Pickups: Three Texas Special single-coil
Controls: Master volume, two tone
Switches: Five-position pickup selector with white switch tip
Case: Tweed rectangular hardshell case with red plush lining and handwritten tie-on label 'WHITEY VO65024 L + L' and adhesive label 'Fender Strat WHITEY L + L White - C. Shop - Texas Specials'

This was the only Eric Clapton Signature Model Stratocaster made during the 1990s for Eric that had Texas Special pickups instead of the Gold Lace Sensor pickups that he preferred. About a year later Eric had Fender's Custom Shop build him virtually identical guitars with Olympic White finishes (page 16) to pay tribute to his friend Jimmie Vaughan, only this time the guitars were equipped with Lace Sensors.

Clapton played this guitar primarily during rehearsals.

1993 FENDER STRATOCASTER ERIC CLAPTON SIGNATURE MODEL

Serial No: A-755
Body: Mahogany back and sides, maple top, f-holes, sunburst finish
Neck: Mahogany, 19 frets, rosewood fingerboard with dot inlays
Bridge: Rosewood, nickel-plated trapeze tailpiece
Pickups: One P-90 single-coil
Controls: One volume, one tone
Case: Grey hardshell contour case with handwritten tie-on label 'Gibson L48 Early '50s #755' and adhesive paper label similarly inscribed

The successor to the Gibson ES-100 model, the ES-125 was Gibson's least expensive electric archtop when post-war production of the model resumed in 1946. The ES-125 was a favourite of many early, aspiring electric blues guitarists, including B.B. King, who was photographed playing an ES-125 when performing for a radio broadcast on WDIA in Memphis.

Clapton purchased this ES-125 in Atlanta, Georgia, and he is seen playing it in the promotional video for 'Motherless Child'. Although the original tailpiece was replaced and the pickguard is missing, this guitar possesses a wealth of blues mojo.

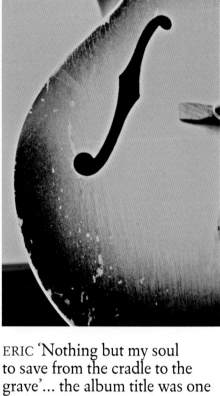

ERIC 'Nothing but my soul to save from the cradle to the grave'... the album title was one of those things you wake up in the middle of the night and run downstairs and write down.

This album was paying respect to the records the way I heard and felt about them, so, when I was singing and playing, I was trying to be me being Freddie King. Of course, that didn't happen, because it still came out as me, but I did it as much as I could. I did everything to try and be as true to my recollection of the experience as possible: in the way we recorded it all on the floor at the same time, with the instruments I played, and with the way I sang it.

With *From The Cradle* I really retraced my steps back to John Mayall's Blues Breakers.

Playlist:
From The Cradle, 1994
Highlight:
'Motherless Child' video

Opposite:
Clapton photographed during the filming of the promotional video for 'Motherless Child' in 1994.

ERIC I love this model of guitar.

244　1947 GIBSON ES-125

LOT 1 CHRISTIE'S 1999

Serial No: 536346
Body: Indian rosewood body with spruce top, natural finish, white binding with seven-layer black and white purfling (front) and five-layer black and white purfling (back)
Neck: Mahogany, 20 frets, bound ebony fingerboard with hexagonal abalone inlays
Bridge: Ebony 'belly' pin bridge
Pickguard: Black
Tuners: Gold-plated with ebony buttons
Case: Black hardshell contour case with blue plush lining and handwritten adhesive paper label 'Martin 12 Str.- Blonde J.40 #536346'

Eric Clapton used this guitar to perform 'Motherless Child', which was his arrangement of the traditional blues song 'Motherless Child Blues', originally recorded by Robert 'Barbecue Bob' Hicks in 1927. To perform the song, Clapton tuned the guitar to open G and placed a capo at the guitar's fourth fret.

ERIC I used this guitar for 'Motherless Child', the number that opened the show on the From The Cradle Tour.

I used to come out and start with just an acoustic guitar, and I think that really worked. I like to see people do that because it's very intimate that way. If I go to see somebody perform, I want to feel like they're just singing for me. More than that; I want to feel like they're singing for themselves, actually. That's what I want to see, and I hope that's what the audience wants.

Clapton playing 'Motherless Child' during his 1994-5 From The Cradle Tour.

Gigs:
1994-5 From The Cradle Tour
Oct. 3, 1994-
Oct. 13, 1995

Serial No: A32176
Factory Order No:
S92615
Body: Double cutaway
thinline semi-hollow,
maple, f-holes, maple
centre block, natural finish
Neck: Mahogany, 22 frets,
bound rosewood
fingerboard with dot inlays
Headstock: Crown
peghead inlay
Bridge: Nickel-plated
Tune-o-matic with
stop tailpiece
Pickguard: Black five-ply
(black/white/black/
white/black)
Pickups: Two humbucking
Controls: Two volume,
two tone
Switches: Three-position
pickup selector
Additional: Bag containing
six Kluson Deluxe tuners in
guitar case
Case: Brown hardshell
contour case lined in pink
plush and handwritten
tie-on label 'Gibson 335 '59
Blonde "Dot" Ser
#A.32176'

ES-335 guitars made from 1958 through 1962 – distinguishable by
the dot fingerboard inlays – are collectible for their PAF humbucking
pickups and stop tailpieces. The most desirable 'dot neck' ES-335
guitars have a blonde or natural finish like this example, which was
produced in limited numbers between 1958 and 1960.

Clapton played this vintage ES-335 frequently during the 1994-5
From The Cradle 'Blues' Tour. Clarence 'Gatemouth' Brown, who
was the opening act for several shows on this tour, also played
this guitar when he joined Clapton on stage to perform 'Sweet
Home Chicago'.

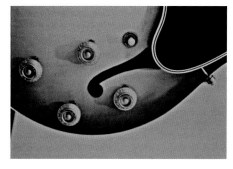

ERIC I used this guitar occasionally
on the Blues Tour.

Gigs:
1994-5 From The
Cradle Tour
Oct. 3, 1994-
Oct. 13, 1995

1959 GIBSON ES-335TDN

Serial No: A15241
Factory Order No:
Y531715
Body: Laminated maple,
bound hollowbody, single
sharp Florentine cutaway,
f-holes, sunburst finish
Neck: Mahogany, 19 frets,
bound rosewood
fingerboard with double
parallelogram inlays
Headstock: Crown
peghead inlay
Bridge: Gold-plated Les
Paul combination
trapeze/bridge tailpiece
Pickguard: Clear
single-ply with cream back
painting and embossed
gold floral design
Pickups: Two cream
P-90 single-coil
Controls: Two volume,
two tone
Switches: Three-position
pickup selector
Case: Brown hardshell
contour case with
handwritten tie-on label
'Gibson 295 '53 Sunburst
P.90s Ser #A.15241' and
adhesive paper label
similarly inscribed

The concept for the ES-295 was inspired by an ES-175 with
a custom gold finish that Les Paul asked Gibson to make and that
he presented to a disabled guitarist in 1951. A few changes were
made to the electronics and hardware, and the ES-295 was later
introduced in 1952 as the hollowbody counterpart to the solidbody
Gibson Les Paul model. The model played a crucial role in the
development of rock and roll when Scotty Moore played a Gibson
ES-295 on the early records he made with Elvis Presley.

This ES-295 is an extremely rare custom variant that has a sunburst
finish instead of the stock gold finish. Gibson also made a handful
of ES-295s with cherry red and Argentine Grey finishes.

ERIC If I'm trying to evoke something from
the Fifties, I'll use an old Gibson. They're
quite tricky to play because I use fairly thick
strings on them, so they're louder and fatter.
But it means that when I go to bend a note,
I'm not going to be able to do exactly what
I want. It's pretty resistant, so I end up
playing – or attempting to play – a little
like T-Bone Walker, with that kind of
sound. It's more of an implied bend than
a full bend; I don't really get to the note I'm
trying to bend to. I half get there and then
the string is too stiff. I love those Alnicos,
but I have to dicker a lot with pickups so
the bottom end isn't overwhelming, because
they're really rich bass pickups.

I have to let down the bottom end, and then
raise up some of the pegs in the pickup to
get up to the E string and the B string.

I'LL PLAY FOR YOU

247   1953 GIBSON ES-295

Serial No: A 24857
Factory Order No:
V 4815 3
Body: Maple back and
sides, spruce top, bound,
thinline, single round
Venetian cutaway, bound
f-holes, sunburst finish
Neck: Two-piece maple
with mahogany strip,
22 frets, bound ebony
fingerboard with
block inlays
Headstock: Multi-bound,
pearl Gibson logo,
flowerpot inlay
Bridge: Gold-plated
Tune-o-matic with
rosewood base,
gold-plated triple-loop
trapeze tailpiece
Pickguard: Multi-bound
imitation tortoiseshell
Pickups: Two Alnico V
single-coil
Controls: Two volume,
two tone
Switches: Three-position
pickup selector
Case: Brown hardshell
contour case with pink
plush lining and
handwritten tie-on label
'Gibson Byrdland '57
sunburst Alnicos
Ser. #A.24857' and
adhesive paper label
similarly inscribed

The Byrdland is named after guitarists Billy Byrd and Hank Garland, who helped Gibson develop this model in 1955. Featuring a hollow body only 2¼ inches deep, the Byrdland was Gibson's first thinline model. Other distinctive features include a short 23½ inch scale, narrow nut width and Alnico V pickups. The latter was only offered on upscale Gibson models, which also included the Les Paul Custom, L-5CES, and Super 400CES.

Clapton used this guitar to play 'Reconsider Baby' on his *From The Cradle* album and tour.

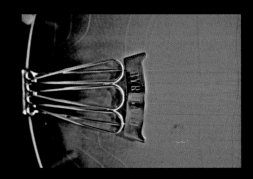

ERIC I played period numbers on this guitar such as 'Reconsider Baby'.

Playlist:
From The Cradle, 1994
Gigs:
1994-5 From
The Cradle Tour
Oct. 3, 1994-
Oct. 13, 1995

Royal Albert Hall
London, UK
Feb.-Mar. 1995

LOT 72 BONHAMS 2011

Serial No: 21579002
Body: Flame maple back and sides, spruce top, bound thinline, single round Venetian cutaway, bound f-holes, natural finish
Neck: Three-piece flame maple with two mahogany strips, 22 frets, bound ebony fingerboard with block inlays
Headstock: Multi-bound, pearl Gibson logo, flowerpot inlay
Bridge: Gold-plated Tune-o-matic with rosewood base with pearl inlays, gold-plated triple-loop trapeze tailpiece
Pickguard: Multi-bound imitation tortoiseshell
Pickups: Two Alnico V single-coil
Controls: Two volume, two tone
Switches: Three-position pickup selector
Additional: Various accessories including manufacturer's warranty and Gibson Custom Certificate Of Authenticity
Case: Black hardshell contour case with purple plush lining and tie-on label

The Gibson Custom Shop still produces a limited number of Byrdland guitars built to original 1950s specifications. Most modern-day Gibson Byrdland guitars feature a pair of humbucking pickups, but Clapton had a pair of his favourite mid 1950s-style Alnico V single-coil pickups installed on this guitar.

This model is similar to the Gibson Byrdland played on Clapton's From The Cradle Tour.

Nippon Budokan
Tokyo, Japan
Oct. 13, 1995

Clapton playing Howlin' Wolf's 'Forty Four' with his 1955 Gibson Byrdland, similar to this guitar, on the last night of his From The Cradle Tour.

I'LL PLAY FOR YOU

LOT 40 CHRISTIE'S 2004

Serial No: A 24590
Factory Order No:
W5028 1
Body: Maple back and
sides, spruce top, bound
thinline, single round
Venetian cutaway, bound
f-holes, sunburst finish
Neck: Maple, 22 frets,
bound rosewood
fingerboard with double
parallelogram inlays
Headstock: Bound,
crown inlay
Bridge: Gold-plated
Tune-o-matic on
rosewood base,
gold-plated 'W-shaped'
tubular trapeze
tailpiece with
pointed-end crossbar
Pickguard: Black five-ply
(black/white/black/
white/black)
Pickups: Two P-90
single-coil
Controls: Two volume,
two tone
Switches: Three-position
pickup selector
Label: 'Style ES-350 T/
Gibson Guitar/Number
A-24590 is hereby/
Guaranteed/against
faulty workmanship and
materials./Gibson
Inc/Kalamazoo
Michigan,/U.S.A.'
Case: Original hardshell
case with adhesive tape
inscribed 'Auction
#24/ES350T.Cedar [sic]
Top./#A24590'

While most Gibson ES-350T thinline guitars have laminated
maple tops, Gibson made a few early models with solid spruce
tops similar to the Gibson Byrdland, which the ES-350T was
based on. Considering that this guitar has a 1955 factory order
number (identifiable by the 'W') but a 1956 serial number, it's
likely that it was built in 1955 but not shipped until 1956.
In fact, records show that Gibson shipped only one sunburst
ES-350T and one blonde ES-350TN in 1955. Gibson ink
stamped the factory order number on guitars early during the
production process, while serial numbers were assigned after
the guitar was finished and ready for shipment. The spruce top,
'T' designation (instead of the 'TD' designation Gibson used later
in 1956), and 1955 factory order number suggest that this may
be one of the earliest ES-350T guitars that Gibson produced.

ERIC This is one that I regret
selling. It was well used.

Gigs:
1994-5 From
The Cradle Tour
Oct. 3, 1994-
Oct. 13, 1995

I'LL PLAY FOR YOU

Serial No: A32333
Factory Order No: S1765 29
Body: Double cutaway thinline semi-hollow, maple, f-holes, maple centre block, sunburst finish
Neck: Mahogany, 22 frets, bound rosewood fingerboard with dot inlays
Headstock: Crown peghead inlay
Bridge: Nickel-plated Tune-o-matic with stop tailpiece
Pickguard: Black five-ply (black/white/black/white/black)
Pickups: Two humbucking
Controls: Two volume, two tone
Switches: Three-position pickup selector
Case: Brown hardshell contour case with pink plush lining and handwritten tie-on label 'Gibson. ES. 335 "Dot" '60. Sunburst. Ser. #A.32333' and adhesive paper label similarly inscribed

The sunburst finish Gibson ES-335TD is the most common version of the original dot neck ES-335 model. Gibson produced about 1,900 ES-335TD guitars between 1958 and 1962, compared to about 1,000 cherry finish ES-335TDC guitars between 1960 and 1962 and only 209 blonde finish ES-335TDN guitars, which were only made from 1958 until 1960.

Although Clapton's blonde 1959 ES-335TDN (page 247) is more collectible than this ES-335TD, he preferred the tone of this instrument and played it frequently on stage. During the From The Cradle Tour, he often used the guitar to perform the songs 'Third Degree', 'Reconsider Baby' and 'Sinner's Prayer'.

Gigs:
1994-5 From The Cradle Tour
Oct. 3, 1994-
Oct. 13, 1995

Madison Square Garden
New York, USA
Oct. 1995

ERIC One for each song...

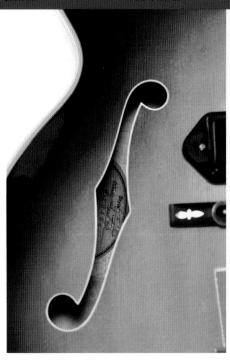

Serial No: A 22494
Factory Order No: V 2798 8
Body: Maple back and sides, spruce top, ivoroid binding, single round Venetian cutaway, sunburst finish
Neck: Maple with mahogany centre strip, 20 frets, multi-bound ebony fingerboard with block inlays
Headstock: Multi-bound, pearl Gibson logo, flowerpot inlay
Bridge: Rosewood, gold-plated L-5 trapeze tailpiece with silver insert, Allen wrench tension adjustment hole, and engraved 'L5'
Pickguard: Multi-bound imitation tortoiseshell
Pickups: Two Alnico V single-coil
Controls: Two volume, two tone
Switches: Three-position pickup selector
Label: 'Style L-5-CES/ Gibson Guitar/Number A-22494 is hereby/ Guaranteed/against faulty workmanship and materials./Gibson Inc/ Kalamazoo Michigan,/U.S.A.'
Case: Period hardshell case with adhesive tape inscribed 'Gibson '56 L5/S. Burst Alnicos/#22494'

Gibson introduced two flagship electric archtop guitar models in 1951 – the Super 400CES and the L-5CES. Both models were essentially identical to Gibson's archtop acoustic Super 400C and L-5C guitars with the exception of the pickups, switches and controls. Initially Gibson offered the L-5CES with P-90 single-coil pickups, but in late 1953 they introduced a second variant with stronger Alnico V magnet single-coil pickups.

This guitar was a spare for the blonde L-5CES that was one of Clapton's main guitars on his From The Cradle Tour.

ERIC **This is another guitar that I regret selling. It's stunning.**

I love those Alnico pickups, they are the best studio pickups... my favourites for when you want that rich blues sound. In the live situation they're just a little bit more difficult to manage than the humbucking pickups. They don't have the same kind of fluidity, in terms of the left hand, because their set-up has a different playability. At some point, when you get to the volume you need – and given that the rest of the band are playing fairly loud – the feedback is pretty uncontrollable at the bottom end. But in a studio, where you're playing in much more easily managed dynamics, they're the best-sounding pickups in the world for me.

Playlist:
From The Cradle, 1994
Me and Mr Johnson, 2004
Gigs:
Spare on 1994-5
From The Cradle Tour
Oct. 3, 1994-
Oct. 13, 1995
Spare on 2001
Reptile Tour
Feb. 3-Dec. 15, 2001

Opposite:
NBC Television Studio 8H
Rockefeller Plaza
New York, USA
Sept. 24, 1994

Eric Clapton performs with a sunburst Gibson on *Saturday Night Live.* Andy Fairweather Low is playing an L-5 similar to this model.

I'LL PLAY FOR YOU

LOT 5 CHRISTIE'S 1999

Serial No: A35535
Body: Double cutaway thinline semi-hollow, maple, f-holes, maple centre block, natural finish
Neck: Mahogany, 22 frets, bound rosewood fingerboard with dot inlays
Headstock: Crown peghead inlay
Bridge: Chrome-plated Tune-o-matic with stop tailpiece
Pickguard: Black five-ply (black/white/black/white/black)
Pickups: Two humbucking
Controls: Two volume and two tone
Switches: Three-position pickup selector
Case: Black hardshell contour case with red plush lining and handwritten adhesive paper label 'Gibson '85 335 # A35535 Blonde Reissue'

Gibson produced only 209 ES-335 guitars with a natural (also known as 'blonde') finish and dot fingerboard inlays from 1958 until 1960. Due to demand and soaring prices on the vintage guitar market, Gibson introduced the ES-335 DOT reissue in 1982, which offered many of the same features as the original dot neck version.

This 1985 Gibson ES-335 DOT was a backup spare for the original 1959 ES-335 TDN (page 247) that Clapton played on the From The Cradle Tour.

Gigs:
Spare on 1994-5
From The Cradle Tour
Oct. 3, 1994-
Oct. 13, 1995

1985 GIBSON ES-335 DOT

LOT 48 CHRISTIE'S 1999

Serial No: A25591
Factory Order No: U 7131 1
Body: Maple back and sides, spruce top, bound thinline, single round Venetian cutaway, bound f-holes, sunburst finish
Neck: Two-piece maple with mahogany strip, 22 frets, bound ebony fingerboard with block inlays
Headstock: Multi-bound, pearl Gibson logo, flowerpot inlay
Bridge: Gold-plated Tune-o-matic with rosewood base, gold-plated triple-loop trapeze tailpiece
Pickguard: Multi-bound imitation tortoiseshell
Pickups: Two Alnico V single-coil
Controls: Two volume, two tone
Switches: Three-position pickup selector
Case: Brown hardshell contour case with pink plush lining and handwritten tie-on label 'Gibson Byrdland '57 Sunburst Alnicos Ser # A25591'

This 1957 Byrdland is almost identical to Clapton's 1956 Byrdland, although the finish has faded slightly more to give its colour a warm amber glow. Clapton purchased this guitar in Texas and played it during rehearsals. He also brought it on the From The Cradle Tour as a spare slide guitar.

ERIC I got this guitar in Texas and used it for rehearsing.

Gigs:
Spare on 1994-5
From The Cradle Tour
Oct. 3, 1994-
Oct. 13, 1995
Spare on 2001
Reptile Tour
Feb. 3-Dec. 15, 2001

254   1957 GIBSON BYRDLAND

I'LL PLAY FOR YOU

LOT 38 CHRISTIE'S 2004, LOT 74 BONHAMS 2011

Serial No: A 2597
Body: Maple back and sides, spruce top, ivoroid binding, single round Venetian cutaway, natural finish
Neck: Maple with mahogany centre strip, 20 frets, multi-bound rosewood fingerboard with block inlays
Headstock: Multi-bound, pre-war script Gibson logo, flowerpot inlay
Bridge: Rosewood, gold-plated L-5 trapeze tailpiece with silver insert, Allen wrench tension adjustment hole, and engraved 'L5'
Pickguard: Multi-bound imitation tortoiseshell
Pickups: Two Alnico V single-coil
Controls: Two volume, two tone
Switches: Three-position pickup selector
Label: 'Style L-5-P/Gibson Guitar/Number A-2597 is hereby/Guaranteed/against faulty workmanship and materials./Gibson Inc/Kalamazoo Michigan/U.S.A.'
Case: Original Gibson hardshell case and cover, case with adhesive tape inscribed 'Gibson 1948 - Proto-Alnico P 90/'48 L.5 #A2597'

This guitar is almost identical to the 1948 Premier discussed previously (page 238), but sometime after this guitar was built in 1948 a pair of Alnico V single-coil pickups, four volume and tone controls, and a three-position pickup selector were installed on the guitar. Because the placement of all of these parts matches that of the L-5CES, which Gibson introduced in 1951, the modifications likely took place at the Gibson factory. The Alnico V pickups with distinctive rectangular polepieces, which Gibson offered on the L-5CES only from late 1953 through 1957, suggest that the modifications may have been made during the mid 1950s.

Clapton acquired this guitar as a spare for his main L-5CES. He played it on *From The Cradle* and the subsequent tour. It was bought in the 2004 Crossroads auction, then generously donated to the 2011 auction by Shamir Deen.

ERIC I had two blondes in my collection. The grain on the top is a little bit more accentuated on this than on the one I didn't sell. There's not a lot to choose between the two of them; they both had plenty of use.

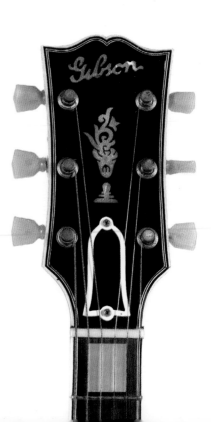

Playlist:
From The Cradle, 1994
Gigs:
1994-5 From The Cradle Tour
Oct. 3, 1994-
Oct. 13, 1995

LOT 27 CHRISTIE'S 1999

Serial No: T028
Body: Nickel-plated brass, grid pattern lattice upper body soundholes, three internal resonating cones with triangular-shaped cover plate and trapezoid and triangular mesh grilles, T-shaped handrest
Neck: Mahogany, 19 frets, bound ebony fingerboard with dot inlays
Headstock: Slotted, imitation mother-of-pearl overlay
Bridge: Maple, nickel-plated trapeze tailpiece
Case: Black hardshell contour case with red plush lining and adhesive paper label 'Beltona'

Gigs:
1994-5 From The Cradle Tour
Oct. 3, 1994-
Oct. 13, 1995

Steve Evans and Bill Johnson formed Beltona Resonator Instruments in 1990 in the UK with the goal of producing reproductions of classic resonator instruments with modern improvements that they developed themselves. Their first instruments were tri-cone models like this example, which were based on metal-body tri-cone guitars produced by National during the late 1920s and 30s.

Clapton purchased this guitar from Charlie Chandler while recording *From The Cradle* at Olympic Studios in London.

LOT 22 BONHAMS 2011

Body: Flame maple, grid pattern lattice upper body soundholes, three internal resonating cones with triangular-shaped cover plate and trapezoid and triangular mesh grilles, T-shaped handrest, sunburst finish
Neck: Flame maple, 19 frets, bound ebony fingerboard with dot inlays
Headstock: Slotted, ebony veneer, pearloid inlays
Bridge: Maple, nickel-plated trapeze tailpiece
Label: Signed and dated inside the body by Mark Lewis
Case: Black hardshell contour case with black plush lining, handwritten label

Mike Lewis originally was a cabinet maker until one day a friend asked him to build a guitar similar to a National tricone but with a body made of wood instead of metal. Lewis took on the task and was very pleased with the results, so decided to go into business making guitars. Lewis has enjoyed much success as a guitar maker, building resonator instruments in his Paris, France, workshop that are sold under the Fine Resophonic brand.

In 1995 when Clapton's From The Cradle Tour stopped in Paris, Clapton invited Lewis to come backstage before the concert. Lewis brought one of his first Model 1 Wood Body Triplate guitars, which he had made a few years earlier in 1992. In fact, this is the only Model 1 guitar Lewis ever made that has the 'Lewis' name on the headstock, as immediately after its completion he adopted the name Fine Resophonic. Clapton bought the guitar on the spot and used it to play a few songs during the remainder of the tour.

Gigs:
1994-5 From The Cradle Tour
Oct. 3, 1994-
Oct. 13, 1995

I'LL PLAY FOR YOU

Serial No: 40802437
Body: Maple back and sides, spruce top, single round cutaway, bound f-holes, natural finish
Neck: Maple, 20 frets, bound ebony fingerboard with block inlays
Headstock: Pearl 'vase' inlays engraved 'Designed by D'Aquisto'
Bridge: Ebony, ebony trapeze tailpiece
Pickguard: Bound ebony
Pickups: One humbucking
Controls: One volume, one tone
Tuners: Gold-plated, ebony buttons
Case: Black hardshell contour case with orange plush lining and handwritten tie-on label 'F. D'Aquisto Blonde 1 P.U. # 40802437'

James D'Aquisto was an apprentice to master archtop luthier John D'Angelico. After D'Angelico passed away in 1964, D'Aquisto produced guitars under his own name, carrying on D'Angelico's tradition of expert craftsmanship and meticulous attention to detail while developing his own innovations and designs. In 1984, D'Aquisto collaborated with Fender to produce affordable versions of his archtop jazz guitars, which were manufactured in Japan.

Fender gave this guitar to Eric in the mid 1980s, but it wasn't used on any of his albums until the late 1990s.

Playlist:
Retail Therapy, 1997
Pilgrim, 1998

ERIC As an experiment, Simon Climie and I tried to record an album of electronic dance music anonymously, under the name T.D.F. We felt we had a licence to explore because we were going to make music for a fashion show.

I used this guitar for a jazz number on *Retail Therapy* and on the *Pilgrim* album.

ON THE ROAD

Serial No: V006423
Body: Alder, black finish
Neck: Maple with skunk-stripe truss rod routing, 22 frets, maple fingerboard with dot inlays
Bridge: Blocked synchronised tremolo
Pickguard: White single-ply
Pickups: Three Gold Fender Lace Sensors
Controls: Master volume, two tone, TBX/MDX active circuitry
Switches: Five-position pickup selector with white switch tip
Case: Original hardshell contour case with adhesive tape inscribed '(L.Brks/Apollo) E.C. Custom Strat/ Blk. #V006423'

The idea for this guitar was conceived backstage during rehearsals for Clapton's appearance at New York's Apollo Theater on June 15th, 1993, when Clapton discussed a few modifications that he wanted to make to his signature model Stratocaster with Larry Brooks and John Page of the Fender Custom Shop. Brooks built this Eric Clapton Signature Model Strat in 1996. During this period the Fender Custom Shop made Eric several Strats without his signature on the headstock, although the stock production models retained that feature.

Clapton played this guitar frequently during the late 1990s. It was one of his main stage guitars on the Pilgrim Tour and was played on a number of significant appearances.

Opposite:
Clapton playing this guitar on the USA leg of the 1998 Pilgrim Tour.

ERIC I think the changes were to the neck and some finishing. I liked it; it got my approval.

Gigs:
1998 Pilgrim Tour
Mar. 30-Dec. 11, 1998
A Very Special Christmas at The White House (TV)
The White House, Washington, USA
Dec. 17, 1998
Central Park in Blue: Sheryl Crow & Friends (TV)
Central Park
New York, USA
Sept. 14, 1999
The Concert of The Century for VH1 Save The Music Campaign (TV)
The White House
Washington, USA
Oct. 23, 1999
1999 Japan Tour
Nov. 9-30, 1999
Highlight:
Eric Clapton & Friends for Crossroads Centre Antigua
Madison Square Garden
New York, USA
June 30, 1999

Serial No: EC1
Body: Alder, 23-carat gold leaf with clear polyester finish
Neck: Maple with skunk-stripe truss rod routing, 22 frets, maple fingerboard with dot inlays, neck plate engraved 'EC1/Fender 50th/Anniversary'
Bridge: Blocked gold-plated synchronised tremolo
Pickguard: White single-ply, dated '10-15-96' on underside
Pickups: Three Gold Fender Lace Sensors
Controls: Master volume, two tone, TBX/MDX active circuitry
Switches: Five-position pickup selector with white switch tip
Case: Original hardshell case with adhesive tape inscribed 'gold leaf 50th Anniv/Fender-Strat #E.C.1'

In 1996, Fender celebrated the company's 50th anniversary by making a variety of special edition guitars. Of all the Fender 50th Anniversary Strats that Fender made in 1996 (not to be confused with the guitars Fender made in 2004 in celebration of the Stratocaster's 50th anniversary), none of them can top this rare example covered with genuine 23-carat gold leaf. Clapton came up with the idea for the gold leaf Strat, and only three examples were made – one for Clapton, one for his 'number one fan', and one for Fender CEO Bill Schultz.

Fender Custom Shop master builder Mark Kendrick made this gold leaf Strat, which was delivered to Clapton at The Complex Theater in Hollywood, California, in late 1996. It was Clapton's main stage guitar in 1997, and he played it frequently during recording sessions and special concert appearances, including the Music for Montserrat concert at London's Royal Albert Hall on September 15th, 1997, where he used it on the songs 'The Same Old Blues' and 'Hey Jude' with an all-star line up that included Phil Collins, Elton John, Mark Knopfler, Paul McCartney and Sting. It was also Eric's main Strat on his *Pilgrim* album and a backup guitar for his 1998 Pilgrim Tour.

Playlist:
B.B. King: *Deuces Wild* 1997
Pilgrim, 1998
Gigs:
Legends 1997 Jazz Festival Tour
July 3-17, 1997
1997 Far East Tour
Oct. 9-31,1997
1998 Pilgrim Tour
Mar. 30-Dec. 11, 1998
Highlight:
Music for Montserrat Benefit Concert
Royal Albert Hall
London, UK
Sept. 15, 1997

ERIC This got played a lot, all over the place. It was exactly what I thought it would be. The only reason I stopped playing it is that sometimes guitars require too much attention, or they stop being working tools. I've always just reverted to guitars that can sublimate themselves to the work. I've worked with Crash graffiti guitars (page 306), which are quite elaborate, but they're not as ornate as this.

There's one guy, my number one fan, in a great restaurant I go to in Tokyo. He asked Fender to make a copy of it. They said they only would if I gave permission, so there is another one.

Opposite:
Eric Clapton playing this guitar, which was used as the main stage instrument for his tour of Japan and Korea in 1997.

ERIC A lovely, beautiful guitar.
I wanted that kind of gesso look.

LOT 70 CHRISTIE'S 1999

1989 FENDER STRATOCASTER ERIC CLAPTON SIGNATURE MODEL

Serial No: SE926567
Body: Alder, custom gold sparkle finish with airbrush snow leopard and scenery
Neck: Maple with skunk-stripe truss rod routing, 22 frets, maple fingerboard with dot inlays. Custom Shop neckplate.
Bridge: Blocked synchronised tremolo
Pickguard: White single-ply
Pickups: Three Gold Fender Lace Sensors
Controls: Master volume, two tone, TBX active circuitry
Switches: Five-position pickup selector with white switch tip
Case: Tweed rectangular hardshell case with red plush lining and handwritten adhesive paper label 'Fender Strat. #S.E.926567 "Snow Leopard" White & Gold E.C.Model'

This signature model Stratocaster with an unusual Asian-inspired custom finish is somewhat of a mystery: Clapton says that he has no recollection of how, or why, he acquired the guitar.

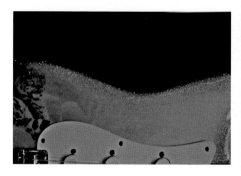

LOT 50 CHRISTIE'S 1999

1994 FENDER STRATOCASTER 40TH ANNIVERSARY CONCERT EDITION

Body: Alder, wine red finish, gold-plated metal tremolo engraved back plate cover
Neck: Birdseye maple with skunk-stripe truss rod routing, 21 frets, maple fingerboard with dot inlays, engraved neck plate
Headstock: Printed transfer 'Custom Shop F USA' on back
Bridge: Blocked synchronised tremolo
Pickguard: White single-ply
Pickups: Three single-coil
Controls: One volume, two tone
Additional: Gold-plated tremolo arm and bridge cover, strap, lead and Fender certificate
Case: Tweed rectangular hardshell case with red plush lining, handwritten label 'Fender Red Strat. Dark Blood – 40th Anniv Ltd Edit #11-of 40'

In 1994 Fender celebrated the 40th anniversary of the Stratocaster by offering a variety of limited-edition instruments, but the 'Concert Edition' model, produced to also celebrate the *Curves, Contours and Body Horns* documentary, is the rarest 40th anniversary Strat model they made that year. Only 40 of these guitars were made, and most were presented to Fender VIPs like Clapton.

ERIC I played this guitar at home.

Serial No: 7070
Body: Rosewood back and sides, cedar top, boxwood binding with abalone purfling, natural finish
Neck: Mahogany, 20 frets, ebony fingerboard with abalone 'leaf' inlays
Headstock: Lowden logo inlaid in pearl
Bridge: Rosewood pinless bridge
Soundhole: Abalone inlaid rosette
Case: Original hardshell case with adhesive tape inscribed 'Auction #42/ Lowden O-38'

Madison Square Garden
New York, USA
Feb. 26, 1997

Eric Clapton and Babyface pictured performing 'Change The World' at the Grammy Awards.

At 18, George Lowden says that he fancied himself as 'Ireland's answer to Eric Clapton and Jimi Hendrix'. Soon, however, he realised that he was better at making guitars than playing them, and in 1973 he decided to pursue a professional career as a luthier. By 1980 demand for his guitars had grown to the point where he had his instruments manufactured in Japan, but in 1985 he decided to move production back to Northern Ireland. Lowden developed a reputation as a builder of fine steel-string acoustics with balanced tone, lush resonance, and sweet harmonic overtones that are particularly beloved by fingerstyle Celtic music players.

Irish singer-songwriter Paul Brady gave Clapton this guitar as a gift. Clapton played it during the 39th Grammy Awards ceremony at Madison Square Garden on February 27th, 1997, performing 'Change The World' with producer Kenneth 'Babyface' Edmonds. Clapton won two awards for the song that evening – 'Record of the Year' and 'Best Male Pop Vocal Performance' – and its songwriters Gordon Kennedy, Wayne Kirkpatrick and Tommy Simms took home the 'Song of the Year' award. Clapton also won a 'Best Rock Instrumental Performance' Grammy that night along with Robert Cray, Buddy Guy, Dr. John, B.B. King, Art Neville, Bonnie Raitt and Jimmie Vaughan for 'SRV Shuffle'.

Playlist:
Pilgrim, 1997
Highlight:
1997 Grammy Awards
Madison Square Garden
New York, USA
Feb. 26, 1997

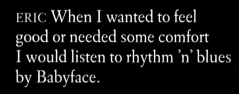

ERIC When I wanted to feel good or needed some comfort I would listen to rhythm 'n' blues by Babyface.

This is a beautiful guitar with a great tone. Look at the wood – it's fabulous. This was used all the way through *Pilgrim*, on every track virtually.

LOT 51 CHRISTIE'S 2004

Serial No: 49808
Body: Mahogany with maple top, natural finish
Neck: Mahogany, 22 frets, rosewood fingerboard with shell inlays
Headstock: Terry C. McInturff logo, wooden truss rod cover, back inscribed 'Custom made/-for-/Eric Clapton/April 1998/Terry C. McInturff'
Bridge: Gold-plated Tune-o-matic with stop tailpiece
Pickups: Two humbucking with gold-plated covers, one single-coil
Controls: One volume, one tone
Switches: Five-position pickup selector
Additional: Original warranty card registered to the name of Eric Clapton and an unopened letter from Terry C. McInturff Guitars addressed to Eric Clapton
Case: Original hardshell case with adhesive tape

Terry McInturff started building guitars in 1977 while he was attending the Roberto-Venn School of Luthiery. Over the next two decades he worked as a repairman, restoring vintage Epiphone, Gibson, Martin and Washburn guitars, and as a master craftsman for several guitar companies, including Hamer. In 1996 he formed TCM Guitars in North Carolina, where he leads a small workshop of highly skilled craftsmen that manufacture high-end electric solidbody guitars.

McInturff personally made this custom TCM Glory Standard guitar for Clapton in 1998. He presented the guitar to Eric after one of Eric's concert appearances in North Carolina that year.

LOT 69 CHRISTIE'S 1999

Serial No: Custom No.11
Body: Steel, chrome finish, single cutaway
Neck: Birdseye maple, mauve finish, 24 frets, ebony fingerboard with dot inlays
Pickguard: Chrome-plated steel, engraved 'CORIDA Paris-Zenith 3 & 4 Mars. 1990'
Pickups: Three Lace Sensors
Controls: One volume, one tone
Switches: Three-position pickup selector
Bridge: Stamped steel baseplate, six adjustable saddles, engraved 'ashtray' bridge baseplate cover
Additional: Black strap
Case: Tweed rectangular hardshell case with orange plush lining and handwritten tie-on label 'E.C. James Trussart Chrome Body Custom Telecaster #11' and adhesive paper label inscribed 'James Trussart Custom Made For E.C. Chrome – Tele Deville # 11'

James Trussart started making his distinctive hollow steel-body guitars in Paris, France, during the 1980s. His guitars are based on classic Fender and Gibson designs with a little inspiration from National and Dobro resonator guitars as well. His instruments feature unorthodox finishes from weathered-looking 'rust-o-matic' finishes, which involve actual rust ageing, to flashy chrome-plating like that on this Steel Deville that he made in 1990 and gave to Clapton as a gift when he visited Paris.

264

ON THE ROAD

LOT 25 BONHAMS 2011

Serial No: 049907045
Body: Masonite over plywood frame, Turquoise Metalflake finish
Neck: Maple, 21 frets, rosewood fingerboard with dot inlays
Headstock: Back of headstock signed by Eric Clapton in silver felt pen
Bridge: Adjustable with six metal saddles
Pickguard: White single-ply
Pickups: Three 'lipstick tube' cylindrical-shaped single-coil
Controls: One concentric volume/tone
Switches: Six-position 'Selectomatic' pickups selector, 'Blow' (all pickups on) on/off
Additional: Cardboard box with handwritten label

The original Danelectro company shuttered its doors in 1969, but in the late 1990s the Evets Corporation purchased the rights to the Danelectro name and started producing a line of guitars based on their original models. The DC-3 was one of the first guitars that the company offered, with production lasting from 1998 until 2001. The DC-3 was not a reissue but rather a new model that was based on the double cutaway shorthorn guitars that Danelectro originally made between 1958 and 1969. The DC-3 most closely resembled Danelectro's 6036/6037/6038 models, but instead of having three sets of concentric volume/tone controls (one set for each pickup), it featured a new six-position 'Selectomatic' pickup selector and 'Blow' on/off switch that engaged all three pickups at once while bypassing the 'Selectomatic' settings. Danelectro gave this guitar to Clapton in the 1990s.

LATE 1990s DANELECTRO DC-3

LOT 5 BONHAMS 2011

Serial No: 2629360
Covering: Beige, oxblood speaker cloth
Speakers: One 8-inch
Switches: Power on/off
Controls: Overdrive, level, bass, middle, treble
Inputs: One
Outputs: Headphone
Additional: Amp signed on the back by Eric Clapton in black felt pen, original cardboard box

The 15-watt Honeytone HT-50 was one of several solid-state amps that Danelectro introduced during the late 1990s. Knowing that Clapton often used small amps in the studio, Danelectro also sent this amp to Clapton as a gift.

LATE 1990s DANELECTRO HONEYTONE HT-50 AMPLIFIER

LOT 48 BONHAMS 2011

Serial No: 002098
Body: Mahogany, ash top, bound, sunburst finish
Neck: Mahogany, 22 frets, bound rosewood fingerboard with abalone dot inlays and 'EC' inlaid at 12th fret
Headstock: Rosewood veneer, abalone vertical 'Rowan' inlay, signed by Eric Clapton
Bridge: Gold-plated Gotoh strings-through-body tailpiece with six adjustable saddles
Pickups: Four Lace Sensor single-coil set up as two humbuckers
Controls: One volume, two tone, Musitech mid-range booster circuitry
Switches: Five-position pickup selector
Additional: Certificate of Authenticity and manufacturer's warranty
Case: Tweed rectangular hardshell case with brown plush lining, label inscribed 'Custom Handmade in Texas'

Michael Rowan of Garland, Texas, started building guitars as a hobby in 1996, but thanks to encouraging feedback he received from guitarists that he showed his instruments to, he decided to go into business as a full-time luthier. This guitar is one of the first Journeyman models that Rowan made. Rowan gave this guitar to Clapton on May 22nd, 1998, when Clapton was in Dallas, Texas, to play a concert at Reunion Arena.

1998 MICHAEL ROWAN JOURNEYMAN

LOT 4 CHRISTIE'S 1999

Serial No: EC 98-2
Body: Ash with flamed maple top, sunburst finish
Neck: Maple with skunk-stripe truss rod routing, 22 frets, maple fingerboard with dot inlays, Custom Shop neckplate
Bridge: Blocked synchronised tremolo
Pickguard: White single-ply
Pickups: Three Gold Fender Lace Sensors
Controls: Master volume, two tone, TBX active circuitry
Switches: Five-position pickup selector with white switch tip
Case: Black hardshell contour case with black plush lining and handwritten adhesive paper label 'Red Flametop E.C. Fender-Strat. #E.C.-98-2'

Fender Custom Shop Senior Master Builder J.W. Black made several fancy custom variations of Clapton's Signature Model Stratocaster during the late 1990s, including this example with a flamed maple top and vibrant cherry sunburst finish. Eric played this guitar occasionally but sold it at the 1999 Christie's auction about a year after he received it.

1998 FENDER STRATOCASTER ERIC CLAPTON SIGNATURE MODEL

266

Body: Copper back and sides engraved with figure of a knight in a landscape with a castle and inscriptions 'To Eric, best wishes/From Brian Knight' and 'Excalibur', mahogany top, natural finish
Neck: Mahogany, 20 frets, ebony fingerboard with custom inlays
Headstock: Bound, 'Coppertone' logo, knight helmet inlay, two half-moon cutouts
Bridge: Rosewood pin bridge, pearl inlays
Case: Case with adhesive tape inscribed 'Brian Knight AC 6/ Coppertone #none'

Brian Knight (1939-2001) was a singer, slide guitarist and harmonica player who served an early role in Britain's burgeoning blues-rock scene during the early 1960s. He formed a band with Brian Jones, Geoff Bradford, Ian Stewart and Dick Taylor that broke up when Jones teamed up with Mick Jagger and Keith Richards to form The Rolling Stones. After that Knight and Bradford formed Blues By Six with drummer Charlie Watts, performing at London clubs like the Marquee and 100 Club and backing touring American bluesmen when they performed in the UK. Knight temporarily stopped making music in 1966 but returned to the blues circuit in the early 1970s and recorded several albums for independent labels during the 1980s and 90s.

The story of this guitar is a mystery. A similar jumbo six-string acoustic with the same distinctive body and headstock shapes appears on the cover of Knight's 1988 album *Good Time Down The Road*, but it has a different finish, fingerboard inlays, bridge and soundhole design, and the peghead is completely solid, unlike the guitar here which has two cutouts. Whether this guitar was originally made for Knight and later engraved with Knight's message to Clapton, or commissioned by Knight as a gift for Clapton is unknown. It's also unknown if the 'Coppertone' name on the headstock refers to the guitar's maker or the unorthodox copper body materials, which apparently are inspired by a resonator guitar's design.

Serial No: 108218
Body: Rosewood back and sides, spruce top, natural finish
Neck: Mahogany, 20 frets, ebony fingerboard with dot inlays
Headstock: Solid
Bridge: Ebony 'belly' pin bridge
Pickguard: Imitation tortoiseshell
Case: Later circa 1968 hardshell case stencilled in white 'MEL TAYLOR' and with adhesive tape inscribed 'Auction #32/D-28 Acoustic'

By 1934 the design of Martin's dreadnought guitars transformed to a 14-fret neck and a body with squared-off shoulders. Martin dreadnought models with this design, like the D-18 and D-28, quickly became Martin's most popular models. This style of dreadnought is the most copied flat-top steel-string acoustic guitar design. The 14-fret Martin D-28 with a Brazilian rosewood body and herringbone purfling that Martin produced until early 1947, when it exhausted its supply of German herringbone trim, is the most desirable version of the D-28. Some collectors feel that this 1948 example was produced a year too late, but it is still a fine instrument for both players and collectors.

This D-28 appears in a photograph that was used for the cover of the 'Pilgrim' CD single released in the UK. Clapton also played this guitar on stage at the September 15th, 1997, Music for Montserrat concert at London's Royal Albert Hall to perform 'Broken Hearted'. Ventures drummer Mel Taylor previously owned this guitar, which was sold to Clapton by Fat Rick's Vintage Guitar Emporium on New King's Road in Fulham.

Playlist:
Pilgrim, 1998
Gigs:
Music for Montserrat Benefit Concert
Royal Albert Hall London, UK
Sept. 15, 1997
Highlight:
'Broken Hearted'

Opposite:
Royal Albert Hall London, UK
Sept. 15, 1997

Clapton playing 'Broken Hearted' on this guitar at Music For Montserrat.

ERIC This guitar belonged to one of The Ventures.

Body: Rosewood back and sides, spruce top, natural finish
Neck: Cedar, 19 frets, ebony fingerboard
Headstock: Slotted
Bridge: Rosewood tie bridge
Pickguard: Transparent protective golpeador plate
Rosette: Multi-coloured marquetry
Label: 'Constructor/de Guitars/José Ramírez/Conceptión/Jerónima, No.2/1882 Madrid/1992/No.11-145/F656-PA/Clase 1a.'
Case: Hardshell case with adhesive tape inscribed 'Auction #47/Ramirez Flam' [sic]

José Ramírez established a guitar-making workshop in Madrid in 1890. His grandson, José Ramírez III, became the shop's supervisor in 1957 and developed several innovations that improved the guitar's volume output and clarity, such as longer scale lengths, a larger sound box, asymmetrical bracing and new finishing techniques. Numerous guitar makers were inspired by or imitated these innovations, which are considered standards of classical guitar construction today. Andrés Segovia was one of many performers who played José Ramírez III guitars on the concert stage.

Clapton purchased this guitar in London in 1992.

Playlist:
Pilgrim, 1998
Other 1990s recordings

ERIC This was used a lot, on just about everything. It was the first Ramírez I ever had. Once I got onto the pure flamenco guitars I didn't look back really. But this was on *Pilgrim* and every record after it in the Nineties. It's a great guitar... fantastic.

Opposite (above): Clapton is pictured playing this guitar during rehearsals for his 1998 Pilgrim Tour.

Opposite (below): He was pictured with the same guitar for a promotional shoot on Oct. 2, 2000.

LOT 35 CHRISTIE'S 2004

Serial No: 91287001
Body: Maple back and sides, spruce top, ivoroid binding, sunburst finish
Neck: Maple, 19 frets, bound ebony fingerboard with block inlays
Headstock: Multi-bound, pearl 'The Gibson' logo, pearl flowerpot inlay, black three-ply truss rod cover (black/white/black)
Bridge: Rosewood with triangular inlays, gold-plated trapeze tailpiece
Pickguard: Multi-bound imitation tortoiseshell
Label: 'Style Guitar/ Gibson '34 L-5/Number 91287001 is hereby/ Guaranteed/against faulty workmanship and materials./Gibson Custom/Nashville Tennessee,/U.S.A.'
Case: Hardshell case with adhesive tape inscribed 'Gibson Lloyd Loar '34 reissue/L.5. '34 Custom Shop'

In late 1934, Gibson increased the size of the L-5's body width from 16 inches to 17 inches and replaced the top's internal parallel bracing with X-bracing, resulting in an archtop with a bold, commanding voice suited to the big band era. Many collectors call this version the 'advanced' L-5 to distinguish it from its Lloyd Loar-designed 16-inch body predecessor. The Gibson Custom Shop reissued the L-5, built to 1934 specifications, in the mid 1990s as part of its Historical Collection, paying tribute to one of the most influential modern archtop guitar designs. Thanks to Gibson's modern serial number system we can determine that this guitar was completed on May 8th, 1997.

Clapton admired this guitar's authentic details. He played this guitar on several tracks on his *Pilgrim* album.

Playlist:
Pilgrim, 1998

ERIC This is a beautiful guitar. The detail on the inlays, machine heads, and so on is wonderful.

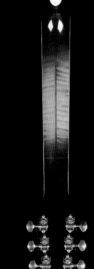

Body: Rosewood back and sides, spruce top, five-ply binding, natural finish
Neck: Walnut, 21 frets plus zero fret at nut, ebony fingerboard with dot inlays
Headstock: Slotted, Dupont logo stamp
Bridge: Ebony 'moustache' floating bridge, brass trapeze tailpiece
Soundhole: 'Petite bouche'-style oval
Label: 'Maurice Dupont/Luthier/20, Port-Boutiers/16100 Cognac (France)/Modèle MD 30 Date Oct 1995'
Additional: Original dealer's price tag and two letters, undated, to Eric Clapton with text pertaining to the setup and adjustment of the guitar, signed 'Fred' (Walecki)
Case: Hardshell case with adhesive tape inscribed 'Auction #5/Dupont/ Maca 'f' Style'

In 1986, Maurice Dupont made his first copy of a Selmer Modèle Jazz like the guitar that Django Reinhardt played. Today he makes a variety of guitars in his workshop in Cognac, France, including several models that Selmer enthusiasts consider the most accurate and faithful recreations of Selmer's original guitars.

Clapton purchased this guitar in 1995 from vintage guitar dealer Fred Walecki at Westwood Music in Los Angeles, California. Although Clapton hoped to find an original Selmer Modèle Jazz guitar, he settled for the next best alternative when he was unable to find a Selmer that met his liking. Selmer made only about 600 Modèle Jazz guitars (in both the early D-hole and later 'petite bouche' oval-hole styles) so demand is very high, especially since the collectors and players who own one rarely part with them. Clapton used his Dupont Modèle MD-30 to record a few overdubs on his *Pilgrim* album.

Playlist:
Pilgrim, 1998

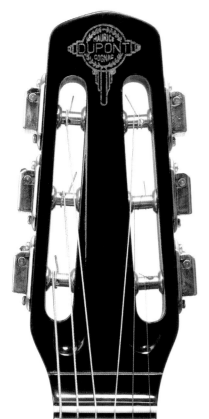

ERIC This came from LA. It would have been bought out of my love for Django Reinhardt and Gypsy guitar playing.

Body: Rosewood back and sides, spruce top, ivoroid binding with herringbone purfling and herringbone back stripe, nickel-plated cover plate with four fan-shaped cut-outs, two upper bout soundhole grilles, three soundholes under fingerboard, natural finish
Neck: Mahogany, round, 19 frets, bound ebony fingerboard with dot inlays
Headstock: Solid, Dobro logo decal
Bridge: 'Spider' with maple saddles, nickel-plated trapeze tailpiece
Case: Original hardshell case with adhesive tape inscribed 'Wood Body Dobro'

During the 1930s the Dobro Manufacturing Company sold metal resonators to the Regal Musical Instrument Company of Chicago. In exchange, Regal supplied Dobro with wood bodies that Dobro used to make some of their guitar models. When Dobro moved their factory from Los Angeles to Chicago in 1936, Regal made the majority of the bodies used for Dobro's wood-body guitars, and by August of 1937 Regal gained exclusive rights to manufacture Dobro instruments.

Regal made this custom Dobro, which resembles the Dobro Model 45, sometime during the late 1930s. The most unusual features of this guitar are its rosewood body and herringbone purfling and backstripe, which were inspired by Martin's Style 28 guitars. The shape of the peghead, which has a distinct peaked curve instead of a smooth arc, is also a feature commonly found on Regal's high-end instruments during this time. The number of Dobros that Regal made with these features is unknown.

Clapton purchased this rare Dobro sometime during the late 1990s. He used it to play Robert Johnson's 'Ramblin' On My Mind' at The Concert of the Century held at the White House on October 23rd, 1999, and brought it on the Japan leg of his Pilgrim Tour in November 1999 to perform the same song. He also played it during several recording sessions between 1999 and 2004.

Gigs:
The Concert of The Century for VH1 Save The Music Campaign
The White House
Washington, USA
Oct. 23, 1999
1999 Japan Tour
Nov. 9-30, 1999
Highlight:
Robert Johnson's 'Ramblin' On My Mind'

Opposite:
The Concert of The Century for VH1 Save The Music Campaign
The White House
Washington, USA
Oct. 23, 1999

LOT 6 CHRISTIE'S 1999

Serial No: 571028
Body: Indian Rosewood back and sides with herringbone purfling, Sitka spruce top, natural finish
Neck: Mahogany, 20 frets, ebony fingerboard with slotted-diamond inlays
Bridge: Ebony 'belly' pin bridge
Pickguard: Imitation tortoiseshell
Case: Black hardshell contour case with green plush lining and handwritten adhesive paper label 'Martin. OM-28 #571028'

The OM-28 was Martin's first Orchestra Model guitar and first model with a neck that met the body at the 14th fret – a specification requested by plectrum banjo player Perry Bechtel, who wanted a six-string guitar with additional frets clear of the body. Produced from 1929 until 1933 when the model's designation was changed to 000-28, the OM-28 is considered the first modern flat-top steel string guitar.

Clapton recorded several songs on his *Pilgrim* album with this 1996 OM-28 VR, a reissue model Martin started producing in 1990 based on the original, vintage OM-28.

Playlist:
Pilgrim, 1998

ERIC This guitar had a fabulous sound. I found it hard to part with this one.

LOT 33 CHRISTIE'S 1999

Serial No: EK-8816
Body: Mahogany back and sides, spruce top, checker binding, f-holes, sunburst finish
Neck: Mahogany, 19 frets, rosewood fingerboard with dot inlays
Bridge: Rosewood, nickel-plated trapeze tailpiece
Pickguard: Bound imitation tortoiseshell
Additional: Multi-coloured string/strap
Case: Brown softshell contour case with brown felt lining and handwritten adhesive paper label '1938 – Bound Check Body S.Burst F.Holes Gibson-Kalamazoo 8816'

Gibson debuted their 'budget' brand Kalamazoo guitars during the Great Depression. The KG-32, introduced in 1939, was Kalamazoo's top-of-the-line archtop model, and it possessed many similar attributes to the Gibson L-50 of this era, including the 'open book' headstock shape, which was a signature Gibson characteristic.

Clapton purchased this guitar in Memphis, Tennessee, primarily for collecting purposes. He says that the guitar was in the studio when he was recording his *Pilgrim* album; however it is unknown whether he actually played it on any tracks.

ERIC This was around during the *Pilgrim* sessions.

Playlist:
Pilgrim, 1998

1996 MARTIN OM-28 VR

1997 FENDER STRATOCASTER ERIC CLAPTON SIGNATURE MODEL

EST: $4,000 – $6,000   PRICE: $16,730

LOT 81 CHRISTIE'S 2004

Serial No: 7950067
Body: Alder, custom black finish with VW logo
Neck: Maple with skunk-stripe truss rod routing, 22 frets, maple fingerboard with dot inlays
Bridge: Blocked synchronised tremolo
Pickguard: White single-ply
Pickups: Three Gold Fender Lace Sensors
Controls: Master volume, two tone, TBX/MDX active circuitry
Switches: Five-position pickup selector with white switch tip
Additional: Guitar output cable, owner's manual and manufacturer's 'hang tags' A large collection of promotional material from Eric Clapton's 1998 European and Japanese tours donated by Virginia Lohle
Case: Original hardshell tweed case with adhesive tape

When the Volkswagen Sound Foundation (a programme to promote aspiring musical talent) sponsored Eric's 1998 Pilgrim Tour, Fender produced a special run of Eric Clapton Signature Model Stratocasters with VW Sound Foundation logo graphics. Most of these guitars were given to VIPs after concert performances, but at the end of the tour Volkswagen presented one of the guitars to Clapton in appreciation of his support of the programme.

1997 FENDER STRATOCASTER ERIC CLAPTON SIGNATURE MODEL

1960 GIBSON ES-330TD

EST: $3,000 – $5,000   PRICE: $24,000

LOT 34 CHRISTIE'S 1999

Factory Order No: R 4560 32
Body: Maple, hollow thinline, double cutaway, f-holes, sunburst finish
Neck: Mahogany, 22 frets, bound rosewood fingerboard with dot inlays
Bridge: Nickel-plated Tune-o-matic, nickel-plated 'raised diamond' trapeze tailpiece
Pickguard: Black five-ply (black/white/black/white/black)
Pickups: Two P-90 single-coil
Controls: Two volume, two tone
Switches: Three-position pickup selector
Case: Black Guild hardshell contour case with grey plush lining and handwritten adhesive paper label 'Gibson ES 330TD '60 Sunburst 2 P90s Ser#4560-32'

When Gibson introduced the ES-330 in 1959, some guitarists viewed it as a budget version of the ES-335, although it actually has few features in common with that model. The biggest differences are its entirely hollow body, a neck that meets the body at the 17th fret instead of the 19th, and a pair of single-coil P-90 pickups instead of humbuckers. The ES-330 is almost identical to the Gibson-made Epiphone Casino introduced in 1961, which was a favourite of The Beatles.

Record producer John Porter gave this ES-330 to Eric as a gift after they worked together on Taj Mahal's 1996 album, *Phantom Blues*.

1960 GIBSON ES-330TD

LOT 9 CHRISTIE'S 1999

Serial No: 92285623
Body: Double cutaway thinline semi-hollow, maple, no f-holes, maple centre block, black finish
Neck: Maple, 22 frets, bound ebony fingerboard with block inlays
Headstock: Lucille inlay, gold-plated 'B.B. King' truss rod cover
Bridge: Gold-plated Tune-o-matic, TP-6 stop tailpiece with adjustable fine tuners
Pickguard: Imitation tortoiseshell pickguard signed in gold felt pen, 'B.B. King'
Pickups: Two humbucking with gold-plated covers
Controls: Two volume, two tone
Switches: Three-position pickup selector, six-position Vari-Tone
Case: Brown hardshell contour case with pink plush lining and handwritten label 'Gibson "Lucille" # 92285623 B.B. King signed'

The Gibson B.B. King Lucille model is based on Gibson's ES-355 model, which had been B.B. King's favourite guitar ever since he bought his first one in 1959. In 1980, Gibson introduced the B.B. King Custom, which was similar to King's ES-355 guitars except it had no f-holes. In 1988 Gibson renamed the B.B. King Custom as the B.B. King Lucille after the name that King has called his main guitars since 1949, when he was almost killed in a fire started by two men arguing over a woman named Lucille.

Clapton purchased this 1995 Gibson B.B. King Lucille model, featuring a pickguard autographed by King, at a charity auction in the mid 1990s for his personal collection.

ERIC There was a lot of talk about me collaborating with B.B.; we'd been friends for a long time and we'd always make reference to the fact that, one day, we must make a record together.

LOT 32 BONHAMS 2011

Serial No: 10579, Model 308A
Covering: Black Tolex, black speaker cloth
Plate: Lab Series logo
Speakers: Two 12-inch Fender
Switches: Bright (channel 1), bright (channel 2), compressor on/off, power on/off (rear panel)
Controls: Volume, bass, midrange, treble (channel 1); volume, bass, frequency, midrange, treble, six-position rotary multi-filter switch, reverb (channel 2); compressor, master
Inputs: Hi, lo (channel 1); hi, lo (channel 2), power amp (effects loop return)
Outputs: Speaker, preamp (effects loop send)
Footswitch inputs: Reverb

In the late 1970s, Norlin Music Inc. owned both Gibson and synthesiser manufacturer Moog. In 1977 Norlin introduced Lab Series guitar amplifiers, which were designed by Moog engineers and incorporated uncommon features that included a parametric midrange equaliser, multi-filter with six preset EQ settings, and built-in compressor. Although Lab Series amps were essentially Moog products, they were marketed by Gibson and sold primarily through Gibson dealers. Norlin discontinued the first series of Lab amps in 1979 and introduced the Gibson-branded Lab Series 2 amps, which were made for Gibson by Garnet, in 1980.

The 100-watt L5 combo featuring two 12-inch speakers is B.B. King's favourite amp. Although many guitarists –particularly those who play blues – disparage solid-state amps, the L5 caused many players to reconsider their attitudes thanks to its warm, robust tones and impressive volume output. This Lab Series L5 is a very early version featuring an uncommon copper-coloured control panel. Most Lab Series amps have black control panels. This example's 12-inch Fender speakers are not stock.

Left:
Café Au Go Go
New York, USA
Sept. 1967

B.B. King and Eric
Clapton jam with members
of the Paul Butterfield
Blues Band.

Below:
Apollo Theater
New York, USA
June 15, 1993

These photographs of
B.B. King with Clapton
show him playing a similar,
but not identical Gibson.

ERIC We sometimes had three, maybe four, guitarists on the floor, including B.B. and myself, and the drummer and bass player and keyboards and everything, and we were sitting opposite one another, singing live. Most of *Riding With The King* was done first, second take – absolutely live. There was very little to do in terms of mixing or putting the record together.

Serial No: 90697017
Body: Maple back and sides, spruce top, multiple-layer binding, bound f-holes, single round Venetian cutaway, sunburst finish
Neck: Maple, 20 frets, multiple-layer bound ebony fingerboard with block inlays
Headstock: Multiple-layer binding, pearl Gibson logo, flowerpot inlay, black three-ply (black/white/black) truss rod cover engraved 'Custom L-5'
Bridge: Gold-plated Tune-o-matic on ebony base with pearl inlays, gold-plated L-5 trapeze tailpiece with silver insert engraved 'Wes Montgomery', Allen wrench tension adjustment hole, and engraved 'L5'
Pickguard: Multi-bound imitation tortoiseshell
Pickups: Single humbucking with gold-plated cover
Controls: One volume, one tone
Label: 'Style: Wes Montgomery, Number: 90697017, is hereby Guaranteed against ...'
Case: Brown hardshell contour case with dark pink plush lining and pink satin dust cover

In 1963, jazz guitarist Wes Montgomery special-ordered a Gibson L-5CES with a single humbucking pickup in the neck position and a rounded Venetian cutaway (Gibson was making the L-5 with the pointed Florentine cutaway during this period). Later in the 1960s Gibson made Montgomery another two L-5CES guitars with these same specifications as well as a handful of similar custom instruments for customers who requested the features they saw on Montgomery's guitar. This model was Montgomery's main guitar, used to record the highly influential jazz records he made during the 1960s until his death in 1968.

To pay tribute to Montgomery, the Gibson Custom Shop introduced the Wes Montgomery L-5CES model built to the exact specifications that Montgomery requested in the 1960s. The Gibson Custom Shop still builds this model today.

Clapton used this Wes Montgomery L-5CES to record tracks for his *Reptile* album.

Opposite: Eric photographed with a similar L-5 on Jan. 8, 2001, during rehearsals for his Reptile Tour.

Playlist:
Reptile, 2001

ERIC *Reptile* is an electric
unplugged album! I used a Gibson
L-5. I just love that tone. The sound
and phrasing on the track 'Reptile'
comes a bit from Gilberto and a bit
from B.B. King – that woolly tone
he'll occasionally use. I wanted that
guitar to personify the album,
so I put it all over the record.

LOT 45 CHRISTIE'S 2004

Serial No: CS1 1280
Body: Mahogany with carved maple top, sunburst finish
Neck: Mahogany, 22 frets, bound rosewood fingerboard with crown inlays
Headstock: Pearl Gibson logo, 'Les Paul model' in gold paint, Gibson Custom Shop stamp on reverse
Bridge: Nickel-plated Tune-o-matic with stop tailpiece
Pickguard: White single-ply
Pickups: Two humbucking with nickel-plated covers
Controls: Two volume, two tone
Switches: Three-position pickup selector
Case: Original hardshell case with adhesive tape inscribed 'Auction #25/Hist Re-Issue/L Paul'

Clapton's use of a sunburst Gibson Les Paul Standard (page 52) on John Mayall's *Blues Breakers With Eric Clapton* album played a significant role in making the original 1958-60 Les Paul Standard one of the most desirable and collectible electric guitars ever. However, after recording that album Clapton rarely used a Les Paul Standard ever again, playing one for a brief spell with Cream and performing with one only on infrequent occasions ever since. One of those rare instances was Clapton's August 7th, 2001, concert in Portland, where he replaced his usual Fender Stratocaster with this 2001 Gibson Historical Collection Les Paul Standard to perform his set that night.

Gigs:
Rose Garden Arena
Portland, Oregon, USA
Aug. 7, 2001

ERIC On the Reptile Tour I changed from a Strat to a Gibson. A lot of the reason why was in my head. Sometimes I'll get a nostalgic yearning for something, or maybe the amps are giving me trouble. It's never the guitars, it's often the amp.

The combination of the Fender and this amp was not working, or it wasn't warm enough or something. The thing with Gibsons has always been their warmth. I'd go to them for the bottom end, the midrange and so on. Perhaps it was just my ears were tired, or I was tired, or I wanted a change.

Serial No: 040
Body: Alder, custom
iridescent purple/
blue DuPont
Chromalusion finish
Neck: Maple with
skunk-stripe truss rod
routing, 22 frets, maple
fingerboard with dot
inlays, neck plate
engraved 'Custom Shop/
USA', back of headstock
inscribed '040/
Todd Krause'
Bridge: Blocked
synchronised tremolo
Pickguard: White
single-ply
Pickups: Three Fender
Vintage Noiseless
single-coil
Controls: Master volume,
two tone
Switches: Five-position
pickup selector with white
switch tip
Case: Original case with
adhesive tape inscribed
'Fender C/Shop
Strat/'Rainbow Rod' #40'

In addition to being a European sports car enthusiast, Clapton also owns a variety of custom street rods built by Roy Brizio Street Rods of South San Francisco, California. When Brizio loaned his 1932 Ford Model B Roadster to the photo shoot for Clapton and B.B. King's *Riding With The King* album, Clapton became enamoured with the Ford's dazzling paint job, which transforms to different colours depending on the angle of view and the light hitting it. After the photo session, Clapton commissioned the Fender Custom Shop to make him a Stratocaster finished with the same DuPont Chromalusion paint that Brizio used on that deuce coupé. Fender Custom Shop master builder Todd Krause built the guitar.

Clapton played this Strat in the studio while recording *Reptile* and brought it on his 2001 tour as a backup guitar.

ERIC This is Brizio paint. It's the same colour as Roy Brizio's hot rod that we were driving for *Riding With The King*.

Playlist:
Reptile, 2001
Gigs:
2001 Reptile Tour
Feb. 3–Dec. 15, 2001

Serial No: 1511
Covering: Cream Tolex, oxblood speaker cloth
Speakers: Three Fender 10-inch V1030 ceramic
Switches: Fat, power on/off, standby
Controls: Dwell, mix, tone, volume, treble, bass, mid, speed, intensity
Inputs: Two
Outputs: Speaker, external speaker
Footswitch input: One
Other: Effects loop (send, return)

When Fender established its amplifier Custom Shop at the company's headquarters in Scottsdale, Arizona, in 1993 under the direction of Bruce Zinky (formerly of Matchless Amplifier Company), the initial goal allegedly was to build an amp that Fender would be proud to offer to Eric Clapton. The first amp that Zinky developed and Fender introduced later that year was the Vibro King, a 60-watt combo featuring an unusual 3x10 speaker configuration based on that of the 1954-60 Fender Bandmaster combo and a built-in tube-powered spring reverb circuit based on Fender's standalone Reverb Unit produced from 1961-66. Producing incredibly fat, rich, and warm clean tones and gorgeous, smooth reverb, the Vibro King was hailed by professional players and collectors alike as an instant classic that deserved a prominent place in history alongside the best amps Fender ever made.

Fender was indeed proud to offer the Vibro King to Clapton, who owned both this 1995 model and a 2001 model, which British amp tech Denis Cornell modified with a circuit that boosted the amps' midrange frequencies. Clapton started using the Vibro King on tour in 2001 when he needed an amp that provided a better match than his Fender Twins to the Vintage Noiseless pickups he was starting to use. Clapton was using the Vibro King as his main stage amp on August 17th and 18th, 2001, during his concerts at the Staples Center in Los Angeles, California, which were filmed and recorded for the live *One More Car, One More Rider* DVD and double album.

Playlist:
One More Car, One More Rider, 2002
Gigs:
2001 Reptile Tour
Feb. 3-Dec. 15, 2001
Highlight:
Staples Center
Los Angeles
California, USA
Aug. 17-18, 2001

Staples Center
Los Angeles
California, USA
Aug. 2001

Clapton is seen using these amps in the live video *One More Car, One More Rider*, recorded at the Staples Center concerts and released in Nov. 2002.

DOWN TO THE CROSSROADS

EST: $9,000 – $12,000   PRICE: $4,800

Serial No: 2752
Covering: Cream Tolex, oxblood speaker cloth, 'flat' Fender logo
Speakers: Three 10-inch Jensen alnico
Switches: Fat, power on/off, standby
Controls: Dwell, mix, tone, volume, treble, bass, mid, speed, intensity
Inputs: Two
Outputs: Speaker, external speaker
Footswitch input: One
Other: Effects loop (send, return)

Vibro King extension speaker cabinet
Serial No: CR-276981
Housing: Closed-back
Covering: Cream Tolex, oxblood speaker cloth
Speakers: Two 12-inch
Details: 'Flat' Fender logo

ERIC At the start of a tour there's the whole thing of actually playing, getting up on stage and getting your ears back. Developing that, being on stage; the space and volume and the balances of it all. The music will then start to fuel it, and it gains its own momentum, really.

Playlist:
One More Car, One More Rider, 2002
Gigs:
2001 Reptile Tour
Feb. 3–Dec. 15, 2001
Highlight:
Staples Center
Los Angeles
California, USA
Aug. 17–18, 2001

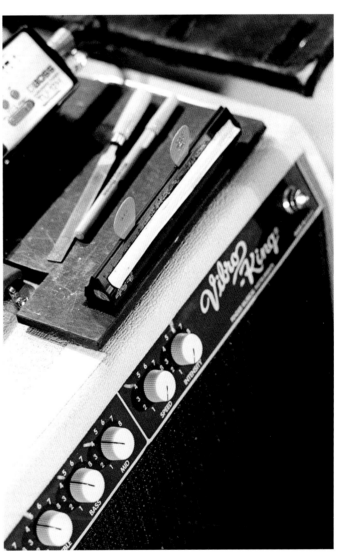

Clapton's amp photographed during rehearsals on Jan. 8, 2001.

Serial No:
M-2003-22-1169-A
Covering: Stitched cream
leather, grey speaker cloth
Logo: Black script Marshall
Speakers: Two Celestion
G12 T652 alnico
Switches: Power
on/off, standby
Controls: Speed, intensity,
presence, bass, middle,
treble, volume I, volume II
Inputs: Four
Other: Gold-plated
footswitch
Additional: In original
shipping carton with
documentation stating
'number 23 of 40'

The Marshall 1962JAG Limited Edition combo guitar amplifier resulted from a very special collaboration between two British icons – Marshall Amplification and Jaguar Cars Ltd – in celebration of Marshall's 40th anniversary. This amp, which essentially is a reproduction of the 45-watt Marshall 1962 (made in 1965 and 1966 – 1962 is just the model number) 2x12 'Bluesbreaker' combo that Clapton used to record John Mayall's *Blues Breakers With Eric Clapton* album, is distinguished by its gorgeous cream leather covering and detailed stitching – the same materials and craftsmanship featured in Jaguar cars. Other distinguishing features include the gold-plated control plate, screws, handle mounts, and footswitch and a specification plate featuring the Jaguar logo. Marshall made only 40 of these commemorative amps.

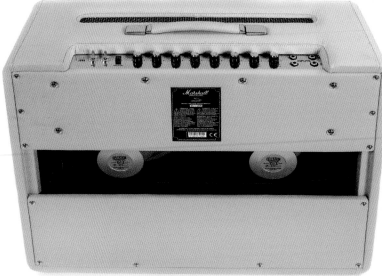

2005 FENDER BLUES JUNIOR

EST: $400 - $600   PRICE: $1,400

LOT 44 BONHAMS 2011

Serial No: B-256474
Covering: Black Tolex, silver speaker cloth
Plate: Fender
Speakers: One 12-inch Fender
Switches: Power on/off, fat
Controls: Reverb, master, middle, bass, treble, volume
Inputs: One
Footswitch input: Fat

Making its debut in 1995 – two years after Fender's Blues De Ville and Blues Deluxe models – the Blues Junior may have been the last Blues Series amp model that Fender introduced but it quickly became the line's most popular model. The Blues Junior has remained in continuous production while the Blues De Ville and Blues Deluxe were discontinued in 1997 when Hot Rod series models replaced them (although they were reissued in 2006 due to popular demand).

Featuring a 15-watt circuit driven by two EL84 power tubes and three 12AX7 preamp tubes, the Blues Junior provides 'big amp' features like three-band EQ and reverb in a compact 1x12 combo package that makes it a perfect for recording or playing small gigs.

2005 FENDER BLUES JUNIOR

A BROWN SOUN 2X12 SPEAKER CABINET

EST: $750 - $1,000   PRICE: $3,200

LOT 27 BONHAMS 2011

Cabinet: Semi-open back with oval back panel cutout
Covering: Red Tolex, brown basketweave speaker cloth
Plate: Brown logo
Speakers: Two 12-inch Tone Tubby alnico
Label: Inscribed 'Committed to a tone – A Brown Soun Inc'

In 1974 John Harrison moved to the San Francisco Bay Area and opened a speaker repair and reconing shop called A Brown Soun. This shop was one of several cottage-industry companies established during the late 1960s and early 1970s that catered to the Bay Area's burgeoning music scene, led by artists like The Grateful Dead and Carlos Santana. A Brown Soun soon started making its own brand of custom speaker cabinets, working with independent speaker manufacturers to produce a product that duplicated the sound quality of vintage speakers but with improved performance characteristics.

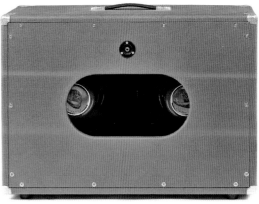

Body: Walnut, natural finish
Neck: Maple with skunk-stripe truss rod routing, 21 frets, maple fingerboard with dot inlays
Headstock: 'Eric' transfer, back of the headstock inscribed 'Built by Will Louthe', signed by Eric Clapton in black felt pen
Bridge: Strings-through-body gold-plated Fender baseplate with six adjustable brass saddles
Pickguard: Black three-ply (black/white/black)
Pickups: Three single-coil
Controls: One volume, two tone
Switches: Five-position pickup selector
Other: Gold-plated Schaller M6 Mini tuners, brass nut
Case: Black rectangular hardshell case with bright pink plush lining, handwritten labels inscribed with various details including '"Eric" Strat Made By Will Louthe Maple Neck Brass Nut'

Of all the guitars sold in the Crossroads auctions, this is the most mysterious. It appears to be a typical 'parts'-caster made from a prefabricated Stratocaster-style neck and body likely produced by a company like Warmoth or Schecter in the 1980s. The bridge, stamped 'Fender USA', is consistent with parts made in the mid 1980s, and the Schaller tuners are stamped 'Made in W. Germany', suggesting they were made prior to the reunification of Germany in 1990. All of this guitar's parts appear consistent with this period.

The only person named Will Louthe we could find with any connection to Clapton is an Irish electrician and lighting technician who worked in the film industry in Britain and the USA. Louthe was an engineer for the 1985 Live Aid broadcast, but it's unknown if he worked in London, or in Philadelphia at the John F. Kennedy Stadium show that Clapton performed at. Louthe also worked on U2's *Rattle and Hum* film and the *Queen Live at Wembley '86* documentary, so had connections to the music industry. Unfortunately, Louthe passed away on October 19th, 2009, so we were unable to confirm if he made Clapton this guitar.

Body: Ash, Transparent Amber finish, signed on the body by Eric Clapton in black felt pen
Neck: Maple, 22 frets, rosewood fingerboard with dot inlays
Headstock: Tunerless hollowed-out design
Bridge: Floyd Rose SpeedLoader double-locking tremolo
Pickguard: Black three-ply (black/white/black)
Pickups: One Red humbucking (bridge), two Vintage single-coil (middle, neck)
Controls: One volume
Switches: Five-position pickup selector
Case: Black Floyd Rose rectangular hardshell case with black plush lining

Floyd Rose is best known for the innovative double-locking tremolo system he invented in the late 1970s featuring clamps in the nut and bridge that prevented strings from going out of tune. In 2003 Rose introduced an improvement to his original tremolo design called the SpeedLoader, which made the process of changing strings much faster and easier. To properly showcase his innovation, Rose also offered his first line of electric guitars called the Redmond Series. In addition to the new Floyd Rose SpeedLoader tremolo bridge and locking nut, the Redmond guitars featured a distinctive tunerless design and a purely decorative hollowed-out headstock.

Guitarists praised the convenience and performance of the new design; however, they were less enthusiastic about the special proprietary strings mandatory for the SpeedLoader system, which were both expensive and hard to find. Rose discontinued his Redmond Series guitars a few years after their introduction (the special strings followed suit in 2010) and developed new guitar models that allowed guitarists to use standard guitar strings with the SpeedLoader system.

LOT 54 BONHAMS 2011

Serial No: 91703343
Body: Mahogany, bound flame maple top, single pointed cutaway, sunburst finish
Neck: Mahogany, 22 frets, bound ebony fingerboard with crest 'pineapple' inlays
Headstock: Crown peghead inlay
Bridge: Strings-through-body gold-plated baseplate with six adjustable saddles
Pickups: Mini humbucking (neck), slanted humbucking (bridge)
Controls: One volume, one tone/pull coil tap
Switches: Five-position pickup selector
Case: Black hardshell contour case with black plush lining, handwritten label with various inscriptions including 'Gibson Nighthawk Sunburst'

Gibson designed its Nighthawk model guitars to provide players with the familiar feel of a Les Paul but with a lighter, slimmed-down body that is more comfortable to play. Gibson also developed a versatile wiring configuration that provided a wide variety of humbucking and single-coil tones. The bridge humbucker produces fat, sustaining Les Paul-like tones, the neck mini humbucker delivers the distinctive midrange snarl of a Firebird, and various coil-splitting settings produce tones similar to a Stratocaster or Telecaster. Many guitarists praised the Nighthawk as one of Gibson's best new solidbody guitar designs since the early 1960s.

1993 GIBSON NIGHTHAWK CUSTOM

1995 FENDER JAM

LOT 36 BONHAMS 2011

Serial No: LO-653703
Covering: Black carpet, black speaker cloth
Speakers: One 12-inch
Switches: Normal bright, normal full, drive crunch, drive lead, chorus on/off, power on/off
Controls: Contour, volume, reverb, chorus rate, chorus depth
Inputs: Two ¼ inch, two RCA, power amp (effects loop return)
Outputs: Preamp (effects loop send), headphone

The JAM is a small practice amp that Fender introduced in 1990 along with the similar HOT and RAD models – all of which were designed for young beginning guitarists. The key selling point of the JAM amp was its push-button controls that instantly produced preset distortion tones at low volume levels ideal for bedroom jamming. With its built-in chorus and reverb effects, headphone jack, and stereo inputs for a cassette or CD player, the Fender JAM was designed more for practice than performance or recording applications. It also featured a low-cost solid-state design and durable carpet covering similar to amps made by Crate, which was one of Fender's biggest competitors in the entry-level amp category at that time. Fender discontinued the JAM model in 1996 as tastes progressed towards more traditional designs.

1995 FENDER JAM

Serial No: DC-2
Covering: Tweed, brown speaker cloth
Plate: Cornell
Speakers: Two 12-inch Tone Tubby
Switches: Power on/off, standby, output 20/80
Controls: Treble, bass, volume
Inputs: Two
Label: Plaque on back panel stamped 'DC-2'
Case: Flight case

Because Clapton was quite pleased with the modification work that Denis Cornell had performed on his Fender Vibro King amps (page 284), Clapton commissioned Cornell to build a custom amp for him. Clapton wanted an amp that was similar to his favourite tweed Fender Twin (page 224) but with a completely different circuit. The amp Cornell made featured an 80-watt circuit similar to a Twin's with four 6L6GT power tubes, two 12AX7 preamp tubes and one 12AT7, but it also included a switch for reducing output power to 20 watts and a very simple two-band EQ section.

Cornell described the amp's features: 'With very few components in the signal path to corrupt the tone, its simplicity is its strength. The natural tone and response can only be a result of that no-fuss design. The two Tone Tubby [made by A Brown Soun of San Rafael, California] speakers enhance its response, resulting in the perfect blues sound.'

While the cabinet's dimensions are similar to those of a 'big box' Twin, the 12-inch speakers are mounted in the cabinet at a slightly offset angle instead of directly side-by-side.

Cornell made two Custom 80 amps for Eric with serial numbers DC-1 and DC-2. Both were Clapton's main stage amps from 2002 through 2004, including his performance at the Concert for George, on November 29th, 2002, at London's Royal Albert Hall.

ERIC George and I met when I was in The Yardbirds. We talked about guitar strings and guitars and music and became friends.

Musically we were kindred spirits. That's what joined us together, because he loved what I did, and he couldn't do it, while I loved what he did, but I couldn't do it. I mean there's no way I can play the slide the way he did: he was fantastic, the first man who had the idea of playing a melody, instead of just trying to play like Elmore James. He achieved that, and just doing that was enough.

Opposite:
The Concert for George
Royal Albert Hall
London, UK
Nov. 29, 2002

Eric playing with Ringo Starr and Dhani Harrison at the 2002 memorial concert for George Harrison. This amp can be seen to the left of Eric.

Playlist:
Concert for George, 2002
Gigs:
2002-2004 Tours
Jubilee 2002: Party at the Palace (TV)
Buckingham Palace
London, UK
June 3, 2002
John Mayall & Friends: A Tribute To John Mayall For His 70th Birthday (in aid of UNICEF)
King's Dock
Liverpool, UK
July 19, 2003
Eric Clapton's Crossroads Guitar Festival
June 4-6, 2004
Highlight:
The Concert for George
Royal Albert Hall
London, UK
Nov. 29, 2002

Serial No: 547943
Body: Rosewood back and sides, spruce top, multi-ply ivoroid binding, natural finish
Neck: Mahogany, 20 frets, bound ebony fingerboard with pearl 'snowflake' inlays
Headstock: Solid
Bridge: Ebony 'belly' pin bridge
Soundhole: Pearl inlaid rosette
Pickguard: Imitation tortoiseshell
Tuners: Gold-plated with ebony buttons
Pickups: Internal piezo transducer
Case: Original hardshell case with adhesive tape inscribed 'Martin 12 string/J.40 # 547943'

Playlist:
From The Cradle, 1994
Concert for George, 2002
Gigs:
1994-5 From The Cradle Tour
Oct. 3, 1994-Oct. 13, 1995
Highlight:
The Concert for George
Royal Albert Hall
London, UK
Nov. 29, 2002

Opposite:
The Concert for George
Royal Albert Hall
London, UK
Nov. 29, 2002

Eric during his rendition of 'My Sweet Lord' with Jeff Lynne, Tessa Niles, Sam Brown, Mark Mann, Albert Lee and Dhani Harrison.

This custom Martin 12-string is essentially identical to the Martin J12-40 model that Clapton used to play 'Motherless Child' on his From The Cradle Tour with the exception of its 'snowflake' fingerboard inlays, which are similar to those on Martin's earliest D-45 guitars. Clapton used this guitar to record 'Motherless Child' on *From The Cradle,* and he occasionally played this guitar as an alternate for the J12-40 on that tour. Clapton also used this guitar to perform 'My Sweet Lord' at the Concert for George.

ERIC When George's death was still a recent thing, I wanted to know what was going to happen. Brian Roylance and I were having dinner; I'd been away in Japan and I'd come back to get the latest news. I asked him, 'Is there going to be a benefit or is anyone going to play?' and he said, 'No, not unless you do.' I thought, 'Oh my God, nothing's going to happen unless we do something.'

I immediately thought, 'If this was me what would I want?' and I suppose in a selfish way I thought, 'Well, what goes around comes around and I'd like to be remembered in this way – with a bunch of people that I love, playing songs.' Not necessarily my songs in my case because I don't really like my songs as much, but George's songs, they're evergreens. So I just thought it would be great and I had no idea how big it should be but it took shape very quickly. We thought the Albert Hall would be good and it was easy to pick people because there was a definite group that was always involved with George's life at one stage or another that came and went. All I wanted to do was share our love for George and his music.

Serial No: 892351
Body: Rosewood back and sides, spruce top, ivoroid binding with herringbone purfling, natural finish
Neck: Mahogany, 20 frets, ebony fretboard with 'slotted diamond' inlays, 'Eric Clapton' signature inlay between 19th and 20th frets
Headstock: Solid
Bridge: Ebony 'belly' pin bridge
Soundhole: Herringbone rosette
Pickguard: Imitation tortoiseshell
Case: Original hardshell case with adhesive tape inscribed 'Auction #45 serial 892351/Martin 000-28' and '1 of 4 New/000-28EC/Dhani/For Italy'

When Martin's limited-edition 000-42EC model based on the 000-42 guitar that Clapton used for his *Unplugged* performance (page 230) sold out within days of its release in 1995, Martin followed it up by introducing the 000-28EC in 1996. This stock production model, which has Style 28 features that are less elaborate than those of the 000-42EC, remains in Martin's catalogue today and is one of the company's bestselling guitars.

Martin Director of Artist Relations Dick Boak sent four 000-28EC guitars, including this one, to Clapton when Eric told him that he needed more acoustic guitars for the Concert for George rehearsals. Various guitarists played them during rehearsals, including Albert Lee and George's son Dhani Harrison.

Highlight:
The Concert for George
Royal Albert Hall
London, UK
Nov. 29, 2002

The Concert for George
Royal Albert Hall
London, UK
Nov. 29, 2002

Eric is playing this guitar or a similar Martin acoustic onstage with fellow guitarists Jeff Lynne, Andy Fairweather Low, Dhani Harrison, Paul McCartney and Mark Mann.

ERIC This was one of the first signatures from the second series.

EST: $6,000 - $8,000   PRICE: $16,730

Body: Cypress back and sides, spruce top, rosewood binding, natural finish
Neck: Cedar, 19 frets, ebony fingerboard
Headstock: Solid
Bridge: Rosewood tie bridge
Rosette: Multi-coloured marquetry
Pickups: Internal Carlos pickup
Label: 'Gerundino/ Luthier/Beunavista [sic] 4 (Quemadero)/ Almería-España-año 1976' stamped internally 'Gerundino/Luthier/ Almería', maker's signature on label
Case: Hardshell case with adhesive tape inscribed 'Auction #56/Gerundino'

Spanish luthier Gerundino Fernández García (1931-2006) opened his workshop in Almería, Spain, in 1960, building an average of 10 to 12 guitars a year until his retirement in 1999. Gerundino Fernández is considered one of the best flamenco guitar luthiers of the 20th century, and many renowned flamenco guitarists, including Juan Martin, Paco Peña and Tomatito, favour his instruments.

This guitar was bought for the rehearsals for the Concert for George and has been used at home a little.

ERIC A great guitar. I loved it – the playability of it was phenomenal. The neck, and the feel, and the action were perfect. But I found that thing with the pegs a bit intimidating.

Highlight:
The Concert for George
Royal Albert Hall
London, UK
Nov. 29, 2002

During rehearsals for the Concert for George with Gary Brooker, Jeff Lynne, Andy Fairweather Low and Dhani Harrison. Eric is playing the Martin on the previous page. His 1930s dobro and one of his Strats painted by Crash (page 306) can also be seen in this shot.

DOWN TO THE CROSSROADS

Body: Brazilian rosewood back and sides, cedar top, bound, natural finish
Neck: Cedar, 19 frets, ebony fingerboard
Headstock: Solid, rosewood veneer
Bridge: Rosewood tie bridge
Pickguard: Transparent protective golpeador plate
Soundhole: Multi-coloured marquetry
Label: 'Gerundino/ Luthier/Beunavista [sic] 4/ El Quemadero/Almería/ España/año 1980' with initials 'GFG' handwritten sideways
Additional: Guitar strap
Case: Black hardshell contour case with black plush lining, handwritten label inscribed with various details including 'Gerundino With "Banjo" Pegs'

Although this Gerundino Fernández flamenco guitar looks almost identical to the other Fernández flamenco guitar, it is designed for flamenco players who prefer the warmer character and wider tonal range of a classical guitar over the bright, percussive tones of traditional flamenco guitars made from cypress and spruce. The model is called 'Negra' in reference to the deep, dark colour of its Brazilian rosewood back and sides. Rosewood body guitars like this one provide excellent volume output and enhanced treble and bass response, while the cedar top produces warm, rich tones that contrast the percussive attack and brighter treble tones produced by guitars with spruce tops. Many traditional flamenco guitarists prefer single-piece wood friction tuning pegs like those on this guitar over the geared tuning pegs used on modern instruments.

Serial No: 213689
Body: Rosewood back and sides, spruce top, imitation tortoiseshell back and top binding, natural finish
Neck: Mahogany, 20 frets, rosewood fingerboard with dot inlays
Headstock: Slotted
Bridge: Rosewood 'belly' pin bridge
Pickguard: Imitation tortoiseshell
Additional: Three guitar picks, one inscribed 'Nelson Wilbury', one inscribed 'George Harrison/My Sweet Lord', the other 'George Harrison' and an OM symbol
Case: Hardshell case decorated on the lid with an OM sticker, tie-on label printed with an OM logo, inscribed with the guitar details

George Harrison kept this guitar at Friar Park, his home in Henley-on-Thames, Oxfordshire, for about 10 years before he gave it as a gift to Clapton. Martin 00-21 guitars were very popular in the 1950s and 60s, when they were often seen in the hands of performers like Elvis Presley and the Kingston Trio. With its Brazilian rosewood back and sides, small 00-size body, and 12-fret neck, this guitar produces a very sweet and well-balanced tone that is ideal for fingerstyle playing.

LOT 23 BONHAMS 2011

Body: Alder, single resonator cone, nickel-plated cover with six diamond-shaped cutouts, red finish
Neck: Maple, 18 frets, maple fingerboard with mother-of-pearl dot inlays
Bridge: Maple 'biscuit' bridge, nickel-plated trapeze tailpiece
Pickguard: Mother-of-pearl
Case: Handmade wooden case with blue velvet lining, handwritten label with various inscriptions including 'Lewis Dobrouke, Mini Dobro Style Uke'

Mike Lewis of Fine Resophonic in Paris, France, gave Clapton this solidbody resonator ukulele as a gift when Clapton purchased a Model 1 Wood Body Triplate guitar from him in 1995. The sharp attack, loud volume output and metallic tone of a resonator instrument provide a stunning complement to the ukulele's inherent brash character.

CIRCA 1920s G HOUGHTON & SONS MELODY MAJOR MANDOLIN-BANJO   EST: $300 - $500   PRICE: $3,200

LOT 20 BONHAMS 2011

Body: Wood resonator, 11-inch vellum head with 16 tension hooks
Neck: Walnut, 17 frets, ebony fingerboard with mother-of-pearl dot inlay
Headstock: Metal plate with upside-down 'Melody Major' logo, embossed gold lion maker's mark with 'British Made' banner
Tuners: Brass with bone buttons
Bridge: Maple with nickel fret saddle, nickel-plated trapeze tailpiece
Case: Black softshell carrying case, handwritten label

George Houghton started producing Reliance brand banjos and zither-banjos in Birmingham in 1888. Although his instruments were inexpensive, they were very well made and featured various improvements, like the 'unwarpable' neck that he patented in the 1890s. As the popularity of his instruments increased, Houghton changed the company name to G. Houghton & Sons and expanded production over the years to include other instruments like banjo-mandolins and banjo-ukuleles. G. Houghton & Sons produced instruments in Birmingham until 1962, when George Houghton (son of the founder) closed the shop and started making banjos for John E. Dallas & Sons Ltd. in Kent.

DOWN TO THE CROSSROADS

Serial No: 00035
Body: Ash, blonde finish
Neck: Maple, 24 frets, maple fingerboard with dot inlays
Bridge: Stamped steel baseplate, two adjustable saddles
Pickguard: Anodised aluminium
Pickups: One single-coil
Controls: One volume, one tone
Additional: Original output cable, leather strap, strings, manufacturer's warranty 'hang tag', and salesman sheet
Case: Original hardshell tweed case with adhesive tape inscribed 'Auction 317/Fender Mandolin'

While Leo Fender inventions like the first production solidbody guitar (Broadcaster/Telecaster) and the first electric bass guitar (Precision Bass) are still going strong, some of his innovations were not quite as long-lasting. The solidbody Fender Electric Mandolin is one example, although it managed to be successful enough to remain in continuous production for 20 years from its introduction in 1956 until its discontinuation in 1976. Unlike a traditional mandolin, which has four double courses of strings, the Fender Electric Mandolin has only four strings.

Clapton purchased this Fender Electric Mandolin, which came complete with the original tags, papers and accessories that it originally shipped with back in 1957, for his collection.

ERIC The mandolin was a relatively recent acquisition. It's a beautiful thing – stunning.

What little I know about mandolins is that they are the business, what the real genuine Nashville guys would use if they weren't using an acoustic Gibson or whatever. I also love that gold anodised finish on the scratchplate with that colour, that ivory paint.

I was always trying to find mandolins and I would end up trying to tune them like guitars. I never understood the tuning – it's upside down like a violin tuning. I try now and then to play a mandolin but it doesn't work for me. It was another experiment that didn't really pay off.

Body: Poplar with hollow chambers, asymmetrical shape with swept-back cutaways and contour horn, red and black crackle finish
Neck: Poplar, 21 frets, Brazilian rosewood fingerboard with dot inlays
Bridge: Rosewood 'buzz' bridge
Pickguard: Clear Plexiglas with printed lettering 'Vincent Bell, Signature Design Electric Sitar'
Pickups: Three 'lipstick tube' cylindrical-shaped single-coil
Controls: Three volume, three tone
Other: 13 sympathetic 'drone' strings with two rosewood bridges, Plexiglas armrest plate
Case: Brown Tolex rectangular hardshell case with yellow plush lining and handwritten tie-on label 'Coral Sitar N.S.N.' and adhesive paper label similarly inscribed

Danelectro of Neptune, New Jersey, made Silvertone guitars for Sears as well as the Coral brand, which offered the revolutionary Vincent Bell Coral Sitar from 1967 until 1969. Invented by session musician Vincent Bell, the Coral Sitar featured an unusual 'buzz' bridge and 13 sympathetic 'drone' strings that produced a good, electrified approximation of a sitar's distinctive sound.

Pete Townshend borrowed this guitar from Eric for a couple of years.

ERIC I guess everybody who's played a string instrument has had an influence on me. All the Indian musicians I've heard and all the blues musicians I've heard have influenced me. There are lots of other idioms I haven't even touched on, fields of music I haven't even been near. I experimented with this sitar; it has a great sound. I found it difficult to part with this instrument.

Eric is pictured with sitar player Ravi Shankar's daughter Anoushka, at rehearsals for the Concert for George.

Serial No: 538170
Body: Rosewood back and sides, spruce top, multi-ply ivoroid binding, black finish
Neck: Mahogany, 20 frets, bound ebony fingerboard with Style 45 pearl hexagonal inlays
Headstock: Solid
Bridge: Ebony 'belly' pin bridge
Soundhole: Pearl inlaid rosette
Pickguard: Black single-ply
Case: Case with adhesive tape inscribed 'Auction #36/Black Martin J-40/#538170'

The Martin J-40 is essentially an M-38 with a deeper body that matches the depth of a Martin D-size dreadnought. Because its body is also wider and longer than a dreadnought, it is a true jumbo guitar. When Martin introduced the J-40 in 1985, it became an instant success, favoured by many bluegrass guitarists for its powerful bass and piano-like tone. Martin started offering the J-40 with a black finish (the only colour beyond natural or sunburst that Martin offered at that time) in 1988.

Clapton purchased this guitar after he saw a similar black J-40 in the Martin catalogue. He played it occasionally in the recording studio, including during the sessions for *Me and Mr. Johnson*.

Playlist:
Me and Mr. Johnson, 2004

Japan, Nov. 2003

Eric Clapton with a Bellezza Nera guitar. A photograph from this shoot was used as the inspiration for Sir Peter Blake's painting on the cover of *Me and Mr. Johnson*.

LOT 25 CHRISTIE'S 1999

Serial No: 60616
Body: Mahogany back
and sides, arched spruce
top, red mahogany
sunburst finish
Neck: Mahogany, 19 frets,
bound ebony fingerboard
with dot inlays
Headstock: Floral inlay,
script 'The Gibson' logo
Bridge: Rosewood,
nickel-plated
trapeze tailpiece
Pickguard: Celluloid,
imitation tortoiseshell
Soundhole: Round
Case: Black hardshell
contour case with red
plush lining and
handwritten tie-on label
'1924 Gibson L3 60616'
and adhesive paper label
similarly inscribed

Although the handwritten label for this guitar identifies it as
a 1924 L-3, it actually has several distinguishing features and a serial
number that suggest it was made in 1920. While the original bridge
and trapeze tailpiece were possibly replaced with later versions
– a common modification – the floral inlay and 'The Gibson' logo
on the headstock, lack of an adjustable truss rod, and distinctive
red mahogany sunburst finish narrow down its date of manufacture
to between 1918 and 1922.

Clapton likely purchased this guitar because it reminded him of
the L-1 that Robert Johnson is seen holding in a studio portrait
photographed in the mid 1930s. However, the L-3 differs from the
L-1 in several significant ways, including its arched top (the L-1 is
a flat-top guitar) and floating bridge/trapeze tailpiece instead of
the L-1's pin bridge.

ERIC It was quite hard to play.

ERIC Robert Johnson is the most
important influence I've had in
my life and always will be. First
of all I was really intimidated by
his music, especially the
technique; it didn't make any
sense to me at all. It was very
random – he'd sing a line then
play a line, then do bits
underneath. It took me a long
time to understand the depth
of the Robert Johnson records.

I have never actually sat down and played
Robert Johnson unaccompanied. I can
play Big Bill Broonzy's stuff, but there's
something very symmetrical about his
music – once you learn the fingerpicking
pattern, it's easy. But Robert's music
is so asymmetrical, and there is always
something new going on. I find it very
difficult to play by myself. While playing
a line on the low strings Robert Johnson
would simultaneously pick little reference
notes on the high strings. I've heard
countless electric guitar players do that.
It was like Johnson was playing electric
guitar before there were electric guitars;
that's the bizarre thing.

Most of *Me and Mr. Johnson* was done
either on a Strat or vintage Gibsons, like
a Byrdland and an L-5 with the alnico
pickups. Those are Fifties guitars. Then
there were also a couple of Martins. There's
an OM-45 that I had – a pretty old one –
and I used the Martin signature guitars
a lot – the 000-42ECB and 000-28ECB.
So that's about it, really. There wasn't a lot
of equipment involved.

Body: Flame maple, bound, upper bout f-holes, single resonator cone, nickel-plated cover plate with 'chicken foot' cutouts, natural finish
Neck: Flame maple, 19 frets, bound ebony fingerboard with dot inlays
Headstock: Slotted
Bridge: Maple 'biscuit' bridge, nickel-plated trapeze tailpiece
Label: Signed and dated inside the body by Mark Lewis
Case: Black hardshell contour case with red plush lining, handwritten label with various inscriptions including 'Blonde Maple Dobro With Highlander'

When Clapton played in Paris, France, on April 6th, 2004, Mike Lewis dropped by again to show Clapton more of the resonator guitars he makes. Clapton purchased this stunning single-cone resonator guitar made of beautifully figured 'flame' curly maple from him during this visit. Clapton put the guitar to good use a few months later when he played it on sessions and performances that were filmed for the *Sessions for Robert J.* DVD. Doyle Bramhall II also played this guitar (left-handed) on tour with Clapton from 2004 through 2009.

Playlist:
Sessions for Robert J.
2004
Gigs:
World Tours
2004-2009

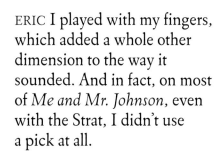

ERIC I played with my fingers, which added a whole other dimension to the way it sounded. And in fact, on most of *Me and Mr. Johnson*, even with the Strat, I didn't use a pick at all.

When I'm using my fingers, I've got much more control about how subtle it could be. When you play live, I think there's something about using your fingers that gives it more intimacy. If I play with a pick, it's a stage approach. I always use the same standard heavy pick; I'm going for maximum attack and volume.

Serial No: B-050344
Covering: Varnished flame maple cabinet, wheat speaker cloth with three gold-plated metal strips, back covered with red velour, signed by makers on bottom of cabinet
Plate: Fender Custom Instruments Corona California
Speakers: One 12-inch
Switches: Power on/off, fat
Controls: Reverb, master, middle, bass, treble, volume
Inputs: One
Label: Plaque stamped 'Woody Jr, Made in USA'
Case: Brown/black textured custom flight case with stickers including 'Eric Clapton & Stevie Winwood USA 2008 LOAD-IN POSITION OFF STAGE DOCK, STAY ON TRUCK'

The wood cabinet of this small Fender combo amp is based on those used on Leo Fender's first amps bearing the Fender brand name made from 1946 until 1948; however, this amp's exquisitely figured flame maple is much fancier than anything available to Fender during the early post-World War II years. The maple cabinet gives this amp a significant edge in tone that's as beautiful as its external appearance. Despite the attention to detail in the cabinetry work, the electronics are rather mundane and consist of a standard Fender Blues Junior chassis.

Clapton used this amp on his 2004 tour in support of his *Me and Mr. Johnson* album. The amp had the perfect look and sound for songs that needed to replicate the primitive vibe of the 1930s and 1940s era.

ERIC The 2004 Crossroads guitar auction was when I finally parted with Blackie (page 122) and the cherry red Gibson ES-335 that I had had ever since The Yardbirds (page 26). The day before the festival I went to see them both on display, and bid them farewell. It was hard. We had travelled a lot of miles together, and I knew I would never find another instrument that could take the place of either of these.

Opposite:
Eric Clapton's Crossroads
Guitar Festival
Fair Park
Dallas, Texas, USA
June 5, 2004

Clapton using this amp
with his Crash guitar.
He sat on the drum riser
to join J.J. Cale in
his performance of
'After Midnight'.

Gigs:
2004 Tour
Mar. 24-Aug. 2, 2004
Highlight:
Eric Clapton's Crossroads
Guitar Festival
Fair Park & Cotton Bowl
Stadium
Dallas, Texas, USA
June 4-6, 2004

Serial No: 390
Body: Alder, polychrome custom finish
Neck: Maple with skunk-stripe truss rod routing, 22 frets, maple fingerboard with dot inlays, rear of headstock inscribed '390/Todd Krause'
Bridge: Blocked synchronised tremolo
Pickguard: Black single-ply with painted graphics
Pickups: Three Fender Vintage Noiseless single-coil
Controls: Master volume, two tone
Switches: Five-position pickup selector with black switch tip
Case: Hardshell case

Gigs:
One Generation 4 Another
Royal Albert Hall
London, UK
Mar. 15, 2004
2004 Tour
Mar. 24-May 11, 2004
Highlight:
Eric Clapton's Crossroads
Guitar Festival
Fair Park & Cotton Bowl
Stadium
Dallas, Texas, USA
June 4-6, 2004

Opposite:
Olympiahalle
Munich, Germany
Mar. 31, 2004

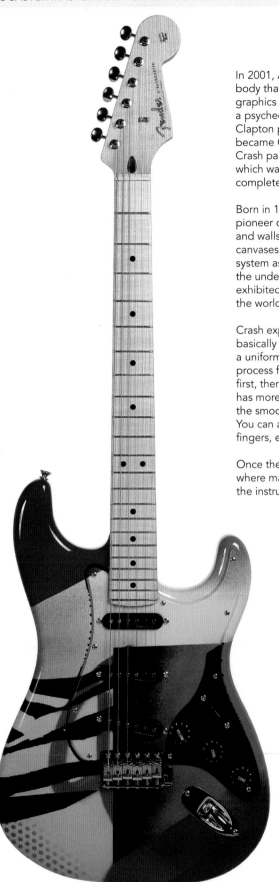

DOWN TO THE CROSSROADS

In 2001, American graffiti artist John 'Crash' Matos gave Eric a guitar body that he had painted as a gift. This guitar with its bold, colourful graphics is the modern equivalent of the 1964 Gibson SG with a psychedelic motif painted by the Dutch art collective The Fool that Clapton played in Cream (page 61). The Crash guitar immediately became Clapton's main stage guitar, and over the next few years Crash painted several more guitars for Clapton, including this one, which was the third instrument Crash painted for Clapton and completed in 2004.

Born in 1961 in New York City, Crash has been described as a true pioneer of the Graffiti art movement. Subway cars, basketball courts and walls of buildings in run-down neighbourhoods were his canvases. In the words of one biographer: 'Using the IRT subway system as his launching pad, Crash established a visual link between the underground street life and the world above.' His works are now exhibited and collected by private and public collections throughout the world.

Crash explained how he creates his designs on Eric's guitars: 'First, basically I prime the Fender body in flat white Krylon spray paint for a uniform undercoat. I usually give it quite a few coats. Then the process for painting is a bit confusing. I start with the smaller details first, then build up to the larger areas. Every place that is painted has more than two or three coats. The idea is to break the surface of the smooth wood. Otherwise it would look like a simple paint job. You can actually feel the grooves of the surfaces with your fingers, even after thorough clear coating has been done.'

Once the body was painted, it was sent to the Fender Custom Shop where master builders Todd Krause and Mark Kendrick completed the instrument.

ERIC I became very close to the graffiti writer Crash in the early Nineties, and bought a lot of his work.

There were a few guys – Crash, Futura, Lee, Daze and Haze. These guys used to paint subways, until it was outlawed and the city found a way to make the new trains with a chemical treatment so that the paint won't stay on it. Crash was a train painter when he was 14. Now he's legit and he paints on canvas, but still uses spray paint. When we became friends, I asked him to paint a couple of Strats for me. I have a collection of new Strats and each one has been painted by one of these famous graffiti artists. I use them because they're exciting.

ERIC It's the multi-coloured Strat that's probably the one that's most recognised now. That was the first of its kind. Crash made another one especially for the 2004 guitar festival. I played it for the first part of the tour and then put it into the auction. He painted that guitar to be the spearhead guitar for the whole campaign. But I'd never part with the original.

2004 FENDER ACOUSTASONIC JUNIOR DSP

EST: $300 - $500   PRICE: $4,000

LOT 107 BONHAMS 2011

2004 FENDER ACOUSTASONIC JUNIOR DSP

Serial No: M1400896
Covering: Brown Tolex, wheat speaker cloth
Plate: Acoustasonic-Junior, 'flat' Fender logo
Speakers: Two 8-inch, high-frequency tweeter
Switches: Phase (two), power on/off, ground lift
Controls: Volume, treble, mid, bass, feedback notch, string dynamics, FX select, FX level (channel 1), volume, treble, bass, FX select, FX level, line-out level
Inputs: Instrument, mic, line/instrument
Outputs: Balanced line (XLR)
Footswitch inputs: One
Other: Stereo effects loop (send, return), black vinyl cover

The Fender Acoustasonic Junior DSP may look like an early 1960s brown Tolex Fender amp, but its resemblance to a vintage amp stops there. The Acoustasonic Junior DSP features two 40-watt amps, separate microphone and instrument channels, and two built-in digital effects processors (one per channel) with Vibratone, chorus, reverb/chorus, chorus/delay, delay, reverb/delay, plate, room, and hall presets. Designed specifically for amplifying acoustic guitars and microphones, the Acoustasonic amp is like a miniature PA system in a combo amp configuration.

Clapton ordered this amp from Fender on June 3rd, 2004, one day before the opening of his first Crossroads Guitar Festival in Dallas, Texas. Fender delivered the amp to him at Centennial Hall-Fair Park in Dallas, which is located next to Cotton Bowl Stadium where the concert took place.

2003 GIBSON LES PAUL R4 SINGLE PICKUP

EST: $4,500 - $6,500   PRICE: $17,000

LOT 53 BONHAMS 2011

2003 GIBSON LES PAUL R4 SINGLE PICKUP

Serial No: 4 3307
Body: Mahogany, maple top, bound, single cutaway, gold finish
Neck: Mahogany, 22 frets, bound rosewood fingerboard with crown inlays
Headstock: Pearl Gibson logo, silk-screened gold paint 'Les Paul Model'
Bridge: Nickel-plated stud wrap-around tailpiece/bridge
Pickups: One 'soapbar' P-90 single-coil
Controls: One volume, one tone
Additional: Gibson Certificate of Authenticity
Case: Black Gibson hardshell contour case with claret plush lining and handwritten label

Staples High School
Westport
Connecticut, USA
Mar. 27, 1968

Eric playing a goldtop Gibson Les Paul on tour with Cream.

In 2003 the Gibson Custom Shop made only 28 of these Les Paul 1954 reissue goldtop guitars in an unusual single-pickup configuration, which are a hybrid of Gibson's 1954 goldtop Les Paul Standard and the single-pickup 1954 Les Paul Junior. This guitar provides a combination of the Les Paul Junior's simplicity with the more complex tonal character of the goldtop Les Paul Standard's carved maple top.

Clapton bought it during the 2004 Crossroads Guitar Festival.

DOWN TO THE CROSSROADS

2004 FENDER STRATOCASTER 'ACOUSTIC' PROTOTYPE

EST: $3,000 - $4,000

PRICE: $12,000

LOT 59 BONHAMS 2011

Body: Alder, black finish
Neck: Maple with skunk-stripe truss rod routing, 22 frets, maple fingerboard with dot inlays, Custom Shop logo engraved neck plate, neck butt pencil-marked '05-04 Todd Krause'
Headstock: Back of the headstock inscribed 'Todd Krause Fender Custom Shop'
Bridge: Blocked synchronised tremolo
Pickguard: White single-ply
Pickups: Three Vintage Noiseless single-coil, bridge piezos
Controls: One volume, two tone, one piezo pickup volume
Switches: Five-position pickup selector, piezo on/off toggle
Case: Black Fender hardshell contour case with black plush lining, handwritten label inscribed 'Fender E.C. Strat Black. AC/EL T.K. Proto.'

This guitar is essentially a standard Fender Stratocaster with a custom bridge featuring built-in piezo pickups that produce tones similar to an acoustic steel-string guitar. Numerous companies introduced guitars with similar bridges during the 1990s, and Fender decided it was time to try developing their own version. Fender sent this prototype to Clapton for evaluation purposes.

The 'acoustic' Stratocaster never made it into production, probably because Fender and Roland had been working in secret partnership since 1997 to develop new products like the VG Stratocaster, which was announced in 2007 along with the formal public unveiling of their partnership. The VG Stratocaster's modelling technology, which enabled it to produce the tones of numerous guitars including several very realistic-sounding acoustic guitars, made a piezo bridge guitar like this prototype obsolete.

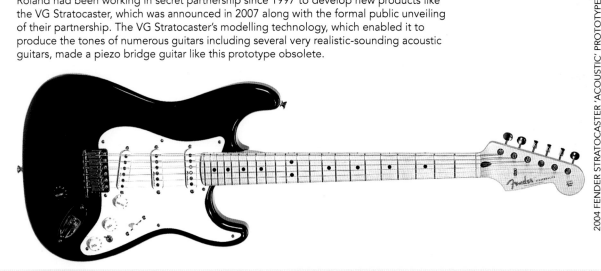

2004 FENDER STRATOCASTER 'ACOUSTIC' PROTOTYPE

2004 FENDER ACOUSTASONIC STRATOCASTER

EST: $2,200 - $2,800

PRICE: $12,000

LOT 108 BONHAMS 2011

Body: Alder, graphite top, hollowbody, Sapphire Blue Transparent metallic finish
Neck: Maple with skunk-stripe truss rod routing, 22 frets, maple fingerboard with dot inlays, neck butt stamped 'Clapton JUN 14 2004'
Headstock: Back of the headstock with Fender Custom Shop and Eric Clapton transfers, signed by Eric Clapton in black felt pen
Bridge: Asymmetrical rosewood pin bridge
Soundhole: Dual-angled elliptical
Pickups: Three bridge-saddle Fishman piezo
Controls: One volume, one tone
Case: Black Fender hardshell contour case with black plush lining, handwritten label inscribed 'Fender-Acoustasonic "Acoustic Strat" Blue "Stratosonic"'

Fender designed the Acoustasonic Stratocaster to combine the comfort of a solidbody electric guitar with an instrument that sounded as good unplugged as it did amplified. The key to the Acoustasonic Stratocaster's design is its unique dual soundhole that helps the guitar project sound like a full-size acoustic while maintaining the compact size and feedback-resistant benefits of an electric-acoustic instrument.

Fender introduced the Acoustasonic Stratocaster in 2003. The production model featured a rosewood fingerboard and an 'Acoustasonic' decal on the headstock, but this example has a maple fingerboard Strat neck that was made for Eric by the Fender Custom Shop in 2004. All of the remaining features appear to be stock.

DOWN TO THE CROSSROADS

2004 FENDER ACOUSTASONIC STRATOCASTER

Serial No: 1000305
Body: Maple back and sides, spruce top, herringbone purfling, white finish
Neck: Mahogany neck, 20 frets, bound ebony fingerboard with mother-of-pearl snowflake inlays and mother-of-pearl 'Bellezza Bianca' inlay between 19th and 20th frets
Headstock: Solid, bound, pearl 'fern' inlay
Bridge: Ebony 'belly' pin bridge
Pickguard: Black single-ply
Soundhole: Custom slotted-diamond inlay rosette
Label: 'CF Martin & Co. Bellezza Bianca', signed by C.F. Martin IV, Eric Clapton, Hiroshi Fujiwara and Dick Boak, inscribed 'Prototype 3 of 4'
Case: Black hardshell contour case with bottle green plush lining, handwritten label with various inscriptions including 'MARTIN PROTO 'BIANCA' 1000305...3 OF 4'

Playlist:
Sessions for Robert J. 2004 (DVD)
Highlight:
Today (TV)
NBC Television Studio
New York, USA
Nov. 18, 2005

Many companies that make acoustic guitars have offered instruments in a wide variety of colours, but for decades Martin only offered their steel-string flat-top guitars with natural or sunburst finishes as well as a few rare models with black finish options. In 2004 Clapton convinced Martin to break with tradition by making white Bellezza Bianca guitars in addition to the black Bellezza Nera guitars that they were building for him.

The Bellezza Nera and Bellezza Bianca were the products of an unusual collaboration between Clapton, Martin and Hiroshi Fujiwara, a DJ/musician/producer/designer who helped introduce club music and fashion to Japan in the 1990s. Clapton and Fujiwara conceived the Bellezza guitar, and Martin made four prototypes in black (Bellezza Nera) and an additional four prototypes in white (Bellezza Bianca). Clapton is seen playing one of his Bellezza Nera guitars on the cover of his *Me and Mr. Johnson* album, and several Bellezza Martins appeared in videos shot for the *Sessions for Robert J.* DVD/CD package that Fujiwara produced. Clapton also played one of his Bellezza Bianca guitars during a performance of 'Back Home' on NBC's *Today* show that aired on Friday, November 18th, 2005.

The Bellezza guitars are 000-size instruments with numerous distinctive features, including a unique slotted-diamond rosette inlay pattern and 'fern' headstock inlay pattern previously only found on four 1902 00-45 guitars and Martin's 000-42EC Eric Clapton signature models. Martin offered a limited-edition run of 476 Bellezza Nera guitars in the summer of 2004, and in 2006 they followed that up with a limited-edition run of 410 Bellezza Bianca guitars.

PAIR OF LATE 1950s FENDER TWIN AMPLIFIERS

EST: $2,000 - $3,000   PRICE: $12,000, $16,000

LOT 52, 82 CHRISTIE'S 1999

Covering: Tweed, 'oxblood' brown speaker cloth
Plate: Fender Twin-Amp
Speakers: Two 12-inch
Switches: Ground, power, standby
Controls: Presence, mid, bass, treble, bright volume, normal volume
Inputs: Four

Fender Twin amplifiers produced between 1958 and 1960 are nicknamed 'big box' Twins because they are 2½ inches wider than the previous version. Although the 'big box' Twin was also 1½ inches shorter than its predecessor, it earned the 'big box' name for its more rectangular-looking dimensions. The 'big box' cabinet allowed Fender to place both 12-inch speakers directly next to each other instead of in the diagonal configuration found on previous models. Fender also changed the Twin's circuit significantly to almost double the power output, replacing the 12AY7 preamp tubes with 12AX7s, the pair of 6L6 power amp tubes with a quartet of 5881s, and the pair of 5U4GA rectifier tubes with either a mercury vapour 83 (5F8 circuit) or GZ-34 (5F8-A circuit).

This matching pair of late 1950s 'big box' Twins was likely used for live performance. 'Big box' Twin amps provide very loud volume output with considerable clean headroom desired by players who love the distinctively punchy and warm clean tones and harmonically rich overdrive produced by Fender tweed amps.

1994 FENDER BLUES DE VILLE 212

EST: $600 - $900   PRICE: $1,400

LOT 41 BONHAMS 2011

Serial No: T-053838
Covering: Tweed, brown speaker cloth
Plate: Fender
Speakers: Two 12-inch ceramic
Switches: Power on/off, standby, drive select, bright
Controls: Presence, reverb, master, middle, bass, treble, drive, volume
Inputs: Two
Footswitch input: One
Other: Effects loop (power amp in, preamp out)

When Fender reissued the tweed 4x10 '59 Bassman in 1990, they discovered that a new generation of guitarists loved the vintage styling but still wanted the modern features and technology that they had become accustomed to during the three decades since Fender last produced their original tweed designs. In 1993 Fender introduced the Blues De Ville, which featured classic tweed styling and top-mounted controls in a chrome-plated chassis but also provided features that modern guitarists considered essential, like high-gain overdrive, a master volume control, channel switching, and an effects loop.

The first Fender Blues De Ville amp was a 4x10 combo designed to appeal to Bassman and Super Reverb players. A year later in 1994 Fender introduced the Blues De Ville 212, which has two 12-inch speakers like a Twin but features a less powerful circuit driven by two 6L6 power tubes to produce 60 watts of output. The lower power rating is actually preferable for the modern blues players Fender was targeting with the Blues De Ville, as it makes it easier to achieve power tube overdrive at more comfortable stage volume levels than a Twin could.

LOT 93 BONHAMS 2011

Serial No: ECT2 and ECT3
Covering: Tweed, 'oxblood' brown speaker cloth
Plate: Fender Twin-Amp
ECT2 speakers: Two 12-inch 1972 blue label Fender ceramic with annotations 'Tim Myer 3-97' on both speakers.
ECT3 speakers: Two 12-inch Jensen C12N ceramic
Switches: Power on/off, standby
Controls: Presence, bass, treble, bright volume, normal volume
Inputs: Four
ECT2 valves: Three 12AY7, one 12AX7 preamp and phase inverter, two Ruby 6L6GC-STR and two Mesa 6L6GC-STR415 power amp
ECT3 valves: Four 12AX7 preamp and phase inverter, two Philips 6L6WBG power amp
Label: ECT2 inscribed 'Built by John Suhr for Eric Clapton 5/97' in red and 'ECT2' in black; ECT3 inscribed 'Built by John Suhr for Eric Clapton 6/97'
Case: Custom-built flight case that transports the two amps together

In 1997 Clapton loaned Fender his César Díaz-modified 1957 Fender Twin amp (page 224) so they could build him reproductions that he could use on tour. Amp technician John Suhr of the Fender Custom Shop built four reproductions for Eric, making slight modifications to each circuit and experimenting with different speakers to provide even better sound and performance than the original.

Del Breckenfeld, Fender's director of artist relations, said: 'Eric considered his 1957 Twin the Holy Grail of amps, but since he only had one he was afraid of damaging it on tour. Our mission was to clone that amp, which was a quite difficult task. We first analysed the amp's specs then we searched for old parts. After all that, it still didn't sound right. At that point, John Page of the Fender Custom Shop suggested that we make a cabinet from old pine. We found some that came from an old church floor, and that made the difference. Eric loved them and declared them to be exact replicas. He gave one to B.B. King as a gift.'

These amps became Clapton's main stage amps the moment that he received them. They first appeared on stage with Clapton during his European Jazz Festival Tour in July 1997. He also used these amps on his 1998-9 Pilgrim Tour, the 2001 Reptile Tour, and the 2005 Cream Reunion at the Royal Albert Hall.

Playlist:
Royal Albert Hall London May 2-3-5-6, 2005, 2005
Gigs:
1998 Pilgrim Tour Mar. 30-Dec. 11, 1998
2001 Reptile Tour Feb. 3-Dec. 15, 2001
Highlights:
Legends 1997 Jazz Festival Tour July 3-17, 1997
Cream 2005 London Reunion Concerts May 2-6, 2005
Cream 2005 New York City Reunion Concerts Oct. 24-26, 2005

Opposite:
Bray Film Studios Windsor, Berkshire, UK Apr. 14, 2005

Clapton using these amps during rehearsals for the Cream Reunion Concerts.

ERIC It was basically either of the two Fender Twin amps that I used. One was an original Fifties blonde tweed model that was rewired and restored. That got used a lot. Then there was the copy that Fender made for me. They made a copy that had all the same materials, basically. It was a lot more robust and I could use that on the road, too.

1958 FENDER TWIN AMPLIFIER

EST: $2,000 - $3,000   PRICE: $23,900

LOT 71 CHRISTIE'S 2004

Serial No: A00502
Covering: Tweed, 'oxblood' brown speaker cloth
Plate: Fender Twin amp
Speakers: Two 12-inch
Switches: Ground, power, standby
Controls: Presence, mid, bass, treble, bright volume, normal volume
Inputs: Four

During the 1950s, Fender frequently modified their amp circuits as they constantly strived to improve the tone, volume output and performance of their amps. The Fender Twin amp with the 5F8-A circuit was the last Twin model with tweed covering, and many Fender amp enthusiasts consider it the best version of all as it combines the warmth of Fender tweed amps with the increased efficiency of Fender's late 1950s designs.

This 1958 5F8-A Twin was one of Clapton's favourite amps. Clapton's tweed Twins were usually modified by César Díaz to increase their output, and since the late 1980s they were his preferred amps in the recording studio. When Clapton started performing an increasing number of traditional blues songs during his concerts, starting with his 1991 series of performances at the Royal Albert Hall, he used his Fender Twin amps more frequently on stage as well. By 1995 he was using tweed late 1950s Twins on stage almost exclusively.

Playlist:
Recording since the late 1980s
24 Nights, 1991
Gigs:
1991 Royal Albert Hall Feb. 5-Mar. 9, 1991
World Tours 1990-1997

CIRCA 2004 AMP STAND

EST: $750 - $1,000   PRICE: $7,000

LOT 137 BONHAMS 2011

Construction: Welded aluminium frame with single removable wood shelf, black finish
Case: Custom-made flight case with various stickers

Clapton had grown so fond of the Fender Twin amps he used during the late 1990s and 2000s that he couldn't bear to part with them when he got back together with his old Cream bandmates for several reunion shows in 2005. To take the place of the Marshall stacks that he used on stage with Cream in the 1960s (page 55), Clapton had this custom amp stand built that allowed him to stack two tweed Fender Twin amps vertically for a similar visual effect. He used this rack at Cream's Royal Albert Hall and Madison Square Garden performances in 2005.

Playlist:
Royal Albert Hall London May 2-3-5-6, 2005, 2005
Gigs:
Cream 2005 London Reunion Concerts May 2-6, 2005
Cream 2005 New York City Reunion Concerts Oct. 24-26, 2005

Opposite:
Cream Reunion Concert Royal Albert Hall London, UK May 5, 2005

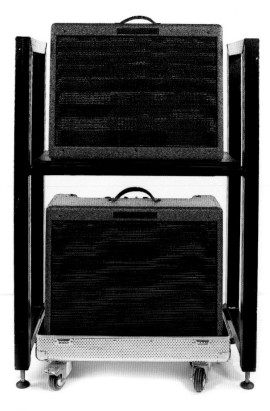

ILFORD HP5 PLUS   ILFORD HP5 PLUS   9 7 1 4   ILFORD HP5 PLUS   ILFORD

ILFORD HP5 PLUS   9 7 1 4   ILFORD HP5 PLUS

2006 TAYLOR T5 CUSTOM

Serial No: 20060901515
Body: Sapele, spruce top, multiple-layer binding, bound segmented f-holes, Honey Sunburst finish
Neck: Sapele, 21 frets, bound ebony fingerboard with 'artist series' mother-of-pearl inlays
Headstock: Solid, bound, ebony veneer
Bridge: Ebony 'belly' pin bridge
Pickups: T5 CMR air-coil rear (bridge), T5 dynamic neck, T5 dynamic body sensor
Controls: One volume, one bass, one treble
Switches: Five-position pickup selector
Case: Black Taylor mock-crocodile hardshell contour case with black plush lining, handwritten label with various inscriptions including 'TAYLOR LTUITAR [sic]'

The Taylor T5 is a hybrid electric/acoustic guitar with a thin, semi-hollow body made from a routed-out slab of sapele (an African tone wood similar to mahogany). Taylor's standard AT5 comes with either a spruce or maple top, while the T5 Custom is available with a selection of top woods that include spruce (like this example), cocobolo, koa, Makassar ebony, maple or walnut. This body design combined with active two-band EQ, a humbucking bridge pickup, and internally mounted neck humbucker and body sensor pickups enables the T5 to produce a wide variety of amplified solidbody, hollowbody and acoustic guitar tones.

Taylor Guitars are made in El Cajon, California (near San Diego), which is about 30 miles south of Escondido.

1966 FENDER SUPER REVERB

Serial No: A-15064, PL date code on tube chart
Covering: Black Tolex, silver speaker cloth
Speakers: Three 'Fender Special Design' CTS alnico-magnet 10-inch, one Rola ceramic-magnet 10-inch
Switches: Bright (channel 1), bright (channel 2)
Controls: Volume, treble, bass (channel 1); volume, treble, middle, bass, reverb, speed, intensity (channel 2)
Inputs: Four (two Normal channel, two Vibrato channel)
Other: Chrome tilt legs
Label: Tape at the bottom of the cabinet inscribed 'S.L. MAIN A15064'
Case: Black flight case with stickers, the top with white tape inscribed 'Derek Trucks EC Band, Fender 4x10 Super Rev !!Fragile!! E.C. To New York Crossroads '07' and sticker printed 'Load-In Position', inscribed 'Stage'

Guitarist Derek Trucks (Allman Brothers Band, Derek Trucks Band, Tedeschi Trucks Band) and Clapton first played music together during the recording sessions for *The Road to Escondido*. Clapton later hired Trucks to tour as a member of his band in 2006 and 2007 and invited the Derek Trucks Band to perform at the 2007 Crossroads Guitar Festival in Chicago. For the 2006 and 2007 tours Clapton loaned Trucks this 1966 Fender Super Reverb amplifier, which Trucks used as his main stage amp alongside his own Fender Super Reverb amp.

The 'blackface' mid-1960s Fender Super Reverb is a favourite of many modern blues guitarists, including Stevie Ray Vaughan, who used this model as his main amp for several years. The Super Reverb provides the volume output and punch of the beloved 1950s tweed 4x10 Fender Bassman, but with greater clean headroom, tighter bottom end, and the addition of reverb and tremolo effects. Thanks to this amp's tube chart date code (PL) we can determine that it was built in December 1966.

Gigs:
Used by Derek Trucks 2006-2007

Royal Albert Hall
London, UK
May 25, 2006

Derek Trucks playing with Clapton and using this amp.

EST: $300 - $400   PRICE: $7,000

Serial No: B-232117
Covering: Black Tolex, silver speaker cloth
Plate: Fender
Speakers: One 10-inch
Switches: Power on/off
Controls: One volume, one tone
Inputs: One
Additional: Signed by Eric Clapton on the back in black felt pen

Fender introduced the Pro Junior in 1994. Featuring a 10-inch speaker and a 15-watt circuit with two EL-84 power tubes and two 12AX7 preamp tubes, the Pro Junior was the smallest all-tube amp in Fender's line at the time. Like the Fender Champ, which it resembles in concept although the circuit is quite different, the Pro Junior is often used in the studio by guitarists who love the harmonically rich distortion and focused midrange of small tube amps. Some players – including Jeff Beck – have even used Pro Juniors on stage.

ERIC **On most of** *The Road to Escondido,* **I played a Strat and an L-5.**

Gigs:
World Tours
Feb. 25, 2008-
June 30, 2009

Royal Albert Hall
London, UK
May 17, 2009

Clapton with this amp on the drum riser to his stage right. The amplifier was used for the songs 'Anytime For You' and 'Over the Rainbow'.

Serial Nos: AB 025456, AB 025457, AB 025444
Covering: Tweed, 'oxblood' brown speaker cloth stencilled with 'Crossroads Antigua' and sun motif designed by Clapton
Plate: Fender Twin amp
Speakers: Two 12-inch Fender Special Design by Weber/Eminence alnico
Switches: Power on/off, standby
Controls: Presence, bass, treble, bright volume, normal volume
Inputs: Four
Label: Plaque on back panel engraved 'Fender Limited Edition, This hand-built amplifier is one of only fifty made to benefit the Crossroads Antigua Foundation'
Details: One red dot sticker and purple tape on the top of cabinet
Additional: Unused cover, spare leather handle, instruction manual

The Fender '57 Crossroads Twin amp is a limited-edition amplifier that Fender only sold packaged along with the Fender Eric Clapton Crossroads Stratocaster model (overleaf). Only 50 of these amps were produced. The amp is essentially a '57 Twin reissue inspired by and built to Eric's specifications but also featuring custom speaker cloth graphics with Clapton's hand-drawn Crossroads Antigua sun logo.

This particular amp was used on stage at the 2007 Crossroads Guitar Festival in Chicago by various guitarists who performed at the festival. This and the other two amps pictured here were part of the limited run of 50 '57 Crossroads Twins.

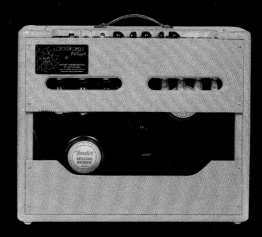

Highlight:
Eric Clapton's Crossroads Guitar Festival
Toyota Park
Bridgeville, Illinois, USA
July 28, 2007

Eric Clapton's Crossroads Guitar Festival
Fair Park
Dallas, Texas, USA
June 4, 2004

Eric pictured playing his Crash guitar (page 306) through a similar amplifier in 2004.

Serial No: MK476
Body: Alder, black finish, white printed Crossroads sun logo and 'Crossroads Antigua', signed in various inks by 22 of the artists who participated in the Crossroads Festival, Chicago, on June 26, 2010, including Eric Clapton, Jeff Beck, Steve Winwood, Albert Lee, Robert Cray, Sheryl Crow, Jimmy Vaughan, Doyle Bramhall II, and Joe Bonamassa
Neck: Maple with skunk-stripe truss rod routing, 22 frets, maple fingerboard with dot inlays, neck plate stamped with 'This Master Built Stratocaster® Guitar is 1 of only 100 made to benefit The Crossroads Antigua Foundation' and Fender Custom Shop logo
Headstock: Back of the headstock printed with 'Mark Kendrick Fender Custom Shop MK476' transfer and 'Eric Clapton Blackie' transfer
Bridge: Blocked synchronised tremolo
Pickguard: White single-ply
Pickups: Three Vintage Noiseless single-coil
Controls: One volume, two tone, TBX/MDX active circuitry
Switches: Five-position pickup selector
Additional: Black leather Fender guitar strap stamped with the Crossroads sun logo and 'Crossroads Antigua', two black guitar picks stamped with the Crossroads sun logo and 'One Day At A Time', unopened bag containing various items, including guitar cable, Fender cleaning cloth and Owner's Manual
Case: Anvil flight case with black plush lining, lid stencilled in white with the Crossroads sun logo and 'Crossroads Antigua'

About a month prior to Eric Clapton's second Crossroads Guitar Festival on July 28th, 2007, in Chicago, Fender announced the limited-edition Eric Clapton Crossroads Stratocaster model with production limited to only 100 guitars. The guitar, nicknamed the 'Sun Strat', was based on the Eric Clapton Signature Model Stratocaster that Clapton was playing at this time but also featured Clapton's hand-drawn sun logo that he created for the Crossroads Centre in Antigua. Fender paired 50 of these guitars with the limited edition Crossroads '57 Twin amp, while the remaining 50 were sold separately. The guitar/amp packages and individual guitars went on sale eight days before the 2007 festival, and Fender donated all profits from the project to the Crossroads Centre.

Clapton and John Mayer appeared on the television show *Good Morning America* in July 2007, performing a version of 'Crossroads'. Both played Crossroads Strats. Clapton kept the very first Crossroads Strat, numbered 1 of 100, and brought it to the 2010 Crossroads Guitar Festival in Chicago where he had several of the festival's performers autograph it.

ERIC My Strats have the stage strings on them, but I'm not sure what that is. Maybe an .011 or .010.

Highlight:
Good Morning America
Concert Series (TV)
Bryant Park
New York, USA
July 20, 2007

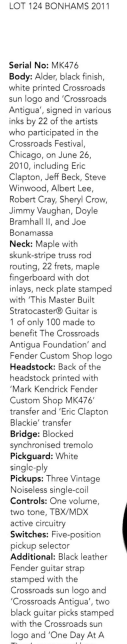

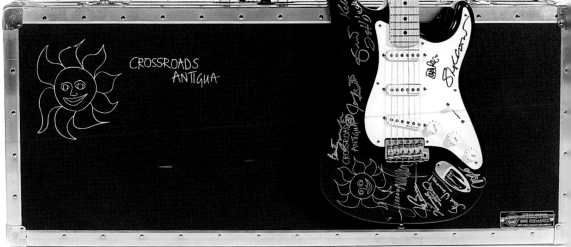

Bryant Park
New York, USA
July 20, 2007

Eric photographed during
a live television
appearance on ABC TV's
Good Morning America
with John Mayer.

Serial No: 1279975
Body: Rosewood back and sides, spruce top, natural finish
Neck: Mahogany, 20 frets, bound ebony fingerboard with dot inlays
Headstock: Solid
Bridge: Ebony 'belly' pin bridge
Pickguard: Black single-ply
Additional: Empty string envelope inscribed in an unknown hand in black felt pen 'OPEN "G," D-G-D-G-B-D, capo@4th, F#-F'
Case: Black hardshell contour case with green plush lining

When it comes to his choice of 12-string Martins for concert performances, Clapton often switches between Martin dreadnought models and Martin jumbo models. For example, for his 1992 MTV *Unplugged* performance he used a Martin D12-20 dreadnought 12-string with rounded upper bout shoulders and a 12-fret neck, but on his 1994-5 From the Cradle Tour and 2002 Concert for George performance he used a Martin J12-40 jumbo 12-string (page 292). For his 2008 summer tour, Clapton switched back to a Martin dreadnought 12-string, using a D12-28 (essentially Martin's 12-string version of a D-28, featuring square upper bout shoulders and a 14-fret neck) to perform 'Motherless Child'. As previously, he tuned the guitar to open G and placed a capo at the fourth fret to perform the song.

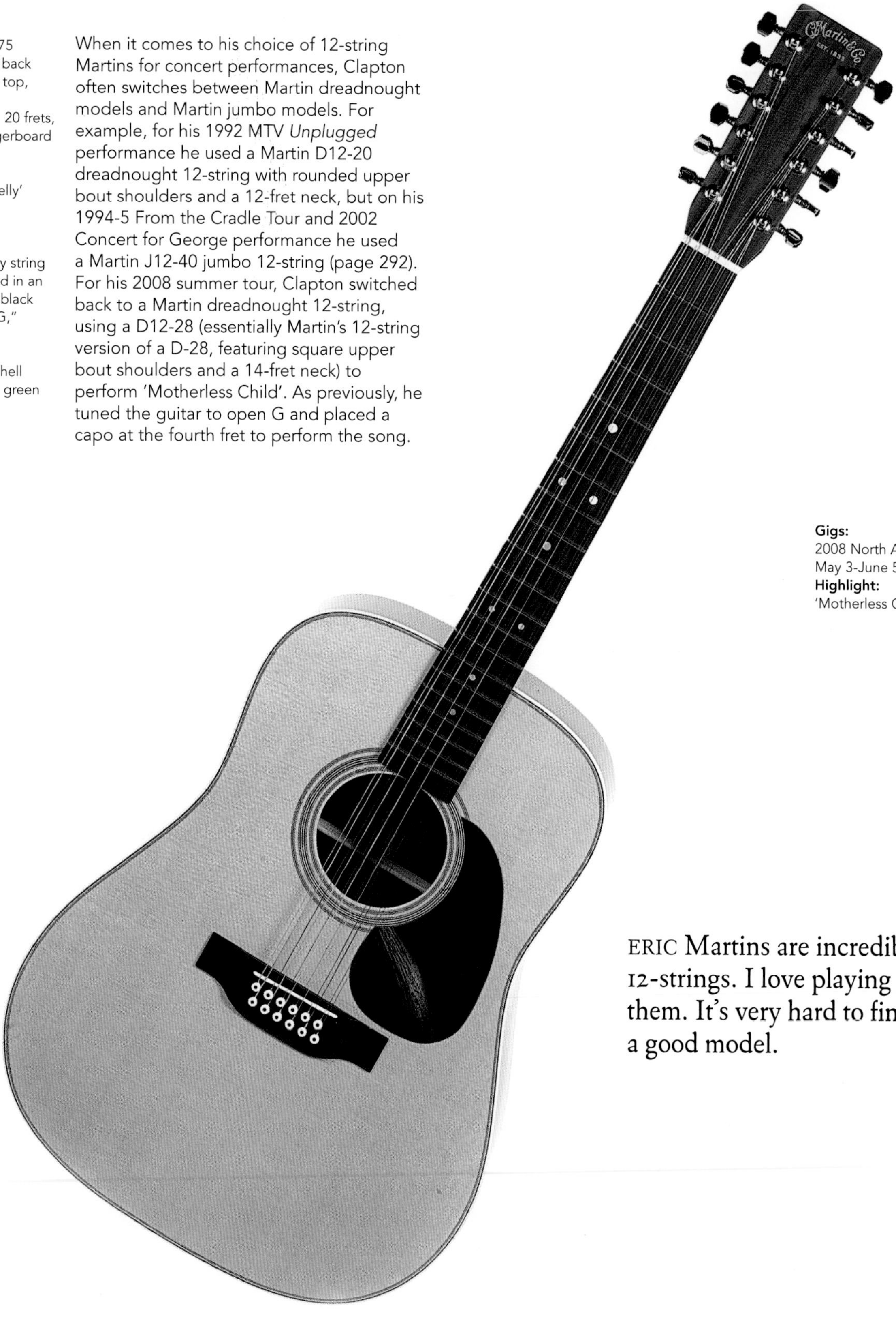

Gigs:
2008 North American Tour
May 3-June 5, 2008
Highlight:
'Motherless Children'

ERIC Martins are incredible 12-strings. I love playing them. It's very hard to find a good model.

2007 FENDER VG STRATOCASTER

EST: $3,000 - $4,000   PRICE: $15,000

LOT 60 BONHAMS 2011

Body: Alder, black finish
Neck: Maple with skunk-stripe truss rod routing, 22 frets, maple fingerboard with dot inlays, neck butt pencil-marked '06-07 Todd Krause'
Headstock: Inscribed 'Todd Krause Fender Custom Shop', signed by Clapton
Bridge: Blocked synchronised tremolo
Pickguard: White three-ply (white/black/white)
Pickups: Three single-coil, Roland GK-2 hexaphonic
Controls: One volume, one tone
Switches: Five-position pickup selector, six-position rotary tuning selector, five-position rotary model selector
Other: Battery and VG electronics compartments, staggered-height tuners
Additional: Black Fender leather guitar strap, 2007 Owner's Manual
Case: Fender tweed rectangular hardshell case with orange plush lining

The Fender VG Stratocaster was the first announced product that was the result of 10 years of prior collaboration between Fender and Japan's Roland Corporation, best known for its synthesisers, Boss-brand effects pedals and JC-120 Jazz Chorus guitar amplifiers. The VG Stratocaster featured Roland's 'Virtual Guitar' technology installed in the familiar and comfortable platform of Fender's beloved Stratocaster guitar. In addition to providing the Strat's normal passive single-coil pickup tones, the VG Stratocaster also featured Roland modelling technology that enabled it to produce a variety of Stratocaster, Telecaster, humbucking and acoustic guitar tones. Guitarists could also instantly select alternate drop D, open G, D modal, baritone and 12-string tunings without having to retune the guitar's strings.

Fender Custom Shop master builder Todd Krause sent this VG Stratocaster to Eric in 2007 for evaluation purposes.

2007 FENDER ROLAND READY STRATOCASTER

EST: $3,000 - $4,000   PRICE: $12,000

LOT 61 BONHAMS 2011

Body: Alder, black finish
Neck: Maple with skunk-stripe truss rod routing, 22 frets, maple fingerboard with dot inlays, neck butt pencil-marked '06-07 Todd Krause'
Headstock: Back of headstock inscribed 'Todd Krause Fender Custom Shop', signed by Clapton
Bridge: Blocked synchronised tremolo
Pickguard: White three-ply (white/black/white)
Pickups: Three single-coil, Roland GK-2 hexaphonic
Controls: One guitar volume, one guitar tone, one GK-2 volume
Switches: Five-position pickup selector, up button, down button, guitar/mix/synth
Other: Staggered-height tuners
Additional: Black leather Fender guitar strap, a guitar cable, Fender cleaning cloth and Owner's Manual
Case: Fender tweed rectangular hardshell case with orange plush lining

The Fender Roland Ready Stratocaster is a standard Strat with a built-in Roland GK-2 hexaphonic pickup and controls designed for use with Roland's popular guitar synth and V-Guitar systems that make it easy to switch between traditional electric guitar tones and synthesiser sounds in an instant. The Roland Ready Strat provides guitarists with a plug-and-play instrument that is more convenient than Roland's previous option, which required guitarists to install the synth pickup on their instruments themselves or with assistance from a repair shop. Thanks to the Stratocaster's popularity and affordable price, this proved to be a very popular option for guitarists who wanted to experiment with guitar synths as well as dedicated guitar synth players who preferred the Strat as their guitar of choice.

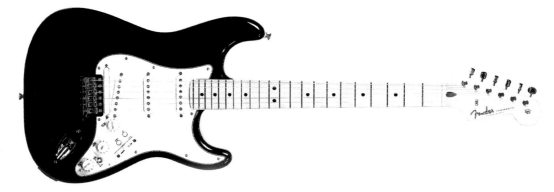

CREAM OF CLAPTON

Serial No: CZ512926
Body: Alder, Daphne Blue finish
Neck: Maple with skunk-stripe truss rod routing, 22 frets, maple fingerboard with dot inlays
Headstock: Back of the headstock with printed 'Todd Krause Fender Custom Shop' transfer
Bridge: Blocked synchronised tremolo
Pickguard: White single-ply
Pickups: Three Vintage Noiseless single-coil
Controls: One volume, two tone, TBX/MDX active circuitry
Switches: Five-position pickup selector
Case: Black Fender hardshell contour case with black plush lining, handwritten label inscribed 'Fender Daphne Blue CZ512926'

Fender settled on Black (page 194), Olympic White (page 16), Pewter (page 181) and Torino Red (page 190) as the available finish colours for the Eric Clapton Stratocaster. Of course, Clapton's personal tastes in finish colours have changed more often over the years, and the Fender Custom Shop has always happily obliged his requests for new and unusual colours.

In 2008, Clapton asked the Fender Custom Shop to build him two Strats finished in Daphne Blue – a pastel light blue shade. Clapton has used a Daphne Blue Stratocaster as his main guitar frequently since he first received those Strats later in 2008, including his performance at the 2010 Crossroads Guitar Festival.

Gigs:
2008-2011
Highlight:
Eric Clapton's Crossroads Guitar Festival
Toyota Park
Bridgeville, Illinois, USA
June 26, 2010

Left:
Eric's 1932 Ford roadster.

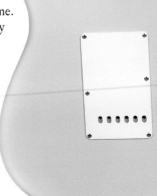

ERIC I was playing that right up until the auction. It's a 1950s doo-wop colour we took from a hot rod Roy Brizio built for me. The car is a 1932 roadster but without any roof – it's completely open. I've still got it; it's a lovely car.

123445 # 3

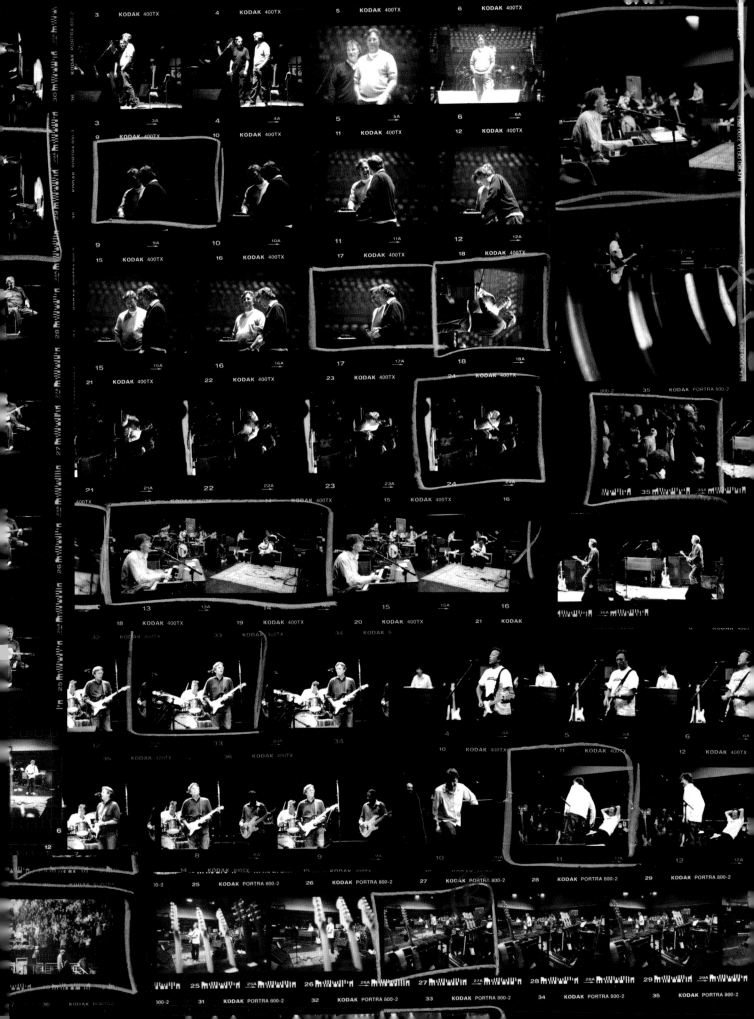

ERIC I've still got some
nice guitars that I can play.
Not as many as I had.

GIGOGRAPHY

In the 1960s, not all gigs were advertised in the press, dates would be added or cancelled without notice and tour diaries were rarely kept. Jam sessions and guest appearances can still occasionally go undocumented.

Eric Clapton: Early Appearances Autumn / Winter 1962
EC, sometimes accompanied by guitarist Dave Brock, played in the folk pubs, clubs and coffeehouses around Kingston-upon-Thames and Richmond-upon-Thames. Confirmed venues include The Crown in Kingston and L'Auberge in Richmond

The Roosters
Jan-Aug 63: Rehearsing at the Prince of Wales in New Malden, The Roosters played private parties and less than two dozen gigs primarily in Greater London. Venues included the Carfax Ballroom in Oxford, the Ricky Tick Clubs in Kingston, Reading, West Wickham and Windsor, the Wooden Bridge Hotel in Guildford, the Jazz Cellar in Kingston, The Scene in Ham Yard, Soho and Uncle Bonnie's Chinese Jazz Club in Brighton. Confirmed dates:
15 Jul 63: Marquee Club, Oxford Street, Soho, Central London (England)
20 Jul 63: Ricky Tick Club, St. John's Ambulance Hall, Chatham Street, Reading, Berkshire (England)

Casey Jones & The Engineers
Sep 63: EC plays seven gigs over several weeks on the Northern Beat and Cabaret Circuit. The first show was at the Civic Hall in Macclesfield, Cheshire. Performances followed at The Oasis and the Belle Vue Amusement Park, both in Manchester. At the Civic Hall and The Oasis gigs, The Engineers were also required to back cabaret singer Polly Perkins

The Yardbirds – U.K. Club & Ballroom Circuit
13 Oct 63: CrawDaddy Club, Richmond Athletic Association Grounds, Twickenham Road, Richmond-upon-Thames, Surrey (England) – EC is recruited to join The Yardbirds earlier this month. He goes to see them perform at this gig and agrees to join
18 Oct 63: Studio '51, Great Newport Street, Leicester Square, Central London (England) – likely EC's first official gig with The Yardbirds
19 Oct 63: CrawDaddy Club, Star Hotel, London Road, Croydon, South London (England)
20 Oct 63: Studio '51, Great Newport Street, Leicester Square, Central London (England)
20 Oct 63: CrawDaddy Club, Richmond Athletic Association Grounds, Twickenham Road, Richmond-upon-Thames, Surrey (England)
27 Oct 63: CrawDaddy Club, Richmond Athletic Association Grounds, Twickenham Road, Richmond-upon-Thames, Surrey (England)
2 Nov 63: CrawDaddy Club, Star Hotel, London Road, Croydon, South London (England)
3 Nov 63: CrawDaddy Club, Richmond Athletic Association Grounds, Twickenham Road, Richmond-upon-Thames, Surrey (England)
8 Nov 63: CrawDaddy Club, Edwina's, Seven Sisters Road, Finsbury Park, North London (England)
9 Nov 63: CrawDaddy Club, Star Hotel, London Road, Croydon, South London (England)
10 Nov 63: CrawDaddy Club, Richmond Athletic Association Grounds, Twickenham Road, Richmond-upon-Thames, Surrey (England)
15 Nov 63: CrawDaddy Club, Edwina's, Seven Sisters Road, Finsbury Park, North London (England)
16 Nov 63: CrawDaddy Club, Star Hotel, London Road, Croydon, South London (England)
17 Nov 63: CrawDaddy Club, Richmond Athletic Association Grounds, Twickenham Road, Richmond-upon-Thames, Surrey (England)
20 Nov 63: Ricky Tick Club, The Star & Garter, Peascod Street, Windsor, Berkshire (England)
22 Nov 63: CrawDaddy Club, Edwina's, Seven Sisters Road, Finsbury Park, North London (England)
23 Nov 63: CrawDaddy Club, Star Hotel, London Road, Croydon, South London (England)
24 Nov 63: CrawDaddy Club, Richmond Athletic Association Grounds, Twickenham Road, Richmond-upon-Thames, Surrey (England)
29 Nov 63: CrawDaddy Club, Edwina's, Seven Sisters Road, Finsbury Park, North London (England)
30 Nov 63: CrawDaddy Club, Star Hotel, London Road, Croydon, South London (England)
1 Dec 63: CrawDaddy Club, Richmond Athletic Association Grounds, Twickenham Road, Richmond-upon-Thames, Surrey (England)
6 Dec 63: CrawDaddy Club, Edwina's, Seven Sisters Road, Finsbury Park, North London (England)
7 Dec 63: CrawDaddy Club, Star Hotel, London Road, Croydon, South London (England) – before their performance, the band rehearses with Sonny Boy Williamson for the next night's gig
8 Dec 63: CrawDaddy Club, Richmond Athletic Association Grounds, Twickenham Road, Richmond-upon-Thames, Surrey (England) – with Sonny Boy Williamson
13 Dec 63: Club A'Gogo, Percy Street, Newcastle-upon-Tyne, Northumberland (England)
13 Dec 63: Downbeat Club, Carliol Square, Newcastle-upon-Tyne, Northumberland (England) – probable all-nighter
14 Dec 63: CrawDaddy Club, Star Hotel, London Road, Croydon, South London (England)
15 Dec 63: Guildford Civic Hall, London Road, Guildford, Surrey (England)
17 Dec 63: Ricky Tick Club, The Star & Garter, Peascod Street, Windsor, Berkshire (England) – with Sonny Boy Williamson
20 Dec 63: Ricky Tick Club, Plaza Ballroom, Guildford, Surrey (England)
21 Dec 63: CrawDaddy Club, Star Hotel, London Road, Croydon, South London (England)
22 Dec 63: Olympia Ballroom, Reading, Berkshire (England) – Roger Pearce fills in for EC at this afternoon gig as he had scheduled time off over the Christmas holiday. EC is reportedly in the audience
22 Dec 63: CrawDaddy Club, Richmond Athletic Association Grounds, Twickenham Road, Richmond-upon-Thames, Surrey (England) – with Sonny Boy Williamson. EC on holiday, Roger Pearce fills in on guitar
24 Dec 63: Ricky Tick Club, The Star & Garter, Peascod Street, Windsor, Berkshire (England) – EC on holiday, Roger Pearce fills in on guitar
28 Dec 63: CrawDaddy Club, Star Hotel, London Road, Croydon, South London (England) – EC on holiday, Roger Pearce fills in on guitar
29 Dec 63: CrawDaddy Club, Richmond Athletic Association Grounds, Twickenham Road, Richmond-upon-Thames, Surrey (England) – EC on holiday, Roger Pearce fills in on guitar
4 Jan 64: CrawDaddy Club, Star Hotel, London Road, Croydon, South London (England) – EC returns to the band
5 Jan 64: CrawDaddy Club, Richmond Athletic Association Grounds, Twickenham Road, Richmond-upon-Thames, Surrey (England)
7 Jan 64: Ricky Tick Club, The Star & Garter, Peascod Street, Windsor, Berkshire (England)
11 Jan 64: CrawDaddy Club, Star Hotel, London Road, Croydon, South London (England)
12 Jan 64: CrawDaddy Club, Richmond Athletic Association Grounds, Twickenham Road, Richmond-upon-Thames, Surrey (England)
14 Jan 64: Ricky Tick Club, The Star & Garter, Peascod Street, Windsor, Berkshire (England)
17 Jan 64: Ricky Tick Club, Plaza Ballroom, Guildford, Surrey (England) – with Sonny Boy Williamson
18 Jan 64: CrawDaddy Club, Star Hotel, London Road, Croydon, South London (England)
19 Jan 64: CrawDaddy Club, Richmond Athletic Association Grounds, Twickenham Road, Richmond-upon-Thames, Surrey (England)
20 Jan 64: Toby Jug Hotel, Hook Rise South, Tolworth, Surrey (England)
21 Jan 64: Ricky Tick Club, The Star & Garter, Peascod Street, Windsor, Berkshire (England)

The Yardbirds – "The Big R&B Night"
22 Jan 64: The Cavern Club, Mathew Street, Liverpool, Merseyside (England) with Sonny Boy Williamson

The Yardbirds – U.K. Club & Ballroom Circuit cont'd
23 Jan 64: Marquee Club, Oxford Street, Soho, Central London (England)
24 Jan 64: Ricky Tick Club, St. John's Ambulance Hall, Chatham Street, Reading, Berkshire (England)
25 Jan 64: CrawDaddy Club, Star Hotel, London Road, Croydon, South London (England)
26 Jan 64: CrawDaddy Club, Richmond Athletic Association Grounds, Twickenham Road, Richmond-upon-Thames, Surrey (England)
27 Jan 64: Toby Jug Hotel, Hook Rise South, Tolworth, Surrey (England)
28 Jan 64: Ricky Tick Club, The Star & Garter, Peascod Street, Windsor, Berkshire (England)

The Yardbirds – "Cyril Davies Benefit Night"
28 Jan 64: The Flamingo, Wardour Street, Soho, Central London (England)

The Yardbirds – U.K. Club & Ballroom Circuit cont'd
30 Jan 64: Marquee Club, Oxford Street, Soho, Central London (England)
31 Jan 64: Ricky Tick Club, St. John's Ambulance Hall, Chatham Street, Reading, Berkshire (England)
1 Feb 64: Ricky Tick Club, Pearce Hall, Marlow Road, Maidenhead, Berkshire (England) – with Sonny Boy Williamson
2 Feb 64: CrawDaddy Club, Richmond Athletic Association Grounds, Twickenham Road, Richmond-upon-Thames, Surrey (England)
3 Feb 64: Coronation Hall, Denmark Road, Kingston-upon-Thames, Surrey (England)
4 Feb 64: Ricky Tick Club, Plaza Ballroom, Guildford, Surrey (England)
6 Feb 64: Marquee Club, Oxford Street, Soho, Central London (England)
7 Feb 64: Ricky Tick Club, St. John's Ambulance Hall, Chatham Street, Reading, Berkshire (England)

8 Feb 64: Ricky Tick Club, Pearce Hall, Marlow Road, Maidenhead, Berkshire (England)
8 Feb 64: Galaxy Club, Town Hall, Basingstoke, Hampshire (England)
9 Feb 64: CrawDaddy Club, Richmond Athletic Association Grounds, Twickenham Road, Richmond-upon-Thames, Surrey (England)
11 Feb 64: Coronation Hall, Denmark Road, Kingston-upon-Thames, Surrey (England)
13 Feb 64: Marquee Club, Oxford Street, Soho, Central London (England)
14 Feb 64: CrawDaddy Club, Star Hotel, London Road, Croydon, South London (England)
15 Feb 64: CrawDaddy Club, Richmond Athletic Association Grounds, Twickenham Road, Richmond-upon-Thames, Surrey (England)
16 Feb 64: Olympia Ballroom, Reading, Berkshire (England)
16 Feb 64: Ricky Tick Club, Pearce Hall, Marlow Road, Maidenhead, Berkshire (England)
18 Feb 64: Ricky Tick Club, Plaza Ballroom, Guildford, Surrey (England)
20 Feb 64: Marquee Club, Oxford Street, Soho, Central London (England)

The Yardbirds – "National Jazz Federation Presents A Cyril Davies Benefit Concert"
21 Feb 64: Fairfield Halls, Park Lane, Croydon, South London (England) – with Sonny Boy Williamson and others

The Yardbirds – U.K. Club & Ballroom Circuit cont'd
22 Feb 64: Ricky Tick Club, Pearce Hall, Marlow Road, Maidenhead, Berkshire (England)
23 Feb 64: CrawDaddy Club, Richmond Athletic Association Grounds, Twickenham Road, Richmond-upon-Thames, Surrey (England)
26 Feb 64: The Cavern Club, Mathew Street, Liverpool, Merseyside (England) lunchtime

The Yardbirds – "R&B Festival No. 2"
26 Feb 64: The Cavern Club, Mathew Street, Liverpool, Merseyside (England) evening show with Sonny Boy Williamson

The Yardbirds – U.K. Club & Ballroom Circuit cont'd
27 Feb 64: Marquee Club, Oxford Street, Soho, Central London (England)

The Yardbirds – "Birmingham's 1st British Rhythm & Blues Festival"
28 Feb 64: Town Hall, Victoria Square, Birmingham, West Midlands (England) with Sonny Boy Williamson

The Yardbirds – U.K. Club & Ballroom Circuit cont'd
29 Feb 64: Ricky Tick Club, Pearce Hall, Marlow Road, Maidenhead, Berkshire (England)
1 Mar 64: CrawDaddy Club, Richmond Athletic Association Grounds, Twickenham Road, Richmond-upon-Thames, Surrey (England)
3 Mar 64: Coronation Hall, Denmark Road, Kingston-upon-Thames, Surrey (England)
3 Mar 64: Town Hall, Alexandra Road, Farnborough, Hampshire (England) with Sonny Boy Williamson
5 Mar 64: Marquee Club, Oxford Street, Soho, Central London (England) the venue's last night at this location
6 Mar 64: Telephone House, Wimbledon, Northwest London (England)
7 Mar 64: Ricky Tick Club, Pearce Hall, Marlow Road, Maidenhead, Berkshire (England)
8 Mar 64: The Refectory, Finchley Road, Golders Green, Northwest London (England)
8 Mar 64: CrawDaddy Club, Richmond Athletic Association Grounds, Twickenham Road, Richmond-upon-Thames, Surrey (England)
11 Mar 64: CrawDaddy Club, Star Hotel, London Road, Croydon, South London (England)
13 Mar 64: Marquee Club, Wardour Street, Soho, Central London (England) with Sonny Boy Williamson; opening night of the venue's new location
14 Mar 64: CrawDaddy Club, Star Hotel, London Road, Croydon, South London (England)
15 Mar 64: CrawDaddy Club, Richmond Athletic Association Grounds, Twickenham Road, Richmond-upon-Thames, Surrey (England)
20 Mar 64: Marquee Club, Wardour Street, Soho, Central London (England)
21 Mar 64: CrawDaddy Club, Star Hotel, London Road, Croydon, South London (England)
22 Mar 64: CrawDaddy Club, Richmond Athletic Association Grounds, Twickenham Road, Richmond-upon-Thames, Surrey (England)
27 Mar 64: Marquee Club, Wardour Street, Soho, Central London (England)
28 Mar 64: Star Club, Star Hotel, London Road, Croydon, South London (England)
29 Mar 64: CrawDaddy Club, Richmond Athletic Association Grounds, Twickenham Road, Richmond-upon-Thames, Surrey (England) – Brian Jones fills in for vocalist Keith Relf
3 Apr 64: Marquee Club, Wardour Street, Soho, Central London (England)
4 Apr 64: St. Peter's Hall, Kingston-upon-Thames, Surrey (England)
5 Apr 64: CrawDaddy Club, Richmond Athletic Association Grounds, Twickenham Road, Richmond-upon-Thames, Surrey (England)
6 Apr 64: The Refectory, Finchley Road, Golders Green, Northwest London (England)

6 Apr 64: Town Hall, Queen Victoria Road, High Wycombe, Buckinghamshire (England)
10 Apr 64: Marquee Club, Wardour Street, Soho, Central London (England)
11 Apr 64: Star Club, Star Hotel, London Road, Croydon, South London (England)
12 Apr 64: CrawDaddy Club, Richmond Athletic Association Grounds, Twickenham Road, Richmond-upon-Thames, Surrey (England)
17 Apr 64: Marquee Club, Wardour Street, Soho, Central London (England)
18 Apr 64: Star Club, Star Hotel, London Road, Croydon, South London (England)
19 Apr 64: CrawDaddy Club, Richmond Athletic Association Grounds, Twickenham Road, Richmond-upon-Thames, Surrey (England)
20 Apr 64: The Cellar Club, High Street, Kingston-upon-Thames, Surrey (England)
23 Apr 64: Town Hall, Queen Victoria Road, High Wycombe, Buckinghamshire (England)
24 Apr 64: Unknown Venue, Unknown Location (Wales)
25 Apr 64: Town Hall, Abergavenny, Monmouth (Wales)
26 Apr 64: CrawDaddy Club, Richmond Athletic Association Grounds, Twickenham Road, Richmond-upon-Thames, Surrey (England)
27 Apr 64: Bluesville R&B, The Manor House, Finsbury Park, North London (England)
28 Apr 64: Star Club, Star Hotel, London Road, Croydon, South London (England)
30 Apr 64: Olympia Ballroom, Reading, Berkshire (England)
1 May 64: Marquee Club, Wardour Street, Soho, Central London (England)
2 May 64: Star Club, Star Hotel, London Road, Croydon, South London (England)
3 May 64: CrawDaddy Club, Richmond Athletic Association Grounds, Twickenham Road, Richmond-upon-Thames, Surrey (England)
4 May 64: Bromel Club, Bromley Court Hotel, Bromley Hill, Bromley, Kent (England)
6 May 64: The Refectory, Finchley Road, Golders Green, Northwest London (England)
8 May 64: Marquee Club, Wardour Street, Soho, Central London (England)
9 May 64: Star Club, Star Hotel, London Road, Croydon, South London (England)
10 May 64: CrawDaddy Club, Richmond Athletic Association Grounds, Twickenham Road, Richmond-upon-Thames, Surrey (England)
11 May 64: The Cellar Club, High Street, Kingston-upon-Thames, Surrey (England)
13 May 64: Party for Lord Ted Willis, Private Home, Chiselhurst, Kent (England)
13 May 64: Bromel Club, Bromley Court Hotel, Bromley Hill, Bromley, Kent (England)
15 May 64: Marquee Club, Wardour Street, Soho, Central London (England)
16 May 64: Star Club, Star Hotel, London Road, Croydon, South London (England)
17 May 64: CrawDaddy Club, Richmond Athletic Association Grounds, Twickenham Road, Richmond-upon-Thames, Surrey (England)
21 May 64: Town Hall, Queen Victoria Road, High Wycombe, Buckinghamshire (England)

The Yardbirds – "Ready Steady Go" Television Show (ITV-Rediffusion)
22 May 64: Associated-Rediffusion Studios, Television House, Kingsway, Central London (England) – television broadcast date, probably pre-recorded (Season 1, Episode #43)

The Yardbirds – U.K. Club & Ballroom Circuit cont'd
22 May 64: Marquee Club, Wardour Street, Soho, Central London (England)
24 May 64: CrawDaddy Club, Richmond Athletic Association Grounds, Twickenham Road, Richmond-upon-Thames, Surrey (England)
25 May 64: The Cellar Club, High Street, Kingston-upon-Thames, Surrey (England)

The Yardbirds – "Discs A Go Go" Television Show (TWW/ITV)
27 May 64: TV Wales & West Studios, Television Centre, Bath Road, Brislington, Bristol (England) – likely pre-recording date for 1 Jun television broadcast

The Yardbirds – U.K. Club & Ballroom Circuit cont'd
27 May 64: Beckenham Ballroom, Beckenham, Southeast London (England)
29 May 64: Marquee Club, Wardour Street, Soho, Central London (England)
31 May 64: CrawDaddy Club, Richmond Athletic Association Grounds, Twickenham Road, Richmond-upon-Thames, Surrey (England)
3 Jun 64: The Twisted Wheel Club, Whitworth Street, Manchester (England)
5 Jun 64: Marquee Club, Wardour Street, Soho, Central London (England)
6 Jun 64: Trade Union Hall, Watford, Hertfordshire (England)
7 Jun 64: CrawDaddy Club, Richmond Athletic Association Grounds, Twickenham Road, Richmond-upon-Thames, Surrey (England)
8 Jun 64: The Cellar Club, High Street, Kingston-upon-Thames, Surrey (England)
9 Jun 64: Town Hall, Queen Victoria Road, High Wycombe, Buckinghamshire (England)
10 Jun 64: Blue Moon, Church Road, Hayes, Middlesex (England)
11 Jun 64: Brighton Dome, Church Street, Brighton, East Sussex (England)
12 Jun 64: Marquee Club, Wardour Street, Soho, Central London (England)
13 Jun 64: Fleur de Lys, Hayes, Middlesex (England)

The Yardbirds – "All Nite Rave"
13 Jun 64: Club Noreik, High Road, Tottenham, North London (England)

The Yardbirds – U.K. Club & Ballroom Circuit cont'd
14 Jun 64: Wimbledon Palais, Merton High Street, Wimbledon, Northwest London (England)

The Yardbirds – "The Cool Spot" Television Show (BBC TV)
Jun 64: Nottingham Ice Stadium, Nottingham, Nottinghamshire (England)
possible appearance as acts unable to appear had their records choreographed by ice
skaters; pre-recorded mid-month for 7 Jul television broadcast (Episode #1)

The Yardbirds – U.K. Club & Ballroom Circuit cont'd
16 Jun 64: University Hall, Cambridge University, Cambridge (England)
18 Jun 64: The Twisted Wheel Club, Whitworth Street, Manchester (England)
19 Jun 64: Marquee Club, Wardour Street, Soho, Central London (England)
20 Jun 64: Uxbridge Showground, Uxbridge, Middlesex (England)

The Yardbirds – "West London Jazz Festival"
20 Jun 64: Osterley Rugby Club Ground, Tentelow Lane, Norwood Green,
West London (England)

The Yardbirds – U.K. Club & Ballroom Circuit cont'd
21 Jun 64: CrawDaddy Club, Richmond Athletic Association Grounds, Twickenham
Road, Richmond-upon-Thames, Surrey (England)
22 Jun 64: The Cellar Club, High Street, Kingston-upon-Thames, Surrey (England)
23 Jun 64: Assembly Hall, Aylesbury, Buckinghamshire (England)

The Yardbirds – "Discs A Go Go" Television Show (TWW/ITV)
24 Jun 64: TV Wales & West Studios, Television Centre, Bath Road, Brislington, Bristol
(England) – pre-recording date for 29 Jun broadcast

The Yardbirds – U.K. Club & Ballroom Circuit cont'd
25 Jun 64: Attic Club, High Street, Hounslow, West London (England)

The Yardbirds – "Northern Jazz Festival"
26 Jun 64: Redcar Racecourse, Thrush Road, Redcar and Cleveland, North Yorkshire
(England)

The Yardbirds – "Thank Your Lucky Stars" Television Show (ABC TV)
27 Jun 64: Alpha Television Studio, Aston, Birmingham (England) – television
broadcast date; pre-recorded on unknown date (Season 4, Episode #40)

The Yardbirds – U.K. Club & Ballroom Circuit cont'd
28 Jun 64: CrawDaddy Club, Richmond Athletic Association Grounds, Twickenham
Road, Richmond-upon-Thames, Surrey (England)
29 Jun 64: The Cellar Club, High Street, Kingston-upon-Thames, Surrey (England)
30 Jun 64: Casino Hotel, Tags Island, Twickenham, Southwest London (England)
1 Jul 64: Blu-Beat Club, Lord Wakefield Hall, Hayes, Middlesex (England)
3 Jul 64: Marquee Club, Wardour Street, Soho, Central London (England)
5 Jul 64: The Cavern Club, Mathew Street, Liverpool, Merseyside (England)
7 Jul 64: Tuesday Blues Club, Churchill Hall, Hawthorne Avenue, Kenton, Harrow,
Northwest London (England)
8 Jul 64: Blu-Beat Club, Lord Wakefield Hall, Hayes, Middlesex (England)
9 Jul 64: Olympia Ballroom, Reading, Berkshire (England)
10 Jul 64: Marquee Club, Wardour Street, Soho, Central London (England)
11 Jul 64: Rhodes Centre, South Road, Bishop's Stortford, Hertfordshire (England)
12 Jul 64: Scala Ballroom, Kent Road, Dartford, Kent (England)
13 Jul 64: The Sparrowhawk, Edgware, North London (England)
14 Jul 64: Tuesday Blues Club, Churchill Hall, Hawthorne Avenue, Kenton, Harrow,
Northwest London (England)
15 Jul 64: Il Rondo, Silver Street, Leicester, Leicestershire (England)
16 Jul 64: Olympia Ballroom, Reading, Berkshire (England)
17 Jul 64: Marquee Club, Wardour Street, Soho, Central London (England)

The Yardbirds – "2nd Scottish Jazz & Blues Festival"
18 Jul 64: Dam Park Stadium, Ayr, South Ayrshire (Scotland)

The Yardbirds – U.K. Club & Ballroom Circuit cont'd
19 Jul 64: Commodore Cinema Ballroom, Star Street, Ryde, Isle of Wight (England)
20 Jul 64: The Cellar Club, High Street, Kingston-upon-Thames, Surrey (England)
21 Jul 64: Tuesday Blues Club, Churchill Hall, Hawthorne Avenue, Kenton, Harrow,
Northwest London (England)

The Yardbirds – "Go Tell It On The Mountain" TV Show (Granada TV)
22 Jul 64: Granada Studios, Quay Street, Manchester (England)

The Yardbirds – U.K. Club & Ballroom Circuit cont'd
22 Jul 64: The Twisted Wheel Club, Whitworth Street, Manchester (England)
23 Jul 64: The Twisted Wheel Club, Whitworth Street, Manchester (England)
23 Jul 64: Queen's Ballroom, Cleveleys, Lancashire (England)
24 Jul 64: Marquee Club, Wardour Street, Soho, Central London (England)
25 Jul 64: King George's Hall, High Street, Esher, Surrey (England)
26 Jul 64: CrawDaddy Club, Richmond Athletic Association Grounds, Twickenham
Road, Richmond-upon-Thames, Surrey (England)

The Yardbirds – U.K. Club & Ballroom Circuit cont'd
27 Jul 64: Town Hall, Station Road, Clacton-On-Sea, Essex (England)
28 Jul 64: Tuesday Blues Club, Churchill Hall, Hawthorne Avenue, Kenton, Harrow,
Northwest London (England)
29 Jul 64: Bromel Club, Bromley Court Hotel, Bromley Hill, Bromley, Kent (England)
30 Jul 64: The Locarno Ballroom, High Street, Old Town, Swindon (England)
31 Jul 64: Marquee Club, Wardour Street, Soho, Central London (England)
2 Aug 64: CrawDaddy Club, Richmond Athletic Association Grounds, Twickenham
Road, Richmond-upon-Thames, Surrey (England)
4 Aug 64: The Fender Club, Churchill Hall, Hawthorne Avenue, Kenton, Harrow,
Northwest London (England)
5 Aug 64: Town Hall, Castle Circus, Torquay, Devon (England)
6 Aug 64: Flamingo Ballroom, Illogan Highway, Redruth, Cornwall (England)
6 Aug 64: Queen's Ballroom, Barnstaple, Devon (England) – unconfirmed
7 Aug 64: Marquee Club, Wardour Street, Soho, Central London (England) – vocalist
Keith Relf collapses during this show with complications from severe asthma and
misses 6 weeks of gigs. Mick O'Neil, Mike Vernon and Tony Carter fill in
8 Aug 64: Unknown Venue, Unknown Location (England)

The Yardbirds – "4th National Jazz & Blues Festival"
9 Aug 64: Richmond Athletic Association Grounds, Richmond-upon-Thames, Surrey
(England)

The Yardbirds – "International Jazz Days Festival"
14 Aug 64: Unknown Venue, Ascona, Ticino (Switzerland) – exact date(s) performing
unknown
15 Aug 64: Unknown Venue, Ascona, Ticino (Switzerland) – exact date(s) performing
unknown
16 Aug 64: Unknown Venue, Ascona, Ticino (Switzerland) – exact date(s) performing
unknown

The Yardbirds – Swiss "Holiday" Engagement
14 Aug 64: Lido, Locarno, Ticino (Switzerland)
15 Aug 64: Lido, Locarno, Ticino (Switzerland)
16 Aug 64: Lido, Locarno, Ticino (Switzerland)
17 Aug 64: Lido, Locarno, Ticino (Switzerland)
18 Aug 64: Lido, Locarno, Ticino (Switzerland)
19 Aug 64: Lido, Locarno, Ticino (Switzerland)
20 Aug 64: Lido, Locarno, Ticino (Switzerland)
21 Aug 64: Lido, Locarno, Ticino (Switzerland)

The Yardbirds – U.K. Club & Ballroom Circuit cont'd
29 Aug 64: Town Hall, Abergavenny, Monmouthshire (Wales) – unconfirmed

The Yardbirds – "Discs A Go Go" Television Show (TWW/ITV)
2 Sep 64: TV Wales & West Studios, Television Centre, Bath Road, Brislington, Bristol
(England) – likely pre-recording date for 7 Sep broadcast

The Yardbirds – U.K. Club & Ballroom Circuit cont'd
4 Sep 64: Marquee Club, Wardour Street, Soho, Central London (England)
6 Sep 64: CrawDaddy Club, Richmond Athletic Association Grounds, Twickenham
Road, Richmond-upon-Thames, Surrey (England)
8 Sep 64: Tuesday Blues Club, Churchill Hall, Hawthorne Avenue, Kenton, Harrow,
Northwest London (England)
9 Sep 64: Il Rondo, Silver Street, Leicester, Leicestershire (England)
10 Sep 64: Kidderminster Town Hall, Vicar Street, Kidderminster, Worcestershire
(England)
11 Sep 64: Marquee Club, Wardour Street, Soho, Central London (England)
12 Sep 64: Pavilion Gardens Ballroom, St. John's Road, Buxton, Derbyshire (England)
13 Sep 64: CrawDaddy Club, Richmond Athletic Association Grounds, Twickenham
Road, Richmond-upon-Thames, Surrey (England)
15 Sep 64: Town Hall, Queen Victoria Road, High Wycombe, Buckinghamshire
(England)
16 Sep 64: The Bristol Chinese R&B and Jazz Club, The Corn Exchange, Corn Street,
Bristol (England)

The Yardbirds – U.K. & Ireland Package Tour
18 Sep 64: Granada Theatre, Hoe Street, Walthamstow, Northeast London (England)
cancelled
19 Sep 64: Colston Hall, Colston Street, Bristol (England) – cancelled
20 Sep 64: Odeon Theatre, Loampit Vale, Lewisham, South London (England)
cancelled
21 Sep 64: Granada Theatre, Lower Stone Street, Maidstone, Kent (England)
recovered from his illness, vocalist Keith Relf rejoins the band after 6 weeks
22 Sep 64: Granada Theatre, Greenford Road, Greenford, West London (England)
23 Sep 64: Gaumont Theatre, St. Helen's Street, Ipswich, Suffolk (England)
24 Sep 64: Odeon Theatre, High Street, Southend-on-Sea, Essex (England)
25 Sep 64: ABC Cinema, Abbington Street, Northampton, East Midlands (England)
26 Sep 64: Granada Theatre, West Gate, Mansfield, Nottinghamshire (England)
27 Sep 64: Empire Theatre, Lime Street, Liverpool, Merseyside (England)

28 Sep 64: Caird Hall, City Square, Dundee (Scotland)
29 Sep 64: ABC Cinema, Lothian Road, Edinburgh (Scotland)
30 Sep 64: Odeon Theatre, Renfield Street, Glasgow (Scotland)
1 Oct 64: Adelphi Theatre, Middle Abbey Street, Dublin (Ireland)
2 Oct 64: ABC Cinema, Fisherwick Place, Belfast (Northern Ireland)
3 Oct 64: Savoy Theatre, Patrick Street, Cork (Ireland)
4 Oct 64: Globe Theatre (ABC Cinema), High Street, Stockton-on-Tees, Yorkshire (England)
7 Oct 64: ABC Cinema, Warwick Road, Carlisle, Cumbria (England)
8 Oct 64: Odeon Theatre, Ashburner Street, Bolton, Manchester (England)
9 Oct 64: Granada Theatre, St. Peter's Hill, Grantham, Lincolnshire (England)
10 Oct 64: ABC Cinema, Ferensway, Hull, East Riding of Yorkshire (England)
11 Oct 64: Granada Theatre, Barking Road, East Ham, London (England)

The Yardbirds – Booking Independent Of Package Tour
12 Oct 64: Unknown Venue, Hanworth, West London (England)

The Yardbirds – U.K. & Ireland Package Tour cont'd
13 Oct 64: Granada Theatre, St. Peter's Street, Bedford, Bedfordshire (England)
14 Oct 64: Granada Theatre, Brighton Terrace, Brixton, South London (England)
15 Oct 64: Odeon Theatre, Upper High Street, Guildford, Surrey (England)
16 Oct 64: ABC Cinema, Above Bar, Southampton, Hampshire (England)
17 Oct 64: ABC Cinema, St. Aldate Street, Gloucester, Gloucestershire (England)
18 Oct 64: Granada Theatre, Mitcham Road, Tooting, Southwest London (England)

The Yardbirds – "Kingston Student Rag Week"
20 Oct 64: TA Hall, Surbiton Road, Kingston-upon-Thames, Surrey (England)

The Yardbirds – U.K. Club & Ballroom Circuit cont'd
21 Oct 64: The Twisted Wheel Club, Whitworth Street, Manchester (England)
23 Oct 64: Marquee Club, Wardour Street, Soho, Central London (England)
24 Oct 64: Goldhawk Social Club, Goldhawk Road, Shepherd's Bush, West London (England)
25 Oct 64: CrawDaddy Club, Richmond Athletic Association Grounds, Twickenham Road, Richmond-upon-Thames, Surrey (England)
26 Oct 64: Glenlyn Ballroom, Forest Hill, South London (England)

The Yardbirds – "Town and Around" Television Show (BBC 1 TV)
27 Oct 64: Unknown Television Studio, Unknown Location (England) – likely date; pre-recorded for 28 Oct television broadcast

The Yardbirds – "Rhythm & Blues" Radio Show (BBC World Service)
29 Oct 64: BBC Maida Vale Studios, Delaware Road, Maida Vale, West London (England) – pre-recorded for 21 Nov radio broadcast

The Yardbirds – U.K. Club & Ballroom Circuit cont'd
29 Oct 64: The Lakeside R&B Scene, Old Welsh Harp, The Broadway, Hendon, Northwest London (England)
30 Oct 64: Marquee Club, Wardour Street, Soho, Central London (England)
1 Nov 64: CrawDaddy Club, Richmond Athletic Association Grounds, Twickenham Road, Richmond-upon-Thames, Surrey (England)
3 Nov 64: Town Hall, Queen Victoria Road, High Wycombe, Buckinghamshire (England)

The Yardbirds – "Discs A Go Go" Television Show (TWW/ITV)
4 Nov 64: TV Wales & West Studios, Television Centre, Bath Road, Brislington, Bristol, (England) – pre-recorded for 9 Nov television broadcast

The Yardbirds – U.K. Club & Ballroom Circuit cont'd
7 Nov 64: Memorial Hall, Northwich, Cheshire (England)
8 Nov 64: CrawDaddy Club, Richmond Athletic Association Grounds, Twickenham Road, Richmond-upon-Thames, Surrey (England)
10 Nov 64: Tuesday Blues Club, Churchill Hall, Hawthorne Avenue, Kenton, Harrow, Northwest London (England)
11 Nov 64: The Bristol Chinese R&B and Jazz Club, The Corn Exchange, Corn Street, Bristol (England)
14 Nov 64: The Twisted Wheel Club, Whitworth Street, Manchester (England)
19 Nov 64: Worthing Pier Pavilion, Worthing, West Sussex (England)
21 Nov 64: Ricky Tick Club, Plaza Ballroom, Guildford, Surrey (England)
22 Nov 64: Hippodrome, Middle Street, Brighton, East Sussex (England)

The Yardbirds – "Five O'Clock Club" Television Show (ITV-Rediffusion)
24 Nov 64: Associated-Rediffusion Studios, Wembley Drive, Wembley, Northwest London (England) – live television broadcast

The Yardbirds – U.K. Club & Ballroom Circuit cont'd
27 Nov 64: Town Hall, Leamington Spa, Warwickshire (England)
29 Nov 64: CrawDaddy Club, Richmond Athletic Association Grounds, Twickenham Road, Richmond-upon-Thames, Surrey (England)

4 Dec 64: Ricky Tick Club, The Thames Hotel, Barry Avenue, Windsor, Berkshire (England)
5 Dec 64: St George's Hall Ballroom, Hinckley, Leicestershire (England)

The Yardbirds – "Top Beat Show" (BBC 2 TV)
7 Dec 64: Royal Albert Hall, Kensington Gore, Central London (England) pre-recorded for television broadcast on 9 Dec

The Yardbirds – U.K. Club & Ballroom Circuit cont'd
8 Dec 64: Assembly Hall, Crescent Road, Tunbridge Wells, Kent (England)
10 Dec 64: Olympia Ballroom, Reading, Berkshire (England)
12 Dec 64: Peterborough Palais, Peterborough, Cambridgeshire (England)
13 Dec 64: King Mojo Club, Barnsley Road, Sheffield, South Yorkshire (England)
14 Dec 64: Grand Pavilion, The Esplanade, Porthcawl, Bridgend (Wales)
17 Dec 64: Lakeside Ballroom, Hendon, Northwest London (England)
18 Dec 64: Co-Op Hall, Harmer Street, Gravesend, Kent (England)
20 Dec 64: CrawDaddy Club, Richmond Athletic Association Grounds, Twickenham Road, Richmond-upon-Thames, Surrey (England)

The Yardbirds – Opening Act on "Another Beatles Christmas Show"
24 Dec 64: Odeon Theatre, Queen Caroline Street, Hammersmith, West London (England) – 1 show
26 Dec 64: Odeon Theatre, Queen Caroline Street, Hammersmith, West London (England) – 2 shows

The Yardbirds – U.K. Club & Ballroom Circuit cont'd
27 Dec 64: CrawDaddy Club, Richmond Athletic Association Grounds, Twickenham Road, Richmond-upon-Thames, Surrey (England)

The Yardbirds – Opening Act on "Another Beatles Christmas Show" cont'd
28 Dec 64: Odeon Theatre, Queen Caroline Street, Hammersmith, West London (England) – 2 shows

The Yardbirds – Opening Act on "The Beatles For Brady" Benefit Concert
29 Dec 64: Odeon Theatre, Queen Caroline Street, Hammersmith, West London (England) – 1 show

The Yardbirds – Opening Act on "Another Beatles Christmas Show" cont'd
30 Dec 64: Odeon Theatre, Queen Caroline Street, Hammersmith, West London (England) – 2 shows
31 Dec 64: Odeon Theatre, Queen Caroline Street, Hammersmith, West London (England) – 2 shows
1 Jan 65: Odeon Theatre, Queen Caroline Street, Hammersmith, West London (England) – 2 shows
2 Jan 65: Odeon Theatre, Queen Caroline Street, Hammersmith, West London (England) – 2 shows

The Yardbirds – U.K. Club & Ballroom Circuit cont'd
3 Jan 65: CrawDaddy Club, Richmond Athletic Association Grounds, Twickenham Road, Richmond-upon-Thames, Surrey (England)

The Yardbirds – Opening Act on "Another Beatles Christmas Show" cont'd
4 Jan 65: Odeon Theatre, Queen Caroline Street, Hammersmith, West London (England) – 2 shows
5 Jan 65: Odeon Theatre, Queen Caroline Street, Hammersmith, West London (England) – 2 shows
6 Jan 65: Odeon Theatre, Queen Caroline Street, Hammersmith, West London (England) – 2 shows
7 Jan 65: Odeon Theatre, Queen Caroline Street, Hammersmith, West London (England) – 2 shows
8 Jan 65: Odeon Theatre, Queen Caroline Street, Hammersmith, West London (England) – 2 shows
9 Jan 65: Odeon Theatre, Queen Caroline Street, Hammersmith, West London (England) – 2 shows

The Yardbirds – U.K. Club & Ballroom Circuit cont'd
10 Jan 65: CrawDaddy Club, Richmond Athletic Association Grounds, Twickenham Road, Richmond-upon-Thames, Surrey (England)

The Yardbirds – Opening Act on "Another Beatles Christmas Show" cont'd
11 Jan 65: Odeon Theatre, Queen Caroline Street, Hammersmith, West London (England) – 2 shows
12 Jan 65: Odeon Theatre, Queen Caroline Street, Hammersmith, West London (England) – 2 shows
13 Jan 65: Odeon Theatre, Queen Caroline Street, Hammersmith, West London (England) – 2 shows
14 Jan 65: Odeon Theatre, Queen Caroline Street, Hammersmith, West London (England) – 2 shows
15 Jan 65: Odeon Theatre, Queen Caroline Street, Hammersmith, West London (England) – 2 shows

16 Jan 65: Odeon Theatre, Queen Caroline Street, Hammersmith, West London (England) – 2 shows

The Yardbirds – U.K. Club & Ballroom Circuit cont'd
17 Jan 65: CrawDaddy Club, Richmond Athletic Association Grounds, Twickenham Road, Richmond-upon-Thames, Surrey (England)
18 Jan 65: The Pavilion, North Parade Road, Bath, Somerset (England)
20 Jan 65: Bromel Club, Bromley Court Hotel, Bromley Hill, Bromley, Kent (England)
21 Jan 65: Black Cat Club, Woolwich, East London (England)
22 Jan 65: Marquee Club, Wardour Street, Soho, Central London (England)
23 Jan 65: Astoria Ballroom, Bank Street, Rawtenstall, Lancashire (England)
25 Jan 65: Majestic Ballroom, Caversham Road, Reading, Berkshire (England)
29 Jan 65: Trentham Ballroom, Trentham Gardens, Trentham, Stoke-on-Trent, Staffordshire (England)
30 Jan 65: Floral Hall, Morecambe, Lancashire (England)

The Yardbirds – "That's For Me" Television Show (ITV)
1 Feb 65: Associated-Rediffusion Studios, London (England) – live television broadcast

The Yardbirds – U.K. Club & Ballroom Circuit cont'd
1 Feb 65: Marquee Club, Wardour Street, Soho, Central London (England)
5 Feb 65: Dungeon, Stanford Street, Nottingham, East Midlands (England)
6 Feb 65: Whisky A Go Go, Birmingham, West Midlands (England)
7 Feb 65: Cavern Club, Cromford Court, Manchester (England)
8 Feb 65: Town Hall, Basingstoke, Hampshire (England)
9 Feb 65: Town Hall, Queen Victoria Road, High Wycombe, Buckinghamshire (England)
10 Feb 65: Town Hall, Alexandra Road, Farnborough, Hampshire (England)
12 Feb 65: Unknown Venue, Sudbury, Suffolk (England) – unconfirmed
13 Feb 65: Unknown Venue, Catford, South London (England) – unconfirmed
14 Feb 65: Community Centre, Southall, West London (England)
15 Feb 65: Marquee Club, Wardour Street, Soho, Central London (England)
19 Feb 65: Unknown Venue, Guildford, Surrey (England) – unconfirmed
20 Feb 65: Unknown Venue, Leicester, Leicestershire (England) – unconfirmed
21 Feb 65: R&B Rendezvous, Kimbells Ballroom, Osborne Road, Southsea, Portsmouth, Hampshire (England)
23 Feb 65: Unknown Venue, Wallington, Surrey (England) – unconfirmed
26 Feb 65: Leyton Baths, High Road, Leyton, Northeast London (England)
27 Feb 65: Unknown Venue, Southampton, Hampshire (England) - unconfirmed
28 Feb 65: CrawDaddy Club, Richmond Athletic Association Grounds, Twickenham Road, Richmond-upon-Thames, Surrey (England)
2 Mar 65: Town Hall, Lydney, Gloucestershire (England)
3 Mar 65: The Bristol Chinese R&B and Jazz Club, The Corn Exchange, Corn Street, Bristol (England) – EC's last appearance with The Yardbirds

John Mayall's Bluesbreakers – U.K. Club & Ballroom Circuit
6 Apr 65: Unknown Venue, Unknown Location (England) – presumably in the Greater London area, EC debuts with John Mayall
9 Apr 65: King Mojo Club, Barnsley Road, Sheffield, South Yorkshire (England)
10 Apr 65: The Lyric, Laughton Road, Dinnington, South Yorkshire (England)
11 Apr 65: Blue Moon, Church Road, Hayes, Middlesex (England) or Le Metro Club, Birmingham, West Midlands (England) – two gigs advertised but likely one is cancelled due to distance between them

John Mayall's Bluesbreakers – "Grand R&B Concert"
13 Apr 65: Haymarket Theatre, Wote Street, Basingstoke, Hampshire (England)

John Mayall's Bluesbreakers – U.K. Club & Ballroom Circuit cont'd
15 Apr 65: Waterfront Club, Southampton, Hampshire (England)
16 Apr 65: Ricky Tick Club, Plaza Ballroom, Guildford, Surrey (England)
17 Apr 65: The Flamingo, Wardour Street, Soho, Central London (England)
19 Apr 65: King Mojo Club, Barnsley Road, Sheffield, South Yorkshire (England)
22 Apr 65: The Flamingo, Wardour Street, Soho, Central London (England)

John Mayall's Bluesbreakers – "Ready Steady Goes Live!" Television Show (ITV-Rediffusion)
23 Apr 65: Associated-Rediffusion Studio 1, Wembley Drive, Wembley, Northwest London (England) – live television broadcast (Season 2, Episode #34)

John Mayall's Bluesbreakers – U.K. Club & Ballroom Circuit cont'd
23 Apr 65: All Nighter Club at The Flamingo, Wardour Street, Soho, Central London (England)
24 Apr 65: Rendezvous Club, Kingston Road, Oddfellows Hall, Portsmouth, Hampshire (England)

John Mayall's Bluesbreakers – "Saturday Club" Radio Show (BBC Light Programme)
26 Apr 65: BBC Maida Vale Studios, Delaware Road, Maida Vale, West London (England) – pre-recorded for 1 May radio broadcast (Episode #343)

John Mayall's Bluesbreakers – U.K. Club & Ballroom Circuit cont'd
27 Apr 65: Bluesday, Rhodes Centre, South Road, Bishop's Stortford, Hertfordshire (England)
30 Apr 65: The Flamingo, Wardour Street, Soho, Central London (England)
1 May 65: Cubiklub, Slack Street, Rochdale, Lancashire (England)

John Mayall's Bluesbreakers – "Five O'Clock Club" (ITV-Rediffusion)
4 May 65: Associated-Rediffusion Studios, Wembley Drive, Wembley, Northwest London (England) – live television broadcast

John Mayall's Bluesbreakers – U.K. Club & Ballroom Circuit cont'd
8 May 65: The Twisted Wheel Club, Whitworth Street, Manchester (England)
9 May 65: Dungeon, Stanford Street, Nottingham, East Midlands (England)
10 May 65: Bluesville R&B, Manor House Ballroom, Ipswich, Suffolk (England)
14 May 65: The Fender Club, Churchill Hall, Hawthorne Avenue, Kenton, Harrow, Northwest London (England)
14 May 65: Ricky Tick Club, Plaza Ballroom, Guildford, Surrey (England) with headliner John Lee Hooker
15 May 65: Arbour Youth Club, Pyrford, Surrey (England)
15 May 65: All Nighter Club at The Flamingo, Wardour Street, Soho, Central London (England)
16 May 65: Riverside Club, Bridge Road, Cricketers Hotel, Chertsey, Surrey (England)
21 May 65: All Nighter Club at The Flamingo, Wardour Street, Soho, Central London (England)
22 May 65: All Nighter Club at The Flamingo, Wardour Street, Soho, Central London (England)
25 May 65: Klooks Kleek, Railway Hotel, Broadhurst Gardens, Northwest London (England)
28 May 65: Club A'Gogo, Percy Street, Newcastle-upon-Tyne, Northumberland (England)
29 May 65: King Mojo Club, Barnsley Road, Sheffield, South Yorkshire (England)
30 May 65: Kirklevington Country Club, Yarm, Stockton-on-Tees, North Yorkshire (England)
4 Jun 65: Ricky Tick Club, Plaza Ballroom, Guildford, Surrey (England)
4 Jun 65: All Nighter Club at The Flamingo, Wardour Street, Soho, Central London (England)
5 Jun 65: New Georgian, Cowley, Uxbridge, Middlesex (England)
5 Jun 65: All Nighter Club at The Flamingo, Wardour Street, Soho, Central London (England)
6 Jun 65: All Nighter Club at The Flamingo, Wardour Street, Soho, Central London (England)
7 Jun 65: Blue Moon, Church Road, Hayes, Middlesex (England)
9 Jun 65: The Orford Cellar, Anchor Buildings, Red Lion Street, Norwich, Norfolk (England)
10 June 65: Klooks Kleek, Railway Hotel, Broadhurst Gardens, Northwest London (England)
12 Jun 65: Galaxy Club, Town Hall, Basingstoke, Hampshire (England)

John Mayall's Bluesbreakers – "Hull University Hullabaloo Ball"
17 Jun 65: Locarno Ballroom, Hull, Humberside (England)

John Mayall's Bluesbreakers – U.K. Club & Ballroom Circuit cont'd
18 Jun 65: Pontiac Club, Zeeta House, Putney High Street, Putney, Southwest London (England)

John Mayall's Bluesbreakers – "Uxbridge Blues & Folk Festival"
19 Jun 65: Uxbridge Showground, Uxbridge, Middlesex (England)

John Mayall's Bluesbreakers – U.K. Club & Ballroom Circuit cont'd
19 Jun 65: Ricky Tick Club, Clewer Mead, Windsor, Berkshire (England)
20 Jun 65: Galaxy Club, Woburn Park Hotel, Station Road, Addlestone, Surrey (England)

John Mayall's Bluesbreakers – "Leeds University Rag Day Hop"
26 Jun 65: Roundhay Park, Leeds, West Yorkshire (England)

John Mayall's Bluesbreakers – U.K. Club & Ballroom Circuit cont'd
7 Jul 65: Bromel Club, Bromley Court Hotel, Bromley Hill, Bromley, Kent (England)
8 Jul 65: Klooks Kleek, Railway Hotel, Broadhurst Gardens, Northwest London (England)
10 Jul 65: The Flamingo, Wardour Street, Soho, Central London (England)
10 Jul 65: All Nighter Club at The Flamingo, Wardour Street, Soho, Central London (England)
11 Jul 65: Ultra Club, Downs Hotel, Keymer, Hassocks, Sussex (England)
12 Jul 65: Galaxy Club, Town Hall, Basingstoke, Hampshire (England)
14 Jul 65: The Orford Cellar, Anchor Buildings, Red Lion Street, Norwich, Norfolk (England)
15 Jul 65: London College of Fashion, Central London (England)
16 Jul 65: Ricky Tick Club, Plaza Ballroom, Guildford, Surrey (England)

16 Jul 65: All Nighter Club at The Flamingo, Wardour Street, Soho, Central London (England)
18 Jul 65: Gaumont Theatre, Westover Road, Bournemouth, Dorset (England)
19 Jul 65: Galaxy Club, Town Hall, Basingstoke, Hampshire (England)
22 Jul 65: Bowes Lyon House Youth Centre, St. George's Way, Stevenage, Hertfordshire (England)
23 Jul 65: Il Rondo, Silver Street, Leicester, Leicestershire (England)
24 Jul 65: Rhodes Centre, South Road, Bishop's Stortford, Hertfordshire (England)
24 Jul 65: All Nighter Club at The Flamingo, Wardour Street, Soho, Central London (England)
25 Jul 65: Blue Moon, Church Road, Hayes, Middlesex (England)
26 Jul 65: Galaxy Club, Town Hall, Basingstoke, Hampshire (England)
28 Jul 65: Blue Indigo, The Bay Tree Inn, Southampton, Hampshire (England)
29 Jul 65: Klooks Kleek, Railway Hotel, Broadhurst Gardens, Northwest London (England)
30 Jul 65: Bluesville R&B, The Manor House, Finsbury Park, North London (England)
1 Aug 65: The Boat Club, Trentside, West Bridgford, Nottingham, East Midlands (England)
2 Aug 65: Majestic Ballroom, Stow Hill, Newport (Wales)
4 Aug 65: Pontiac Club, Zeeta House, Putney High Street, Putney, Southwest London (England)
7 Aug 65: New Georgian, Cowley, Uxbridge, Middlesex (England)
7 Aug 65: All Nighter Club at The Flamingo, Wardour Street, Soho, Central London (England)
11 Aug 65: Pontiac Club, Zeeta House, Putney High Street, Putney, Southwest London (England)
15 Aug 65: The Cellar Club, High Street, Kingston-upon-Thames, Surrey (England)
16 Aug 65: Bluesville R&B, Manor House Ballroom, Ipswich, Suffolk (England)
18 Aug 65: Pontiac Club, Zeeta House, Putney High Street, Putney, Southwest London (England)
21 Aug 65: The Flamingo, Wardour Street, Soho, Central London (England)
21 Aug 65: All Nighter Club at The Flamingo, Wardour Street, Soho, Central London (England)
22 Aug 65: Galaxy Club, Woburn Park Hotel, Station Road, Addlestone, Surrey (England)
24 Aug 65: Klooks Kleek, Railway Hotel, Broadhurst Gardens, Northwest London (England)
25 Aug 65: Pontiac Club, Zeeta House, Putney High Street, Putney, Southwest London (England)
28 Aug 65: All Nighter Club at The Flamingo, Wardour Street, Soho, Central London (England)
29 Aug 65: Black Prince Hotel, Bexley, Southeast London (England)

The Glands – "Greek Adventure"
EC and some friends form a blues band and set off to play their way around the world. Piling into a Ford Galaxy they head off in September. Arriving in Athens, they get their first job. Although they refer to themselves as The Glands, they bill themselves as The Faces. From 11 October, EC plays with both The Glands (The Faces) and the Igloo Club's house band, The Juniors

7 Oct 65: Igloo Club, Ioannou Drosopoulou, Kipseli, Athens (Greece)
8 Oct 65: Igloo Club, Ioannou Drosopoulou, Kipseli, Athens (Greece)
9 Oct 65: Igloo Club, Ioannou Drosopoulou, Kipseli, Athens (Greece)
10 Oct 65: Igloo Club, Ioannou Drosopoulou, Kipseli, Athens (Greece)
11 Oct 65: Igloo Club, Ioannou Drosopoulou, Kipseli, Athens (Greece)
13 Oct 65: Igloo Club, Ioannou Drosopoulou, Kipseli, Athens (Greece)
14 Oct 65: Igloo Club, Ioannou Drosopoulou, Kipseli, Athens (Greece)
15 Oct 65: Igloo Club, Ioannou Drosopoulou, Kipseli, Athens (Greece)
16 Oct 65: Igloo Club, Ioannou Drosopoulou, Kipseli, Athens (Greece)
17 Oct 65: Igloo Club, Ioannou Drosopoulou, Kipseli, Athens (Greece)
18 Oct 65: Igloo Club, Ioannou Drosopoulou, Kipseli, Athens (Greece)
20 Oct 65: Igloo Club, Ioannou Drosopoulou, Kipseli, Athens (Greece)
21 Oct 65: Igloo Club, Ioannou Drosopoulou, Kipseli, Athens (Greece)
22 Oct 65: Igloo Club, Ioannou Drosopoulou, Kipseli, Athens (Greece)
23 Oct 65: Igloo Club, Ioannou Drosopoulou, Kipseli, Athens (Greece)
24 Oct 65: Cine-Terpsithea, Piraeus, Athens (Greece) – EC gigs with The Juniors
24 Oct 65: Igloo Club, Ioannou Drosopoulou, Kipseli, Athens (Greece)
25 Oct 65: Igloo Club, Ioannou Drosopoulou, Kipseli, Athens (Greece)

John Mayall's Bluesbreakers – U.K. Club & Ballroom Circuit cont'd
6 Nov 65: Unknown Venue, London Airport, Heathrow, West London (England)
EC meets Jack Bruce who has temporarily joined the Bluesbreakers
7 Nov 65: The Flamingo, Wardour Street, Soho, Central London (England)

Eric Clapton jam session with Wilson Pickett
9 Nov 65: Scotch of St. James, Mason's Yard, Central London (England)

John Mayall's Bluesbreakers – U.K. Club & Ballroom Circuit cont'd
11 Nov 65: Klooks Kleek, Railway Hotel, Broadhurst Gardens, Northwest London (England)

12 Nov 65: Bluesville R&B, The Manor House, Finsbury Park, North London (England)
13 Nov 65: The Blue Moon, High Street, Cheltenham, Gloucestershire (England)
14 Nov 65: Ricky Tick Club, Plaza Ballroom, Guildford, Surrey (England)

Eric Clapton jam session with The Spencer Davis Group
16 Nov 65: Marquee Club, Wardour Street, Soho, Central London (England)

John Mayall's Bluesbreakers – U.K. Club & Ballroom Circuit cont'd
17 Nov 65: Scaffold Club, Northampton, East Midlands (England)
19 Nov 65: Zambezi, High Street, Hounslow, West London (England)
20 Nov 65: University, Leicester (England)
21 Nov 65: Red Cross Hall, Sutton, Surrey (England) – the gig may have been moved to the nearby Public Baths in Throwley Road
21 Nov 65: Blue Moon, Church Road, Hayes, Middlesex (England)
22 Nov 65: Galaxy Club, Town Hall, Basingstoke, Hampshire (England)
27 Nov 65: Burton's Dance Hall, Windsor Street, Uxbridge, Middlesex (England)
28 Nov 65: Community Centre, Southall, West London (England) – postponed until 23 Jan 66
28 Nov 65: The Flamingo, Wardour Street, Soho, Central London (England)
29 Nov 65: Majestic Ballroom, Caversham Road, Reading, Berkshire (England)
30 Nov 65: Bowes Lyon House Youth Centre, St. George's Way, Stevenage, Hertfordshire (England)
4 Dec 65: New Barn, Brighton, East Sussex (England)

John Mayall's Bluesbreakers – "The Big R&B Beat Show Of 1965"
6 Dec 65: Bluesville Club, St. Matthew's Baths Hall, Civic Drive, Ipswich, Suffolk (England)

John Mayall's Bluesbreakers – U.K. Club & Ballroom Circuit cont'd
10 Dec 65: Ricky Tick Club, Town Hall, Market Square, Staines, Surrey (England)

John Mayall's Bluesbreakers – "Christmas Dance"
11 Dec 65: Chelsea College of Art, Central London (England)

John Mayall's Bluesbreakers – U.K. Club & Ballroom Circuit cont'd
12 Dec 65: Agincourt Ballroom, London Road, Camberley, Surrey (England)
16 Dec 65: Mistral Club, Sidcup, Kent (England)
17 Dec 65: Il Rondo, Silver Street, Leicester, Leicestershire (England)
18 Dec 65: The Twisted Wheel Club, Whitworth Street, Manchester (England)
19 Dec 65: The Boat Club, Trentside, West Bridgford, Nottingham, East Midlands (England)

John Mayall's Bluesbreakers – "Grand Xmas Party Night"
23 Dec 65: The Refectory, Finchley Road, Golders Green, Northwest London (England)

John Mayall's Bluesbreakers – "Christmas Eve Party"
24 Dec 65: Blue Moon, Cheltenham, Gloucestershire (England)

John Mayall's Bluesbreakers – U.K. Club & Ballroom Circuit cont'd
26 Dec 65: Eel Pie Island Hotel, Eel Pie Island, Twickenham, Southwest London (England)
27 Dec 65: The Flamingo, Wardour Street, Soho, Central London (England)
28 Dec 65: Klooks Kleek, Railway Hotel, Broadhurst Gardens, Northwest London (England)
29 Dec 65: The Orford Cellar, Anchor Buildings, Red Lion Street, Norwich, Norfolk (England)

John Mayall's Bluesbreakers – "New Year's Eve Great Rave"
31 Dec 65: Bluesville R&B, The Manor House, Finsbury Park, North London (England)

John Mayall's Bluesbreakers – U.K. Club & Ballroom Circuit cont'd
1 Jan 66: The Flamingo, Wardour Street, Soho, Central London (England)
1 Jan 66: All Nighter Club at The Flamingo, Wardour Street, Soho, Central London (England)
9 Jan 66: Beachcomber, Lace Market, Nottingham, East Midlands (England)
11 Jan 66: Town Hall, Queen Victoria Road, High Wycombe, Buckinghamshire (England)
13 Jan 66: White Lion Inn, Edgware, North London (England)
16 Jan 66: Bromel Club, Bromley Court Hotel, Bromley Hill, Bromley, Kent (England)
17 Jan 66: Starlite, The Star Hotel, London Road, Croydon, South London (England)
21 Jan 66: Skerne Park Hotel, Darlington, Durham (England)
22 Jan 66: Liverpool University, Liverpool, Merseyside (England)
23 Jan 66: Community Centre, Southall, West London (England)
26 Jan 66: Town Hall, Alexandra Road, Farnborough, Hampshire (England)
28 Jan 66: California Pool Ballroom, Whipsnade Road, Dunstable, Bedfordshire (England)
29 Jan 66: Club A'Gogo, Percy Street, Newcastle-upon-Tyne, Northumberland (England)

31 Jan 66: Bluesville '66, St. Matthew's Baths Hall, Civic Drive, Ipswich, Suffolk (England)
1 Feb 66: The Civic Hall, Grays, Essex (England)
4 Feb 66: Links International Youth Centre, Maxwell Road, Borehamwood, Hertfordshire (England)
5 Feb 66: Ricky Tick Club, Clewer Mead, Windsor, Berkshire (England)
6 Feb 66: Woolwich R&B Club, Shakespeare Hotel, Woolwich, East London (England)
8 Feb 66: Klooks Kleek, Railway Hotel, Broadhurst Gardens, Northwest London (England)

John Mayall's Bluesbreakers – "Jazz Beat" Radio Show (BBC Light Programme)
9 Feb 66: BBC Playhouse Theatre, Northumberland Avenue, West End, Central London (England) – pre-recorded for broadcast on 12 Feb

John Mayall's Bluesbreakers – "Combined Engineering Societies Dance"
11 Feb 66: Avon Room, Birmingham University, Birmingham, West Midlands (England)

John Mayall's Bluesbreakers – U.K. Club & Ballroom Circuit cont'd
12 Feb 66: Regent Street Polytechnic, Central London (England)
13 Feb 66: Beachcomber, Lace Market, Nottingham, East Midlands (England)
15 Feb 66: Fishmonger's Arms, High Road, Wood Green, North London (England)
16 Feb 66: The Orford Cellar, Anchor Buildings, Red Lion Street, Norwich, Norfolk (England)
18 Feb 66: Bluesville '66, The Manor House, Finsbury Park, North London (England)
19 Feb 66: The Flamingo, Wardour Street, Soho, Central London (England)
19 Feb 66: All Nighter Club at The Flamingo, Wardour Street, Soho, Central London (England)
20 Feb 66: Cosmopolitan Club, Carlisle, Cumberland (England)
25 Feb 66: Hermitage Ballroom, Hitchin, Hertfordshire (England)
26 Feb 66: The Twisted Wheel Club, Whitworth Street, Manchester (England)
27 Feb 66: Bromel Club, Bromley Court Hotel, Bromley Hill, Bromley, Kent (England)
4 Mar 66: Blue Friday, Beechwood Court Hotel, Harrogate, Yorkshire (England)
5 Mar 66: Club A'Gogo, Percy Street, Newcastle-upon-Tyne, Northumberland (England)
6 Mar 66: Kirklevington Country Club, Yarm, Stockton-on-Tees, North Yorkshire (England)
11 Mar 66: Blues by Night Club, Royal College of Advanced Technology, Salford, Lancashire (England)
13 Mar 66: The Boat Club, Trentside, West Bridgford, Nottingham, East Midlands (England)

John Mayall's Bluesbreakers – "Saturday Club" Radio Show (BBC Light Programme)
14 Mar 66: BBC Aeolian Hall, New Bond Street, Central London (England) pre-recorded for 19 March broadcast (Episode #389)

John Mayall's Bluesbreakers – U.K. Club & Ballroom Circuit cont'd
17 Mar 66: Ricky Tick Club Night, Harvest Moon Club, Guildford, Surrey (England)
18 Mar 66: The Ram Jam Club, Brixton Road, Brixton, South London (England)
18 Mar 66: All Nighter Club at The Flamingo, Wardour Street, Soho, Central London (England)

John Mayall's Bluesbreakers – "Spring Rite Festival Refectory Dance"
19 Mar 66: University, Southampton, Hampshire (England)

John Mayall's Bluesbreakers – U.K. Club & Ballroom Circuit cont'd
20 Mar 66: Eel Pie Island Hotel, Eel Pie Island, Twickenham, Southwest London (England)
21 Mar 66: Bluesville '66, St. Matthew's Baths Hall, Civic Drive, Ipswich, Suffolk (England)
23 Mar 66: The Orford Cellar, Anchor Buildings, Red Lion Street, Norwich, Norfolk (England)
26 Mar 66: The Flamingo, Wardour Street, Soho, Central London (England)
26 Mar 66: All Nighter Club at The Flamingo, Wardour Street, Soho, Central London (England)
1 Apr 66: Beaconsfield Youth Club, High Wycombe, Buckinghamshire (England)
2 Apr 66: Ricky Tick Club, Windsor, Berkshire (England)

Eric Clapton jam session with Alexis Korner, John Mayall and Duffy Power
2 Apr 66: Les Cousins, Greek Street, Soho, Central London (England)

John Mayall's Bluesbreakers – U.K. Club & Ballroom Circuit cont'd
3 Apr 66: Blue Moon, Church Road, Hayes, Middlesex (England)
4 Apr 66: Carousel Club, Farnborough, Hampshire (England)
5 Apr 66: Fishmonger's Arms, High Road, Wood Green, North London (England)
7 Apr 66: Kave Dwellers Club, Billingham, Durham (England)
8 Apr 66: Bluesville '66, The Manor House, Finsbury Park, North London (England)
9 Apr 66: Assembly Hall, Barking, East London (England)
10 Apr 66: Central R&B Club, Central Hotel, Gillingham, Kent (England)
11 Apr 66: Marquee Club, Wardour Street, Soho, Central London (England)

13 Apr 66: Market Hall, St. Albans, Hertfordshire (England)
15 Apr 66: Zambezi, High Street, Hounslow, West London (England)
16 Apr 66: The Twisted Wheel Club, Whitworth Street, Manchester (England)
17 Apr 66: Beachcomber, Lace Market, Nottingham, East Midlands (England)
18 Apr 66: Woodhall Community Centre, Welwyn Garden City, Hertfordshire (England) EC plays truant
22 Apr 66: The Refectory, Finchley Road, Golders Green, Northwest London (England)
24 Apr 66: Bromel Club, Bromley Court Hotel, Bromley Hill, Bromley, Kent (England)
25 Apr 66: Cooks Ferry Inn, Angel Road, Edmonton, North London (England)
27 Apr 66: Castle Club, Tooting, Southwest London (England)
28 Apr 66: Club A'Gogo, Percy Street, Newcastle-upon-Tyne, Northumberland (England)
29 Apr 66: Il Rondo, Silver Street, Leicester, Leicestershire (England)

John Mayall's Bluesbreakers – "All Nighter R&B" with John Lee Hooker
29 Apr 66: Town Hall, Victoria Square, Birmingham, West Midlands (England)

John Mayall's Bluesbreakers – U.K. Club & Ballroom Circuit cont'd
30 Apr 66: The Flamingo, Wardour Street, Soho, Central London (England)
30 Apr 66: All Nighter Club at The Flamingo, Wardour Street, Soho, Central London (England)
1 May 66: The Orford Cellar, Anchor Buildings, Red Lion Street, Norwich, Norfolk (England)
4 May 66: Casino Club, Walsall, West Midlands (England)
6 May 66: Beachcomber, Lace Market, Nottingham, East Midlands (England)
7 May 66: The Ram Jam Club, Brixton Road, Brixton, South London (England)
8 May 66: King Mojo Club, Barnsley Road, Sheffield, South Yorkshire (England)
9 May 66: Starlite, The Star Hotel, London Road, Croydon, South London (England)
10 May 66: Klooks Kleek, Railway Hotel, Broadhurst Gardens, Northwest London (England)
13 May 66: Town Hall, Oxford, Oxfordshire (England) – guest appearance by Ginger Baker; on the drive back to London Ginger proposes forming a band with EC
14 May 66: Toft's, Grace Hill, Folkestone, Kent (England)
15 May 66: Beachcomber, Lace Market, Nottingham, East Midlands (England)
17 May 66: Fishmonger's Arms, High Road, Wood Green, North London (England)
19 May 66: The Mod Scene Club, County Arms, Blaby, Leicester (England)
20 May 66: Royal College of Advanced Technology, Salford, Lancashire (England)
21 May 66: Ricky Tick Club, Clewer Mead, Windsor, Berkshire (England)
22 May 66: The Flamingo, Wardour Street, Soho, Central London (England)
23 May 66: Atalanta Ballroom, Commercial Road, Woking, Surrey (England) EC possibly plays truant
25 May 66: Castle Club, Tooting, Southwest London (England)
27 May 66: The Refectory, Finchley Road, Golders Green, Northwest London (England)
28 May 66: Mansfield Blues Club, Nottingham, East Midlands (England)
28 May 66: Beachcomber, Lace Market, Nottingham, East Midlands (England)
29 May 66: Eel Pie Island Hotel, Eel Pie Island, Twickenham, Southwest London (England)
30 May 66: Marquee Club, Wardour Street, Soho, Central London (England)
31 May 66: Grand Black Daffodil, Odeon Ballroom, Chesterfield, Derbyshire (England)
1 Jun 66: The Orford Cellar, Anchor Buildings, Red Lion Street, Norwich, Norfolk (England)
3 Jun 66: The Flamingo, Wardour Street, Soho, Central London (England)
4 Jun 66: Floral Hall, Southport, Lancashire (England)
5 Jun 66: Bromel Club, Bromley Court Hotel, Bromley Hill, Bromley, Kent (England)
7 Jun 66: Town Hall, Queen Victoria Road, High Wycombe, Buckinghamshire (England)
8 Jun 66: Town Hall, Alexandra Road, Farnborough, Hampshire (England)
10 Jun 66: The Ram Jam Club, Brixton Road, Brixton, South London (England)
12 Jun 66: Blue Moon, Church Road, Hayes, Middlesex (England)
16 Jun 66: Marquee Club, Wardour Street, Soho, Central London (England)

John Mayall's Bluesbreakers – "Corpus Ball"
17 Jun 66: University, Oxford, Oxfordshire (England)

John Mayall's Bluesbreakers – "Rutlishian Jubilee Fair"
18 Jun 66: Rutlish Grammar School, Merton Park, Southwest London (England)

John Mayall's Bluesbreakers – U.K. Club & Ballroom Circuit cont'd
19 Jun 66: Beachcomber, Lace Market, Nottingham, East Midlands (England)
21 Jun 66: Fishmonger's Arms, High Road, Wood Green, North London (England)

John Mayall's Bluesbreakers – Leeds University Rag Ball
23 Jun 66: University Refectory, Leeds, West Yorkshire (England)

John Mayall's Bluesbreakers – U.K. Club & Ballroom Circuit cont'd
25 Jun 66: The Flamingo, Wardour Street, Soho, Central London (England)
25 Jun 66: All Nighter Club at The Flamingo, Wardour Street, Soho, Central London (England) – after this date, EC fails to show at several gigs as his time with the Bluesbreakers draws to a close

26 Jun 66: Carousel Club, Camp Road, Farnborough, Hampshire (England)
27 Jun 66: Majestic Ballroom, Caversham Road, Reading, Berkshire (England)
1 Jul 66: Bluesville '66, The Manor House, Finsbury Park, North London (England)
2 Jul 66: Blue Moon, Cheltenham, Gloucestershire (England)
3 Jul 66: Bluesette, Leatherhead, Surrey (England)
5 Jul 66: Klooks Kleek, Railway Hotel, Broadhurst Gardens, Northwest London (England)
7 Jul 66: Club A'Gogo, Percy Street, Newcastle-upon-Tyne, Northumberland (England)
8 Jul 66: Ricky Tick Club, Corn Exchange, Newbury, Berkshire (England)
9 Jul 66: Rhodes Centre, South Road, Bishop's Stortford, Hertfordshire (England)
14 Jul 66: Ricky Tick Club, Stoke Hotel, Guildford, Surrey (England) – EC definitely plays this gig
15 Jul 66: Ricky Tick Club, High Street, Hounslow, West London (England) EC definitely plays this gig
16 Jul 66: Cad-Lac Club, Florida Rooms, Brighton, East Sussex (England) EC definitely plays this gig
17 Jul 66: Black Prince Hotel, Bexley, Southeast London (England) EC's last scheduled gig with the Bluesbreakers; possibly cancelled

Cream – Unofficial Debut Concert
30 Jul 66: The Twisted Wheel Club, Whitworth Street, Manchester (England)

Cream – "6th National Jazz & Blues Festival"
31 Jul 66: Balloon Meadow, Royal Windsor Racecourse, Windsor, Berkshire (England)

Cream – U.K. Club & Ballroom Circuit
1 Aug 66: Cooks Ferry Inn, Angel Road, Edmonton, North London (England)
2 Aug 66: Klooks Kleek, Railway Hotel, Broadhurst Gardens, Northwest London (England)

Cream – "Beat 'n' Blues Festival"
6 Aug 66: Town Hall, Castle Circus, Torquay, Devon (England)

Cream – U.K. Club & Ballroom Circuit cont'd
9 Aug 66: Fishmonger's Arms, High Road, Wood Green, North London (England)
12 Aug 66: Bromel Club, Bromley Court Hotel, Bromley Hill, Bromley, Kent (England)
13 Aug 66: Blue Moon, Cheltenham, Gloucestershire (England)
16 Aug 66: Marquee Club, Wardour Street, Soho, Central London (England)
17 Aug 66: The Orford Cellar, Anchor Buildings, Red Lion Street, Norwich, Norfolk (England)
19 Aug 66: The Cellar Club, High Street, Kingston, Surrey (England)
20 Aug 66: King Mojo Club, Barnsley Road, Sheffield, South Yorkshire (England)
21 Aug 66: Unknown Venue, Warrington, Lancashire (England) – probable gig
24 Aug 66: Eel Pie Island Hotel, Eel Pie Island, Twickenham, Southwest London (England)
26 Aug 66: Il Rondo, Silver Street, Leicester, Leicestershire (England)
27 Aug 66: The Ram Jam Club, Brixton Road, Brixton, South London (England)
27 Aug 66: All Nighter Club at The Flamingo, Wardour Street, Soho, Central London (England)
28 Aug 66: Beachcomber, Lace Market, Nottingham, East Midlands (England)
29 Aug 66: Community Centre, Welwyn Garden City, Hertfordshire (England)
1 Sep 66: Concorde, Southampton, Hampshire (England)
2 Sep 66: Bluesville '66, The Manor House, Finsbury Park, North London (England)
4 Sep 66: Ricky Tick Club, Thames Hotel, Windsor, Berkshire (England)
5 Sep 66: Garston, Liverpool, Merseyside (England) – cancelled
7 Sep 66: Town Hall, Alexandra Road, Farnborough, Hampshire (England)
9 Sep 66: Unknown Venue, Folkestone, Kent (England) – probable gig
10 Sep 66: Marquee Dance Club, Birmingham, West Midlands (England) – venue changed from The Penthouse
11 Sep 66: Skyline Ballroom, Kingston-upon-Hull, Humberside (England) – dropped in favour of a gig in Stockport
11 Sep 66: Manor Lounge, Wellington Road South, Stockport, Cheshire (England)
12 Sep 66: Bluesville '66, St. Matthew's Baths Hall, Civic Drive, Ipswich, Suffolk (England)
15 Sep 66: Ricky Tick Club, Corn Exchange, St. Paul's Square, Bedford, Bedfordshire (England)
16 Sep 66: Hermitage Halls, Hermitage Road, Hitchin, Hertfordshire (England)
17 Sep 66: Drill Hall, Grantham, Lincolnshire (England)
18 Sep 66: Blue Moon, Church Road, Hayes, Middlesex (England)
19 Sep 66: Atalanta Ballroom, Commercial Road, Woking, Surrey (England)
23 Sep 66: Ricky Tick Club, Corn Exchange, Newbury, Berkshire (England)
26 Sep 66: Starlite, The Star Hotel, London Road, Croydon, South London (England)
27 Sep 66: Marquee Club, Wardour Street, Soho, Central London (England)
29 Sep 66: Unknown Venue, Newcastle (England) – probable gig
30 Sep 66: Ricky Tick Club, High Street, Hounslow, West London (England)
1 Oct 66: Regent Street Polytechnic, Central London (England) – guest appearance by Jimi Hendrix
2 Oct 66: Kirklevington Country Club, Yarm, Stockton-on-Tees, North Yorkshire (England) – cancelled
3 Oct 66: Wall City Jazz Club, Chester (England) – cancelled

4 Oct 66: Fishmonger's Arms, High Road, Wood Green, North London (England) cancelled
5 Oct 66: Reading University, Reading, Berkshire (England) – cancelled
6 Oct 66: York University, York (England) – cancelled
7 Oct 66: Kings College, Strand, Central London (England)
8 Oct 66: University of Sussex, Brighton, East Sussex (England) – Ginger Baker collapses afterwards from acute exhaustion and influenza
9 Oct 66: Birdcage Club, Eastney Road, Portsmouth, Hampshire (England) – cancelled
12 Oct 66: The Orford Cellar, Anchor Buildings, Red Lion Street, Norwich, Norfolk (England)
13 Oct 66: Club A'Gogo, Percy Street, Newcastle-upon-Tyne, Northumberland (England)
14 Oct 66: Unknown Venue, Newark-on-Trent, Nottinghamshire (England) probable gig
15 Oct 66: Unknown Venue, Sheffield, South Yorkshire (England) – probable gig

Cream – "All Night Rave"
15 Oct 66: Jigsaw, Cromford Court, Manchester (England)

Cream – U.K. Club & Ballroom Circuit cont'd
16 Oct 66: Unknown Venue, Coventry, West Midlands, West Midlands (England) possible gig
17 Oct 66: Majestic Ballroom, Caversham Road, Reading, Berkshire (England)

Cream – "Carnival Dance"
20 Oct 66: St. Giles' Youth Club, Willenhall Baths Assembly Hall, Wolverhampton, West Midlands (England)

Cream – "Bandbeat" Radio Show (BBC World Service)
21 Oct 66: BBC Maida Vale Studio 4, Delaware Road, Maida Vale, West London (England) – pre-recorded for 21 Nov radio broadcast

Cream – U.K. Club & Ballroom Circuit cont'd
21 Oct 66: Bluesville '66, The Manor House, Finsbury Park, North London (England)

Cream – "Union Hop"
22 Oct 66: Leeds University, Leeds, West Yorkshire (England)

Cream – U.K. Club & Ballroom Circuit cont'd
23 Oct 66: Beachcomber, Lace Market, Nottingham, East Midlands (England)
24 Oct 66: Bluesville '66, St. Matthew's Baths Hall, Civic Drive, Ipswich, Suffolk (England)
27 Oct 66: New Yorker Discotheque, Milton Road, Swindon, Wiltshire (England)
28 Oct 66: Il Rondo, Silver Street, Leicester, Leicestershire (England)
29 Oct 66: Bristol University Students Union, Bristol (England)

Cream – "All Night Rave"
29 Oct 66: Midnight City, Bradford Street, Digbeth, Birmingham, West Midlands (England)

Cream – U.K. Club & Ballroom Circuit cont'd
30 Oct 66: Agincourt Ballroom, London Road, Camberley, Surrey (England)
31 Oct 66: Atalanta Ballroom, Commercial Road, Woking, Surrey (England)

Cream – "Ready Steady Go" Television Show (ITV-Rediffusion)
1 Nov 66: Associated-Rediffusion Studio 1, Wembley Drive, Wembley, Northwest London (England) – pre-recorded for 4 November television broadcast (Season 4, Episode #10)

Cream – U.K. Club & Ballroom Circuit cont'd
2 Nov 66: Unknown Venue, Hemel Hempstead (England) – probable gig
3 Nov 66: The Ram Jam Club, Brixton Road, Brixton, South London (England)
4 Nov 66: Unknown Venue, Coventry, West Midlands (England) – the university is the probable location
5 Nov 66: Town Hall, Barking Road, East Ham, East London (England)
7 Nov 66: New Spot Club, Thorngate Ballroom, Gosport, Hampshire (England)

Cream – "Saturday Club" Radio Show (BBC Light Programme)
8 Nov 66: BBC Playhouse Theatre, Northumberland Avenue, West End, Central London (England) – pre-recorded for 12 Nov radio broadcast (Episode #423)

Cream – U.K. Club & Ballroom Circuit cont'd
8 Nov 66: Marquee Club, Wardour Street, Soho, Central London (England)
11 Nov 66: Public Baths, Throwley Road, Sutton, Surrey (England)
12 Nov 66: Liverpool University, Liverpool, Merseyside (England)
13 Nov 66: Redcar Jazz Club, Coatham Hotel, Newcomen Terrace, Redcar, North Yorkshire (England)
15 Nov 66: Klooks Kleek, Railway Hotel, Broadhurst Gardens, Northwest London (England)

17 Nov 66: Unknown Venue, Norwich, Norfolk (England) – the university is the probable location
18 Nov 66: Hoveton Village Hall, Stalham Road, Wroxham, Norfolk (England)
19 Nov 66: Blue Moon, Cheltenham, Gloucestershire (England)

Cream – "Monday Monday" Radio Show (BBC Light Programme)
21 Nov 66: BBC Playhouse Theatre, Northumberland Avenue, West End, Central London (England) – pre-recorded for same day radio broadcast

Cream – U.K. Club & Ballroom Circuit cont'd
21 Nov 66: The Pavilion, North Parade Road, Bath, Somerset (England)
22 Nov 66: The Bristol Chinese R&B and Jazz Club, The Corn Exchange, Corn Street, Bristol (England)
25 Nov 66: California Pool Ballroom, Whipsnade Road, Dunstable, Bedfordshire (England)
26 Nov 66: Corn Exchange, Tindal Square, Chelmsford, Essex (England)
27 Nov 66: Agincourt Ballroom, London Road, Camberley, Surrey (England)

Cream – "Guitar Club" Radio Show (BBC Home Service)
28 Nov 66: BBC Aeolian Hall Studio 2, New Bond Street, Central London (England) pre-recorded for 30 Dec radio broadcast

Cream – U.K. Club & Ballroom Circuit cont'd
28 Nov 66: Atalanta Ballroom, Commercial Road, Woking, Surrey (England)
2 Dec 66: Hornsey Art College, Hornsey, London (England)
3 Dec 66: Birdcage Club, Eastney Road, Portsmouth, Hampshire (England)
2 shows; second cancelled when Ginger Baker collapses ill during first show
4 Dec 66: Starlite Ballroom, Allendale Road, Greenford, Middlesex (England) cancelled
5 Dec 66: Bluesville '66, Baths Hall, Ipswich, Suffolk (England) – cancelled
7 Dec 66: Skyline Ballroom, Kingston-upon-Hull, Humberside (England) – cancelled

Cream – "Rhythm & Blues" Radio Show (BBC World Service)
9 Dec 66: BBC Maida Vale Studio 4, Delaware Road, Maida Vale, West London (England) – pre-recorded for 9 Jan 67 radio broadcast

Cream – U.K. Club & Ballroom Circuit cont'd
9 Dec 66: Bluesville '66, The Manor House, Finsbury Park, North London (England)
10 Dec 66: Isleworth Polytechnic, Isleworth, West London (England)
12 Dec 66: Cooks Ferry Inn, Angel Road, Edmonton, North London (England)
13 Dec 66: University of Exeter, Exeter, Devonshire (England)
14 Dec 66: Bromel Club, Bromley Court Hotel, Bromley Hill, Bromley, Kent (England)
15 Dec 66: University of Sussex, Brighton, East Sussex (England)

Cream – French TV & Radio Show Appearance
16 Dec 66: Unknown locations, Paris (France) – unconfirmed
17 Dec 66: La Locomotive Club, Place Blanche, Paris (France)

Cream – U.K. Club & Ballroom Circuit cont'd
18 Dec 66: Agincourt Ballroom, London Road, Camberley, Surrey (England) cancelled
19 Dec 66: Atalanta Ballroom, Commercial Road, Woking, Surrey (England)
20 Dec 66: Tuesday Beat Session, Malvern Winter Gardens, Grange Road, Malvern, Worcestershire (England)

Cream – "Top of the Pops" Television Show (BBC 1 TV)
21 Dec 66: Lime Grove Studios, Shepherd's Bush, West London (England) pre-recorded for 29 Dec television broadcast (Season 3, Episode #52)

Cream – U.K. Club & Ballroom Circuit cont'd
21 Dec 66: Bromel Club, Bromley Court Hotel, Bromley Hill, Bromley, Kent (England)
22 Dec 66: Worthing Pier Pavilion, Worthing, West Sussex (England)
23 Dec 66: Odeon Theatre, New Street, Birmingham, West Midlands (England)

Cream – "36 Hour Rave"
23 Dec 66: Midnight City, Bradford Street, Digbeth, West Midlands (England)

Cream – "Double Giant Freak-Out Ball"
30 Dec 66: The Roundhouse, Chalk Farm Road, Chalk Farm, Northwest London (England)

Cream – U.K. Club & Ballroom Circuit cont'd
7 Jan 67: Ricky Tick Club, Thames Hotel, Windsor, Berkshire (England)

Cream – "Saturday Club" Radio Show (BBC Light Programme)
10 Jan 67: BBC Playhouse Theatre, Northumberland Avenue, West End, Central London (England) – pre-recorded for 14 Jan radio broadcast (Episode #432)

Cream – U.K. Club & Ballroom Circuit cont'd
10 Jan 67: Marquee Club, Wardour Street, Soho, Central London (England)

Cream – "Top of the Pops" Television Show (BBC 1 TV)
11 Jan 67: Lime Grove Studios, Shepherd's Bush, West London (England) pre-recorded for 12 Jan television broadcast (Season 4, Episode #2)

Cream – U.K. Club & Ballroom Circuit cont'd
13 Jan 67: Guildhall, West Marlands Road, Southampton, Hampshire (England)

Cream – "Lanchester Arts Festival"
14 Jan 67: Lanchester Polytechnic College, Coventry, West Midlands (England)

Cream – U.K. Club & Ballroom Circuit cont'd
15 Jan 67: Ricky Tick Club, High Street, Hounslow, West London (England)

Cream – "Monday Monday" Radio Show (BBC Light Programme)
16 Jan 67: BBC Playhouse Theatre, Northumberland Avenue, West End, Central London (England) – pre-recorded for same day radio broadcast

Cream – U.K. Club & Ballroom Circuit cont'd
18 Jan 67: Town Hall, Stourbridge, West Midlands (England)

Cream – "Leicester College Of Art Arts Ball"
19 Jan 67: Granby Halls, Welford Road, Leicester, Leicestershire (England)

Cream – U.K. Club & Ballroom Circuit cont'd
20 Jan 67: Club A'Gogo, Percy Street, Newcastle-upon-Tyne, Northumberland (England)
21 Jan 67: Floral Hall, Southport, Lancashire (England)
24 Jan 67: The Bristol Chinese R&B and Jazz Club, The Corn Exchange, Corn Street, Bristol (England)

Cream – "Parade Of The Pops" Radio Show (BBC Light Programme)
25 Jan 67: BBC Playhouse Theatre, Northumberland Avenue, West End, Central London (England) – live broadcast

Cream – "Top of the Pops" Television Show (BBC 1 TV)
26 Jan 67: Lime Grove Studios, Shepherd's Bush, West London (England) live television broadcast (Season 4, Episode #4)

Cream – "All Night Rave"
27 Jan 67: Adelphi Ballroom, West Bromwich, Staffordshire (England)

Cream – U.K. Club & Ballroom Circuit cont'd
28 Jan 67: The Ram Jam Club, Brixton Road, Brixton, South London (England)
2 shows

Cream – "All Night Rave"
3 Feb 67: Queen's Hall, Leeds, West Yorkshire (England)

Cream – U.K. Club & Ballroom Circuit cont'd
4 Feb 67: Ewell Technical College, Ewell, Epsom, Surrey (England)

Cream – "Sundays At The Saville"
5 Feb 67: Saville Theatre, Shaftesbury Avenue, Central London (England) – 2 shows

Cream – U.K. Club & Ballroom Circuit cont'd
9 Feb 67: City Hall, Salisbury, Wiltshire (England)
10 Feb 67: Bluesville '67, The Manor House, Finsbury Park, North London (England)
11 Feb 67: Bath Pavilion, Matlock, Derbyshire (England)
15 Feb 67: Ricky Tick Club, Assembly Hall, Aylesbury, Buckinghamshire (England)
17 Feb 67: Woodlands Youth Centre, Basildon, Essex (England)
18 Feb 67: Toft's, Grace Hill, Folkestone, Kent (England)
19 Feb 67: Starlite Ballroom, Greenford, West London (England)
22 Feb 67: Bromel Club, Bromley Court Hotel, Bromley Hill, Bromley, Kent (England)

Cream – "Beat Club" Television Show (ARD TV)
24 Feb 67: Radio Bremen Studios, Bremen (Germany) – pre-recorded for 25 Feb television broadcast (Season 2, Episode #6)

Cream – German Concerts
25 Feb 67: Star Club, Hamburg (Germany)
26 Feb 67: Star Club, Kiel (Germany)

Cream – "Manchester & Salford Students Rag Ball '67"
27 Feb 67: Main Debating Hall, Manchester University, Manchester (England) probable location

Cream – U.K. Club & Ballroom Circuit cont'd
1 Mar 67: Ulster Hall, Belfast (Northern Ireland) – two 45-minute shows

Cream – "Rag Pop Festival"
2 Mar 67: Queen's University Students' Hall, Belfast (Northern Ireland)

Cream – Scandinavian Concerts
6 Mar 67: Ekstra Bladets Pop Pool, Falkoner Teatret, Copenhagen (Denmark)
25 minutes broadcast on 21 Mar as Dansk Beat: Cream by Danish Radio

Cream – "Onkel Thores Stuga" Television Show (SR TV)
7 Mar 67: Unknown Studio, Stockholm (Sweden) – pre-recorded for 19 Mar television broadcast

Cream – Scandinavian Concerts cont'd
7 Mar 67: Konserthuset, Stockholm (Sweden) – 5 songs later broadcast on Sveriges Radio's Konsert Med Cream
8 Mar 67: Cue Club, Lorensbergs Cirkus, Liseberg, Gothenburg (Sweden)

Cream – U.K. Club & Ballroom Circuit cont'd
11 Mar 67: St. George's Ballroom, Hinckley, Leicestershire (England)
12 Mar 67: Tavern Club, East Dereham, Norfolk (England)

Cream – "All Night Rave"
14 Mar 67: Beachcomber, Lace Market, Nottingham, East Midlands (England)

Cream – U.K. Club & Ballroom Circuit cont'd
16 Mar 67: Regent Street Polytechnic, Central London (England)
18 Mar 67: Students' Union, Bristol University, Bristol (England)

Cream – "Monday Monday" Radio Show (BBC Light Programme)
20 Mar 67: BBC Playhouse Theatre, Northumberland Avenue, West End, Central London (England) – pre-recorded for same-day radio broadcast

Cream – U.K. Club & Ballroom Circuit cont'd
21 Mar 67: Marquee Club, Wardour Street, Soho, Central London (England)
22 Mar 67: Locarno Ballroom, Stevenage, Hertfordshire (England)

Cream – Murray the K's "Music in the Fifth Dimension" Show
25 Mar 67: RKO 58th Street Theater, New York, New York (United States) – missed due to travel delays
26 Mar 67: RKO 58th Street Theater, New York, New York (United States) – 5 shows
27 Mar 67: RKO 58th Street Theater, New York, New York (United States) – 5 shows
28 Mar 67: RKO 58th Street Theater, New York, New York (United States) – 5 shows
29 Mar 67: RKO 58th Street Theater, New York, New York (United States) – 5 shows
30 Mar 67: RKO 58th Street Theater, New York, New York (United States) – 5 shows
31 Mar 67: RKO 58th Street Theater, New York, New York (United States) – 5 shows
1 Apr 67: RKO 58th Street Theater, New York, New York (United States) – 5 shows
2 Apr 67: RKO 58th Street Theater, New York, New York (United States) – 5 shows

Cream – U.K. Club & Ballroom Circuit cont'd
7 Apr 67: Municipal Hall, Pontypridd, Glamorgan (Wales) – postponed to 5 May
9 Apr 67: Redcar Jazz Club, Coatham Hotel, Newcomen Terrace, Redcar, North Yorkshire (England)
14 Apr 67: Ricky Tick Club, Plaza, Newbury, Berkshire (England)
15 Apr 67: Rhodes Centre, South Road, Bishop's Stortford, Hertfordshire (England)

Cream – "Daily Express Record Star Show"
16 Apr 67: The Empire Pool and Sports Arena, Wembley, Northwest London (England)

Cream – U.K. Club & Ballroom Circuit cont'd
18 Apr 67: Chinese R&B Jazz Club, The Bristol Chinese R&B and Jazz Club, The Corn Exchange, Corn Street, Bristol (England)
19 Apr 67: Beachcomber, Lace Market, Nottingham, East Midlands (England)

Cream – "Brighton Arts Festival"
21 Apr 67: Brighton Dome, Church Street, Brighton, East Sussex (England)

Cream – U.K. Club & Ballroom Circuit cont'd
22 Apr 67: Ricky Tick Club, High Street, Hounslow, West London (England)
26 Apr 67: Birdcage Club, Eastney Road, Portsmouth, Hampshire (England)
28 Apr 67: University, Edgbaston, Birmingham, West Midlands (England)
29 Apr 67: Leeds University Union, Leeds, West Yorkshire (England)

Cream – German Concerts
1 May 67: Starpalast, Kiel, Germany – likely cancelled
2 May 67: Appearance on Hor Hin-Schau Zu Television Show, Berlin (Germany) probably cancelled

Cream – U.K. Club & Ballroom Circuit cont'd
5 May 67: Municipal Hall, Pontypridd, Glamorgan (Wales) – rescheduled from 7 Apr

Cream – "Sound & Picture City" Television Show (BBC 1 TV)
6 May 67: BBC Television Centre, Studio 4, White City, West London (England) – pre-recorded appearance for unaired pilot episode of Sound and Picture City, snippet used in Watch It on 22 Sept

Cream – Royal Agriculture College Charity Appeal
6 May 67: RAF Station, Chippenham, Wiltshire (England)

Cream – "New Musical Express Poll Winners Concert"
7 May 67: The Empire Pool and Sports Arena, Wembley, Northwest London (England)

Cream – U.K. Club & Ballroom Circuit cont'd
7 May 67: The Swan, Coventry Road, Yardley, Birmingham, West Midlands (England)

Cream – "Beat Club" Television Show (ARD TV)
19 May 67: Radio Bremen Studios, Bremen (Germany) – pre-recorded for 20 May television broadcast (Season 2, Episode #9)

Cream – German Concerts
20 May 67: Berlin Stadium, Berlin (Germany)
21 May 67: Jaguar Club, Scala, Herford (Germany)

Cream – U.K. Club & Ballroom Circuit cont'd
23 May 67: Marquee Club, Wardour Street, Soho, Central London (England)

Cream – "Goldsmiths College Summer Ball"
26 May 67: Goldsmiths College, New Cross, South London (England)

Cream – "May Ball"
27 May 67: Pembroke College, Oxford, Oxfordshire (England)

Cream – "Exeter Eights Week Ball"
27 May 67: Exeter College, Oxford, Oxfordshire (England)

Cream – "Barbecue '67"
29 May 67: Tulip Bulb Auction Hall, Spalding, Lincolnshire (England)

Cream – "Saturday Club" Radio Show (BBC Light Programme)
30 May 67: BBC Playhouse Theatre, Northumberland Avenue, West End, Central London (England) – pre-record appearance for broadcast 3 Jun (Episode #452)

Eric Clapton jam session with Jimi Hendrix, Jack Bruce, Jose Feliciano and Graeme Edge
31 May 67: Speakeasy, Margaret Street, Central London (England) – EC jams with Jimi Hendrix, Jack Bruce, Jose Feliciano and Graeme Edge

Cream – "1st International Festival of Pop Music"
1 Jun 67: Palais des Sports, Paris (France)

Cream – U.K. Club & Ballroom Circuit cont'd
3 Jun 67: The Ram Jam Club, Brixton Road, Brixton, South London (England)
8 Jun 67: Locarno Ballroom, Frogmore Street, Bristol (England)
9 Jun 67: Wolverhampton Civic Hall, North Street, Wolverhampton, West Midlands (England)
10 Jun 67: Wellington Club, East Dereham, Norfolk (England)
11 Jun 67: Starlite Ballroom, Greenford, West London (England)
12 Jun 67: Trinity Hall, Cambridge (England)

Cream – "Top of the Pops" Television Show (BBC 1 TV)
15 Jun 67: Lime Grove Studios, Shepherd's Bush, West London (England) – live broadcast (Season 4, Episode #25)

Cream – U.K. Club & Ballroom Circuit cont'd
16 Jun 67: University of Sussex, Brighton, East Sussex (England)

Cream – "Top of the Pops" Television Show (BBC 1 TV)
21 Jun 67: Lime Grove Studios, Shepherd's Bush, West London (England) pre-recorded for 22 Jun 67 television broadcast, song is not aired (Season 4, Episode #26)

Cream – "Dee Time" Television Show (BBC 1 TV)
22 Jun 67: BBC Dickinson Road Studios, Rusholme, Manchester (England) live broadcast

Cream – "June Ball"
23 Jun 67: Durham University, Durham (England)

Cream – U.K. Club & Ballroom Circuit cont'd
24 Jun 67: Carlton Ballroom, High Street, Erdington, Birmingham, West Midlands (England)

Eric Clapton – "Our World" Worldwide Satellite Television Broadcast with The Beatles
25 Jun 67: EMI Abbey Road Studios, St. John's Wood, Central London (England)

Cream – U.K. Club & Ballroom Circuit cont'd
25 Jun 67: Wheels Discotheque, Reading, Berkshire (England)
27 Jun 67: Tuesday Beat Session, Malvern Winter Gardens, Grange Road, Malvern, Worcestershire (England)
28 Jun 67: Floral Hall, Gorleston-on-Sea, Norfolk (England) – equipment does not arrive and Cream performs "unplugged" on borrowed equipment; makeup gig scheduled for 12 Aug

Cream – "Top of the Pops" Television Show (BBC 1 TV)
29 Jun 67: Lime Grove Studios, Shepherd's Bush, West London (England) – live broadcast (Season 4, Episode #27)

Cream – U.K. Club & Ballroom Circuit cont'd
30 Jun 67: Bluesville '67, The Manor House, Finsbury Park, North London (England)
1 Jul 67: The Upper Cut, Forest Gate Centre, Woodgrange Road, Forest Gate, Northeast London (England)

Cream – "Sundays At The Saville"
2 Jul 67: Saville Theatre, Shaftesbury Avenue, Central London (England) – 2 shows

Cream – U.K. Club & Ballroom Circuit cont'd
7 Jul 67: Ballerina Ballroom, High Street, Nairn (Scotland) – postponed to 10 Jul as equipment van breaks down
8 Jul 67: Beach Ballroom, Beach Promenade, Aberdeen (Scotland)
9 Jul 67: Kinema Ballroom, Pilmuir Street, Dunfermline (Scotland)
10 Jul 67: Ballerina Ballroom, High Street, Nairn (Scotland) – rescheduled from 7 Jul
12 Jul 67: Floral Hall, Gorleston, Great Yarmouth, Norfolk (England)

Cream – "Joe Loss Show" Radio Show (BBC Light Programme)
14 Jul 67: BBC Playhouse Theatre, Northumberland Avenue, West End, Central London (England) – pre-recorded for same-day radio broadcast

Cream – U.K. Club & Ballroom Circuit cont'd
15 Jul 67: Supreme Ballroom, Ramsgate, Kent
4 Aug 67: City Hall, King Edward Street, Perth (Scotland)
5 Aug 67: Market Hall, Carlisle, Cumberland (England)
6 Aug 67: McGoo's, High Street, Edinburgh (Scotland) – EC plays a Fender Stratocaster for the only time while in Cream
7 Aug 67: Locarno Ballroom, Sauchiehall Street, Glasgow (Scotland)
8 Aug 67: Palace Ballroom, Queen's Promenade, Douglas (Isle of Man)
12 Aug 67: Floral Hall, Gorleston, Great Yarmouth, Norfolk (England)

Cream – "7th National Jazz & Blues Festival"
13 Aug 67: Balloon Meadow, Royal Windsor Racecourse, Windsor, Berkshire (England)

Cream – "Explosion '67"
15 Aug 67: Town Hall, Castle Circus, Torquay, England

Cream – U.K. Club & Ballroom Circuit cont'd
17 Aug 67: Speakeasy, Margaret Street, Central London (England)
20 Aug 67: Redcar Jazz Club, Coatham Hotel, Newcomen Terrace, Redcar, North Yorkshire (England) – cancelled

Cream – 1967 U.S. Tour
22 Aug 67: Fillmore Auditorium, Geary Boulevard, San Francisco, California (United States) – 2 shows
23 Aug 67: Fillmore Auditorium, Geary Boulevard, San Francisco, California (United States) – 2 shows
24 Aug 67: Fillmore Auditorium, Geary Boulevard, San Francisco, California (United States) – 2 shows
25 Aug 67: Fillmore Auditorium, Geary Boulevard, San Francisco, California (United States) – 2 shows
26 Aug 67: Fillmore Auditorium, Geary Boulevard, San Francisco, California (United States) – 2 shows
27 Aug 67: Fillmore Auditorium, Geary Boulevard, San Francisco, California (United States) – 2 shows
29 Aug 67: Fillmore Auditorium, Geary Boulevard, San Francisco, California (United States) – 2 shows
30 Aug 67: Fillmore Auditorium, Geary Boulevard, San Francisco, California (United States) – 2 shows
31 Aug 67: Fillmore Auditorium, Geary Boulevard, San Francisco, California (United States) – 2 shows
1 Sep 67: Fillmore Auditorium, Geary Boulevard, San Francisco, California (United States) – 2 shows
2 Sep 67: Fillmore Auditorium, Geary Boulevard, San Francisco, California (United States) – 2 shows

3 Sep 67: Fillmore Auditorium, Geary Boulevard, San Francisco, California (United States) – 2 shows
4 Sep 67: Whisky A Go Go, W. Sunset Boulevard, Los Angeles, California (United States)
5 Sep 67: Whisky A Go Go, W. Sunset Boulevard, Los Angeles, California (United States)
6 Sep 67: Whisky A Go Go, W. Sunset Boulevard, Los Angeles, California (United States)
8 Sep 67: The Psychedelic Supermarket, Commonwealth Avenue, Kenmore Square, Boston, Massachusetts (United States) – 2 shows
9 Sep 67: The Psychedelic Supermarket, Commonwealth Avenue, Kenmore Square, Boston, Massachusetts (United States) – 2 shows
10 Sep 67: The Psychedelic Supermarket, Commonwealth Avenue, Kenmore Square, Boston, Massachusetts (United States) – 2 shows
11 Sep 67: The Psychedelic Supermarket, Commonwealth Avenue, Kenmore Square, Boston, Massachusetts (United States) – 2 shows
12 Sep 67: The Psychedelic Supermarket, Commonwealth Avenue, Kenmore Square, Boston, Massachusetts (United States) – 2 shows
13 Sep 67: The Psychedelic Supermarket, Commonwealth Avenue, Kenmore Square, Boston, Massachusetts (United States) – 2 shows
14 Sep 67: The Psychedelic Supermarket, Commonwealth Avenue, Kenmore Square, Boston, Massachusetts (United States) – 2 shows
15 Sep 67: The Psychedelic Supermarket, Commonwealth Avenue, Kenmore Square, Boston, Massachusetts (United States) – 2 shows
16 Sep 67: The Psychedelic Supermarket, Commonwealth Avenue, Kenmore Square, Boston, Massachusetts (United States) – 2 shows
22 Sep 67: Action House, Austin Boulevard, Island Park, New York (United States)
23 Sep 67: Village Theater, Second Avenue, New York, New York (United States) 2 shows
24 Sep 67: Action House, Austin Boulevard, Island Park, New York (United States)
26 Sep 67: Cafe Au Go Go, Bleecker Street, New York, New York (United States)
27 Sep 67: Cafe Au Go Go, Bleecker Street, New York, New York (United States)
28 Sep 67: Cafe Au Go Go, Bleecker Street, New York, New York (United States)
29 Sep 67: Cafe Au Go Go, Bleecker Street, New York, New York (United States)
30 Sep 67: Village Theater, Second Avenue, New York, New York (United States) early show
30 Sep 67: Cafe Au Go Go, Bleecker Street, New York, New York (United States) late show
1 Oct 67: Cafe Au Go Go, Bleecker Street, New York, New York (United States)
3 Oct 67: Cafe Au Go Go, Bleecker Street, New York, New York (United States)
4 Oct 67: Cafe Au Go Go, Bleecker Street, New York, New York (United States)
5 Oct 67: Cafe Au Go Go, Bleecker Street, New York, New York (United States)
6 Oct 67: Cafe Au Go Go, Bleecker Street, New York, New York (United States)
7 Oct 67: Cafe Au Go Go, Bleecker Street, New York, New York (United States)
8 Oct 67: Cafe Au Go Go, Bleecker Street, New York, New York (United States)
11 Oct 67: Fifth Dimension Club, The Fifth Dimension, W. Huron Street, Ann Arbor, Michigan (United States)
12 Oct 67: Fifth Dimension Club, The Fifth Dimension, W. Huron Street, Ann Arbor, Michigan (United States)
13 Oct 67: Grande Ballroom, Grand River Avenue, Detroit, Michigan (United States)
14 Oct 67: Grande Ballroom, Grand River Avenue, Detroit, Michigan (United States)
15 Oct 67: Grande Ballroom, Grand River Avenue, Detroit, Michigan (United States)

Cream – U.K. Club & Ballroom Circuit cont'd
19 Oct 67: Romano's Ballroom, Queen Street, Belfast (Northern Ireland) postponed to 2 Nov 67

Cream – "Top Gear" Radio Show (BBC Radio One)
24 Oct 67: BBC Aeolian Hall Studio 2, New Bond Street, Central London (England) pre-recorded for radio broadcast on 29 Oct

Cream – "Union Dance"
28 Oct 67: University, Southampton, Hampshire (England)

Cream – "Sundays At The Saville"
29 Oct 67: Saville Theatre, Shaftesbury Avenue, Central London (England) – 2 shows

Cream – U.K. Club & Ballroom Circuit cont'd
1 Nov 67: The Bal Tabarin, Downham Way, Bromley, Kent (England)
2 Nov 67: Romano's Ballroom, Queen Street, Belfast (Northern Ireland) rescheduled from 19 Oct
3 Nov 67: Strand Ballroom, Portstewart (Northern Ireland)
6 Nov 67: Silver Blades Ice Rink, High Road, Streatham, South London (England)

Cream – "Toppop" Television Show (DR TV)
11 Nov 67: TV Byen Studio A, Gladsaxe (Denmark) – pre-recorded for same day television broadcast

Cream – Scandinavian Tour
11 Nov 67: Hit Club, Vejgaard Hallen, Aalborg (Denmark)
12 Nov 67: Falkoner Teatret, Copenhagen (Denmark) – 2 shows

Cream – "Tunnusävel" Television Show (Finnish TV)
13 Nov 67: Pasila TV Studios, Helsinki (Finland) – pre-recorded for later television broadcast

Cream – Scandinavian Tour cont'd
13 Nov 67: Kulttuuritalo, Helsinki (Finland) – 2 shows
14 Nov 67: Konserthuset, Stockholm (Sweden) – 2 shows
15 Nov 67: Lorensbergs Cirkus, Liseberg, Gothenburg (Sweden) – 2 shows
17 Nov 67: Rigoletto, Jönköping (Sweden)
18 Nov 67: Idrottshuset, Örebro (Sweden)

Cream – U.K. Club & Ballroom Circuit cont'd
23 Nov 67: Club A'Gogo, Percy Street, Newcastle-upon-Tyne, Northumberland (England)
24 Nov 67: Marine Ballroom, Central Pier, Morecambe, Lancashire (England)

Cream – "Twice a Fortnight" Television Show (BBC 1 TV)
26 Nov 67: Lime Grove Studio G, Shepherd's Bush, West London (England) pre-recorded for 2 Dec television broadcast

Cream – "Rhythm & Blues" Radio Show (BBC World Service)
28 Nov 67: BBC Maida Vale Studio, Central London (England) – cancelled

Cream – U.K. Club & Ballroom Circuit cont'd
28 Nov 67: Marquee Club, Wardour Street, Soho, Central London (England) cancelled
1 Dec 67: Top Rank Suite, West Street, Brighton, East Sussex (England) – postponed to 19 Jan 68
2 Dec 67: Owen's Union Building, Manchester University, Manchester (England) postponed to 10 Feb 68

Cream – "Union Dance"
9 Dec 67: University, Bristol (England)

Cream – Short U.S. Visit
20 Dec 67: Private Party for Debutante's Ball, Unknown Venue, Chicago, Illinois (United States)
22 Dec 67: Grande Ballroom, Grand River Avenue, Detroit, Michigan (United States)
23 Dec 67: Grande Ballroom, Grand River Avenue, Detroit, Michigan (United States)
24 Dec 67: Grande Ballroom, Grand River Avenue, Detroit, Michigan (United States)

Cream – U.K. Club & Ballroom Circuit cont'd
5 Jan 68: Industrial Club, Norwich, Norfolk (England)

Cream – "Top Gear" Radio Show (BBC Radio One)
9 Jan 68: BBC Aeolian Hall Studio 2, New Bond Street, Central London (England) pre-recorded for 14 Jan radio broadcast

Cream – French Television Appearance
10 Jan 68: Revolution Club, Bruton Place, Mayfair, London (England) rehearsal filmed for French television but never broadcast

Cream – "Fenklup" Television Show (VARA)
13 Jan 68: Dutch TV Studios, Amsterdam (Holland) – likely date; pre-recorded for 19 Jan television broadcast

Cream – U.K. Club & Ballroom Circuit cont'd
14 Jan 68: Redcar Jazz Club, Coatham Hotel, Newcomen Terrace, Redcar, North Yorkshire (England) – cancelled
19 Jan 68: Top Rank Suite, West Street, Brighton, East Sussex (England) reschedule from 1 Dec 67
20 Jan 68: Leeds University Union, Leeds, West Yorkshire (England)
27 Jan 68: St Mary's College, Twickenham, Southwest London (England)
2 Feb 68: Technical College, Nottingham, East Midlands (England)

Cream – "Carnival '68"
3 Feb 68: University College London, Central London (England)

Cream – Short Scandinavian Visit
5 Feb 68: Vognmandsmarken, Copenhagen (Denmark) – movie filming for On A Saturday Night
6 Feb 68: Unknown Roundhouse, Copenhagen (Denmark) – movie filming for On A Saturday Night
7 Feb 68: Tivolis Koncertsal, Copenhagen (Denmark) – 2 shows

Cream – "Arts Ball Goes Hollywood"
9 Feb 68: Leicester University, Leicester, Leicestershire (England)

Cream – U.K. Club & Ballroom Circuit cont'd
10 Feb 68: Owen's Union Building, Manchester University, Manchester (England) rescheduled from 2 Dec 67

Cream – 1968 North American Tour
23 Feb 68: Santa Monica Civic Auditorium, Santa Monica, California (United States) 2 shows
24 Feb 68: Earl Warren Showgrounds, Santa Barbara, California (United States)
25 Feb 68: Swing Auditorium, E Street, San Bernadino, California (United States)
29 Feb 68: Winterland Ballroom, Post Street, San Francisco, California (United States) 2 shows
1 Mar 68: Winterland Ballroom, Post Street, San Francisco, California (United States) 2 shows
2 Mar 68: Winterland Ballroom, Post Street, San Francisco, California (United States) 2 shows
3 Mar 68: Fillmore Auditorium, Geary Boulevard, San Francisco, California (United States) – 2 shows
7 Mar 68: Fillmore Auditorium, Geary Boulevard, San Francisco, California (United States) – 2 shows
8 Mar 68: Winterland Ballroom, Post Street, San Francisco, California (United States) 1 show as band arrived late
9 Mar 68: Winterland Ballroom, Post Street, San Francisco, California (United States) 2 shows
10 Mar 68: Winterland Ballroom, Post Street, San Francisco, California (United States) 2 shows
11 Mar 68: Sacramento Memorial Auditorium, Sacramento, California (United States)
13 Mar 68: Selland Arena, Fresno, California (United States)

Cream – "Romp!!!" Television Show (ABC TV)
14 Mar 68: Unknown Studio, California (United States) – likely date; pre-recorded for broadcast on 21 Apr

Cream – 1968 North American Tour cont'd
15 Mar 68: San Fernando Valley State College, Northridge, California (United States) afternoon
15 Mar 68: Shrine Auditorium, West Jefferson Boulevard, Los Angeles, California (United States)
16 Mar 68: Shrine Auditorium, West Jefferson Boulevard, Los Angeles, California (United States)
17 Mar 68: Phoenix Star Theater, East Van Buren Street, Phoenix, Arizona (United States)
18 Mar 68: Convention Center Arena, Anaheim, California (United States)
19 Mar 68: The Family Dog, West Evans Street, Denver, Colorado (United States) postponed until May 6
21 Mar 68: Beloit College, Beloit, Wisconsin (United States)
22 Mar 68: Clowes Memorial Auditorium, Butler University, Indianapolis, Indiana (United States) – 2 shows
23 Mar 68: Shapiro Athletic Center, Brandeis University, Waltham, Massachusetts (United States)
24 Mar 68: Gymnasium, State University of New York, Stony Brook, New York (United States) – provisional concert postponed until 17 April
26 Mar 68: Union Catholic Regional High School, Martine Avenue, Scotch Plains, New Jersey (United States)
27 Mar 68: Staples High School Auditorium, North Avenue, Westport, Connecticut (United States)
29 Mar 68: Hunter College Auditorium, 68th Street, New York, New York (United States) – 2 shows
30 Mar 68: Music Hall, Fair Park, Dallas, Texas (United States)
31 Mar 68: Houston Music Hall, Houston, Texas (United States)
3 Apr 68: Morris Civic Auditorium, South Bend, Indiana (United States)
5 Apr 68: Back Bay Theatre, Massachusetts Avenue, Boston, Massachusetts (United States)
6 Apr 68: Commodore Ballroom, Thorndike Street, Lowell, Massachusetts (United States)
7 Apr 68: Eastman Theatre, Eastman School of Music, University of Rochester, Rochester, New York (United States) – Cream do not play this gig as their equipment fails to arrive; co-headliners Vanilla Fudge play the show alone
8 Apr 68: Capitol Cinema, Queen Street, Ottawa, Ontario (Canada)
10 Apr 68: Woolsey Hall, Yale University, New Haven, Connecticut (United States)
11 Apr 68: Thee Image, Collins Avenue, Sunny Isles Beach, Florida (United States)
12 Apr 68: Electric Factory, 22nd and Arch Streets, Philadelphia, Pennsylvania (United States)
13 Apr 68: Electric Factory, 22nd and Arch Streets, Philadelphia, Pennsylvania (United States)
14 Apr 68: Electric Factory, 22nd and Arch Streets, Philadelphia, Pennsylvania (United States)
[Break in North American Tour. Dates rescheduled so band could have a rest]

16 Apr 68: Paul Sauvé Arena, Montreal, Quebec (Canada) – postponed to 11 Jun
17 Apr 68: Gymnasium, State University of New York, Stony Brook, New York (United States) – rescheduled from 24 Mar then cancelled
19 Apr 68: Grande Ballroom, Grand River Avenue, Detroit, Michigan (United States) postponed to 7 Jun
20 Apr 68: Grande Ballroom, Grand River Avenue, Detroit, Michigan (United States) postponed to 8 Jun
21 Apr 68: Grande Ballroom, Grand River Avenue, Detroit, Michigan (United States) postponed to 9 Jun
22 Apr 68: Massey Hall, Victoria Street, Toronto, Ontario (Canada) postponed to 5 Jun
[North American Tour resumes]
26 Apr 68: The Cellar, Davis Street at Salem Avenue, Arlington Heights, Illinois (United States)
27 Apr 68: Chicago Coliseum, Wabash Avenue, Chicago, Illinois (United States)
28 Apr 68: Kiel Auditorium (a.k.a. Convention Hall), Clark Avenue, St. Louis, Missouri (United States)
2 May 68: The Factory, Wisconsin State University Field House, Madison, Wisconsin (United States) – cancelled as club closed
3 May 68: The Scene, North 2nd Street, Milwaukee, Wisconsin (United States) 2 shows
4 May 68: The Scene, North 2nd Street, Milwaukee, Wisconsin (United States) 2 shows
5 May 68: New City Opera House, Nicollet Avenue, Minneapolis, Minnesota (United States) – afternoon show
6 May 68: The Family Dog, West Evans Street, Denver, Colorado (United States) rescheduled from 19 Mar
10 May 68: Toledo Sports Arena, Toledo, Ohio (United States)
11 May 68: Akron Civic Center, South Main Street, Akron, Ohio (United States)
12 May 68: Cleveland Music Hall, Lakeside Avenue, Cleveland, Ohio (United States) afternoon show
14 May 68: Veteran's Memorial Auditorium, Columbus, Ohio (United States)
15 May 68: Veteran's Memorial Field House, Huntington, West Virginia (United States)
17 May 68: Anaheim Convention Center Arena, Anaheim, California (United States)
18 May 68: Ice Palace, Las Vegas, Nevada (United States) – cancelled
18 May 68: Anaheim Convention Center Arena, Anaheim, California (United States) gig added
19 May 68: Community Concourse Hall, San Diego, California (United States)

Cream – "The Summer Brothers Smothers Show" Television Show (CBS TV)
20 May 68: CBS Studios, Los Angeles, California (United States) – pre-recorded for 14 July television broadcast

Cream – 1968 North American Tour cont'd
24 May 68: Robertson Gymnasium, University of California, Santa Barbara, California (United States)
25 May 68: San Jose Civic Auditorium, San Jose, California (United States)
27 May 68: Swing Auditorium, E Street, San Bernardino, California (United States)
28 May 68: Pacific Center, Long Beach, California (United States)
29 May 68: Eagles Auditorium, Seventh Avenue, Seattle, Washington (United States)
30 May 68: Eagles Auditorium, Seventh Avenue, Seattle, Washington (United States) afternoon show
31 May 68: Stampede Corral, Stampede Park, Calgary, Alberta (Canada)
1 Jun 68: Sales Pavilion Annex, Edmonton, Alberta (Canada)
2 Jun 68: Pacific Coliseum, Hastings Park, Vancouver, British Columbia (Canada)
5 Jun 68: Massey Hall, Victoria Street, Toronto, Ontario (Canada) rescheduled from 22 Apr
7 Jun 68: Grande Ballroom, Grand River Avenue, Detroit, Michigan (United States) rescheduled from 19 Apr
8 Jun 68: Grande Ballroom, Grand River Avenue, Detroit, Michigan (United States) rescheduled from 20 Apr
9 Jun 68: Grande Ballroom, Grand River Avenue, Detroit, Michigan (United States) rescheduled from 21 Apr
11 Jun 68: Paul Sauvé Arena, Montreal, Quebec (Canada) – rescheduled from 16 Apr
14 Jun 68: Island Garden, Hempstead Turnpike, West Hempstead, New York (United States) – arrive late and only perform 3 songs
15 Jun 68: Oakdale Music Theater, South Turnpike Road, Wallingford, Connecticut (United States) – 2 shows
16 Jun 68: Camden County Music Fair, Borton's Mill Road, Haddonfield, New Jersey (United States)

Eric Clapton jam session with Jimi Hendrix & The Jeff Beck Group
18 Jun 68: Steve Paul's The Scene, West 46th Street, New York City, New York (United States)

Eric Clapton jam session with Ginger Baker & Phil Seaman
10 Aug 68: National Jazz & Blues Festival, Kempton Park Racecourse, Sunbury-on-Thames, Surrey (England)

Cream – 1968 U.S. "Farewell Tour"
4 Oct 68: Oakland-Alameda County Oakland-Alameda County Coliseum, Oakland, California (United States)
5 Oct 68: University Arena, University of New Mexico, Albuquerque, New Mexico (United States)
6 Oct 68: Denver Auditorium Arena, Denver, Colorado (United States)
11 Oct 68: New Haven Arena, New Haven, Connecticut (United States)
12 Oct 68: Olympia Stadium, Detroit, Michigan (United States)

Eric Clapton jam session with John Mayall's Bluesbreakers
12 Oct 68: Grande Ballroom, Grand River Avenue, Detroit, Michigan (United States)
EC sits in with John Mayall's Bluesbreakers

Cream – 1968 U.S. "Farewell Tour" cont'd
13 Oct 68: Chicago Coliseum, Wabash Avenue, Chicago, Illinois (United States)
14 Oct 68: Veteran's Memorial Auditorium, Des Moines, Iowa (United States)
18 Oct 68: The Forum, Inglewood, California (United States)
19 Oct 68: The Forum, Inglewood, California (United States)
20 Oct 68: San Diego Sports Arena, San Diego, California (United States)
24 Oct 68: Sam Houston Coliseum, Houston, Texas (United States)
25 Oct 68: Dallas Memorial Auditorium, Dallas, Texas (United States)
26 Oct 68: Miami Stadium, Miami, Florida (United States) – afternoon show
27 Oct 68: Chastain Park Amphitheater, Atlanta, Georgia (United States) – afternoon show
31 Oct 68: Boston Garden, Boston, Massachusetts (United States) – postponed to 4 Nov but then cancelled and replaced with a gig in Providence, Rhode Island
1 Nov 68: Spectrum, Philadelphia, Pennsylvania (United States)
2 Nov 68: Madison Square Garden, New York City, New York (United States)
3 Nov 68: Civic Center Arena, Baltimore, Maryland (United States)
4 Nov 68: Rhode Island Auditorium, Providence, Rhode Island (United States) 2 shows

Cream – U.K. "Farewell" Concerts
26 Nov 68: Royal Albert Hall, Kensington Gore, Central London (England) – 2 shows

Eric Clapton – The Rolling Stones' "Rock 'n' Roll Circus" Television Show
10 Dec 68: InterTel Studios, Stonebridge Park, Wembley, Northwest London (England)
11 Dec 68: InterTel Studios, Stonebridge Park, Wembley, Northwest London (England)

Eric Clapton – "Super Show" Filming
18 Mar 69: Linoleum Factory, Staines, Surrey (England)
19 Mar 69: Linoleum Factory, Staines, Surrey (England)

Blind Faith – Debut Concert
7 Jun 69: Hyde Park, London (England)

Blind Faith – 1969 Scandinavian Tour
12 Jun 69: Kulttuuritalo, Helsinki (Finland) – 2 shows
14 Jun 69: Njaardhallen, Oslo (Norway)
16 Jun 69: Kungliga Tennishallen, Stockholm (Sweden) – 2 shows possible
18 Jun 69: Konserthallen, Liseberg, Nöjespark, Gothenburg (Sweden)
19 Jun 69: KB Hallen, Copenhagen (Denmark) – 2 shows possible

Blind Faith – "Newport Jazz Festival"
11 Jul 69: Fort Adams State Park, Newport, Rhode Island (United States) cancelled; local authorities revoke permission to perform

Blind Faith – 1969 North American Tour
12 Jul 69: Madison Square Garden, New York City, New York (United States)
13 Jul 69: John F. Kennedy Stadium, Bridgeport, Connecticut (United States)
16 Jul 69: Spectrum, Philadelphia, Pennsylvania (United States)
18 Jul 69: Varsity Stadium, Toronto, Ontario (Canada)
19 Jul 69: The Forum, Montreal, Quebec (Canada)
20 Jul 69: Civic Center Arena, Baltimore, Maryland (United States)
23 Jul 69: War Memorial Stadium, Kansas City, Kansas (United States)
26 Jul 69: Midwest Rock Festival, State Fair Park, West Allis, Wisconsin (United States)
27 Jul 69: International Amphitheater, Chicago, Illinois (United States)
1 Aug 69: Sports Arena, Minneapolis, Minnesota (United States)
2 Aug 69: Olympia Stadium, Detroit, Michigan (United States)
3 Aug 69: Kiel Auditorium (a.k.a. Convention Hall), Clark Avenue, St. Louis, Missouri (United States)
8 Aug 69: Seattle Center Coliseum, Seattle, Washington (United States)
9 Aug 69: Pacific Coliseum, Hastings Park, Vancouver, British Columbia (Canada)
10 Aug 69: Veteran's Memorial Coliseum, Portland, Oregon (United States)
14 Aug 69: Oakland-Alameda County Oakland-Alameda County Coliseum, Oakland, California (United States)
15 Aug 69: The Forum, Inglewood, California (United States)
16 Aug 69: Earl Warren Showgrounds Arena, Santa Barbara, California (United States)
19 Aug 69: Sam Houston Coliseum, Houston, Texas (United States)

20 Aug 69: HemisFair Arena, San Antonio Fairgrounds, San Antonio, Texas (United States)
22 Aug 69: Salt Palace Arena, Salt Lake City, Utah (United States)
23 Aug 69: Arizona Veteran's Memorial Coliseum, Phoenix, Arizona (United States)
24 Aug 69: Hawaii International Center Arena, Honolulu, Hawaii (United States)

Plastic Ono Band – "Toronto Rock 'n' Roll Revival Festival"
13 Sep 69: Varsity Stadium, Toronto, Ontario (Canada)

Delaney & Bonnie & Friends with Eric Clapton – "Price Of Fame (Or Fame At Any Price)" Television Show (BBC 2 TV)
Nov 69: Unknown studio (England) – pre-recorded for 20 Nov television broadcast

Delaney & Bonnie & Friends with Eric Clapton – "Beat Club" Television Show (ARD TV)
26 Nov 69: Radio Bremen Studios, Bremen (Germany) – pre-recorded for 29 Nov television broadcast (Season 5, Episode #3)

Delaney & Bonnie & Friends with Eric Clapton – 1969 German Tour
27 Nov 69: Jahrhunderthalle, Frankfurt am Main Höchst (Germany)
28 Nov 69: Musikhalle, Hamburg (Germany)
29 Nov 69: Sport-Halle, Cologne (Germany)

Delaney & Bonnie & Friends with Eric Clapton – 1969 U.K. Tour
1 Dec 69: Royal Albert Hall, Kensington Gore, Central London (England)
2 Dec 69: Colston Hall, Colston Street, Bristol (England) – 2 shows
3 Dec 69: Town Hall, Victoria Square, Birmingham, West Midlands (England) – 2 shows
4 Dec 69: City Hall, Barkers Pool, Sheffield, South Yorkshire (England) – 2 shows
5 Dec 69: City Hall, Northumberland Road, Newcastle-upon-Tyne, Northumberland (England) – 2 shows
6 Dec 69: Empire Theatre, Lime Street, Liverpool, Merseyside (England) – 2 shows
7 Dec 69: Fairfield Halls, Park Lane, Croydon, South London (England) – 2 shows

Delaney & Bonnie & Friends with Eric Clapton – 1969 Scandinavian Tour
8 Dec 69: Unknown Venue / Location in Scandinavia
9 Dec 69: Unknown Venue / Location in Scandinavia
10 Dec 69: Falkoner Teatret, Copenhagen (Denmark) – pre-recorded for 25 Feb 70 television broadcast on DR TV as "Beat 70"
12 Dec 69: Konserthuset, Gothenburg (Sweden)

Plastic Ono Band – "Peace For Christmas Prom-Pop Concert" for UNICEF
15 Dec 69: Lyceum Ballroom, The Strand, Central London (England)

Delaney & Bonnie & Friends with Eric Clapton – 1970 U.S. Tour
2 Feb 70: Massey Hall, Victoria Street, Toronto, Ontario (Canada) – probably cancelled

Delaney & Bonnie & Friends with Eric Clapton – "The Dick Cavett Show" Television Show (ABC TV)
5 Feb 70: ABC Studio TV-15, Elysee Theatre, New York, New York (United States) pre-recorded for same-day television broadcast

Delaney & Bonnie & Friends with Eric Clapton – 1970 U.S. Tour cont'd
6 Feb 70: Fillmore East, Second Avenue, New York, New York (United States)
7 Feb 70: Fillmore East, Second Avenue, New York, New York (United States)
8 Feb 70: The Boston Tea Party, Lansdowne Street, Boston, Massachusetts (United States) – 2 shows
9 Feb 70: The Boston Tea Party, Lansdowne Street, Boston, Massachusetts (United States) – 2 shows
11 Feb 70: Electric Factory, 22nd and Arch Streets, Philadelphia, Pennsylvania (United States) – 2 shows
12 Feb 70: Symphony Hall, Minneapolis, Minnesota (United States)
13 Feb 70: Ford Auditorium, Detroit, Michigan (United States)
14 Feb 70: Auditorium Theatre, Roosevelt University, Chicago, Illinois (United States)
15 Feb 70: Memorial Hall, Kansas City, Kansas (United States)
19 Feb 70: Fillmore West, Market Street, San Francisco, California (United States)
20 Feb 70: Fillmore West, Market Street, San Francisco, California (United States)
21 Feb 70: Fillmore West, Market Street, San Francisco, California (United States)
22 Feb 70: Fillmore West, Market Street, San Francisco, California (United States)

Eric Clapton jam session with Traffic
5 May 1970: Unknown Venue, Oxford, Oxfordshire (England)

Derek & The Dominos – Debut Concert (in aid of Dr. Spock's Civil Liberties Fund)
14 Jun 70: Lyceum Ballroom, The Strand, Central London (England) – 2 shows

Derek & The Dominos – 1970 U.K. Club Tour (First Leg)
1 Aug 70: Village Blues Club, Lodge Avenue, Dagenham, East London (England)
2 Aug 70: The Place, Bryan Street, Hanley, Stoke-on-Trent, Staffordshire (England)
4 Aug 70: Marquee Club, Wardour Street, Soho, Central London (England) postponed to 11 Aug as band accepts a festival gig in Paris

6 Aug 70: The Penthouse, St. Nicholas' Street, Scarborough, North Yorkshire (England) postponed to 9 Oct as band accepts a festival gig in Paris

Derek & The Dominos – "Popanalia Festival"
5-6 Aug 70: Autoroute De L'Esteral, Biot (France) – leave without playing as riots halt the festival

Derek & The Dominos – 1970 U.K. Club Tour (First Leg) cont'd
7 Aug 70: Mayfair Ballroom, Newgate Street, Newcastle-upon-Tyne, Northumberland (England)
8 Aug 70: California Pool Ballroom, Whipsnade Road, Dunstable, Bedfordshire (England)
9 Aug 70: Mother's, Erdington, High Street, Birmingham, West Midlands (England)
11 Aug 70: Marquee Club, Wardour Street, Soho, Central London (England) rescheduled from 4 Aug
11 Aug 70: Sherwood Rooms, Nottingham (England) – cancelled due to rescheduled Marquee Club date
12 Aug 70: Speakeasy, Margaret Street, Central London (England)
14 Aug 70: Winter Gardens, Grange Road, Malvern, Worcestershire (England)
15 Aug 70: Toft's, Grace Hill, Folkestone, Kent (England)
16 Aug 70: Black Prince Hotel, Bexley, Southeast London (England)
18 Aug 70: The Pavilion, Westover Road, Bournemouth, Dorset (England)
20 Aug 70: Town Hall, Swindon, Wiltshire (England) – postponed to 1 Oct then cancelled
21 Aug 70: Marquay Club, Town Hall, Castle Circus, Torquay, Devon (England)
22 Aug 70: Van Dike Club, Exmouth Road, Plymouth, Devon (England)
[The tour is interrupted for recording sessions in the United States]
20 Sep 70: Fairfield Halls, Park Lane, Croydon, South London (England)
21 Sep 70: De Montfort Hall, Granville Road, Leicester, Leicestershire (England)
22 Sep 70: Portsmouth Guildhall, Guildhall Square, Portsmouth, Hampshire (England) not finalised, dropped from itinerary

Eric Clapton guest appearance with Buddy Guy and Junior Wells (support for The Rolling Stones)
22 Sep 70: L'Olympia Theatre, Paris (France) – radio broadcast

Derek & The Dominos – 1970 U.K. Club Tour (Second Leg)
23 Sep 70: Brighton Dome, Church Street, Brighton, East Sussex (England)
24 Sep 70: Philharmonic Hall, Hope Street, Liverpool, Merseyside (England)
25 Sep 70: Green's Playhouse, Renfield Street, Glasgow (Scotland)
27 Sep 70: Colston Hall, Colston Street, Bristol (England)
28 Sep 70: Free Trade Hall, Peter Street, Manchester (England)
1 Oct 70: Town Hall, Swindon, Wiltshire (England) – rescheduled from 20 Aug then cancelled
2 Oct 70: Trent Polytechnic, Nottingham, East Midlands (England) – cancelled
3 Oct 70: Norwich Lads' Club, King Street, Norwich, Norfolk (England) – possibly cancelled
4 Oct 70: Redcar Jazz Club, Coatham Hotel, Newcomen Terrace, Redcar, North Yorkshire (England)
5 Oct 70: Town Hall, Victoria Square, Birmingham, West Midlands (England)
7 Oct 70: Winter Gardens, Exeter Road, Bournemouth, Dorset (England) – moved forward from 9 Oct
8 Oct 70: University, Liverpool, Merseyside (England)
9 Oct 70: The Penthouse, St. Nicholas' Street, Scarborough, North Yorkshire (England) rescheduled from 6 Aug
10 Oct 70: University, Leeds, West Yorkshire (England)
11 Oct 70: Lyceum Ballroom, The Strand, Central London (England)

Derek & The Dominos – 1970 U.S. Tour
15 Oct 70: Rider College, Trenton, New Jersey (United States)
16 Oct 70: Electric Factory, 22nd and Arch Streets, Philadelphia, Pennsylvania (United States)
17 Oct 70: Electric Factory, 22nd and Arch Streets, Philadelphia, Pennsylvania (United States)
21 Oct 70: Lisner Auditorium, The George Washington University, Washington D.C. (United States)
23 Oct 70: Fillmore East, Second Avenue, New York, New York (United States) 2 shows
24 Oct 70: Fillmore East, Second Avenue, New York, New York (United States) 2 shows
29 Oct 70: Kleinhan's Music Hall, Symphony Circle, Buffalo, New York (United States)
30 Oct 70: Gymnasium, State University of New York, Albany, New York (United States)
31 Oct 70: Alan B. Shepard Convention Center (a.k.a. The Dome), Pacific Avenue, Virginia Beach, Virginia (United States)
1 Nov 70: Civic Auditorium, West Water Street, Jacksonville, Florida (United States)

Derek & The Dominos – "The Johnny Cash Show" (ABC TV)
5 Nov 70: Ryman Auditorium, Fifth Avenue North, Nashville, Tennessee (United States) – pre-recorded appearance for broadcast on 6 Jan 71. While in Nashville, EC buys a handful of Fender Stratocasters at the Sho-Bud Shop from which he will build "Blackie"

Derek & The Dominos – 1970 U.S. Tour cont'd
6 Nov 70: McFarlin Auditorium, Dallas, Texas (United States)
7 Nov 70: Community Center Theater, San Antonio, Texas (United States)
9 Nov 70: Sacramento Memorial Auditorium, Sacramento, California (United States) tentative; postponed until 17 Nov
11 Nov 70: Mammoth Gardens, Denver, Colorado (United States) – cancelled
12 Nov 70: Santa Monica Civic Auditorium, Santa Monica, California (United States) tentative; postponed until 20 Nov
13 Nov 70: University of Nevada, Reno, Nevada (United States)
14 Nov 70: Fairgrounds Coliseum, Salt Lake City, Utah (United States)
17 Nov 70: Sacramento Memorial Auditorium, Sacramento, California (United States)
18 Nov 70: Berkeley Community Theatre, Berkeley High School, Berkeley, California (United States) – guest appearance by Neal Schon
19 Nov 70: Berkeley Community Theatre, Berkeley High School, Berkeley, California (United States) – guest appearance by Neal Schon
20 Nov 70: Santa Monica Civic Auditorium, Santa Monica, California (United States) 2 shows; guest appearance by Delaney Bramlett and Toe Fat (support)
21 Nov 70: Pasadena Civic Auditorium, East Green Street, Pasadena, California (United States) – 2 shows
22 Nov 70: San Diego Community Concourse, San Diego, California (United States)
25 Nov 70: Auditorium Theater, Roosevelt University, Chicago, Illinois (United States)
26 Nov 70: Music Hall, Cincinnati, Ohio (United States) – guest appearance by B.B. King
27 Nov 70: Kiel Opera House, Market Street, St. Louis, Missouri (United States)
28 Nov 70: Allen Theater, E.14 & Euclid Avenue, Cleveland, Ohio (United States) – 2 shows
29 Nov 70: Painters Mill Music Fair, Owings Mills, Maryland (United States)
1 Dec 70: Curtis Hixon Hall, Tampa, Florida (United States) – guest appearance by Duane Allman for the entire show
2 Dec 70: Onondaga War Memorial Auditorium, Syracuse, New York (United States) guest appearance by Duane Allman for the entire show
3 Dec 70: Eastown Theater, Detroit, Michigan (United States)
4 Dec 70: Capitol Theater, Port Chester, New York (United States)
5 Dec 70: Capitol Theater, Port Chester, New York (United States)
6 Dec 70: Gymnasium, Suffolk Community College, Selden, New York (United States)

Eric Clapton jam session with Ringo Starr, Maurice Gibb, Charlie Watts and others
31 Dec 70: Ringo Starr's New Year's Eve Party, Ronnie Scott's, Frith Street, Soho, Central London (England)

Eric Clapton – George Harrison's and Ravi Shankar's "The Concert for Bangladesh"
1 Aug 71: Madison Square Garden, New York City, New York (United States) – 2 shows

Eric Clapton guest appearance with Leon Russell
4 Dec 71: Rainbow Theatre, Seven Sisters Road, Finsbury Park, North London (England) – EC sits in with Leon Russell

Eric Clapton & The Palpitations – "Eric Clapton's Rainbow Concert" (Part of the 11 day "Fanfare For Europe" celebrating Great Britain's entry into the European Economic Community)
13 Jan 73: Rainbow Theatre, Seven Sisters Road, Finsbury Park, North London (England) – 2 shows

Eric Clapton & His Band – Scandinavian Warm-Up Shows for 1974 U.S. Tour
19 Jun 74: Tivoli Gardens, Stockholm (Sweden)
20 Jun 74: KB Hallen, Copenhagen (Denmark)

Eric Clapton & His Band – 1974 U.S. Tour (Leg 1)
28 Jun 74: Yale Bowl, New Haven, Connecticut (United States)
29 Jun 74: Spectrum, Philadelphia, Pennsylvania (United States)
30 Jun 74: Nassau Veterans Memorial Coliseum, Uniondale, New York (United States)
2 Jul 74: International Amphitheatre, Chicago, Illinois (United States)
3 Jul 74: International Amphitheatre, Chicago, Illinois (United States)
4 Jul 74: St. John Arena, Ohio State University, Columbus, Ohio (United States)
5 Jul 74: Three Rivers Stadium, Pittsburgh, Pennsylvania (United States)

Eric Clapton & His Band – "Summerfest At The Stadium"
6 Jul 74: Rich Stadium, Orchard Park, New York (United States) – EC guest appearance with The Band; guest appearance by Freddie King with EC

Eric Clapton & His Band – 1974 U.S. Tour (Leg 1) cont'd
7 Jul 74: Roosevelt Stadium, Jersey City, New Jersey (United States) guest appearance by Freddie King

9 Jul 74: The Forum, Montreal, Quebec (Canada)
10 Jul 74: Civic Center, Providence, Rhode Island (United States)
12 Jul 74: Boston Garden, Boston, Massachusetts (United States)
13 Jul 74: Madison Square Garden, New York City, New York (United States) guest appearance by Todd Rundgren and Dickie Betts
14 Jul 74: Capitol Center, Largo, Maryland (United States)
18 Jul 74: Tempe Stadium, Tempe, Arizona (United States)
19 Jul 74: Long Beach Arena, Long Beach, California (United States) guest appearance by John Mayall
20 Jul 74: Long Beach Arena, Long Beach, California (United States)
21 Jul 74: Cow Palace, San Francisco, California (United States) – 2 shows
23 Jul 74: Denver Coliseum, Denver, Colorado (United States)
24 Jul 74: Denver Coliseum, Denver, Colorado (United States)
25 Jul 74: Kiel Auditorium (a.k.a. Convention Hall), Clark Avenue, St. Louis, Missouri (United States) – 2 shows
27 Jul 74: Mississippi Valley Fairgrounds, Davenport, Iowa (United States)
28 Jul 74: Memorial Stadium, Memphis, Tennessee (United States)
29 Jul 74: Legion Field, Birmingham, Alabama (United States)
31 Jul 74: City Park Stadium, New Orleans, Louisiana (United States)
1 Aug 74: Omni Coliseum, Atlanta, Georgia (United States) – guest appearance by Pete Townshend and Keith Moon
2 Aug 74: Greensboro Coliseum, Greensboro, North Carolina (United States) guest appearance by Pete Townshend and Keith Moon
4 Aug 74: West Palm Beach International Raceway, Palm Beach, Florida (United States) guest appearance by Pete Townshend, Keith Moon and Joe Walsh

Eric Clapton & His Band – 1974 U.S. Tour (Leg 2)
28 Sep 74: Hampton Coliseum, Hampton, Virginia (United States)
29 Sep 74: Nassau Veterans Memorial Coliseum, Uniondale, New York (United States)
30 Sep 74: Boston Garden, Boston, Massachusetts (United States)
1 Oct 74: The Forum, Montreal, Quebec (Canada)
2 Oct 74: Maple Leaf Gardens, Toronto, Ontario (Canada)
4 Oct 74: Capitol Center, Largo, Maryland (United States)
5 Oct 74: Capitol Center, Largo, Maryland (United States)
6 Oct 74: Spectrum, Philadelphia, Pennsylvania (United States)

Eric Clapton & His Band – 1974 Japan Tour
31 Oct 74: Nippon Budokan, Tokyo (Japan)
1 Nov 74: Nippon Budokan, Tokyo (Japan)
2 Nov 74: Nippon Budokan, Tokyo (Japan)
5 Nov 74: Kouseinenkin Kaikan, Osaka (Japan)
6 Nov 74: Kouseinenkin Kaikan, Osaka (Japan)

Eric Clapton & His Band – 1974 European Tour
26 Nov 74: Kongreßzentrum, Hamburg (Germany)
27 Nov 74: Olympiahalle, Munich (Germany)
28 Nov 74: Friedrich-Ebert-Halle, Ludwigshafen (Germany)
29 Nov 74: Grugahalle, Essen (Germany)
30 Nov 74: Ahoy Rotterdam, Rotterdam (Netherlands)
1 Dec 74: Sportpaleis Antwerp, Antwerp (Belgium)
2 Dec 74: Park des Expositions, Paris (France)
4 Dec 74: Odeon Theatre, Queen Caroline Street, Hammersmith, West London (England)
5 Dec 74: Odeon Theatre, Queen Caroline Street, Hammersmith, West London (England)

Eric Clapton & His Band – Hawaiian Warm-Up Shows for New Zealand / Australian Tour
7 Apr 75: Hawaii International Center Arena, Honolulu, Hawaii (United States)
8 Apr 75: Hawaii International Center Arena, Honolulu, Hawaii (United States)

Eric Clapton & His Band – 1975 New Zealand / Australian Tour
11 Apr 75: Western Springs Speedway, Western Springs, Auckland (New Zealand)
15 Apr 75: Festival Hall, Melbourne, Victoria (Australia)
16 Apr 75: Festival Theatre, Adelaide, South Australia (Australia)
17 Apr 75: Hordern Pavilion, R.A.S. Showground, Sydney, New South Wales (Australia)
18 Apr 75: Concert Hall, Sydney Opera House, Sydney, New South Wales (Australia)
19 Apr 75: Hordern Pavilion, R.A.S. Showground, Sydney, New South Wales (Australia)
20 Apr 75: Hordern Pavilion, R.A.S. Showground, Sydney, New South Wales (Australia) unfinished concert due to illness
22 Apr 75: Hordern Pavilion, R.A.S. Showground, Sydney, New South Wales (Australia) free concert to make up for unfinished concert on 20 Apr
23 Apr 75: Festival Hall, Brisbane, Queensland (Australia)
24 Apr 75: Festival Hall, Brisbane, Queensland (Australia)
26 Apr 75: Memorial Drive Park, Adelaide, South Australia (Australia)
28 Apr 75: Entertainment Centre, Perth, Western Australia (Australia)

Eric Clapton & His Band – 1975 U.S. Tour (Leg 1)
14 Jun 75: Tampa Stadium, Tampa, Florida (United States)

15 Jun 75: Jacksonville Veterans' Memorial Coliseum, Jacksonville, Florida (United States)
17 Jun 75: Municipal Auditorium, Mobile, Alabama (United States)
18 Jun 75: Mid-South Coliseum, Memphis, Tennessee (United States)
19 Jun 75: General James White Memorial Coliseum, Knoxville, Tennessee (United States)
20 Jun 75: Charlotte Coliseum, Charlotte, North Carolina (United States)
21 Jun 75: Cincinnati Gardens, Cincinnati, Ohio (United States)

Eric Clapton and The Steel Association guest appearance with The Rolling Stones
22 Jun 75: Madison Square Garden, New York City, New York (United States)

Eric Clapton & His Band – 1975 U.S. Tour (Leg 1) cont'd
23 Jun 75: Niagara Falls International Convention Center, Niagara Falls, New York (United States)
24 Jun 75: Springfield Civic Center, Springfield, Massachusetts (United States)
25 Jun 75: Providence Civic Center, Providence, Rhode Island (United States) guest appearance by Carlos Santana, Armando Peraza and Leon Chancler
26 Jun 75: Saratoga Performing Arts Center, Saratoga Springs, New York (United States)
28 Jun 75: Nassau Veterans' Memorial Coliseum, Uniondale, New York (United States) guest appearance by Carlos Santana, John McLaughlin and Alphonze Mouzon
29 Jun 75: New Haven Veterans' Memorial Coliseum, New Haven, Connecticut (United States) – guest appearance by Carlos Santana, John McLaughlin and Alphonze Mouzon
30 Jun 75: Pittsburgh Civic Center, Pittsburgh, Pennsylvania (United States)
1 Jul 75: Olympia Stadium, Detroit, Michigan (United States)

Eric Clapton & His Band – "Liberty Jam"
3 Jul 75: Memorial Stadium, Baltimore, Maryland (United States) – cancelled, stage destroyed by storm

Eric Clapton & His Band – 1975 U.S. Tour (Leg 1) cont'd
4 Jul 75: Richfield Coliseum, Cleveland, Ohio (United States)
5 Jul 75: Chicago Stadium, Chicago, Illinois (United States)
7 Jul 75: MET Sports Center, Bloomington, Minnesota (United States) guest appearance by Carlos Santana
8 Jul 75: Dane County Coliseum, Madison, Wisconsin (United States)
10 Jul 75: Municipal Auditorium, Kansas City, Missouri (United States)
11 Jul 75: Kiel Auditorium (a.k.a. Convention Hall), Clark Avenue, St. Louis, Missouri (United States)

Eric Clapton guest appearance with the Rolling Stones
12 Jul 75: The Forum, Inglewood, California (United States)

Eric Clapton & His Band – 1975 U.S. Tour (Leg 2)
3 Aug 75: Pacific Coliseum, Hastings Park, Vancouver, British Columbia (Canada) guest appearance by Carlos Santana
4 Aug 75: Portland Coliseum, Portland, Oregon (United States)
5 Aug 75: Seattle Center Coliseum, Seattle, Washington (United States)
6 Aug 75: Spokane Coliseum, Spokane, Washington (United States)
9 Aug 75: Frost Amphitheater, Stanford University, Stanford, California (United States) guest appearance by Carlos Santana
11 Aug 75: Salt Palace Arena, Salt Lake City, Utah (United States)
12 Aug 75: Denver Coliseum, Denver, Colorado (United States)
14 Aug 75: The Forum, Inglewood, California (United States) – guest appearance by Joe Cocker, Keith Moon and Carlos Santana
15 Aug 75: Swing Auditorium, E Street, San Bernardino, California (United States) guest appearance by Carlos Santana and Jerry McGee
16 Aug 75: San Diego Sports Arena, San Diego, California (United States)
17 Aug 75: Tucson Community Center Arena, Tucson, Arizona (United States)
18 Aug 75: Civic Center, El Paso, Texas (United States)
20 Aug 75: Sam Houston Coliseum, Houston, Texas (United States)
21 Aug 75: Tarrant County Convention Center Arena, Fort Worth, Texas (United States)
22 Aug 75: Myriad Convention Center Arena, Oklahoma City, Oklahoma (United States)
23 Aug 75: Assembly Center, Tulsa, Oklahoma (United States)
24 Aug 75: Hirsch Memorial Coliseum, Shreveport, Louisiana (United States)
27 Aug 75: Market Square Arena, Indianapolis, Indiana (United States)
28 Aug 75: Charleston Civic Center, Charleston, West Virginia (United States)
29 Aug 75: Greensboro Coliseum, Greensboro, North Carolina (United States)
30 Aug 75: Norfolk Scope, Norfolk, Virginia (United States) – guest appearance by Poco

Eric Clapton & His Band – 1975 Japan Tour
22 Oct 75: Festival Hall, Osaka (Japan)
23 Oct 75: Festival Hall, Osaka (Japan)
24 Oct 75: Kyoto Kaikan Daiichi Hall, Kyoto (Japan)
27 Oct 75: Kita-Kyushu Shiritsu Sougo Taiikukan, Kita-Kyushu (Japan)

29 Oct 75: Sunpu Kaikan, Shizuoka (Japan)
1 Nov 75: Nippon Budokan, Tokyo (Japan)
2 Nov 75: Nippon Budokan, Tokyo (Japan)

Eric Clapton guest appearance with the Rolling Stones
15 May 76: Granby Halls, Welford Road, Leicester, Leicestershire (England)

Eric Clapton & His Band – 1976 U.K. Tour
29 Jul 76: Pavilion, Hemel Hempstead, Hertfordshire (England)

Eric Clapton & His Band – "Garden Party IX"
31 Jul 76: Crystal Palace Bowl, London (England) – guest appearance by Larry Coryell, Freddie King and Ron Wood

Eric Clapton & His Band – 1976 U.K. Tour cont'd
1 Aug 76: Gaumont Theatre, Southampton, Hampshire (England)
2 Aug 76: Town Hall, Castle Circus, Torquay, Devon (England)
3 Aug 76: ABC Cinema, Plymouth, Devon (England)
5 Aug 76: Odeon Theatre, Birmingham, West Midlands (England) – guest appearance by Van Morrison
6 Aug 76: King's Hall, Belle Vue Amusement Park, Manchester (England) guest appearance by Van Morrison
7 Aug 76: Lancaster University, Lancaster, Lancashire (England)
9 Aug 76: The Apollo, Renfield Street, Glasgow (Scotland)
10 Aug 76: The Apollo, Renfield Street, Glasgow (Scotland)
12 Aug 76: City Hall, Northumberland Road, Newcastle-upon-Tyne, Northumberland (England)
13 Aug 76: Spa Pavilion, Bridlington, East Riding of Yorkshire (England)
15 Aug 76: ABC Cinema, Blackpool, Lancashire (England)
17 Aug 76: Warners Holiday Camp, Hayling Island, West Sussex (England)

Eric Clapton & His Band – 1976 U.S. Tour
5 Nov 76: Bayfront Center, St. Petersburg, Florida (United States)
6 Nov 76: Hollywood Sportatorium, Miami, Florida (United States)
7 Nov 76: Veterans' Memorial Coliseum, Jacksonville, Florida (United States)
9 Nov 76: Omni Coliseum, Atlanta, Georgia (United States)
10 Nov 76: Municipal Auditorium, Mobile, Alabama (United States)
11 Nov 76: Assembly Center, Louisiana State University, Baton Rouge, Louisiana (United States)
12 Nov 76: Convention Center Arena, San Antonio, Texas (United States)
13 Nov 76: Hofeinz Pavilion, Houston, Texas (United States)
15 Nov 76: Convention Center, Dallas, Texas (United States) – guest appearance by Freddie King; recorded for U.S. radio broadcast (King Biscuit Flower Hour / D.I.R. Radio Network)
16 Nov 76: Lloyd Noble Center, Norman, Oklahoma (United States)
18 Nov 76: Pan Am Center, Las Cruces, New Mexico (United States)
19 Nov 76: Arizona State University, Activity Center, Tempe, Arizona (United States)
20 Nov 76: San Diego Sports Arena, San Diego, California (United States)
22 Nov 76: The Forum, Inglewood, California (United States)

Eric Clapton guest appearance at "The Last Waltz" – The Band's Farewell Concert
26 Nov 76: Winterland Ballroom, Post Street, San Francisco, California (United States)

Eric Clapton guest appearance with Ronnie Lane's Slim Chance – "Eddie Earthquake & The Earth Tremors" Charity Concert
14 Feb 77: Cranleigh Village Hall, Village Way, Cranleigh, Surrey (England)

Eric Clapton & His Band – 1977 U.K. Tour
20 Apr 77: De Montfort Hall, Granville Road, Leicester, Leicestershire (England)
21 Apr 77: King-s Hall, Belle Vue Amusement Park, Manchester (England)
22 Apr 77: Victoria Hall, Stoke-on-Trent, Staffordshire (England)
23 Apr 77: The Apollo, Renfield Street, Glasgow (Scotland)
24 Apr 77: City Hall, Northumberland Road, Newcastle-upon-Tyne, Northumberland (England)

Eric Clapton & His Band – "Old Grey Whistle Test" Television Show (BBC 2 TV)
26 Apr 77: BBC Television Theatre, Shepherd's Bush Green, Shepherd's Bush, West London (England) – pre-recorded for later broadcast

Eric Clapton & His Band – 1977 U.K. Tour cont'd
27 Apr 77: Odeon Theatre, Queen Caroline Street, Hammersmith, West London (England)
28 Apr 77: Odeon Theatre, Queen Caroline Street, Hammersmith, West London (England) – guest appearance by Pattie Boyd and Ronnie Lane
29 Apr 77: Rainbow Theatre, Seven Sisters Road, Finsbury Park, North London (England) – guest appearance by Pete Townshend

Eric Clapton & His Band – 1977 European Tour
4 Jun 77: National Stadium, Dublin (Ireland)
6 Jun 77: National Stadium, Dublin (Ireland)

9 Jun 77: Falkoner Teatret, Copenhagen (Denmark)
10 Jun 77: Stadthalle, Bremen (Germany)
11 Jun 77: Groenoordhalle, Leiden (Netherlands)
13 Jun 77: Vorst Forest National, Brussels (Belgium)
14 Jun 77: Le Pavilion, Paris (France) – guest appearance by Ringo Starr
15 Jun 77: Phillipshalle, Düsseldorf (Germany)
17 Jun 77: Rhein-Neckar-Halle, Eppelheim (Germany)
19 Jun 77: Mehrzweckhalle, Wetzikon (Switzerland)
20 Jun 77: Olympiahalle, Munich (Germany)
5 Aug 77: Plaza de Toros, Ibiza (Spain)
11 Aug 77: Nuevo Pabellón Club Juventud, Barcelona (Spain)

Eric Clapton & His Band – 1977 Japan Tour
26 Sep 77: Festival Hall, Osaka (Japan)
27 Sep 77: Ken Taiku-kan, Okayama (Japan)
29 Sep 77: Kyoto Kaikan Daiichi Hall, Kyoto (Japan)
30 Sep 77: Nagoya Shi Kokaido, Nagoya (Japan)
1 Oct 77: Festival Hall, Osaka (Japan)
4 Oct 77: Mokomanai Ice Arena, Sapporo (Japan)
6 Oct 77: Nippon Budokan, Tokyo (Japan)
7 Oct 77: Nippon Budokan, Tokyo (Japan)

Eric Clapton & His Band – 1977 Hawaii Concerts
9 Oct 77: International Center, Honolulu, Hawaii (United States)
10 Oct 77: International Center, Honolulu, Hawaii (United States)

Eric Clapton & His Band – 1978 North American Tour
1 Feb 78: Pacific Coliseum, Hastings Park, Vancouver, British Columbia (Canada)
3 Feb 78: Exhibition Coliseum, Edmonton, Alberta (Canada)
5 Feb 78: Paramount Theatre, Seattle, Washington (United States)
6 Feb 78: WSU Coliseum, Pullman, Washington (United States)
8 Feb 78: Paramount Theatre, Portland, Oregon (United States)
10 Feb 78: Oakland-Alameda County Coliseum, Oakland, California (United States)
11 Feb 78: Santa Monica Civic Auditorium, Santa Monica, California (United States) recorded for U.S. radio broadcast (King Biscuit Flower Hour / D.I.R. Radio Network)
12 Feb 78: Santa Monica Civic Auditorium, Santa Monica, California (United States)
13 Feb 78: Aladdin Theatre, Las Vegas, Nevada (United States)
15 Feb 78: McNichols Arena, Denver, Colorado (United States)
18 Feb 78: Metropolitan Centre, Minneapolis, Minnesota (United States)
19 Feb 78: Hilton Coliseum, University of Iowa, Ames, Iowa (United States)
20 Feb 78: Municipal Auditorium, Kansas City, Kansas (United States)
21 Feb 78: Kiel Auditorium (a.k.a. Convention Hall), Clark Avenue, St. Louis, Missouri (United States)
23 Feb 78: Chicago Stadium, Chicago, Illinois (United States)
24 Feb 78: Louisville Gardens, Louisville, Kentucky (United States)
26 Feb 78: Huntington Civic Center, Huntington, West Virginia (United States)
28 Feb 78: Municipal Auditorium, Nashville, Tennessee (United States)
1 Mar 78: Mid-South Coliseum, Memphis, Tennessee (United States)
2 Mar 78: Boutwell Auditorium, Birmingham, Alabama (United States)
19 Mar 78: Jai Alai Frontun, Miami, Florida (United States)
20 Mar 78: Civic Centre Coliseum, Lakeland, Florida (United States)
21 Mar 78: Civic Centre, Savannah, Georgia (United States)
22 Mar 78: Macon Coliseum, Macon, Georgia (United States)
24 Mar 78: Memorial Coliseum, Charlotte, North Carolina (United States)
25 Mar 78: Carolina Coliseum, Columbia, South Carolina (United States)
26 Mar 78: Von Braun Civic Center, Huntsville, Alabama (United States)
28 Mar 78: Cobo Hall, Detroit, Michigan (United States)
29 Mar 78: Convention Center, Cleveland, Ohio (United States)
31 Mar 78: Civic Center Arena, Baltimore, Maryland (United States)
1 Apr 78: Spectrum, Philadelphia, Pennsylvania (United States)
3 Apr 78: Nassau Veterans' Memorial Coliseum, Uniondale, New York (United States)
5 Apr 78: Civic Center, Springfield, Massachusetts (United States)
7 Apr 78: The Forum, Montreal, Quebec (Canada)
9 Apr 78: Maple Leaf Gardens, Toronto, Ontario (Canada)

Eric Clapton guest appearance at Alexis Korner's 50th Birthday Party
19 Apr 78: Pinewood Studios, The Gatsby Room, Pinewood Road, Iver Heath, Buckinghamshire (England)

Eric Clapton & His Band – 1978 Outdoor Stadium Tour
23 Jun 78: Stadion Feyenoord, Rotterdam (Netherlands) – Festival with Bob Dylan
1 Jul 78: Zeppelinfeld, Nuremberg (Germany) – Festival with Bob Dylan; EC made a guest appearance with Dylan during his set
7 Jul 78: National Stadium, Dublin (Ireland)
8 Jul 78: National Stadium, Dublin (Ireland)

Eric Clapton & His Band – "The Picnic at Blackbushe"
15 Jul 78: Blackbushe Aerodrome, Camberley, Surrey (England) – Festival with Bob Dylan; EC made a guest appearance with Dylan during his set

Eric Clapton & His Band – 1978 European Tour
5 Nov 78: Pabellón Deportivo del Real Madrid, Madrid (Spain)
6 Nov 78: Club Juventus, Barcelona (Spain)
8 Nov 78: Palais des Sports, Lyon (France)
10 Nov 78: Saarlandhalle, Saarbrücken (Germany)
11 Nov 78: Festhalle, Frankfurt (Germany)
12 Nov 78: Olympiahalle, Munich (Germany)
14 Nov 78: Phillipshalle, Düsseldorf (Germany)
15 Nov 78: Kongreßzentrum, Hamburg (Germany)
16 Nov 78: Kongreßzentrum, Hamburg (Germany)
18 Nov 78: Le Pavilion, Paris (France)
19 Nov 78: Vorst Forest National, Brussels (Belgium)
20 Nov 78: Jaap Edenhal, Amsterdam (Netherlands)
24 Nov 78: The Apollo, Renfield Street, Glasgow (Scotland) – guest appearance by Ian Stewart, Jerry Portnoy and Bob Margolin
25 Nov 78: City Hall, Northumberland Road, Newcastle-upon-Tyne, Northumberland (England)
26 Nov 78: Apollo Theatre, Ardwick Green, Manchester (England)
28 Nov 78: Victoria Hall, Bagnall Street, Hanley, Stoke-on-Trent, Staffordshire (England)
29 Nov 78: Gala Ballroom, West Bromwich, West Midlands (England)
1 Dec 78: Gaumont Theatre, Southampton, Hampshire (England)
2 Dec 78: Brighton Centre, King's Road, Brighton, East Sussex (England)
5 Dec 78: Odeon Theatre, Queen Caroline Street, Hammersmith, West London (England)
6 Dec 78: Odeon Theatre, Queen Caroline Street, Hammersmith, West London (England)
7 Dec 78: Guildford Civic Hall, London Road, Guildford, Surrey (England)
guest appearance by George Harrison, Elton John, Pinetop Perkins, Jerry Portnoy and Bob Margolin

Eric Clapton & His Band – 1979 Irish Tour
8 Mar 79: City Hall, Anglesea Street, Cork (Ireland)
9 Mar 79: St. John's Lyn's, Tralee (Ireland)
11 Mar 79: Leisureland, Rockbarton Road, Salthill, Galway (Ireland)
12 Mar 79: Savoy Theatre, Bedford Road, Limerick (Ireland)
13 Mar 79: Baymount, Strandhill, Sligo (Ireland)
15 Mar 79: Downtown Club, Dundalk, Louth (Ireland)
16 Mar 79: Army Camp Drill Hall, Dublin (Ireland)
17 Mar 79: National Stadium, Dublin (Ireland)

Eric Clapton & His Band – 1979 North American Tour (Leg 1)
28 Mar 79: Tucson Community Center Arena, Tucson, Arizona (United States)
29 Mar 79: Civic Center, Albuquerque, New Mexico (United States)
31 Mar 79: Special Events Center, University of Texas, El Paso, Texas (United States)
1 Apr 79: Chaparral Center, Midland, Texas (United States)
3 Apr 79: Lloyd Noble Center, Norman, Oklahoma (United States)
4 Apr 79: Hammons Student Center, Missouri State University, Springfield, Missouri (United States)
6 Apr 79: Tulsa Assembly Center, Tulsa, Oklahoma (United States)
7 Apr 79: Pine Bluff Convention Center Arena, Pine Bluff, Arkansas (United States)
9 Apr 79: The Summit, Houston, Texas (United States)
10 Apr 79: Tarrant County Convention Center Arena, Fort Worth, Texas (United States)
11 Apr 79: Austin Municipal Auditorium, Austin, Texas (United States)
12 Apr 79: San Antonio Convention Center, San Antonio, Texas (United States)
14 Apr 79: Civic Center, Monroe, Louisiana (United States)
15 Apr 79: Municipal Auditorium, New Orleans, Louisiana (United States)
17 Apr 79: Freedom Hall, Johnson City, Tennessee (United States)
18 Apr 79: General James White Memorial Coliseum, Knoxville, Tennessee (United States)
20 Apr 79: Memorial Coliseum, University of Alabama, Tuscaloosa, Alabama (United States)
21 Apr 79: Omni Coliseum, Atlanta, Georgia (United States)
22 Apr 79: Municipal Auditorium, Mobile, Alabama (United States)
24 Apr 79: William & Mary Hall, The College of William & Mary, Williamsburg, Virginia (United States)
25 Apr 79: The Mosque, Richmond, Virginia (United States)
26 Apr 79: Capitol Centre, Landover, Maryland (United States)
28 Apr 79: Providence Civic Center, Providence, Rhode Island (United States)
29 Apr 79: New Haven Veterans Memorial Coliseum, New Haven, Connecticut (United States)
30 Apr 79: Spectrum, Philadelphia, Pennsylvania (United States)

Eric Clapton & His Band – 1979 North American Tour (Leg 2)
25 May 79: Civic Center, Augusta, Maine (United States)
26 May 79: Cumberland County Civic Center, Portland, Maine (United States)
28 May 79: Civic Center, Binghamton, New York (United States)
29 May 79: War Memorial Arena, Syracuse, New York (United States)
30 May 79: War Memorial Coliseum, Rochester, New York (United States)
1 Jun 79: Buffalo Memorial Auditorium, Buffalo, New York (United States)

2 Jun 79: Richfield Coliseum, Cleveland, Ohio (United States)
4 Jun 79: Toledo Sports Arena, Toledo, Ohio (United States)
5 Jun 79: Saginaw Civic Center, Saginaw, Michigan (United States)
7 Jun 79: Riverfront Coliseum, Cincinnati, Ohio (United States)
8 Jun 79: Market Square Arena, Indianapolis, Indiana (United States)
9 Jun 79: Dane County Exposition Center, Madison, Wisconsin (United States)
10 Jun 79: St. Paul Civic Center Arena, St, Paul, Minnesota (United States)
12 Jun 79: Chicago Stadium, Chicago, Illinois (United States)
13 Jun 79: Wings Stadium, Kalamazoo, Michigan (United States)
15 Jun 79: Athletic & Convocation Center, Notre Dame University, South Bend, Indiana (United States)
16 Jun 79: Brown County Veterans' Memorial Coliseum, Green Bay, Wisconsin (United States)
18 Jun 79: Civic Auditorium, Omaha, Nebraska (United States)
19 Jun 79: Kansas Coliseum, Wichita, Kansas (United States)
21 Jun 79: Salt Palace Arena, Salt Lake City, Utah (United States)
23 Jun 79: Spokane Coliseum, Spokane, Washington (United States)
24 Jun 79: Seattle Center Coliseum, Seattle, Washington (United States)

Eric Clapton – The 1979 Parrot Inn Jam Sessions
From the mid-seventies, EC would occasionally stop by The Parrot Inn, Forest Green, Surrey to jam with Gary Brooker and others. During the spring and summer of 1979, when not on the road, EC frequently attended jam sessions at the pub

Eric Clapton & His Band – 1979 "New" Band Warm-Up Concerts
7 Sep 79: Cranleigh Village Hall, Village Way, Cranleigh, Surrey (England)
30 Sep 79: Victoria Hall, Bagnall Street, Hanley, Stoke-on-Trent, Staffordshire (England)

Eric Clapton & His Band – 1979 European Tour
6 Oct 79: Stadthalle, Vienna (Austria)
7 Oct 79: Sporthalle, Linz (Austria)
8 Oct 79: Messecentrum Halle A, Nuremberg (Germany)
10 Oct 79: Palata Pioneer Hala, Belgrade (Yugoslavia)
11 Oct 79: Dom Sportover, Zagreb (Croatia)
12 Oct 79: Dom Sportover, Zagreb (Croatia)
15 Oct 79: Salo Kongresso, Warsaw (Poland)
16 Oct 79: Salo Kongresso, Warsaw (Poland)
17 Oct 79: Halo Sportowa, Krakow (Poland)
18 Oct 79: Halo Sportowa, Krakow (Poland) – cancelled due to riot previous evening

Eric Clapton & His Band – 1979 Israel Tour
21 Oct 79: Heichal Hatarbut, Tel Aviv (Israel)
22 Oct 79: Heichal Hatarbut, Tel Aviv (Israel)
23 Oct 79: Heichal Hatarbut, Tel Aviv (Israel)
25 Oct 79: Heichal Hatarbut, Tel Aviv (Israel)
27 Oct 79: Binyanei Ha'Ooma, Jerusalem (Israel)
29 Oct 79: Binyanei Ha'Ooma, Jerusalem (Israel)

Eric Clapton & His Band – 1979 Far East Tour
16 Nov 79: National Theatre, Bangkok (Thailand)
18 Nov 79: Araneta Coliseum Cinema, Manila (Philippines)
20 Nov 79: Academic Community Hall, Hong Kong (British Hong Kong)
23 Nov 79: Kenmin Bunka Center, Mito (Japan)
25 Nov 79: Nagoya Shi Kokaido, Nagoya (Japan)
26 Nov 79: Kyoto Kaikan Daiichi Hall, Kyoto (Japan)
27 Nov 79: Kouseinenkin Kaikan, Osaka (Japan)
28 Nov 79: Yubinchokin Kaikan, Hiroshima (Japan)
30 Nov 79: Shin-Nittestsu Otani Taiikukan, Kita-Kyushu (Japan)
1 Dec 79: Osaka Furitsu Taiikukan, Osaka (Japan)
3 Dec 79: Nippon Budokan, Tokyo (Japan)
4 Dec 79: Nippon Budokan, Tokyo (Japan)
6 Dec 79: Sangyo Kyoshin Kaikan, Sapporo (Japan)

Eric Clapton & His Band – 1980 "Just One Night" U.K. Tour
2 May 80: New Theatre, George Road, Oxford, Oxfordshire (England)
3 May 80: Brighton Centre, King's Road, Brighton, East Sussex (England)
4 May 80: Bingley Hall, Stafforshire County Showground, West Road, Stafford, Staffordshire (England)
6 May 80: Lancaster University, Lancaster (England)
7 May 80: City Hall, Northumberland Road, Newcastle-upon-Tyne, Northumberland (England)
8 May 80: Odeon Theatre, Clerk Street, Edinburgh (Scotland)
9 May 80: The Apollo, Renfield Street, Glasgow (Scotland)
11 May 80: Deeside Leisure Centre, Chester Road West, Queensferry, Flintshire (Wales)
12 May 80: Coventry Theatre, Hale Street, Coventry, West Midlands (England)
13 May 80: Bristol Hippodrome, St. Augustine's Parade, Bristol (England)
15 May 80: Odeon Theatre, Queen Caroline Street, Hammersmith, West London (England)

16 May 80: Odeon Theatre, Queen Caroline Street, Hammersmith, West London (England)
17 May 80: Odeon Theatre, Queen Caroline Street, Hammersmith, West London (England)
18 May 80: Guildford Civic Hall, London Road, Guildford, Surrey (England) guest appearance by Jeff Beck

Eric Clapton & His Band – 1980 "Just One Night" Scandinavian Tour
19 Sep 80: Aalborghall, Aalborgh (Sweden)
20 Sep 80: Brondbyhallen, Copenhagen (Denmark)
21 Sep 80: Vejlbrisskovhall, Aarhus (Denmark)
23 Sep 80: Olympen, Lund (Sweden)
24 Sep 80: Scandinavium, Gothenburg (Sweden)
25 Sep 80: Drammenshallen, Oslo (Norway)
27 Sep 80: Isstadion, Stockholm (Sweden)
29 Sep 80: Messhall, Helsinki (Finland)

Eric Clapton, Gary Brooker, Henry Spinetti & Friends – Informal Christmas Week Gig
Dec 80: The Parrot Inn, Forest Green, Surrey (England)

Eric Clapton & His Band – 1981 "Another Ticket" U.K. Tour
31 Jan 81: R.D.S. Simmonscourt, Ballsbridge, Dublin (Ireland)
1 Feb 81: Leisureland, Rockbarton Road, Salthill, Galway (Ireland)
2 Feb 81: City Hall, Anglesea Street, Cork (Ireland)
3 Feb 81: Youree Youth Centre, Carlow (Ireland)
25 Feb 81: Rainbow Theatre, Seven Sisters Road, Finsbury Park, North London (England)

Eric Clapton & His Band – 1981 "Another Ticket" U.S. Tour (cut short due to illness)
2 Mar 81: Memorial Coliseum, Portland, Oregon (United States)
3 Mar 81: Spokane Coliseum, Spokane, Washington (United States)
5 Mar 81: Paramount Theater, Pine Street, Seattle, Washington (United States)
6 Mar 81: Paramount Theater, Pine Street, Seattle, Washington (United States)
7 Mar 81: Paramount Theater, Pine Street, Seattle, Washington (United States)
9 Mar 81: MetraPark, Billings, Montana (United States)
10 Mar 81: Four Seasons Arena, Great Falls, Montana (United States)
13 Mar 81: Dane County Exposition Center, Madison, Wisconsin (United States)
14 Mar 81: Arena Auditorium, Duluth, Minnesota (United States) – cancelled
15 Mar 81: Civic Center Arena, St. Paul, Minnesota (United States) – cancelled
17 Mar 81: Hilton Coliseum, Ames, Iowa (United States) – cancelled
19 Mar 81: Britt Brown Arena Kansas Coliseum, Valley Center, Kansas (United States) cancelled
20 Mar 81: Southwest Missouri State University, Springfield, Missouri (United States) cancelled
21 Mar 81: Kemper Arena, Kansas City, Missouri (United States) – cancelled
22 Mar 81: Bob Devaney Sports Center, University Of Nebraska, Lincoln, Nebraska (United States) – cancelled
24 Mar 81: Lousiana State University Assembly Center, Baton Rouge, Louisiana (United States) – cancelled
25 Mar 81: Morris F.X. Jeff Sr. Municipal Auditorium, New Orleans, Louisiana (United States) – cancelled
27 Mar 81: Mid-South Coliseum, Memphis, Tennessee (United States) – cancelled
28 Mar 81: Southern Illinois University Arena, Carbondale, Illinois (United States) cancelled
29 Mar 81: Kiel Auditorium (a.k.a. Convention Hall), Clark Avenue, St. Louis, Missouri (United States) – cancelled
31 Mar 81: Barton Coliseum, Little Rock, Arkansas (United States) – cancelled
1 Apr 81: Hirsch Memorial Coliseum, Shreveport, Louisiana (United States) – cancelled
3 Apr 81: University of Texas Activity Center, Austin, Texas (United States) – cancelled
4 Apr 81: The The Summit, Houston, Texas (United States) – cancelled
5 Apr 81: Reunion Arena, Dallas, Texas (United States) – cancelled
7 Apr 81: Arizona State University Arena, Tempe, Arizona (United States) – cancelled
8 Apr 81: San Diego San Diego Sports Arena, San Diego, California (United States) cancelled
9 Apr 81: Long Beach Arena, Long Beach, California (United States) – cancelled
11 Apr 81: Oakland-Almeda County Oakland-Almeda County Coliseum, Oakland, California (United States) – cancelled
1 May 81: Market Square Arena, Indianapolis, Indiana (United States) – cancelled
2 May 81: Riverfront Coliseum, Cincinnati, Ohio (United States) – cancelled
3 May 81: Joe Louis Arena, Detroit, Michigan (United States) – cancelled
5 May 81: Memorial Coliseum, Fort Wayne, Indiana (United States) – cancelled
7 May 81: Michigan State University Arena, East Lansing, Michigan (United States) cancelled
8 May 81: Chicago Stadium, Chicago, Illinois (United States) – cancelled
9 May 81: Richfield Coliseum, Cleveland, Ohio (United States) – cancelled
10 May 81: Civic Center, Pittsburgh, Pennsylvania (United States) – cancelled
12 May 81: Veterans' Memorial Coliseum, New Haven, Connecticut (United States) cancelled

13 May 81: Broome County Coliseum, Binghamton, New York (United States) cancelled
15 May 81: Nassau Veterans' Memorial Coliseum, Uniondale, New York (United States) cancelled
16 May 81: Civic Center, Providence, Rhode Island (United States) – cancelled
17 May 81: Cumberland County Civic Center, Portland, Maine (United States) cancelled
19 May 81: War Memorial Coliseum, Rochester, New York (United States) – cancelled
20 May 81: Spectrum, Philadelphia, Pennsylvania (United States) – cancelled
22 May 81: Capitol Center, Landover, Maryland (United States) – cancelled
23 May 81: Scope Arena, Norfolk, Virginia (United States) – cancelled
24 May 81: Greensboro Coliseum, Greensboro, North Carolina (United States) cancelled
26 May 81: Charlotte Coliseum, Charlotte, North Carolina (United States) – cancelled
27 May 81: Carolina Coliseum, Columbia, South Carolina (United States) – cancelled
29 May 81: Hollywood Sportatorium, Pembroke Pines, Florida (United States) cancelled
30 May 81: Jacksonville Veterans' Memorial Coliseum, Jacksonville, Florida (United States) – cancelled
31 May 81: Sun Dome, Tampa, Florida (United States) – cancelled
2 Jun 81: Grand Ole Opry, Nashville, Tennessee (United States) – cancelled
4 Jun 81: Mississippi Coliseum, Jackson, Mississippi (United States) – cancelled
5 Jun 81: Municipal Auditorium, Mobile, Alabama (United States) – cancelled
6 Jun 81: Jefferson County Civic Center, Birmingham, Alabama (United States) cancelled
7 Jun 81: Omni Coliseum, Atlanta, Georgia (United States) Coliseum, Atlanta, Georgia (United States) – cancelled

Eric Clapton Guest Appearance – "The Secret Policeman's Other Ball" (Amnesty International Benefit Concert)
9 Sep 81: Theatre Royal, Drury Lane, Covent Garden, Central London (England)
10 Sep 81: Theatre Royal, Drury Lane, Covent Garden, Central London (England)
12 Sep 81: Theatre Royal, Drury Lane, Covent Garden, Central London (England)

Eric Clapton & His Band – 1981 European Tour
7 Oct 81: Messuhalli, Helskinki (Finland)
9 Oct 81: Isstadion, Stockholm (Sweden)
10 Oct 81: Scandinavium, Gothenburg (Sweden)
12 Oct 81: Drammenshallen, Oslo (Norway)
13 Oct 81: Olympen, Lund (Sweden)
15 Oct 81: Forum, Copenhagen (Denmark)
16 Oct 81: Vejlby Risskov Hallen, Aarhus (Denmark)
17 Oct 81: Randers Hallen, Randers (Denmark)

Eric Clapton & His Band – "The John Wile Testimonial"
16 Nov 81: Wolverhampton Civic Hall, North Street, Wolverhampton, West Midlands (England) – date moved forward from 18 Nov

Eric Clapton & His Band – 1981 Japan Tour
27 Nov 81: Niigata Kenmin Kaikan, Niigata (Japan)
30 Nov 81: Aichi Koseinenkin Hall, Nagoya (Japan)
1 Dec 81: Festival Hall, Osaka (Japan)
3 Dec 81: Fukuoka Sunpalace Hall, Fukuoka (Japan)
4 Dec 81: Kyoto Kaikan Daiichi Hall, Kyoto (Japan)
7 Dec 81: Nippon Budokan, Tokyo (Japan)
8 Dec 81: Yokohama Bunka Taiikukan, Yokohama (Japan)
9 Dec 81: Kouseinenkin Kaikan, Tokyo (Japan)

Eric Clapton, Gary Brooker, Henry Spinetti & Friends – Informal Christmas Week Gig
Dec 81: The Parrot Inn, Forest Green, Surrey (England)

Eric Clapton & His Band – 1982 U.S. Tour
5 Jun 82: Paramount Theater, Third Avenue SE, Cedar Rapids, Iowa (United States)
6 Jun 82: Omaha Civic Auditorium Arena, Omaha, Nebraska (United States)
7 Jun 82: Metropolitan Center, Minneapolis, Minnesota (United States)
10 Jun 82: Pine Knob Music Theater, Clarkston, Michigan (United States)
11 Jun 82: Pine Knob Music Theater, Clarkston, Michigan (United States)
12 Jun 82: Buffalo Memorial Auditorium, Buffalo, New York (United States)
13 Jun 82: Blossom Music Center, Cleveland, Ohio (United States)
17 Jun 82: Cumberland County Civic Center, Portland, Maine (United States)
18 Jun 82: Broome County Coliseum, Binghamton, New York (United States)
19 Jun 82: Saratoga Performing Arts Center, Saratoga Springs, New York (United States)
22 Jun 82: Hampton Roads Coliseum, Hampton, Virginia (United States)
23 Jun 82: Charlotte Coliseum, Charlotte, North Carolina (United States)
24 Jun 82: Viking Hall, Bristol, Tennessee (United States)
27 Jun 82: Civic Center, Augusta, Georgia (United States)
28 Jun 82: Jacksonville Veterans' Memorial Coliseum, Jacksonville, Florida (United States)

29 Jun 82: Civic Center, Lakeland, Florida (United States)
30 Jun 82: Hollywood Sportatorium, Pembroke Pines, Florida (United States)
guest appearance by Muddy Waters

Eric Clapton Guest Appearance – "Chas and Dave's Christmas Knees-Up" (ITV)
22 Dec 82: Royal Club, Guildford, Surrey (United Kingdom) – pre-recorded for television broadcast on 25 Dec

Eric Clapton, Gary Brooker, Henry Spinetti & Friends – Informal Christmas Week Gig
Dec 82: The Parrot Inn, Forest Green, Surrey (England)

Eric Clapton & His Band – 1983 "Money & Cigarettes" North American Tour (Leg 1)
1 Feb 83: Paramount Theater, Pine Street, Seattle, Washington (United States)
2 Feb 83: Paramount Theater, Pine Street, Seattle, Washington (United States)
3 Feb 83: Memorial Coliseum, Portland, Oregon (United States)
6 Feb 83: Memorial Auditorium, Sacramento, California (United States)
7 Feb 83: Cow Palace, San Francisco, California (United States)
8 Feb 83: Universal Amphitheater, Hollywood, California (United States)
9 Feb 83: Long Beach Arena, Long Beach, California (United States)
11 Feb 83: Veterans Memorial Coliseum, Phoenix, Arizona (United States)
13 Feb 83: Frank Erwin Center, University of Texas, Austin, Texas (United States)
14 Feb 83: The Summit, Houston, Texas (United States)
15 Feb 83: Reunion Arena, Dallas, Texas (United States)
17 Feb 83: Mid-South Coliseum, Memphis, Tennessee (United States)
18 Feb 83: Henry W. Kiel Municipal Auditorium, St. Louis, Missouri (United States)
19 Feb 83: Hara Arena, Dayton, Ohio (United States)
21 Feb 83: Spectrum, Philadelphia, Pennsylvania (United States) – guest appearance by Ry Cooder
22 Feb 83: Brendan Byrne Arena, East Rutherford, New Jersey (United States)
25 Feb 83: Omni Coliseum, Atlanta, Georgia (United States) Coliseum, Atlanta, Georgia (United States)
26 Feb 83: Louisville Gardens, Louisville, Kentucky (United States)
28 Feb 83: Capitol Centre, Landover, Maryland (United States)
1 Mar 83: The Centrum, Worcester, Massachusetts (United States)
2 Mar 83: Hershey Park Arena, Hershey, Pennsylvania (United States)
3 Mar 83: Civic Arena, Pittsburgh, Pennsylvania (United States)

Eric Clapton & His Band – 1983 "Money & Cigarettes" European Tour
8 Apr 83: Edinburgh Playhouse, Greenside Place, Edinburgh (Scotland)
9 Apr 83: Edinburgh Playhouse, Greenside Place, Edinburgh (Scotland)
11 Apr 83: City Hall, Northumberland Road, Newcastle-upon-Tyne, Northumberland (England)
12 Apr 83: Empire Theatre, Lime Street, Liverpool, Merseyside (England)
14 Apr 83: National Stadium, Dublin (Ireland)
15 Apr 83: National Stadium, Dublin (Ireland)
16 Apr 83: National Stadium, Dublin (Ireland)
20 Apr 83: Stadthalle, Bremen (Germany) – pre-recorded for radio broadcast
21 Apr 83: Grugahalle, Essen (Germany)
23 Apr 83: Ahoy Rotterdam, Rotterdam (Netherlands)
24 Apr 83: Chapitau de Pantin, Paris (France)
26 Apr 83: Sporthalle, Cologne (Germany)
27 Apr 83: Festhalle, Frankfurt (Germany)
29 Apr 83: Rhein Neckar Halle, Eppelheim (Germany)
30 Apr 83: St. Jakobshalle, Basel (Switzerland)
2 May 83: Palaeur, Rome (Italy)
3 May 83: Palazzetto dello Sport, Genoa (Italy)
5 May 83: Sport Palladium, Toulouse (France)
8 May 83: Velodromo de Anoeta, San Sebastian (Spain)
13 May 83: Cornwall Coliseum, Carlyon Bay, St. Austell (England)
14 May 83: Poole Arts Centre, Poole, Dorset (England)
16 May 83: Odeon Theatre, Queen Caroline Street, Hammersmith, West London (England)
17 May 83: Odeon Theatre, Queen Caroline Street, Hammersmith, West London (England)
18 May 83: Odeon Theatre, Queen Caroline Street, Hammersmith, West London (England)
19 May 83: Odeon Theatre, Queen Caroline Street, Hammersmith, West London (England)
21 May 83: Apollo Theatre, Ardwick Green, Manchester (England)
22 May 83: De Montfort Hall, Granville Road, Leicester, Leicestershire (England)
23 May 83: Guildford Civic Hall, London Road, Guildford, Surrey (England)
guest appearance by Chas & Dave, Phil Collins, Paul Brady and Jimmy Page

Eric Clapton & His Band – "Save The Children Benefit Concert"
5 Jun 83: New Victoria Theatre, Wilton Road, Central London (England)

Eric Clapton & His Band – 1983 "Money & Cigarettes" North American Tour (Leg 2)
25 Jun 83: Kingswood Music Theater, Toronto, Ontario (Canada)
27 Jun 83: Pine Knob Music Theater, Detroit, Michigan (United States)

28 Jun 83: Pine Knob Music Theater, Detroit, Michigan (United States)
29 Jun 83: Pine Knob Music Theater, Detroit, Michigan (United States)
1 Jul 83: Saratoga Performing Arts Center, Saratoga Springs, New York (United States)
2 Jul 83: Jones Beach Theater, Jones Beach State Park, Wantagh, New York (United States)
3 Jul 83: Jones Beach Theater, Jones Beach State Park, Wantagh, New York (United States)
5 Jul 83: Merriweather Post Pavilion, Columbia, Maryland (United States)
7 Jul 83: Blossom Music Center, Cleveland, Ohio (United States)
9 Jul 83: Civic Center Arena, St. Paul, Minnesota (United States)

Eric Clapton & His Band – "Summerfest"
10 Jul 83: Henry Maier Festival Park, Milwaukee, Wisconsin (United States)

Eric Clapton & His Band – 1983 "Money & Cigarettes" North American Tour (Leg 2) cont'd
11 Jul 83: Poplar Creek Music Theater, Hoffman Estates, Illinois (United States)
12 Jul 83: Kings Island Timberwolf Theater, Cincinnati, Ohio (United States)
14 Jul 83: Wings Stadium, Kalamazoo, Michigan (United States)
16 Jul 83: Red Rocks Amphitheater, Morrison, Colorado (United States)
17 Jul 83: Red Rocks Amphitheater, Morrison, Colorado (United States)
guest appearance by The Blasters

Eric Clapton Guest Appearance – "The Ronnie Lane Appeal for A.R.M.S. Benefit Concert"
20 Sep 83: Royal Albert Hall, Kensington Gore, Central London (England)

Eric Clapton Guest Appearance – "A Concert In Aid Of The Prince's Trust"
21 Sep 83: Royal Albert Hall, Kensington Gore, Central London (England)

Eric Clapton Guest Appearance – "The Ronnie Lane Appeal for A.R.M.S." U.S. Tour
28 Nov 83: Reunion Arena, Dallas, Texas (United States)
29 Nov 83: Reunion Arena, Dallas, Texas (United States)
1 Dec 83: Cow Palace, San Francisco, California (United States)
2 Dec 83: Cow Palace, San Francisco, California (United States)
3 Dec 83: Cow Palace, San Francisco, California (United States)
5 Dec 83: The Forum, Inglewood, California (United States)
6 Dec 83: The Forum, Inglewood, California (United States)
8 Dec 83: Madison Square Garden, New York City, New York (United States)
9 Dec 83: Madison Square Garden, New York City, New York (United States)

Eric Clapton & His Band – 1984 Europe & Mideast Tour
20 Jan 84: Hallenstadion, Zürich (Switzerland)
21 Jan 84: Hallenstadion, Zürich (Switzerland)
23 Jan 84: Teatro Tenda, Milan (Italy)
24 Jan 84: Teatro Tenda, Milan (Italy)
26 Jan 84: Beogradski Sajam Hala, Belgrade (Serbia)
28 Jan 84: Sporting Of Athens, Athens (Greece)
29 Jan 84: Sporting Of Athens, Athens (Greece)
2 Feb 84: American University, Cairo (Egypt)
5 Feb 84: Binyanei Ha'Ooma, Jerusalem (Israel)
6 Feb 84: Binyanei Ha'Ooma, Jerusalem (Israel)

Roger Waters Featuring Eric Clapton – 1984 "Pros and Cons of Hitch-Hiking" Tour
16 Jun 84: Isstadion, Stockholm (Sweden)
17 Jun 84: Isstadion, Stockholm (Sweden)
19 Jun 84: Ahoy Rotterdam, Rotterdam (Netherlands)
21 Jun 84: Earls Court Exhibition Centre, Earls Court, Central London (England)
22 Jun 84: Earls Court Exhibition Centre, Earls Court, Central London (England)
26 Jun 84: National Exhibition Centre, Birmingham (England)
27 Jun 84: National Exhibition Centre, Birmingham (England)
3 Jul 84: Hallenstadion, Zürich (Switzerland)
6 Jul 84: Palais Omnisports de Paris Bercy, Paris (France)

Eric Clapton Guest Appearance with Bob Dylan
7 Jul 84: Wembley Stadium, Wembley, Northwest London (England)

Roger Waters Featuring Eric Clapton – 1984 "Pros and Cons of Hitch-Hiking" Tour cont'd
17 Jul 84: Civic Center, Hartford, Connecticut (United States)
18 Jul 84: Civic Center, Hartford, Connecticut (United States)
20 Jul 84: Brendan Byrne Arena, East Rutherford, New Jersey (United States)
21 Jul 84: Brendan Byrne Arena, East Rutherford, New Jersey (United States)
22 Jul 84: Brendan Byrne Arena, East Rutherford, New Jersey (United States)
24 Jul 84: Spectrum, Philadelphia, Pennsylvania (United States)
26 Jul 84: Rosemont Horizon, Rosemont, Illinois (United States)
28 Jul 84: Maple Leaf Gardens, Toronto, Ontario (Canada)
29 Jul 84: Maple Leaf Gardens, Toronto, Ontario (Canada)
31 Jul 84: The Forum, Montreal, Quebec (Canada)

Eric Clapton & His Band – 1984 Australia & Far East Tour
13 Nov 84: Hordern Pavilion, R.A.S. Showground, Sydney, New South Wales (Australia)
14 Nov 84: Hordern Pavilion, R.A.S. Showground, Sydney, New South Wales (Australia)
17 Nov 84: Festival Hall, Brisbane, Queensland (Australia)
20 Nov 84: Hordern Pavilion, R.A.S. Showground, Sydney, New South Wales (Australia)
21 Nov 84: Hordern Pavilion, R.A.S. Showground, Sydney, New South Wales (Australia)
23 Nov 84: Sports & Entertainment Centre, Melbourne, Victoria (Australia)
24 Nov 84: Sports & Entertainment Centre, Melbourne, Victoria (Australia)
25 Nov 84: Sports & Entertainment Centre, Melbourne, Victoria (Australia)
28 Nov 84: Entertainment Centre, Perth, Western Australia (Australia)
2 Dec 84: Coliseum, Hong Kong, S.A.R. (China)

Eric Clapton & His Band – 1985 "Behind The Sun" U.K. Tour
27 Feb 85: Edinburgh Playhouse, Greenside Place, Edinburgh (Scotland)
28 Feb 85: Edinburgh Playhouse, Greenside Place, Edinburgh (Scotland)
1 Mar 85: National Exhibition Centre, Birmingham (England)
2 Mar 85: National Exhibition Centre, Birmingham (England)
4 Mar 85: Wembley Arena, Wembley, Northwest London (England)
5 Mar 85: Wembley Arena, Wembley, Northwest London (England)

Eric Clapton & His Band – 1985 "Behind The Sun" Scandinavian Tour
9 Mar 85: Icehall, Helsinki (Finland)
11 Mar 85: Scandinavium, Gothenburg (Sweden)
12 Mar 85: Valbyhallen, Copenhagen (Denmark)
14 Mar 85: Drammenshallen, Oslo (Norway)
15 Mar 85: Isstadion, Stockholm (Sweden)

Eric Clapton & His Band – 1985 "Behind The Sun" North American Tour (Leg 1)
9 Apr 85: Dallas Convention Center Arena, Dallas, Texas (United States)
10 Apr 85: The Summit, Houston, Texas (United States)
11 Apr 85: South Park Meadows, Austin, Texas (United States)
13 Apr 85: Civic Center, Pensacola, Florida (United States)
15 Apr 85: Civic Center, Lakeland, Florida (United States) – guest appearance by George Terry
16 Apr 85: James L. Knight International Center, Miami, Florida (United States)
18 Apr 85: Duke University, Durham, North Carolina (United States)
19 Apr 85: Civic Center, Savannah, Georgia (United States)
20 Apr 85: Omni Coliseum, Atlanta, Georgia (United States), Atlanta, Georgia (United States)
22 Apr 85: Coliseum, Richmond, Virginia (United States) – pre-recorded for radio broadcast
23 Apr 85: Civic Center, Baltimore, Maryland (United States)
25 Apr 85: Brendan Byrne Arena, East Rutherford, New Jersey (United States)
26 Apr 85: Nassau Veterans' Memorial Coliseum, Uniondale, New York (United States)
28 Apr 85: Civic Center, Providence, Rhode Island (United States)
guest appearance by Dick Sims
29 Apr 85: Spectrum, Philadelphia, Pennsylvania (United States)
1 May 85: Hartford Civic Center, Hartford, Connecticut (United States)
2 May 85: Cumberland County Civic Center, Portland, Maine (United States)
3 May 85: The Forum, Montreal, Quebec (Canada)

Eric Clapton Guest Appearance – "Late Night with David Letterman" Television Show (NBC TV)
8 May 85: NBC Television Studio 6A, New York, New York (United States)
pre-recorded for same day television broadcast (Season 4, Show #546)

Eric Clapton & His Band – 1985 "Behind The Sun" North American Tour (Leg 2)
21 Jun 85: Kingswood Music Theater, Toronto, Ontario (Canada)
22 Jun 85: Blossom Music Center, Cleveland, Ohio (United States)
23 Jun 85: Finger Lakes Performing Arts Center, Canandaigua, New York (United States)
25 Jun 85: Saratoga Performing Arts Center, Saratoga, New York (United States)
26 Jun 85: The Centrum, Worcester, Massachusetts (United States)
27 Jun 85: Merriweather Post Pavilion, Columbia, Maryland (United States)
28 Jun 85: Garden State Arts Center, Holmdel, New Jersey (United States)

Eric Clapton & His Band – "Summerfest"
30 Jun 85: Henry Maier Festival Park, Milwaukee, Wisconsin (United States)

Eric Clapton & His Band – 1985 "Behind The Sun" North American Tour (Leg 2) cont'd
1 Jul 85: Louisville Gardens, Louisville, Kentucky (United States)
2 Jul 85: Pine Knob Music Theater, Clarkston, Michigan (United States)
3 Jul 85: Pine Knob Music Theater, Clarkston, Michigan (United States)
5 Jul 85: Poplar Creek Music Theater, Hoffman Estates, Illinois (United States)
6 Jul 85: Indianapolis Sports Center, Indianapolis, Indiana (United States)

7 Jul 85: Riverbend Music Center, Cincinnati, Ohio (United States)
9 Jul 85: Sandstone Amphitheater, Bonner Springs, Kansas (United States)
11 Jul 85: Red Rocks Amphitheater, Morrison, Colorado (United States)

Eric Clapton & His Band – "Live Aid" in aid of Ethiopian Famine Relief (Radio & TV)
13 Jul 85: John F. Kennedy Stadium, Philadelphia, Pennsylvania (United States)
guest appearance by Phil Collins; live worldwide radio and television broadcast

Eric Clapton & His Band – 1985 "Behind The Sun" North American Tour (Leg 2) cont'd
14 Jul 85: Red Rocks Amphitheater, Morrison, Colorado (United States)
17 Jul 85: The Universal Amphitheater, Los Angeles, California (United States)
18 Jul 85: The Universal Amphitheater, Los Angeles, California (United States)
19 Jul 85: The Universal Amphitheater, Los Angeles, California (United States)
21 Jul 85: Compton Terrace at Firebird Lake, Chandler, Arizona (United States)
22 Jul 85: Pacific Amphitheater, Costa Mesa, California (United States)
23 Jul 85: Concord Pavilion, Concord, California (United States) – guest appearance by Carlos Santana
24 Jul 85: Concord Pavilion, Concord, California (United States)
26 Jul 85: Seattle Center Coliseum, Seattle, Washington (United States)
guest appearance by Lionel Richie
27 Jul 85: Pacific Coliseum, Hastings Park, Vancouver, British Columbia (Canada)

Eric Clapton & His Band – 1985 "Behind The Sun" Japan Tour
5 Oct 85: Yoyogi Daiichi Taiikukan, Tokyo (Japan)
6 Oct 85: Yoyogi Daiichi Taiikukan, Tokyo (Japan)
7 Oct 85: Kouseinenkin Kaikan, Osaka (Japan)
9 Oct 85: Nagoya Shimin Kaikan, Nagoya (Japan)
10 Oct 85: Festival Hall, Osaka (Japan)
11 Oct 85: Fukuoka Sunpalace Hall, Fukuoka (Japan)

Eric Clapton & His Band – 1985 "Behind The Sun"Alaska Concert
14 Oct 85: George Sullivan Arena, Anchorage, Alaska (United States)

Eric Clapton & His Band – 1985 "Behind The Sun" U.K. Concert
20 Oct 85: Guildford Civic Hall, London Road, Guildford, Surrey (England)
guest appearances by Phil Collins and Carl Perkins

Eric Clapton Guest Appearance – "Blue Suede Shoes: Carl Perkins & Friends" Television Show (Delilah Films / Cinemax)
21 Oct 85: Limehouse Television Studios, Canary Wharf, West India Docks, London (England) – pre-recorded for later television broadcast

Eric Clapton & His Band – 1985 "Behind The Sun" European Tour
23 Oct 85: Halle des Fêtes, Palais de Beaulieu, Lausanne (Switzerland)
24 Oct 85: Hallenstadion, Zürich (Switzerland)
27 Oct 85: Teatro Tenda, Milan (Italy)
28 Oct 85: Teatro Tenda, Milan (Italy)
29 Oct 85: Palasport, Turin (Italy)
31 Oct 85: Palamaggio, Caserta (Italy)
1 Nov 85: Palaeur, Rome (Italy)
2 Nov 85: Palasport, Genoa (Italy)
4 Nov 85: Teatro Tenda, Bologna (Italy)
5 Nov 85: Palasport, Florence (Italy)
6 Nov 85: Palasport, Padua (Italy)

Eric Clapton Guest Appearance with Buddy Guy and Junior Wells
3 Dec 85: Dingwalls, Middle Yard, Camden Lock, Camden Town, Northwest London (England)

Eric Clapton Guest Appearance with Sting
6 Dec 85: Teatro Tenda, Milan (Italy)

Eric Clapton Guest Appearance with Gary Brooker's Pier Head Restoration Band Benefit Concert in aid of Local Charity
12 Dec 85: The Dickens Pub, High Street, Southend-On-Sea, Essex (England)
13 Dec 85: The Parrot Inn, Forest Green, Surrey (England)

Eric Clapton Guest Appearance with Dire Straits
19 Dec 85: Odeon Theatre, Queen Caroline Street, Hammersmith, West London (England)
22 Dec 85: Odeon Theatre, Queen Caroline Street, Hammersmith, West London (England)

Eric Clapton, Gary Brooker, Mick Fleetwood and Albert Lee – Benefit Concert for Local Charity
23 Dec 85: Village Hall, Dunsfold, Surrey (England)

Eric Clapton Guest Appearance – "Rolling Stones' & Friends' Ian Stewart Memorial Jam Session"
23 Feb 86: 100 Club, Oxford Street, Soho, Central London (England)

Eric Clapton Guest Appearance – "The Prince's Trust 10th Birthday Party"
20 Jun 86: Wembley Arena, Wembley, Northwest London (England)

Eric Clapton & His Band – "Isle of Calf Festival"
3 Jul 86: Kalvoya Island, Sandvika (Norway)

Eric Clapton & His Band – "Roskilde Festival"
4 Jul 86: Festivalpladsen, Roskilde (Denmark)

Eric Clapton Guest Appearance with Otis Rush during "Montreux Jazz Festival" (Swiss Radio)
9 Jul 86: Le Casino, Montreux (Switzerland) – live radio broadcast

Eric Clapton & His Band – "Montreux Jazz Festival" (French Radio)
10 Jul 86: Le Casino, Montreux (Switzerland) – live radio broadcast

Eric Clapton & His Band – "Juan les Pins Jazz Festival"
12 Jul 86: Pinede Gould, Juan les Pins, Antibes (France)

Eric Clapton & His Band – 1986 Concert Video Filming
14 Jul 86: National Exhibition Centre, Birmingham (England) – live rehearsal with audience
15 Jul 86: National Exhibition Centre, Birmingham (England) – filming with audience

Eric Clapton Guest Appearance with Prince
14 Aug 86: The Roof Gardens, Kensington High Street, Central London (England)

Eric Clapton – Bunbury Cricket Club Charity Match Jam Session
15 Aug 86: Finchley Cricket Club, East End Road, Finchley, North London (England)

Eric Clapton Guest Appearance with Tina Turner – "Tearing Us Apart" Video filming
16 Aug 86: Ronnie Scott's, Frith Street, Soho, Central London (England)

Eric Clapton Guest Appearance – "Hail Hail Rock 'n' Roll: Chuck Berry's 60th Birthday Celebration"
16 Oct 86: Fox Theater, North Grand Boulevard, St. Louis, Missouri (United States)
2 shows

Eric Clapton Guest Appearance with Lionel Richie
27 Oct 86: Madison Square Garden, New York City, New York (United States)

Eric Clapton Guest Appearance – "Nightlife with David Brenner" Television Show (King World / Syndicated)
29 Oct 86: Unknown Studio / Upper East Side, New York City, New York (United States) – broadcast date; pre-recorded for in-week televison broadcast

Eric Clapton Guest Appearance with Robert Cray
8 Nov 86: Mean Fiddler, High Street, Harlesden, Northwest London (England)

Eric Clapton & His Band – 1986 U.S. Club Tour
20 Nov 86: Metro Club, Landsdowne Street, Boston, Massachusetts (United States)
21 Nov 86: Metro Club, Landsdowne Street, Boston, Massachusetts (United States)
23 Nov 86: The Ritz, East 11th Street, New York City, New York (United States)
guest appearance by Keith Richards
24 Nov 86: The Ritz, East 11th Street, New York City, New York (United States)

Eric Clapton Guest Appearance with Gary Brooker – Benefit Concert for Local Charity
23 Dec 86: Village Hall, Dunsfold, Surrey (England)

Eric Clapton & His Band – 1987 U.K. Tour
3 Jan 87: Apollo Theatre, Ardwick Green, Manchester (England)
4 Jan 87: Apollo Theatre, Ardwick Green, Manchester (England)
6 Jan 87: Royal Albert Hall, Kensington Gore, Central London (England)
7 Jan 87: Royal Albert Hall, Kensington Gore, Central London (England)
8 Jan 87: Royal Albert Hall, Kensington Gore, Central London (England)
10 Jan 87: Royal Albert Hall, Kensington Gore, Central London (England)
11 Jan 87: Royal Albert Hall, Kensington Gore, Central London (England)
12 Jan 87: Royal Albert Hall, Kensington Gore, Central London (England)

Eric Clapton & His Band – 1987 European Tour
16 Jan 87: Ahoy Rotterdam, Rotterdam (Netherlands)
17 Jan 87: Vorst Forest National, Brussels (Belgium)
18 Jan 87: Le Zenith, Paris (France)
20 Jan 87: Westfalenhalle, Dortmund (Germany)

21 Jan 87: Sporthalle, Hamburg (Germany)
22 Jan 87: Festhalle, Frankfurt (Germany)
23 Jan 87: Olympiahalle, Munich (Germany)
26 Jan 87: Palatrussardi, Milan (Italy)
29 Jan 87: Palaeur, Rome (Italy)
30 Jan 87: Palasport, Florence (Italy)

Eric Clapton & Friends – Benefit Concert for Local Charity
27 Mar 87: Cranleigh Golf & Country Club, Barhatch Lane, Cranleigh, Surrey (England)

Clapton Collins Phillinganes East – 1987 U.S. Tour
11 Apr 87: Oakland-Almeda County Coliseum, Oakland, California (United States)
13 Apr 87: Pacific Amphitheater, Costa Mesa, California (United States)
14 Apr 87: The Forum, Inglewood, California (United States)

Eric Clapton Guest Appearance –"B.B. King & Friends" Television Show (Cinemax)
15 Apr 87: Ebony Showcase Theater, West Washington Boulevard, Los Angeles, California (United States) – pre-recorded for later television broadcast

Clapton Collins Phillinganes East – 1987 U.S. Tour cont'd
16 Apr 87: McNichols Arena, Denver, Colorado (United States)
18 Apr 87: Civic Center, St. Paul, Minnesota (United States)
19 Apr 87: Rosemont Horizon, Rosemont, Illinois (United States)

Eric Clapton Jam Session with Buddy Guy and Robert Cray
19 Apr 87: The Limelight, North Dearborn Street, Chicago, Illinois (United States)

Clapton Collins Phillinganes East – 1987 U.S. Tour cont'd
21 Apr 87: Market Square Arena, Indianapolis, Indiana (United States)
22 Apr 87: Joe Louis Arena, Detroit, Michigan (United States)
23 Apr 87: Richfield Coliseum, Cleveland, Ohio (United States)
25 Apr 87: Capitol Center, Largo, Maryland (United States)
26 Apr 87: Civic Center, Providence, Rhode Island (United States)
27 Apr 87: Madison Square Garden, New York City, New York (United States)

Eric Clapton Guest Appearance with Lionel Richie
6 May 87: Wembley Arena, Wembley, Northwest London (England)

Eric Clapton Guest Appearance – "The Prince's Trust Rock Gala 1987"
5 Jun 87: Wembley Arena, Wembley, Northwest London (England)
6 Jun 87: Wembley Arena, Wembley, Northwest London (England)

Eric Clapton Guest Appearance with Tina Turner
18 Jun 87: Wembley Arena, Wembley, Northwest London (England)

Eric Clapton Guest Appearance – "Island Records' 25th Birthday Party"
4 Jul 87: Pinewood Studios, Pinewood Road, Iver Heath, Buckinghamshire (England)

Eric Clapton – Bunbury Cricket Club Charity Match Jam Session
14 Aug 87: Finchley Cricket Club, East End Road, Finchley, North London (England)

Eric Clapton Guest Appearance with Ronnie Earl's Roomful of Blues
4 Sep 87: Lone Star Cafe, Fifth Avenue, New York City, New York (United States)

Eric Clapton Guest Appearance – "South Bank Show" Television Show (ITV)
6 Oct 87: Ronnie Scott's, Frith Street, Soho, Central London (England) – pre-recorded concert segment with Buddy Guy

Eric Clapton Guest Appearance with Buddy Guy
9 Oct 87: Dingwalls, Middle Yard, Camden Lock, Camden Town, Northwest London (England)

Eric Clapton & His Band – 1987 Australian Tour
23 Oct 87: Entertainment Centre, Sydney, New South Wales (Australia)
24 Oct 87: Entertainment Centre, Brisbane, Queensland (Australia)
27 Oct 87: Sports & Entertainment Centre, Melbourne, Victoria (Australia)

Eric Clapton & His Band – 1987 Japan Tour
2 Nov 87: Nippon Budokan, Tokyo (Japan)
4 Nov 87: Nippon Budokan, Tokyo (Japan)
5 Nov 87: Nippon Budokan, Tokyo (Japan)
7 Nov 87: Aichi Ken Taiikukan, Nagoya (Japan)
9 Nov 87: Osaka-Jo Hall, Osaka (Japan)

Eric Clapton Guest Appearance with Gary Brooker – Benefit Concert for Local Charity
19 Dec 87: Village Hall, Dunsfold (England)

Eric Clapton & His Band – 1988 U.K. Tour
22 Jan 88: National Exhibition Centre, Birmingham (England)

23 Jan 88: National Exhibition Centre, Birmingham (England)
25 Jan 88: Royal Albert Hall, Kensington Gore, Central London (England)
26 Jan 88: Royal Albert Hall, Kensington Gore, Central London (England)
27 Jan 88: Royal Albert Hall, Kensington Gore, Central London (England)
29 Jan 88: Royal Albert Hall, Kensington Gore, Central London (England)
30 Jan 88: Royal Albert Hall, Kensington Gore, Central London (England)
31 Jan 88: Royal Albert Hall, Kensington Gore, Central London (England)
2 Feb 88: Royal Albert Hall, Kensington Gore, Central London (England)
3 Feb 88: Royal Albert Hall, Kensington Gore, Central London (England)
4 Feb 88: Royal Albert Hall, Kensington Gore, Central London (England)
7 Feb 88: Guildford Civic Hall, London Road, Guildford, Surrey (England)

Eric Clapton Guest Appearance – "The Prince's Trust Rock Gala 1988"
5 Jun 88: Royal Albert Hall, Kensington Gore, Central London (England)
6 Jun 88: Royal Albert Hall, Kensington Gore, Central London (England)

Eric Clapton Guest Appearance with Dire Straits
8 Jun 88: Odeon Theatre, Queen Caroline Street, Hammersmith, West London (England)
9 Jun 88: Odeon Theatre, Queen Caroline Street, Hammersmith, West London (England)

Eric Clapton Guest Appearance with Dire Straits – "Nelson Mandela 70th Birthday Tribute Concert"(Radio & TV)
11 Jun 88: Wembley Stadium, Wembley, Northwest London (England)
live worldwide radio and television broadcast

Eric Clapton Guest Appearance – Benefit Concert in aid of King Edward VII Hospital
2 Jul 88: Wintershall Estate, Bramley, Guildford, Surrey (England)

Eric Clapton & His Band – 1988 North American Tour
1 Sep 88: Starplex Amphitheater, Dallas, Texas (United States)
2 Sep 88: Lakefront Arena, New Orleans, Louisiana (United States)
4 Sep 88: Civic Arena, Pittsburgh, Pennsylvania (United States)
6 Sep 88: Meadowlands Arena, East Rutherford, New Jersey (United States)
7 Sep 88: Spectrum, Philadelphia, Pennsylvania (United States)
8 Sep 88: Capitol Centre, Largo, Maryland (United States)
10 Sep 88: Civic Center, Hartford, Connecticut (United States)
11 Sep 88: Nassau Veterans' Memorial Coliseum, Uniondale, New York (United States)
13 Sep 88: Great Woods Center For The Performing Arts, Mansfield, Massachusetts (United States)
14 Sep 88: Great Woods Center For The Performing Arts, Mansfield, Massachusetts (United States)
16 Sep 88: The Palace of Auburn Hills, Auburn Hills, Michigan (United States)
17 Sep 88: Alpine Valley Music Theater, East Troy, Wisconsin (United States)
19 Sep 88: Fiddler's Green, Denver, Colorado (United States)
21 Sep 88: Shoreline Amphitheater, Mountain View, California (United States)
22 Sep 88: ARCO Arena, Sacramento, California (United States)
23 Sep 88: Irvine Meadows Amphitheater, Laguna Hills, California (United States)

Eric Clapton Guest Appearance with Little Feat
24 Sep 88: The Pantages, Hollywood Boulevard, Los Angeles, California (United States)

Eric Clapton Guest Appearance with Elton John
25 Sep 88: Hollywood Bowl, Hollywood, California (United States)

Eric Clapton & His Band – 1988 North American Tour cont'd
26 Sep 88: Memorial Coliseum, Portland, Oregon (United States)
27 Sep 88: Tacoma Dome, Tacoma, Washington (United States)
28 Sep 88: Pacific Coliseum, Hastings Park, Vancouver, British Columbia (Canada)
30 Sep 88: Olympic Saddledome, Calgary, Alberta (Canada)
1 Oct 88: Saskatchewan Place, Saskatoon, Saskatchewan (Canada)
3 Oct 88: Winnipeg Arena, Winnipeg, Manitoba (Canada)
4 Oct 88: MET Sports Center, Minneapolis, Minnesota (United States)
6 Oct 88: The Forum, Montreal, Quebec (Canada)
7 Oct 88: Maple Leaf Gardens, Toronto, Ontario (Canada)
8 Oct 88: Coops Coliseum, Hamilton, Ontario (Canada)

Eric Clapton Guest Appearance with Jack Bruce
11 Oct 88: The Bottom Line, West 4th Street, New York, New York (United States)

Eric Clapton & His Band with Elton John & Mark Knopfler – "Eric Clapton's 25th Anniversary" Japan Tour
31 Oct 88: Rainbow Hall, Nagoya (Japan)
2 Nov 88: Tokyo Dome, Tokyo (Japan) – pre-recorded for television broadcast in Japan (NHK BS)
4 Nov 88: Nippon Budokan, Tokyo (Japan)
5 Nov 88: Osaka Stadium, Osaka (Japan)

Eric Clapton Guest Appearance – Benefit Concert
28 Nov 88: Hard Rock Café, Old Park Lane, London (England)

Eric Clapton Guest Appearance with Gary Brooker – Benefit Concert for Local Charity
23 Dec 88: Village Hall, Dunsfold, Surrey (England)

Eric Clapton Guest Appearance with Womack & Womack
10 Jan 89: Dingwalls, Middle Yard, Camden Lock, Camden Town, Northwest London (England)

Eric Clapton & His Band – 1989 U.K. Tour
16 Jan 89: City Hall, Barker's Pool, Sheffield (England)
17 Jan 89: City Hall, Northumberland Road, Newcastle-upon-Tyne, Northumberland (England)
18 Jan 89: Edinburgh Playhouse, Greenside Place, Edinburgh (Scotland)
20 Jan 89: Royal Albert Hall, Kensington Gore, Central London (England)
21 Jan 89: Royal Albert Hall, Kensington Gore, Central London (England)
22 Jan 89: Royal Albert Hall, Kensington Gore, Central London (England)
24 Jan 89: Royal Albert Hall, Kensington Gore, Central London (England)
25 Jan 89: Royal Albert Hall, Kensington Gore, Central London (England)
26 Jan 89: Royal Albert Hall, Kensington Gore, Central London (England)
28 Jan 89: Royal Albert Hall, Kensington Gore, Central London (England)
29 Jan 89: Royal Albert Hall, Kensington Gore, Central London (England)
30 Jan 89: Royal Albert Hall, Kensington Gore, Central London (England)
1 Feb 89: Royal Albert Hall, Kensington Gore, Central London (England)
2 Feb 89: Royal Albert Hall, Kensington Gore, Central London (England)
3 Feb 89: Royal Albert Hall, Kensington Gore, Central London (England)

Eric Clapton Guest Appearance with Carl Perkins
9 May 89: Bottom Line, West 4th Street, New York City, New York (United States)

Eric Clapton – "1st International Rock Awards" (TV / United States)
31 May 89: Lexington Armory, Lexington Avenue, New York City, New York (United States) – broadcast information unknown

Eric Clapton Guest Appearance with Gary Brooker's Band du Lac – Benefit Concert in aid of Cancer Relief Macmillan Fund
1 Jul 89: Wintershall Estate, Bramley, Guildford, Surrey (England)

Eric Clapton & His Band – 1989 Europe, Israel & Africa Tour
6 Jul 89: Statenhal, The Hague (Netherlands)
7 Jul 89: Statenhal, The Hague (Netherlands)
9 Jul 89: Hallenstadion, Zürich (Switzerland)
10 Jul 89: Hallenstadion, Zürich (Switzerland)
13 Jul 89: Merrill Hassenfeld's Amphitheatre at Sultan's Pool, Jerusalem (Israel)
14 Jul 89: Zemach Amphitheatre, Zemach (Israel)
15 Jul 89: Caesarea Amphitheatre, Caesarea (Israel)
17 Jul 89: Caesarea Amphitheatre, Caesarea (Israel)
23 Jul 89: Somhlolo National Stadium, Lobamba (Swaziland)
25 Jul 89: Harare International Conference Center, Harare (Zimbabwe)
26 Jul 89: Harare International Conference Center, Harare (Zimbabwe)
28 Jul 89: Boipuso Hall, Gaborone (Botswana)
30 Jul 89: Estadio da Machava, Maputo (Mozambique)

Eric Clapton Guest Appearance with Zucchero (TV / Italy)
28 Sep 89: Da Campo Boario, Rome (Italy) – broadcast information unknown

Eric Clapton Guest Appearance with Elton John
7 Oct 89: Madison Square Garden, New York City, New York (United States)

Eric Clapton Guest Appearance with The Rolling Stones
10 Oct 89: Shea Stadium, Flushing, New York City, New York (United States)
19 Oct 89: Coliseum, Los Angeles, California (United States)

Eric Clapton Guest Appearance – "Night Music" Television Show (Broadway Video / Syndicated)
25 Oct 89: Chelsea Television Studios, West 26th Street, New York, New York (United States) – broadcast date; was pre-recorded for later broadcast

Eric Clapton Guest Appearance with Pete Townshend – "Saturday Matters with Sue Lawley" Televison Show (BBC 1 TV)
28 Oct 89: BBC Television Centre, White City, West London (England) – broadcast date; was pre-recorded for later broadcast

Eric Clapton Guest Appearance – "Parents For Safe Food Benefit Concert"
18 Nov 89: Royal Albert Hall, Kensington Gore, Central London (England)

Eric Clapton Guest Appearance with Tina Turner
26 Nov 89: Reform Club, Pall Mall, Central London (England)

Eric Clapton Guest Appearance with The Rolling Stones – "The Rolling Stones: Terrifying" (Pay-Per-View Cable TV)
19 Dec 89: Convention Hall, Boardwalk, Atlantic City, New Jersey (United States) live television broadcast

Eric Clapton Guest Appearance with Gary Brooker – Benefit Concert for Local Charity
23 Dec 89: Chiddingfold Ex-Servicemen's Club, Woodside Road, Chiddingfold, Surrey (England)

Eric Clapton & His Band – 1990 "Journeyman" U.K. Tour
14 Jan 90: National Exhibition Centre, Birmingham (England)
15 Jan 90: National Exhibition Centre, Birmingham (England)
16 Jan 90: National Exhibition Centre, Birmingham (England)
18 Jan 90: Royal Albert Hall, Kensington Gore, Central London (England)
4-Piece Band
19 Jan 90: Royal Albert Hall, Kensington Gore, Central London (England)
4-Piece Band
20 Jan 90: Royal Albert Hall, Kensington Gore, Central London (England)
4-Piece Band
22 Jan 90: Royal Albert Hall, Kensington Gore, Central London (England)
4-Piece Band
23 Jan 90: Royal Albert Hall, Kensington Gore, Central London (England)
4-Piece Band
24 Jan 90: Royal Albert Hall, Kensington Gore, Central London (England)
4-Piece Band; guest appearance by Phil Collins; pre-recorded for radio broadcast (U.S.)
26 Jan 90: Royal Albert Hall, Kensington Gore, Central London (England)
13-Piece Band
27 Jan 90: Royal Albert Hall, Kensington Gore, Central London (England)
13-Piece Band
28 Jan 90: Royal Albert Hall, Kensington Gore, Central London (England)
13-Piece Band
30 Jan 90: Royal Albert Hall, Kensington Gore, Central London (England)
13-Piece Band
31 Jan 90: Royal Albert Hall, Kensington Gore, Central London (England)
13-Piece Band
1 Feb 90: Royal Albert Hall, Kensington Gore, Central London (England)
13-Piece Band
3 Feb 90: Royal Albert Hall, Kensington Gore, Central London (England)
Blues Band; live radio broadcast (BBC Radio One)
4 Feb 90: Royal Albert Hall, Kensington Gore, Central London (England) – Blues Band
5 Feb 90: Royal Albert Hall, Kensington Gore, Central London (England) – Blues Band
8 Feb 90: Royal Albert Hall, Kensington Gore, Central London (England)
Orchestra Night
9 Feb 90: Royal Albert Hall, Kensington Gore, Central London (England)
Orchestra Night
10 Feb 90: Royal Albert Hall, Kensington Gore, Central London (England)
Orchestra Night; live radio broadcast (BBC Radio One)

Eric Clapton & His Band – 1990 "Journeyman" European Tour
14 Feb 90: Icehall, Helsinki (Finland)
16 Feb 90: Globen, Stockholm (Sweden)
17 Feb 90: Skedsmohollen, Oslo (Norway)
19 Feb 90: KB Hallen, Copenhagen (Denmark)
20 Feb 90: Sporthalle, Hamburg (Germany)
22 Feb 90: Vorst Forest National, Brussels (Belgium)
23 Feb 90: Grugahlle, Essen (Germany)
24 Feb 90: Statenhal, Den Haag (Netherlands)
26 Feb 90: Palatrussardi, Milan (Italy)
27 Feb 90: Palatrussardi, Milan (Italy)
1 Mar 90: Olympiahalle, Munich (Germany)
3 Mar 90: Le Zenith, Paris (France)
4 Mar 90: Le Zenith, Paris (France)
5 Mar 90: Festhalle, Frankfurt (Germany)

Eric Clapton & His Band – "Saturday Night Live" Television Show (NBC TV)
24 Mar 90: NBC Television Studio 8H, Rockefeller Plaza, New York City, New York
live television broadcast (Season 15, Episode #17)

Eric Clapton & His Band – 1990 "Journeyman" U.S. Tour (Leg 1)
28 Mar 90: Omni Coliseum, Atlanta, Georgia (United States), Atlanta, Georgia (United States)
30 Mar 90: Charlotte Coliseum, Charlotte, North Carolina (United States)
31 Mar 90: Dean E. Smith Center, Chapel Hill, North Carolina (United States)
2 Apr 90: Madison Square Garden, New York City, New York (United States)
guest appearance by Darryl Hall
3 Apr 90: Meadowlands Arena, East Rutherford, New Jersey (United States)
4 Apr 90: Spectrum, Philadelphia, Pennsylvania (United States)
6 Apr 90: Nassau Veterans' Memorial Coliseum, Uniondale, New York (United States)

7 Apr 90: Carrier Dome, Syracuse, New York (United States)
9 Apr 90: Centrum, Worcester, Massachusetts (United States)
10 Apr 90: Centrum, Worcester, Massachusetts (United States)
12 Apr 90: Hartford Civic Center, Hartford, Connecticut (United States)
13 Apr 90: Hartford Civic Center, Hartford, Connecticut (United States)
15 Apr 90: The Palace of Auburn Hills, Auburn Hills, Michigan (United States)
guest appearance by Stevie Ray Vaughan
16 Apr 90: Riverfront Coliseum, Cincinnati, Ohio (United States)
17 Apr 90: Richfield Coliseum, Cleveland, Ohio (United States)
19 Apr 90: Market Square Arena, Indianapolis, Indiana (United States)
20 Apr 90: Hilton Coliseum, Ames, Iowa (United States)
21 Apr 90: St. Louis Arena, St. Louis, Missouri (United States)
23 Apr 90: Lakefront Arena, New Orleans, Louisiana (United States)
24 Apr 90: The Summit, Houston, Texas (United States)
25 Apr 90: Reunion Arena, Dallas, Texas (United States)
27 Apr 90: McNichols Arena, Denver, Colorado (United States)
29 Apr 90: Tingley Coliseum, Albuquerque, New Mexico (United States)
30 Apr 90: Arizona State University Activity Center, Tempe, Arizona (United States)
1 May 90: The Forum, Inglewood, California (United States) – guest appearance
by George Harrison
3 May 90: San Diego Sports Arena, San Diego, California (United States)
4 May 90: Pacific Ampitheater, Costa Mesa, California (United States)
5 May 90: Shoreline Ampitheater, Mountain View, California (United States)

Eric Clapton – "2nd International Rock Awards"(TV / United States)
6 Jun 90: Lexington Armory, New York, New York (United States) – broadcast
information unknown

**Eric Clapton & His Band – "Knebworth 1990: The Nordoff Robbins Silver Clef
Award Winners' Concert" (Radio & TV)**
30 Jun 90: Knebworth '90, Knebworth Park, Knebworth, Hertfordshire (England)
guest appearances by Elton John and Mark Knopfler; broadcast live on television
and radio

Eric Clapton & His Band – 1990 "Journeyman" U.S. Tour (Leg 2)
21 Jul 90: Miami Arena, Miami, Florida (United States)
22 Jul 90: Miami Arena, Miami, Florida (United States)
23 Jul 90: Miami Arena, Miami, Florida (United States)
25 Jul 90: Orlando Arena, Orlando, Florida (United States)
27 Jul 90: Suncoast Dome, St. Petersburg, Florida (United States)
28 Jul 90: Lakewood Ampitheater, Atlanta, Georgia (United States)
30 Jul 90: Starwood Amphitheater, Nashville, Tennessee (United States)
31 Jul 90: Mid-South Coliseum, Memphis, Tennessee (United States)
2 Aug 90: Greensboro Coliseum, Greensboro, North Carolina (United States)
3 Aug 90: Capitol Center, Landover, Maryland (United States)
4 Aug 90: Capitol Center, Landover, Maryland (United States)
6 Aug 90: Meadowlands Arena, East Rutherford, New Jersey (United States)
7 Aug 90: Meadowlands Arena, East Rutherford, New Jersey (United States)
9 Aug 90: Great Woods Center for the Performing Arts, Mansfield, Massachusetts
(United States)
10 Aug 90: Great Woods Center for the Performing Arts, Mansfield, Massachusetts
(United States)
11 Aug 90: Great Woods Center for the Performing Arts, Mansfield, Massachusetts
(United States)
13 Aug 90: Saratoga Performing Arts Center, Saratoga Springs, New York (United
States)
14 Aug 90: Spectrum, Philadelphia, Pennsylvania (United States)
15 Aug 90: Spectrum, Philadelphia, Pennsylvania (United States)
17 Aug 90: Nassau Veterans' Memorial Coliseum, Uniondale, New York (United States)
18 Aug 90: Nassau Veterans' Memorial Coliseum, Uniondale, New York (United States)
21 Aug 90: Blossom Music Center, Cleveland, Ohio (United States)
22 Aug 90: Pine Knob Music Theater, Detroit, Michigan (United States)
23 Aug 90: Riverbend Music Center, Cincinnati, Ohio (United States)
25 Aug 90: Alpine Valley Music Theater, East Troy, Wisconsin (United States)
guest appearance by Jeff Healey
26 Aug 90: Alpine Valley Music Theater, East Troy, Wisconsin (United States) – guest
appearances by Stevie Ray Vaughan, Jimmie Vaughan, Buddy Guy and Robert Cray
28 Aug 90: Sandstone Ampitheater, Bonner Springs, Kansas (United States)
29 Aug 90: St. Louis Arena, St. Louis, Missouri (United States)
31 Aug 90: Thompson-Boling Arena, Knoxville, Tennessee (United States)
1 Sep 90: Oak Mountain Amphitheater, Birmingham, Alabama (United States)

Eric Clapton & His Band – 1990 "Journeyman" South American Tour
29 Sep 90: Estadio Nacional, Santiago (Chile) – pre-recorded for television broadcast
in Chile
3 Oct 90: Estadio Centenario, Montevideo (Uruguay) – pre-recorded for television
broadcast in Uruguay
5 Oct 90: Estadio River Plate, Buenos Aires (Argentina) – pre-recorded for television
broadcast in Argentina
7 Oct 90: Praca da Apoteose, Rio de Janeiro (Brazil)

9 Oct 90: Ginasio Nilson Nelson, Brasilia (Brazil)
11 Oct 90: Ginasio Mineirinho, Belo Horizonte (Brazil)
13 Oct 90: Estadio Orlando Scarpelli, Florianopolis (Brazil)
16 Oct 90: Ginasio Gigantinho, Porto Alegre (Brazil)
19 Oct 90: Olympia, São Paulo (Brazil) – pre-recorded for television broadcast in Brazil
20 Oct 90: Olympia, São Paulo (Brazil) – pre-recorded for television broadcast in Brazil
21 Oct 90: Olympia, São Paulo (Brazil) – pre-recorded for television broadcast in Brazil

Eric Clapton & His Band – 1990 "Journeyman" New Zealand / Australia Tour
7 Nov 90: Supertop, Auckland (New Zealand)
8 Nov 90: Supertop, Auckland (New Zealand)
10 Nov 90: Royal Theatre, Canberra (Australia)
12 Nov 90: Festival Theatre, Adelaide, South Australia (Australia)
13 Nov 90: Festival Theatre, Adelaide, South Australia (Australia)
15 Nov 90: National Tennis Centre, Melbourne, Victoria (Australia)
16 Nov 90: Entertainment Centre, Sydney, New South Wales (Australia)
17 Nov 90: Entertainment Centre, Sydney, New South Wales (Australia)
19 Nov 90: Entertainment Centre, Brisbane, Queensland (Australia)

Eric Clapton & His Band – 1990 "Journeyman" Far East Tour
24 Nov 90: Singapore Indoor Stadium, Kallang (Singapore)
26 Nov 90: Negara Stadium, Kuala Lumpur (Malaysia)
29 Nov 90: Hong Kong Coliseum, Kowloon, Hong Kong S.A.R. (China)
4 Dec 90: Nippon Budokan, Tokyo (Japan)
5 Dec 90: Nippon Budokan, Tokyo (Japan)
6 Dec 90: Nippon Budokan, Tokyo (Japan)
9 Dec 90: Yoyogi Daiichi Taiikukan, Tokyo (Japan)
10 Dec 90: Rainbow Hall, Nagoya (Japan)
11 Dec 90: Osaka-Jo Hall, Osaka (Japan)
13 Dec 90: Yokohama Arena, Yokohama (Japan)

Eric Clapton & His Band – 1991 Warm-Up Shows
31 Jan 91: The Point Theatre, North Wall Quay, Dublin (Ireland)
2 Feb 91: The Point Theatre, North Wall Quay, Dublin (Ireland)

Eric Clapton & His Band – 1991 Royal Albert Hall Dates "24 Nights"
5 Feb 91: Royal Albert Hall, Kensington Gore, Central London (England)
4-Piece Band
6 Feb 91: Royal Albert Hall, Kensington Gore, Central London (England)
4-Piece Band
7 Feb 91: Royal Albert Hall, Kensington Gore, Central London (England)
4-Piece Band
9 Feb 91: Royal Albert Hall, Kensington Gore, Central London (England)
4-Piece Band
10 Feb 91: Royal Albert Hall, Kensington Gore, Central London (England)
4-Piece Band
11 Feb 91: Royal Albert Hall, Kensington Gore, Central London (England)
4-Piece Band
13 Feb 91: Royal Albert Hall, Kensington Gore, Central London (England)
9-Piece Band
14 Feb 91: Royal Albert Hall, Kensington Gore, Central London (England)
9-Piece Band
15 Feb 91: Royal Albert Hall, Kensington Gore, Central London (England)
9-Piece Band
17 Feb 91: Royal Albert Hall, Kensington Gore, Central London (England)
9-Piece Band; live radio broadcast (BBC Radio One)
18 Feb 91: Royal Albert Hall, Kensington Gore, Central London (England)
9-Piece Band
19 Feb 91: Royal Albert Hall, Kensington Gore, Central London (England)
9-Piece Band
23 Feb 91: Royal Albert Hall, Kensington Gore, Central London (England)
13-Piece Band
24 Feb 91: Royal Albert Hall, Kensington Gore, Central London (England)
13-Piece Band
25 Feb 91: Royal Albert Hall, Kensington Gore, Central London (England)
13-Piece Band; live radio broadcast (BBC Radio One)
27 Feb 91: Royal Albert Hall, Kensington Gore, Central London (England)
13-Piece Band
28 Feb 91: Royal Albert Hall, Kensington Gore, Central London (England)
13-Piece Band
1 Mar 91: Royal Albert Hall, Kensington Gore, Central London (England)
13-Piece Band
3 Mar 91: Royal Albert Hall, Kensington Gore, Central London (England)
Orchestra Night
4 Mar 91: Royal Albert Hall, Kensington Gore, Central London (England)
Orchestra Night
5 Mar 91: Royal Albert Hall, Kensington Gore, Central London (England)
Orchestra Night
7 Mar 91: Royal Albert Hall, Kensington Gore, Central London (England)
Orchestra Night

8 Mar 91: Royal Albert Hall, Kensington Gore, Central London (England)
Orchestra Night
9 Mar 91: Royal Albert Hall, Kensington Gore, Central London (England)
Orchestra Night

Eric Clapton Guest Appearance with Buddy Guy
4 Sep 91: The Roxy Theater, West Sunset Boulevard, West Hollywood, California
(United States)

Eric Clapton Guest Appearance – "The Sunday Comics" Television Show (FOX)
26 Sep 91: The Palace, Vine Street, Hollywood, California (United States)
pre-recorded for television broadcast on 29 Sep

**"Rock Legends: George Harrison with Eric Clapton & His Band" – 1991
Japan Tour**
1 Dec 91: Yokohama Arena, Yokohama (Japan)
2 Dec 91: Osaka-Jo Hall, Osaka (Japan)
3 Dec 91: Osaka-Jo Hall, Osaka (Japan)
5 Dec 91: Nagoya International Showcase Hall, Nagoya (Japan)
6 Dec 91: Hiroshima Sun Plaza, Hiroshima (Japan)
9 Dec 91: Fukuoka International Center Hall, Fukuoka (Japan)
10 Dec 91: Osaka-Jo Hall, Osaka (Japan)
11 Dec 91: Osaka-Jo Hall, Osaka (Japan)
12 Dec 91: Osaka-Jo Hall, Osaka (Japan)
14 Dec 91: Tokyo Dome, Tokyo (Japan)
15 Dec 91: Tokyo Dome, Tokyo (Japan)
17 Dec 91: Tokyo Dome, Tokyo (Japan) – guest appearance by Dhani Harrison

Eric Clapton & His Band – "Unplugged" Television Show (MTV)
16 Jan 92: Bray Film Studios – Soundstage #1, Windsor, Berkshire (United Kingdom)
pre-recorded for later television broadcast

Eric Clapton – "Sue Lawley: Eric Clapton" Television Show (ITV)
25 Feb 92: EC's Home, Chelsea, Central London (England) – television broadcast
date; pre-recorded on unknown date

Eric Clapton & His Band – 1992 U.K. Tour
1 Feb 92: Brighton Centre, Brighton (England)
3 Feb 92: National Indoor Arena, Birmingham (England)
4 Feb 92: National Indoor Arena, Birmingham (England)
5 Feb 92: National Indoor Arena, Birmingham (England)
7 Feb 92: Sheffield Arena, Sheffield (England)
8 Feb 92: Sheffield Arena, Sheffield (England)
12 Feb 92: Royal Albert Hall, Kensington Gore, Central London (England)
13 Feb 92: Royal Albert Hall, Kensington Gore, Central London (England)
14 Feb 92: Royal Albert Hall, Kensington Gore, Central London (England)
16 Feb 92: Royal Albert Hall, Kensington Gore, Central London (England)
17 Feb 92: Royal Albert Hall, Kensington Gore, Central London (England)
18 Feb 92: Royal Albert Hall, Kensington Gore, Central London (England)
22 Feb 92: Royal Albert Hall, Kensington Gore, Central London (England)
23 Feb 92: Royal Albert Hall, Kensington Gore, Central London (England)
24 Feb 92: Royal Albert Hall, Kensington Gore, Central London (England)
26 Feb 92: Royal Albert Hall, Kensington Gore, Central London (England)
27 Feb 92: Royal Albert Hall, Kensington Gore, Central London (England)
28 Feb 92: Royal Albert Hall, Kensington Gore, Central London (England)
2 Mar 92: Scottish Exhibition and Conference Centre, Glasgow (Scotland)
3 Mar 92: Scottish Exhibition and Conference Centre, Glasgow (Scotland)

Eric Clapton & His Band – 1992 U.S. Tour (Leg 1)
25 Apr 92: Reunion Arena, Dallas, Texas (United States)
27 Apr 92: Lakefront Arena, New Orleans, Louisiana (United States)
28 Apr 92: Jefferson County Civic Center, Birmingham, Alabama (United States)
29 Apr 92: The Pyramid, Memphis, Tennessee (United States)
1 May 92: Thompson-Boling Arena, Knoxville, Tennessee (United States)
2 May 92: Charlotte Coliseum, Charlotte, North Carolina (United States)
4 May 92: Spectrum, Philadelphia, Pennsylvania (United States)
5 May 92: Spectrum, Philadelphia, Pennsylvania (United States)
6 May 92: Civic Center, Hartford, Connecticut (United States)
8 May 92: Meadowlands Arena, East Rutherford, New Jersey (United States)
10 May 92: Capitol Center, Largo, Maryland (United States)
11 May 92: Dean E. Smith Center, Chapel Hill, North Carolina (United States)
13 May 92: Rosemont Horizon, Rosemont, Illinois (United States)
14 May 92: Rosemont Horizon, Rosemont, Illinois (United States)
16 May 92: Bradley Center, Milwaukee, Wisconsin (United States)
17 May 92: Target Center, Minneapolis, Minnesota (United States)
19 May 92: Market Square Arena, Indianapolis, Indiana (United States)
20 May 92: Richfield Coliseum, Cleveland, Ohio (United States)
21 May 92: Riverfront Coliseum, Cincinnati, Ohio (United States)
23 May 92: Omni Coliseum, Atlanta, Georgia (United States), Atlanta, Georgia
(United States)

24 May 92: Suncoast Dome, St. Petersburg, Florida (United States)
25 May 92: Miami Arena, Miami, Florida (United States)

Eric Clapton – "Rhythm of Fashion Show"
29 May 92: The Great Room, Grosvenor House Hotel, Park Lane, Mayfair,
Central London (England)

Eric Clapton & His Band – 1992 Belgian Concerts
14 Jun 92: Flanders Expo, Ghent (Belgium)
15 Jun 92: Flanders Expo, Ghent (Belgium)
16 Jun 92: Flanders Expo, Ghent (Belgium)

Elton John and Eric Clapton & His Band – 1992 Double-Bill Tour
18 Jun 92: Hippodrome de Vincennes, Paris (France)
19 Jun 92: Feyenoord Stadium, Rotterdam (Netherlands)

Eric Clapton & His Band – 1992 German Concerts
21 Jun 92: Olympiahalle, Munich (Germany)
22 Jun 92: Waldbuhne, Berlin (Germany)
23 Jun 92: Westfalenhalle, Dortmund (Germany)

Elton John and Eric Clapton & His Band – 1992 Double-Bill Tour cont'd
26 Jun 92: Wembley Stadium, Wembley, Northwest London (England)
27 Jun 92: Wembley Stadium, Wembley, Northwest London (England)
28 Jun 92: Wembley Stadium, Wembley, Northwest London (England)
3 Jul 92: Stade de la Pontaise, Lausanne (Switzerland)
4 Jul 92: St. Jakobshalle, Basel (Switzerland)
6 Jul 92: Stadio Communale, Bologna (Italy)
10 Jul 92: Stadio Brianteo, Monza (Italy)

Eric Clapton & His Band – 1992 "Montreux Jazz Festival"
12 Jul 92: Casino de Montreux, Montreux (Switzerland)

Eric Clapton & His Band – 1992 U.S. Tour (Leg 2)
11 Aug 92: Civic Arena, Pittsburgh, Pennsylvania (United States)

Eric Clapton Guest Appearance with Little Feat
13 Aug 92: Meadowbrook Music Theater, Rochester Hills, Michigan (United States)

Eric Clapton & His Band – 1992 U.S. Tour (Leg 2) cont'd
14 Aug 92: The Palace of Auburn Hills, Auburn Hills, Michigan (United States)
17 Aug 92: Great Woods Center For The Performing Arts, Mansfield, Massachusetts
(United States)
18 Aug 92: Great Woods Center For The Performing Arts, Mansfield, Massachusetts
(United States)
19 Aug 92: Saratoga Performing Arts Center, Saratoga, New York (United States)

Elton John and Eric Clapton & His Band – 1992 Double-Bill Tour cont'd
21 Aug 92: Shea Stadium, Flushing, New York City, New York (United States)
22 Aug 92: Shea Stadium, Flushing, New York City, New York (United States)

Eric Clapton & His Band – 1992 U.S. Tour (Leg 2) cont'd
24 Aug 92: Poplar Creek Music Theater, Hoffman Estates, Illinois (United States)
25 Aug 92: Riverport Amphitheater, St. Louis, Missouri (United States)

Elton John and Eric Clapton & His Band – 1992 Double-Bill Tour cont'd
29 Aug 92: Dodger Stadium, Los Angeles, California (United States)
30 Aug 92: Dodger Stadium, Los Angeles, California (United States)

Eric Clapton & His Band – 1992 U.S. Tour (Leg 2) cont'd
3 Sep 92: Shoreline Amphitheater, Mountain View, California (United States)
4 Sep 92: Shoreline Amphitheater, Mountain View, California (United States)
6 Sep 92: Tacoma Dome, Tacoma, Washington (United States)

Eric Clapton Guest Appearance – 9th Annual MTV Video Music Awards (MTV)
9 Sep 92: Pauley Pavilion, Westwood Plaza, Los Angeles, California (United States)
live television broadcast

**Eric Clapton Guest Appearance – "Columbia Records Celebrates the Music of Bob
Dylan" (Radio & TV)**
16 Oct 92: Madison Square Garden, New York City, New York (United States)
live radio and pay-per-view television broadcast

Eric Clapton & Friends – New Year's Eve Dance (Private Event)
31 Dec 92: Woking, Surrey (England)

Eric Clapton Guest Appearance – "1993 Rock & Roll Hall of Fame Induction Ceremony" (TV)
12 Jan 93: The Century Plaza, Avenue Of The Stars, Los Angeles, California (United States) – Cream is inducted into the Hall of Fame; pre-recorded for television broadcast

Eric Clapton & His Band – 1993 Royal Albert Hall Dates
20 Feb 93: Royal Albert Hall, Kensington Gore, Central London (England)
21 Feb 93: Royal Albert Hall, Kensington Gore, Central London (England)
22 Feb 93: Royal Albert Hall, Kensington Gore, Central London (England)
23 Feb 93: Royal Albert Hall, Kensington Gore, Central London (England)

Eric Clapton – "The 35th Annual Grammy Awards" (CBS TV)
24 Feb 93: Shrine Auditorium, West Jefferson Boulevard, Los Angeles, California (United States) – live television broadcast

Eric Clapton & His Band – 1993 Royal Albert Hall Dates cont'd
26 Feb 93: Royal Albert Hall, Kensington Gore, Central London (England) guest appearances by Buddy Guy and Jimmie Vaughan
27 Feb 93: Royal Albert Hall, Kensington Gore, Central London (England)
1 Mar 93: Royal Albert Hall, Kensington Gore, Central London (England)
2 Mar 93: Royal Albert Hall, Kensington Gore, Central London (England)
3 Mar 93: Royal Albert Hall, Kensington Gore, Central London (England)
5 Mar 93: Royal Albert Hall, Kensington Gore, Central London (England)
6 Mar 93: Royal Albert Hall, Kensington Gore, Central London (England)
7 Mar 93: Royal Albert Hall, Kensington Gore, Central London (England)

Eric Clapton Guest Appearance – "The Apollo Theater Hall of Fame" Television Show (NBC TV)
15 Jun 93: Apollo Theater, West 125th Street, New York City, New York (United States) pre-recorded for 4 Aug television broadcast

Eric Clapton Guest Appearance with The Ruins Band (members of Queen, Pink Floyd, Genesis) – "Cowdray Ruins Concert in aid of King Edward VII Hospital"
18 Sep 93: Cowdray Park, Midhurst, West Sussex (United Kingdom)

Eric Clapton & His Band – "Chemical Dependency Centre Benefit Concerts"
1 Oct 93: National Exhibition Centre, Birmingham (England)
2 Oct 93: National Exhibition Centre, Birmingham (England) – guest appearances by Joe Cocker and ZZ Top
3 Oct 93: Sheffield Arena, Sheffield (England) – guest appearances by Joe Cocker, ZZ Top and Nine Below Zero

Eric Clapton & His Band – 1993 Far East Tour
9 Oct 93: Hong Kong Coliseum, Hong Kong, Hong Kong S.A.R. (China)
10 Oct 93: Hong Kong Coliseum, Hong Kong, Hong Kong S.A.R. (China)
12 Oct 93: Yokohama Arena, Yokohama (Japan)
13 Oct 93: Yokohama Arena, Yokohama (Japan)
14 Oct 93: Rainbow Hall, Nagoya (Japan)
17 Oct 93: Fukuoka International Center Hall, Fukuoka (Japan)
18 Oct 93: Osaka-Jo Hall, Osaka (Japan)
19 Oct 93: Osaka-Jo Hall, Osaka (Japan)
21 Oct 93: Nippon Budokan, Tokyo (Japan)
22 Oct 93: Nippon Budokan, Tokyo (Japan)
23 Oct 93: Yokohama Arena, Yokohama (Japan)
25 Oct 93: Nippon Budokan, Tokyo (Japan)
26 Oct 93: Nippon Budokan, Tokyo (Japan)
27 Oct 93: Nippon Budokan, Tokyo (Japan)
30 Oct 93: Yokohama Arena, Yokohama (Japan)
31 Oct 93: Yokohama Arena, Yokohama (Japan)

Eric Clapton & Friends – New Year's Eve Dance (Private Event)
31 Dec 93: Woking, Surrey (England)

Eric Clapton Guest Appearance – "1994 Rock & Roll Hall of Fame Induction Ceremony"
19 Jan 94: The Grand Ballroom, Waldorf Astoria Hotel, Park Avenue, New York City, New York (United States) – EC inducts The Band

Eric Clapton & His Band – 1994 U.K. Dates
16 Feb 94: Apollo Theatre, Ardwick Green, Manchester (England)
20 Feb 94: Royal Albert Hall, Kensington Gore, Central London (England)
21 Feb 94: Royal Albert Hall, Kensington Gore, Central London (England)
22 Feb 94: Royal Albert Hall, Kensington Gore, Central London (England)
24 Feb 94: Royal Albert Hall, Kensington Gore, Central London (England)
25 Feb 94: Royal Albert Hall, Kensington Gore, Central London (England)
26 Feb 94: Royal Albert Hall, Kensington Gore, Central London (England)

Eric Clapton & His Band – "Children in Crisis Benefit Concert"
28 Feb 94: Royal Albert Hall, Kensington Gore, Central London (England)

Eric Clapton & His Band – 1994 U.K. Dates cont'd
1 Mar 94: Royal Albert Hall, Kensington Gore, Central London (England)
2 Mar 94: Royal Albert Hall, Kensington Gore, Central London (England)
4 Mar 94: Royal Albert Hall, Kensington Gore, Central London (England)
5 Mar 94: Royal Albert Hall, Kensington Gore, Central London (England)
6 Mar 94: Royal Albert Hall, Kensington Gore, Central London (England)

Eric Clapton & His Band – "T.J. Martell Foundation Gala Concert"
2 May 94: Avery Fisher Hall, Lincoln Center Plaza, Columbus Avenue, New York City, New York (United States)

Eric Clapton & His Band – "Saturday Night Live" Television Show (NBC TV)
24 Sep 94: NBC Television Studio 8H, Rockefeller Plaza, New York City, New York (United States) – live television broadcast (Season 20, Episode #1)

Eric Clapton & His Band – "Final Tour Rehearsal" Televison Show (VH1)
28 Sep 94: Manhattan Center Studios, 34th Street, New York City, New York (United States) – pre-recorded for later television broadcast

Eric Clapton & His Band – 1994 "From The Cradle" North American Tour
3 Oct 94: The Forum, Montreal, Quebec (Canada)
5 Oct 94: Maple Leaf Gardens, Toronto, Ontario (Canada)
6 Oct 94: Maple Leaf Gardens, Toronto, Ontario (Canada)
8 Oct 94: Madison Square Garden, New York City, New York (United States)
9 Oct 94: Madison Square Garden, New York City, New York (United States)
10 Oct 94: Madison Square Garden, New York City, New York (United States)
12 Oct 94: USAir Arena, Landover, Maryland (United States)
13 Oct 94: Hartford Civic Center, Hartford, Connecticut (United States)
14 Oct 94: Centrum, Worcester, Massachusetts (United States)
16 Oct 94: Civic Arena, Pittsburgh, Pennsylvania (United States)
17 Oct 94: Riverfront Coliseum, Cincinnati, Ohio (United States)
18 Oct 94: Gateway Arena, Cleveland, Ohio (United States)
20 Oct 94: The Palace of Auburn Hills, Auburn Hills, Michigan (United States)
21 Oct 94: United Center, Chicago, Illinois (United States)
23 Oct 94: Market Square Arena, Indianapolis, Indiana (United States)
24 Oct 94: Bradley Center, Milwaukee, Wisconsin (United States)
26 Oct 94: Kiel Center, St. Louis, Missouri (United States)
28 Oct 94: Kemper Arena, Kansas City, Missouri (United States)
30 Oct 94: McNichols Arena, Denver, Colorado (United States)
31 Oct 94: McNichols Arena, Denver, Colorado (United States)
2 Nov 94: America West Arena, Phoenix, Arizona (United States)
3 Nov 94: Great Western Forum, Inglewood, California (United States)
4 Nov 94: San Jose Arena, San Jose, California (United States)

Eric Clapton & His Band – 1994 U.S. Blues Club Tour
7 Nov 94: The Fillmore, Geary Boulevard, San Francisco, California (United States)
8 Nov 94: The Fillmore, Geary Boulevard, San Francisco, California (United States)
9 Nov 94: The Fillmore, Geary Boulevard, San Francisco, California (United States)
11 Nov 94: House of Blues, Sunset Boulevard, West Hollywood, California (United States)
12 Nov 94: House of Blues, Sunset Boulevard, West Hollywood, California (United States)
13 Nov 94: House of Blues, Sunset Boulevard, West Hollywood, California (United States)
16 Nov 94: Buddy Guy's Legends, South Wabash, Chicago, Illinois (United States)
17 Nov 94: Buddy Guy's Legends, South Wabash, Chicago, Illinois (United States)
18 Nov 94: Buddy Guy's Legends, South Wabash, Chicago, Illinois (United States)
21 Nov 94: House of Blues, New Orleans, Louisiana (United States)
22 Nov 94: House of Blues, New Orleans, Louisiana (United States)
23 Nov 94: House of Blues, New Orleans, Louisiana (United States)
26 Nov 94: Irving Plaza, Irving Place, New York City, New York (United States)
27 Nov 94: Irving Plaza, Irving Place, New York City, New York (United States)
28 Nov 94: Irving Plaza, Irving Place, New York City, New York (United States)

Eric Clapton & Friends – New Year's Eve Dance (Private Event)
31 Dec 94: Woking, Surrey (England)

Eric Clapton & His Band – 1995 "From The Cradle" U.K. Tour
15 Feb 95: Scottish Exhibition and Conference Centre (SECC), Glasgow (Scotland)
16 Feb 95: Sheffield Arena, Sheffield (England)
19 Feb 95: Royal Albert Hall, Kensington Gore, Central London (England)
20 Feb 95: Royal Albert Hall, Kensington Gore, Central London (England)
21 Feb 95: Royal Albert Hall, Kensington Gore, Central London (England)
23 Feb 95: Royal Albert Hall, Kensington Gore, Central London (England)
24 Feb 95: Royal Albert Hall, Kensington Gore, Central London (England)
25 Feb 95: Royal Albert Hall, Kensington Gore, Central London (England)
27 Feb 95: Royal Albert Hall, Kensington Gore, Central London (England)
28 Feb 95: Royal Albert Hall, Kensington Gore, Central London (England)
1 Mar 95: Royal Albert Hall, Kensington Gore, Central London (England)
3 Mar 95: Royal Albert Hall, Kensington Gore, Central London (England)

4 Mar 95: Royal Albert Hall, Kensington Gore, Central London (England)
5 Mar 95: Royal Albert Hall, Kensington Gore, Central London (England)
7 Mar 95: National Indoor Arena, Birmingham (England)

Eric Clapton & His Band – 1995 "From The Cradle" European Tour
5 Apr 95: Spektrum, Oslo (Norway)
7 Apr 95: Spektrum, Oslo (Norway)
8 Apr 95: Globen, Stockholm (Sweden)
10 Apr 95: Forum, Copenhagen (Denmark)
11 Apr 95: Forum, Copenhagen (Denmark)
13 Apr 95: Deutschlandhalle, Berlin (Germany)
14 Apr 95: Stadthalle, Bremen (Germany)
15 Apr 95: Flanders Expo, Ghent (Belgium)
17 Apr 95: Ahoy Rotterdam, Rotterdam (Netherlands)
18 Apr 95: Ahoy Rotterdam, Rotterdam (Netherlands)
19 Apr 95: MECC, Maastricht (Netherlands)
21 Apr 95: Palais Omnisports de Paris Bercy, Paris (France)
22 Apr 95: Palais Omnisports de Paris Bercy, Paris (France)
24 Apr 95: Festhalle, Frankfurt (Germany)
25 Apr 95: Westfalenhalle, Dortmund (Germany)
27 Apr 95: Olympiahalle, Munich (Germany)
28 Apr 95: Hallenstadion, Zürich (Switzerland)
30 Apr 95: Palaeur, Rome (Italy)
1 May 95: Fila Forum, Milan (Italy)
2 May 95: Fila Forum, Milan (Italy)
4 May 95: Palau Sant Jordi, Barcelona (Spain)
5 May 95: Palau Sant Jordi, Barcelona (Spain)

Eric Clapton Guest Appearance – "A Tribute To Stevie Ray Vaughan" (PBS TV)
11 May 95: KLRU Television Studio 6A, Austin, Texas (United States)
pre-recorded for later television broadcast

Eric Clapton Guest Appearance – Stevie Ray Vaughan Tribute Concert
12 May 95: Austin Music Hall, Nueces Street, Austin, Texas (United States)

Eric Clapton & His Band – 1995 "From The Cradle" U.S. Tour
28 Aug 95: Reunion Arena, Dallas, Texas (United States)
30 Aug 95: Frank Erwin Center, Austin, Texas (United States)
31 Aug 95: The Summit, Houston, Texas (United States)
2 Sep 95: Omni Coliseum, Atlanta, Georgia (United States), Atlanta, Georgia (United States)
3 Sep 95: Thompson-Boling Arena, Knoxville, Tennessee (United States)
5 Sep 95: Miami Arena, Miami, Florida (United States)
6 Sep 95: Miami Arena, Miami, Florida (United States)
7 Sep 95: Thunderdome, St. Petersburg, Florida (United States)
9 Sep 95: Dean E. Smith Center, Chapel Hill, North Carolina (United States)
10 Sep 95: Charlotte Coliseum, Charlotte, North Carolina (United States)
11 Sep 95: USAir Arena, Landover, Maryland (United States)
13 Sep 95: Spectrum, Philadelphia, Pennsylvania (United States)
14 Sep 95: Spectrum, Philadelphia, Pennsylvania (United States)
15 Sep 95: The Centrum, Worcester, Massachusetts (United States)
17 Sep 95: Madison Square Garden, New York City, New York (United States)
18 Sep 95: Madison Square Garden, New York City, New York (United States)
19 Sep 95: Nassau Veterans' Memorial Coliseum, Uniondale, New York (United States)
21 Sep 95: Memorial Auditorium, Buffalo, New York (United States)
23 Sep 95: The Palace of Auburn Hills, Auburn Hills, Michigan (United States)
24 Sep 95: United Center, Chicago, Illinois (United States)

Eric Clapton & His Band – 1995 "From The Cradle" Japan Tour
1 Oct 95: Yoyogi Daiichi Taiikukan, Tokyo (Japan)
2 Oct 95: Yoyogi Daiichi Taiikukan, Tokyo (Japan)
3 Oct 95: Yoyogi Daiichi Taiikukan, Tokyo (Japan)
5 Oct 95: Yoyogi Daiichi Taiikukan, Tokyo (Japan)
6 Oct 95: Yoyogi Daiichi Taiikukan, Tokyo (Japan)
8 Oct 95: Osaka-Jo Hall, Osaka (Japan)
9 Oct 95: Osaka-Jo Hall, Osaka (Japan)
11 Oct 95: Nippon Budokan, Tokyo (Japan)
12 Oct 95: Nippon Budokan, Tokyo (Japan)
13 Oct 95: Nippon Budokan, Tokyo (Japan)

Eric Clapton Guest Appearance with Jools Holland and His Rhythm & Blues Orchestra – "Jools Holland's Hootenanny" Television Show (BBC 2 TV)
13 Dec 95: BBC Television Centre, White City, West London (England)
pre-recorded for television broadcast on 31 Dec / 1 Jan

Eric Clapton Guest Appearance with Gary Brooker – Benefit Concert for Local Charity
15 Dec 95: Chiddingfold Ex-Servicemen's Club, Woodside Road, Chiddingfold, Surrey (England)

16 Dec 95: Chiddingfold Ex-Servicemen's Club, Woodside Road, Chiddingfold, Surrey (England)

Eric Clapton & Friends – New Year's Eve Dance (Private Event)
31 Dec 95: Woking, Surrey (England)

Eric Clapton Guest Appearance with Dr. John
11 Jan 96: Ronnie Scott's, Frith Street, Soho, Central London (England)
13 Jan 96: Ronnie Scott's, Frith Street, Soho, Central London (England)

Eric Clapton & His Band – 1996 Royal Albert Hall Warm-Up Date
16 Feb 96: Nynex Arena, Manchester (England)

Eric Clapton & His Band – 1996 Royal Albert Hall Dates
18 Feb 96: Royal Albert Hall, Kensington Gore, Central London (England)
19 Feb 96: Royal Albert Hall, Kensington Gore, Central London (England)
20 Feb 96: Royal Albert Hall, Kensington Gore, Central London (England)
22 Feb 96: Royal Albert Hall, Kensington Gore, Central London (England)
23 Feb 96: Royal Albert Hall, Kensington Gore, Central London (England)
24 Feb 96: Royal Albert Hall, Kensington Gore, Central London (England)
26 Feb 96: Royal Albert Hall, Kensington Gore, Central London (England)
27 Feb 96: Royal Albert Hall, Kensington Gore, Central London (England)
guest appearance by Zucchero
28 Feb 96: Royal Albert Hall, Kensington Gore, Central London (England)
1 Mar 96: Royal Albert Hall, Kensington Gore, Central London (England)
2 Mar 96: Royal Albert Hall, Kensington Gore, Central London (England)
3 Mar 96: Royal Albert Hall, Kensington Gore, Central London (England)

Eric Clapton Guest Appearance – "The Prince's Youth Business Trust 10th Anniversary: A Royal Gala"
19 Mar 96: Royal Albert Hall, Kensington Gore, Central London (England)

Eric Clapton & Dr. John – "VH1 Duets" Television Show (VH1)
9 May 96: Roseland Ballroom, West 52nd Street, New York City, New York (United States) pre-recorded for later television broadcast

Eric Clapton Guest Appearance with Buddy Guy
28 May 96: Shepherd's Bush Empire, Shepherd's Bush Green, Shepherd's Bush, West London (England)

Eric Clapton Guest Appearance – "Pavarotti & Friends for War Child Foundation"
20 Jun 96: Parco Novi Sad, Modena (Italy)

Eric Clapton & His Band – "Masters of Music Concert for The Prince's Trust"
29 Jun 96: Hyde Park, London (England) – EC headlines multi-act benefit concert bill

Eric Clapton Guest Appearance – "Giorgio Armani Party"
12 Sep 96: Lexington Armory, Lexington Avenue, New York City, New York (United States)

Eric Clapton Guest Appearance with Sheryl Crow
18 Nov 96: Shepherd's Bush Empire, Shepherd's Bush Green, Shepherd's Bush, West London (England)
19 Nov 96: Shepherd's Bush Empire, Shepherd's Bush Green, Shepherd's Bush, West London (England)
26 Nov 96: Shepherd's Bush Empire, Shepherd's Bush Green, Shepherd's Bush, West London (England)

Eric Clapton & Friends – New Year's Eve Dance (Private Event)
31 Dec 96: Woking, Surrey (England)

Eric Clapton & Kenneth "Babyface" Edmonds – "The 39th Annual Grammy Awards" (CBS TV)
26 Feb 97: Madison Square Garden, New York City, New York (United States)

Legends – 1997 Jazz Festival Tour
3 Jul 97: Montreux Jazz Festival, Auditorium Stravinski, Montreux (Switzerland) final rehearsal with invited guests
4 Jul 97: Montreux Jazz Festival, Auditorium Stravinski, Montreux (Switzerland)
5 Jul 97: Jazz a Vienne, Theatre Romain, Vienne (France) – television broadcast
7 Jul 97: Cemil Topuzlu Amphitheatre, Istanbul (Turkey)
8 Jul 97: Jazz Fest Wien, Stadthalle, Vienna (Austria)
9 Jul 97: Copenhagen Jazz Festival, Tivoli Gardens, Copenhagen (Denmark)

Eric Clapton Guest Appearance with Robert Cray
11 Jul 97: North Sea Jazz Festival, Statenhal, The Hague (Netherlands)

Legends – 1997 Jazz Festival Tour cont'd
11 Jul 97: North Sea Jazz Festival, Statenhal, The Hague (Netherlands)

12 Jul 97: Moldejazz Jazz Festival, Romsdal Museum, Molde, Møre og Romsdal (Norway)
13 Jul 97: Villa Fidelia, Spello (Italy)
15 Jul 97: Red Cliffs of Arbatax, Sardinia (Italy)
17 Jul 97: Polideportivo de Mendizorroza, Vitoria (Spain)

Eric Clapton Guest Appearance – "Music for Montserrat" Benefit Concert
15 Sep 97: Royal Albert Hall, Kensington Gore, Central London (England)

Eric Clapton Guest Appearance with Kenneth "Babyface" Edmonds – "Babyface Unplugged" Television Show (MTV)
25 Sep 97: Manhattan Center Studios, 34th Street, New York City, New York (United States) – pre-recorded for later television broadcast

Eric Clapton & His Band – 1997 Far East Tour
9 Oct 97: Olympic Gymnasium, Seoul (South Korea)
10 Oct 97: Olympic Gymnasium, Seoul (South Korea)
13 Oct 97: Nippon Budokan, Tokyo (Japan)
14 Oct 97: Nippon Budokan, Tokyo (Japan)
16 Oct 97: Nippon Budokan, Tokyo (Japan)
17 Oct 97: Nippon Budokan, Tokyo (Japan)
20 Oct 97: Marine Messe, Fukuoka (Japan)
21 Oct 97: Osaka-Jo Hall, Osaka (Japan)
22 Oct 97: Osaka-Jo Hall, Osaka (Japan)
24 Oct 97: Green Arena, Hiroshima (Japan)
25 Oct 97: Rainbow Hall, Nagoya (Japan)
27 Oct 97: Nippon Budokan, Tokyo (Japan) – pre-recorded for television broadcast in Japan (DirecTV)
28 Oct 97: Nippon Budokan, Tokyo (Japan)
30 Oct 97: Nippon Budokan, Tokyo (Japan)
31 Oct 97: Nippon Budokan, Tokyo (Japan)

Eric Clapton & Friends – New Year's Eve Dance (Private Event)
31 Dec 97: Woking, Surrey (England)

Eric Clapton & His Band – 1998 "Pilgrim" North American Tour (Leg 1)
30 Mar 98: Civic Center, St. Paul, Minnesota (United States)
2 Apr 98: Kemper Arena, Kansas City, Missouri (United States)
3 Apr 98: Kiel Center, St. Louis, Missouri (United States)
5 Apr 98: Mark of the Quad Cities, Moline, Illinois (United States)
6 Apr 98: Bradley Center, Milwaukee, Wisconsin (United States)
8 Apr 98: The Palace of Auburn Hills, Auburn Hills, Michigan (United States)
9 Apr 98: United Center, Chicago, Illinois (United States)
10 Apr 98: United Center, Chicago, Illinois (United States)
12 Apr 98: Gund Arena, Cleveland, Ohio (United States)
14 Apr 98: Fleet Center, Boston, Massachusetts (United States)
15 Apr 98: Corestates Center, Philadelphia, Pennsylvania (United States)
16 Apr 98: MCI Center, Washington, District of Columbia (United States)
18 Apr 98: Madison Square Garden, New York City, New York (United States)
19 Apr 98: Madison Square Garden, New York City, New York (United States)
20 Apr 98: Madison Square Garden, New York City, New York (United States)
22 Apr 98: Charlotte Coliseum, Charlotte, North Carolina (United States)
23 Apr 98: Thompson-Boling Arena, Knoxville, Tennessee (United States)
25 Apr 98: Miami Arena, Miami, Florida (United States)
26 Apr 98: Ice Palace, Tampa, Florida (United States)
11 May 98: Civic Arena, Pittsburgh, Pennsylvania (United States)
12 May 98: The Crown, Cincinnati, Ohio (United States)
14 May 98: Dean E. Smith Center, Chapel Hill, North Carolina (United States)
16 May 98: Nashville Arena, Nashville, Tennessee (United States)
17 May 98: The Pyramid, Memphis, Tennessee (United States)
19 May 98: Compaq Center, Houston, Texas (United States)
20 May 98: The Superdome, New Orleans, Louisiana (United States)
22 May 98: Reunion Arena, Dallas, Texas (United States)
23 May 98: Alamo Dome, San Antonio, Texas (United States)
25 May 98: America West Arena, Phoenix, Arizona (United States)
26 May 98: Cox Arena, San Diego, California (United States)
27 May 98: Great Western Forum, Inglewood, California (United States)
29 May 98: Arrowhead Pond, Anaheim, California (United States)
30 May 98: MGM Grand Garden Arena, Las Vegas, Nevada (United States)
1 Jun 98: San Jose Arena, San Jose, California (United States)
2 Jun 98: ARCO Arena, Sacramento, California (United States)
4 Jun 98: Idaho Center, Nampa, Idaho (United States)
5 Jun 98: Rose Garden, Portland, Oregon (United States)
6 Jun 98: Key Arena, Seattle, Washington (United States)

Eric Clapton & His Band – "World Convention of Narcotics Anonymous Concert"
5 Sep 98: San Jose University Center, San Jose, California (United States)

Eric Clapton & His Band – 1998 "Pilgrim" North American Tour (Leg 2)
6 Sep 98: New Arena, Oakland, California (United States)

8 Sep 98: General Motors Place, Vancouver, British Columbia (Canada)
10 Sep 98: Canadian Airlines Saddledome, Calgary, Alberta (Canada)
11 Sep 98: Edmonton Coliseum, Edmonton, Alberta (Canada)
15 Sep 98: Corel Center, Ottawa, Ontario (Canada)
17 Sep 98: Sky Dome, Toronto, Ontario (Canada)
18 Sep 98: Molson Center, Montreal, Quebec (Canada)

Eric Clapton & His Band – 1998 "Pilgrim" European Tour
13 Oct 98: National Exhibition Centre Arena, Birmingham (England)
15 Oct 98: Earls Court Exhibition Centre, Earls Court, Central London (England)
16 Oct 98: Earls Court Exhibition Centre, Earls Court, Central London (England) guest appearances by B.B. King and Bonnie Raitt
17 Oct 98: Earls Court Exhibition Centre, Earls Court, Central London (England)
19 Oct 98: Olympiahalle, Munich (Germany)
20 Oct 98: Festhalle, Frankfurt (Germany)
23 Oct 98: Palasport Casselecchio, Bologna (Italy)
24 Oct 98: Fila Forum, Milan (Italy)
26 Oct 98: Palau Sant Jordi, Barcelona (Spain)
27 Oct 98: Le Dome, Marseille (France)
29 Oct 98: Le Zenith, Paris (France)
30 Oct 98: Le Zenith, Paris (France)
31 Oct 98: Hallenstadion, Zürich (Switzerland)
2 Nov 98: Flanders Expo, Gent (Belgium)
3 Nov 98: Ahoy Rotterdam, Rotterdam (Netherlands)
4 Nov 98: Ahoy Rotterdam, Rotterdam (Netherlands)
20 Nov 98: Max Schmeling Halle, Berlin (Germany)
21 Nov 98: Max Schmeling Halle, Berlin (Germany)
23 Nov 98: Thialf Stadium, Heerenveen (Netherlands)
25 Nov 98: Spektrum, Oslo (Norway)
27 Nov 98: Hartwall Arena, Helsinki (Finland)
28 Nov 98: Hartwall Arena, Helsinki (Finland)
30 Nov 98: Scandinavium, Gothenburg (Sweden)
2 Dec 98: Globen, Stockholm (Sweden)
3 Dec 98: Forum, Copenhagen (Denmark)
4 Dec 98: Forum, Copenhagen (Denmark)
6 Dec 98: Ostseehalle, Kiel (Germany)
7 Dec 98: Kölnarena, Cologne (Germany)
9 Dec 98: Westfalenhalle, Dortmund (Germany)
10 Dec 98: Messehalle 2, Hannover (Germany)
11 Dec 98: Messehalle 2, Hannover (Germany)

Eric Clapton Guest Appearance – "After New Year's Eve with David Sanborn" Television Show (ABC TV)
14 Dec 98: Unitel Television Studio 55, Ninth Avenue, New York City, New York (United States) – pre-recorded for broadcast on 1 Jan 99

Eric Clapton Guest Appearance – "A Very Special Christmas at The White House" Television Show (TNT)
17 Dec 98: The White House, Pennsylvania Avenue, Washington, District of Columbia (United States) – pre-recorded for 20 Dec television broadcast

Eric Clapton Guest Appearance with B.B. King and George Benson – "30th NAACP Image Awards" (Fox Network)
14 Feb 99: Pasadena Civic Auditorium, East Green Street, Pasadena, California (United States) – pre-recorded for 4 Mar television broadcast

Eric Clapton Guest Appearance with B.B. King – "The 41st Annual Grammy Awards" (CBS TV)
24 Feb 99: Shrine Auditorium, West Jefferson Boulevard, Los Angeles, California (United States) – live television broadcast

Eric Clapton Guest Appearance – "1999 Rhythm & Blues Foundation Pioneer Awards"
25 Feb 99: Sony Pictures Studios, West Washington Boulevard, Culver City, California (United States)

Eric Clapton Guest Appearance – "1999 Rock & Roll Hall of Fame Induction Ceremony" (VH1)
15 Mar 99: The Grand Ballroom, Waldorf Astoria Hotel, Park Avenue, New York City, New York (United States) – pre-recorded for television broadcast

Eric Clapton Guest Appearance – "Giorgio Armani Party"
12 Jun 99: Quixote Studios, North Fuller Avenue, West Hollywood, California (United States)

"Eric Clapton & Friends for Crossroads Centre Antigua"
30 Jun 99: Madison Square Garden, New York City, New York (United States)

Eric Clapton Guest Appearance – "Central Park in Blue: Sheryl Crow & Friends" Television Show (Fox Network / FX)
14 Sep 99: East Meadow, Central Park, New York City, New York (United States) live television broadcast

Eric Clapton Guest Appearance – "The Concert of The Century for VH1 Save The Music Campaign" (VH1)
23 Oct 99: The White House, Pennsylvania Avenue, Washington, District of Columbia (United States) – pre-recorded for later television broadcast

Eric Clapton Guest Appearance – "Phoenix House and M.A.P. Allegro Awards Gala"
2 Nov 99: Universal City Hilton Towers Hotel, Universal Hollywood Drive, Universal City, California (United States)

Eric Clapton & His Band – "Japan Tour Rehearsals" (NDR 2 Hamburg)
4 Nov 99: The Complex, Los Angeles, California (United States) – pre-recorded for later radio broadcast

Eric Clapton & His Band – 1999 Japan Tour
9 Nov 99: Nippon Budokan, Tokyo (Japan)
11 Nov 99: Aichi Ken Taiikukan, Nagoya (Japan)
13 Nov 99: Marine Messe, Fukuoka (Japan)
15 Nov 99: Osaka-Jo Hall, Osaka (Japan)
16 Nov 99: Osaka-Jo Hall, Osaka (Japan)
17 Nov 99: Osaka-Jo Hall, Osaka (Japan)
19 Nov 99: Nippon Budokan, Tokyo (Japan)
20 Nov 99: Nippon Budokan, Tokyo (Japan)
22 Nov 99: Nippon Budokan, Tokyo (Japan)
24 Nov 99: Yokohama Arena, Yokohama (Japan) – pre-recorded for television broadcast in Japan (NHK BS)
26 Nov 99: Nippon Budokan, Tokyo (Japan)
27 Nov 99: Nippon Budokan, Tokyo (Japan)
29 Nov 99: Nippon Budokan, Tokyo (Japan)
30 Nov 99: Nippon Budokan, Tokyo (Japan)

New Year's Eve Dance – Private Event
31 Dec 99: Woking, Surrey (England)

Curtis Mayfield Memorial Service (Private Event)
22 Feb 00: First African Methodist Episcopal Church Of Los Angeles, South Harvard Boulevard, Los Angeles, California (United States)

Eric Clapton Guest Appearance – "2000 Rock & Roll Hall of Fame Induction Ceremony" (VH1)
6 Mar 00: The Grand Ballroom, Waldorf Astoria Hotel, Park Avenue, New York City, New York (United States) – EC is the only person to be inducted three times into the Hall of Fame (Yardbirds '92, Cream '93, EC '00); pre-recorded for television broadcast

Eric Clapton Guest Appearance with B.B. King
19 Mar 00: B.B. King's Blues Club, Universal Center Drive, Universal City, California (United States)

Eric Clapton Guest Appearance with Bobby Whitlock – "Later... with Jools Holland" TV Show (BBC 2 TV)
25 Apr 00: BBC Television Centre, White City, West London (England) – live television broadcast; also pre-recorded for extended re-broadcast

Eric Clapton Guest Appearance with Carlos Santana
28 Apr 00: Nippon Budokan, Tokyo (Japan)

Eric Clapton Guest Appearance with Dr. John
23 May 00: Blue Note, Tokyo (Japan)

Eric Clapton & Friends – New Year's Eve Dance (Private Event)
31 Dec 00: Woking, Surrey (England)

Eric Clapton Guest Appearance – "Wyclef Jean Foundation Benefit Concert"
19 Jan 01: Carnegie Hall, 57th Street, New York, New York (United States)

Eric Clapton & His Band – 2001 "Reptile" U.K. Tour
3 Feb 01: Royal Albert Hall, Kensington Gore, Central London (England)
4 Feb 01: Royal Albert Hall, Kensington Gore, Central London (England)
6 Feb 01: Royal Albert Hall, Kensington Gore, Central London (England)
7 Feb 01: Royal Albert Hall, Kensington Gore, Central London (England) cancelled due to illness
9 Feb 01: Royal Albert Hall, Kensington Gore, Central London (England)
10 Feb 01: Royal Albert Hall, Kensington Gore, Central London (England)
12 Feb 01: Sheffield Arena, Sheffield (England)

14 Feb 01: Manchester Evening News Arena, Manchester (England)
16 Feb 01: National Exhibition Centre, Birmingham (England)

Eric Clapton & His Band – 2001 "Reptile" European Tour
20 Feb 01: Pavilhão Atlântico, Lisbon (Portugal)
22 Feb 01: Palacio de los Deportes, Madrid (Spain)
23 Feb 01: Palacio de los Deportes, Madrid (Spain)
25 Feb 01: Palau Sant Jordi, Barcelona (Spain)
26 Feb 01: Le Zenith, Toulouse (France)
28 Feb 01: Palasport, Florence (Italy)
2 Mar 01: Filaforum, Milan (Italy)
3 Mar 01: BPA Palas, Pesaro (Italy)
5 Mar 01: Hallenstadion, Zürich (Switzerland)
6 Mar 01: Schleyerhalle, Stuttgart (Germany)
8 Mar 01: Cologne Arena, Cologne (Germany)
9 Mar 01: Festhalle, Frankfurt (Germany)
20 Mar 01: Palais Omnisports de Paris Bercy, Paris (France)
21 Mar 01: Palais Omnisports de Paris Bercy, Paris (France)
23 Mar 01: Flanders Expo, Ghent (Belgium)
25 Mar 01: Ahoy Rotterdam, Rotterdam (Netherlands)
26 Mar 01: Ahoy Rotterdam, Rotterdam (Netherlands)
28 Mar 01: Forum, Copenhagen (Denmark)
29 Mar 01: Forum, Copenhagen (Denmark) – guest appearance by Doyle Bramhall II
31 Mar 01: Scandinavium, Gothenburg (Sweden)
1 Apr 01: Spektrum, Oslo (Norway)
3 Apr 01: Globen, Stockholm (Sweden)
5 Apr 01: Hartwall Arena, Helsinki (Finland)
6 Apr 01: Hartwall Arena, Helsinki (Finland)
8 Apr 01: Ice Palace, St. Petersburg (Russia)
10 Apr 01: The State Kremlin Palace, Moscow (Russia)
11 Apr 01: The State Kremlin Palace, Moscow (Russia)
10 May 01: Reunion Arena, Dallas, Texas (United States)

Eric Clapton & His Band – 2001 "Reptile" North American Tour (Leg 1)
12 May 01: Alamo Dome, San Antonio, Texas (United States)
14 May 01: Compaq Center, Houston, Texas (United States)
15 May 01: New Orleans Arena, New Orleans, Louisiana (United States)
18 May 01: National Car Rental Center, Sunrise, Florida (United States)
19 May 01: Ice Palace Arena, Tampa, Florida (United States)
21 May 01: Philips Arena, Atlanta, Georgia (United States)
22 May 01: The Pyramid, Memphis, Tennessee (United States)
24 May 01: Gaylord Entertainment Center, Nashville, Tennessee (United States)
25 May 01: Charlotte Coliseum, Charlotte, North Carolina (United States)
27 May 01: MCI Center, Washington, District of Columbia (United States)
30 May 01: Bryce Jordan Center, State College, Pennsylvania (United States)
1 Jun 01: Nationwide Arena, Columbus, Ohio (United States)
2 Jun 01: Conseco Fieldhouse, Indianapolis, Indiana (United States)
4 Jun 01: Gund Arena, Cleveland, Ohio (United States)
6 Jun 01: The Palace of Auburn Hills, Auburn Hills, Michigan (United States)
9 Jun 01: Air Canada Centre, Toronto, Ontario (Canada)
11 Jun 01: Fleet Center, Boston, Massachusetts (United States)
12 Jun 01: Fleet Center, Boston, Massachusetts (United States)
15 Jun 01: HSBC Arena, Buffalo, New York (United States)
16 Jun 01: Pepsi Arena, Albany, New York (United States)
17 Jun 01: First Union Center, Philadelphia, Pennsylvania (United States)
21 Jun 01: Madison Square Garden, New York City, New York (United States)
22 Jun 01: Madison Square Garden, New York City, New York (United States)
23 Jun 01: Madison Square Garden, New York City, New York (United States)

Eric Clapton Guest Appearance with Gary Brooker's Band du Lac – Benefit Concert in aid of HASTE (Heart and Stroke Trust Endeavour)
7 Jul 01: Wintershall Estate, Bramley, Guildford, Surrey (England)

Eric Clapton & His Band – 2001 "Reptile" North American Tour (Leg 2)
17 Jul 01: Xcel Energy Center, St. Paul, Minnesota (United States)
19 Jul 01: Fargo Dome, Fargo, North Dakota (United States)
21 Jul 01: Bradley Center, Milwaukee, Wisconsin (United States)
22 Jul 01: Savvis Center, St. Louis, Missouri (United States)
24 Jul 01: United Center, Chicago, Illinois (United States) – guest appearance by Buddy Guy
25 Jul 01: United Center, Chicago, Illinois (United States)
27 Jul 01: Mark of the Quad Cities, Moline, Illinois (United States)
28 Jul 01: Kemper Arena, Kansas City, Missouri (United States)
30 Jul 01: Pepsi Center, Denver, Colorado (United States)
1 Aug 01: Delta Center, Salt Lake City, Utah (United States)
2 Aug 01: Idaho Center, Nampa, Idaho (United States)
4 Aug 01: Key Arena, Seattle, Washington (United States)
5 Aug 01: General Motors Place, Vancouver, British Columbia (Canada)
7 Aug 01: Rose Garden Arena, Portland, Oregon (United States)
10 Aug 01: ARCO Arena, Sacramento, California (United States)

11 Aug 01: Oakland Arena, Oakland, California (United States)
13 Aug 01: Thomas & Mack Center, Las Vegas, Nevada (United States)
15 Aug 01: America West Arena, Phoenix, Arizona (United States)
17 Aug 01: Staples Center, Los Angeles, California (United States)
18 Aug 01: Staples Center, Los Angeles, California (United States)

Eric Clapton & His Band – 2001 "Reptile" South American Tour
4 Oct 01: Estadio Nacional, Santiago (Chile) – pre-recorded for television broadcast in Chile
6 Oct 01: Estadio River Plate, Buenos Aires (Argentina) – pre-recorded for television broadcast in Argentina
8 Oct 01: Cilindro Municipal, Montevideo (Uruguay)
10 Oct 01: Estadio Olimpico, Porto Alegre (Brazil)
11 Oct 01: Estadio do Pacaembu, São Paulo (Brazil)
13 Oct 01: Praca da Apoteose, Rio de Janeiro (Brazil) – pre-recorded for television broadcast in Brazil
16 Oct 01: Estacionamiento del Poliedro, Caracas (Venezuela)
19 Oct 01: Foro Sol, Mexico City (Mexico)

Eric Clapton Guest Appearance with Buddy Guy – "The Concert for New York City" (VH1)
20 Oct 01: Madison Square Garden, New York City, New York (United States) – live radio and television broadcast and radio simulcast

Eric Clapton & His Band – 2001 "Reptile" Japan Tour
19 Nov 01: Osaka-Jo Hall, Osaka (Japan)
21 Nov 01: Osaka-Jo Hall, Osaka (Japan)
22 Nov 01: Osaka-Jo Hall, Osaka (Japan)
24 Nov 01: Aichi Ken Taiikukan, Nagoya (Japan)
26 Nov 01: Marine Messe, Fukuoka (Japan)
28 Nov 01: Nippon Budokan, Tokyo (Japan)
29 Nov 01: Nippon Budokan, Tokyo (Japan)
30 Nov 01: Nippon Budokan, Tokyo (Japan)
3 Dec 01: Nippon Budokan, Tokyo (Japan)
4 Dec 01: Nippon Budokan, Tokyo (Japan) – pre-recorded for television broadcast on 20 Dec in Japan (NHK BS)
5 Dec 01: Nippon Budokan, Tokyo (Japan)
8 Dec 01: Grande 21, Sendai (Japan)
10 Dec 01: Nippon Budokan, Tokyo (Japan)
11 Dec 01: Nippon Budokan, Tokyo (Japan)
14 Dec 01: Yokohama Arena, Yokohama (Japan)
15 Dec 01: Yokohama Arena, Yokohama (Japan)

Eric Clapton & Friends – New Year's Eve Dance (Private Event)
31 Dec 01: Woking, Surrey (England)

Eric Clapton Guest Appearance – "Jubilee 2002: Party at the Palace" (BBC 1 TV / BBC Radio Two)
3 Jun 02: Buckingham Palace Gardens, London (England) – live television broadcast and radio simulcast

Eric Clapton & His Band – "Ferrari Maserati Festival"
3 Aug 02: Brands Hatch Circuit, Fawkham, Longfield, Kent (England)

Eric Clapton Guest Appearance – "5th Annual Carl Wilson Foundation Benefit Concert"
6 Oct 02: UCLA Royce Hall, Los Angeles, California (United States)

Eric Clapton Guest Appearance – "8th Annual BET Walk of Fame Gala Honouring Stevie Wonder" (BET)
19 Oct 02: Black Entertainment Television Studio 2, Washington, District of Columbia (United States) – pre-recorded for later television broadcast

Eric Clapton – "The Concert for George" (in aid of the Material World Foundation)
29 Nov 02: Royal Albert Hall, Kensington Gore, Central London (England)
EC also served as the show's musical director

Eric Clapton & His Band – "Ferrari Victory Concert" (Private Event)
14 Dec 02: Palamalaguti di Bologna (Italy)

Eric Clapton Guest Appearance with Gary Brooker's No Stiletto Shoes – Benefit Concert for Local Charity
20 Dec 02: Village Hall, Dunsfold, Surrey (England)

Eric Clapton & Friends – New Year's Eve Dance (Private Event)
31 Dec 02: Woking, Surrey (England)

Eric Clapton – "Birkdale School: An Evening with Eric Clapton" Concert (Private Event)
18 Mar 03: Birkdale School, Sheffield (England)

Eric Clapton & Friends – "Teenage Cancer Trust 2003" Benefit Concert
25 Mar 03: Royal Albert Hall, Kensington Gore, Central London (England)

Eric Clapton Guest Appearance – "Willie Nelson & Friends: Live & Kickin'" (TNT)
9 Apr 03: Beacon Theatre, Broadway, New York City, New York (United States) pre-recorded for 26 May television broadcast

Eric Clapton Guest Appearance – "Pavarotti & Friends S.O.S. Iraq" / War Child Foundation Benefit Concert (TV)
27 May 03: Parco Novi Sad, Modena (Italy) – television broadcast

Eric Clapton Guest Appearance – "Blowin' The Blues Away: A Gala Evening Celebrating The Blues And Jazz"
2 Jun 03: Apollo Theater, West 125th Street, New York City, New York (United States)

Eric Clapton Guest Appearance – "John Mayall & Friends: A Tribute To John Mayall For His 70th Birthday" (in aid of UNICEF)
19 Jul 03: King's Dock, Liverpool, Merseyside (England)

Eric Clapton & His Band – 2003 "Just For You" Japan Tour
15 Nov 03: Green Arena, Hiroshima (Japan)
17 Nov 03: Osaka-Jo Hall, Osaka (Japan)
19 Nov 03: Osaka-Jo Hall, Osaka (Japan)
20 Nov 03: Osaka-Jo Hall, Osaka (Japan)
22 Nov 03: Rainbow Hall, Nagoya (Japan)
24 Nov 03: Saitama Super Arena, Saitama (Japan)
26 Nov 03: Yokohama Arena, Yokohama (Japan)
27 Nov 03: Yokohama Arena, Yokohama (Japan)
29 Nov 03: Nippon Budokan, Tokyo (Japan)
30 Nov 03: Nippon Budokan, Tokyo (Japan)
2 Dec 03: Nippon Budokan, Tokyo (Japan)
3 Dec 03: Nippon Budokan, Tokyo (Japan)
5 Dec 03: Grande 21, Sendai (Japan)
7 Dec 03: Sapporo Dome, Sapporo (Japan)
9 Dec 03: Nippon Budokan, Tokyo (Japan)
10 Dec 03: Nippon Budokan, Tokyo (Japan)
12 Dec 03: Nippon Budokan, Tokyo (Japan)
13 Dec 03: Nippon Budokan, Tokyo (Japan)

Eric Clapton Guest Appearance with Gary Brooker's No Stiletto Shoes – Benefit Concert for Local Charity
20 Dec 03: Chiddingfold Ex-Servicemen's Club, Woodside Road, Chiddingfold, Surrey (England)

Eric Clapton & Friends – New Year's Eve Dance (Private Event)
31 Dec 03: Woking, Surrey (England) – EC cancelled his appearance but not event

Eric Clapton Guest Appearance with Gary Brooker & Friends – "The Last Fling 1962-2004"
4 Jan 04: Guildford Civic Hall, London Road, Guildford, Surrey (England)

Eric Clapton Guest Appearance – "One Generation 4 Another: In Aid of The Lord Taverners"
15 Mar 04: Royal Albert Hall, Kensington Gore, Central London (England)

Eric Clapton & His Band – 2004 European Tour
24 Mar 04: Palau Sant Jordi, Barcelona (Spain)
26 Mar 04: Zenith d'Auvergne, Cournon d'Auvergne (France)
28 Mar 04: Hallenstadion, Zürich (Switzerland)
30 Mar 04: Hallenstadion, Zürich (Switzerland)
31 Mar 04: Olympiahalle, Munich (Germany)
2 Apr 04: Preaussag Arena, Hannover (Germany)
3 Apr 04: Colorline Arena, Hamburg (Germany)
6 Apr 04: Palais Omnisports Paris Bercy, Paris (France)
8 Apr 04: Festhalle, Frankfurt (Germany)
9 Apr 04: Sportpaleis, Antwerp (Belgium)
11 Apr 04: Ahoy Halle, Rotterdam (Netherlands)
12 Apr 04: Ahoy Halle, Rotterdam (Netherlands)
14 Apr 04: Westfallenhalle, Dortmund (Germany)
15 Apr 04: Cologne Arena, Cologne (Germany)
17 Apr 04: Parken, Copenhagen (Denmark)
23 Apr 04: The Point Theatre, North Wall Quay, Dublin (Ireland)
24 Apr 04: Odyssey Arena, Queen's Quay, Belfast (Northern Ireland) – live radio broadcast on BBC Radio Two and webcast
26 Apr 04: Scottish Exhibition and Conference Centre, Glasgow (Scotland)
27 Apr 04: Telewest Arena, Newcastle (England)

29 Apr 04: Manchester Evening News Arena, Manchester (England)
30 Apr 04: National Exhibition Centre, Birmingham (England)
2 May 04: Hallam FM Arena, Sheffield (England)
4 May 04: Royal Albert Hall, Kensington Gore, Central London (England)
5 May 04: Royal Albert Hall, Kensington Gore, Central London (England)

Eric Clapton Guest Appearance with Zucchero – "Zu & Company" Benefit Concert for United Nation's UNHCR Fund (RAI-2)
6 May 04: Royal Albert Hall, Kensington Gore, Central London (England)
live television broadcast in Italy

Eric Clapton & His Band – 2004 European Tour cont'd
7 May 04: Royal Albert Hall, Kensington Gore, Central London (England)
8 May 04: Royal Albert Hall, Kensington Gore, Central London (England)
10 May 04: Royal Albert Hall, Kensington Gore, Central London (England)
11 May 04: Royal Albert Hall, Kensington Gore, Central London (England)

"Eric Clapton's Crossroads Guitar Festival" (Sirius Satellite Radio – U.S.)
4 Jun 04: Fair Park, Dallas, Texas (United States) – live radio broadcast
5 Jun 04: Fair Park, Dallas, Texas (United States) – live radio broadcast
6 Jun 04: Fair Park & Cotton Bowl Stadium, Dallas, Texas (United States) – live radio broadcast

Eric Clapton & His Band – 2004 U.S. Tour
9 Jun 04: Ford Center, Norman, Oklahoma (United States)
11 Jun 04: Alltel Arena, Little Rock, Arkansas (United States)
12 Jun 04: New Orleans Arena, New Orleans, Louisiana (United States)
14 Jun 04: St. Petersburg Times Forum, Tampa, Florida (United States)
15 Jun 04: Office Depot Center, Sunrise, Florida (United States)
16 Jun 04: Jacksonville Veterans Memorial Arena, Jacksonville, Florida (United States)
18 Jun 04: Philips Arena, Atlanta, Georgia (United States)
19 Jun 04: Bi-Lo Center, Greenville, South Carolina (United States)
21 Jun 04: MCI Center, Washington, District of Columbia (United States)
23 Jun 04: Pepsi Arena, Albany, New York (United States)
26 Jun 04: Wachovia Center, Philadelphia, Pennsylvania (United States)
28 Jun 04: Madison Square Garden, New York City, New York (United States)
29 Jun 04: Madison Square Garden, New York City, New York (United States)
30 Jun 04: Madison Square Garden, New York City, New York (United States)
3 Jul 04: Tweeter Center For The Performing Arts, Mansfield, Massachusetts (United States)
4 Jul 04: Tweeter Center For The Performing Arts, Mansfield, Massachusetts (United States)
7 Jul 04: Air Canada Center, Toronto, Ontario (Canada)
9 Jul 04: HSBC Arena, Buffalo, New York (United States)
10 Jul 04: Gund Arena, Cleveland, Ohio (United States)
12 Jul 04: Nationwide Arena, Columbus, Ohio (United States)
13 Jul 04: The Palace of Auburn Hills, Auburn Hills, Michigan (United States)
15 Jul 04: Conseco Field House, Indianapolis, Indiana (United States)
17 Jul 04: United Center, Chicago, Illinois (United States)
18 Jul 04: Xcel Energy Center, Minneapolis, Minnesota (United States)
20 Jul 04: Bradley Center, Milwaukee, Wisconsin (United States)
22 Jul 04: Qwest Center, Omaha, Nebraska (United States)
24 Jul 04: Pepsi Center, Denver, Colorado (United States)
27 Jul 04: Key Arena, Seattle, Washington (United States)
28 Jul 04: Rose Garden Arena, Portland, Oregon (United States)
30 Jul 04: HP Pavilion, San Jose, California (United States)
31 Jul 04: HP Pavilion, San Jose, California (United States)
2 Aug 04: Hollywood Bowl, Los Angeles, California (United States)

Eric Clapton Guest Appearance with The Crickets
4 Aug 04: House of Blues, Sunset Boulevard, West Hollywood, California (United States)

Eric Clapton Guest Appearance – "A Tribute To The King by Scotty Moore & Friends"
2 Dec 04: EMI Abbey Road Studios, St. John's Wood, Northwest London (England)

Eric Clapton Guest Appearance with Jools Holland and His Rhythm & Blues Orchestra – "Jools Holland's Hootenanny" Television Show (BBC 2 TV)
16 Dec 04: BBC Television Centre, White City, West London (England)
pre-recorded for television broadcast on 31 Dec / 1 Jan

Eric Clapton Guest Appearance with Gary Brooker's No Stiletto Shoes – Benefit Concert for Local Charity
18 Dec 04: Chiddingfold Ex-Servicemen's Club, Woodside Road, Chiddingfold, Surrey (England)

Eric Clapton & Friends – New Year's Eve Dance (Private Event)
31 Dec 04: Woking, Surrey (England)

Eric Clapton Guest Appearance with Roger Waters – "Tsunami Aid: A Concert of Hope" (NBC and Affiliated Networks / Clear Channel Radio)
15 Jan 05: BBC Television Centre, White City, West London (England)
pre-recorded for same day television and radio broadcast in the United States

Eric Clapton Guest Appearance with with Jools Holland and His Rhythm & Blues Orchestra – "Tsunami Relief Cardiff" (BBC Red Button / BBC 2 TV / BBC Radio Wales)
22 Jan 05: Millennium Stadium, Cardiff, Wales (United Kingdom) – live radio and television broadcast

Eric Clapton Guest Appearance with Jools Holland and His Rhythm & Blues Orchestra – "Comic Relief Red Nose Night" (BBC 1 TV)
11 Mar 05: BBC Television Centre, White City, West London (England)
live television broadcast

Eric Clapton Guest Appearance – "2005 Rock and Roll Hall of Fame Induction Ceremony" (VH1)
14 Mar 05: Waldorf Astoria Hotel, Park Avenue, New York City, New York (United States)
EC and B.B. King induct Buddy Guy; pre-recorded for television broadcast

Eric Clapton Guest Appearance with John Mayer and UB40 – "Teenage Cancer Trust 2005" Benefit Concert
8 Apr 05: Royal Albert Hall, Kensington Gore, Central London (England)

Cream – 2005 London Reunion Concerts
2 May 05: Royal Albert Hall, Kensington Gore, Central London (England)
3 May 05: Royal Albert Hall, Kensington Gore, Central London (England)
5 May 05: Royal Albert Hall, Kensington Gore, Central London (England)
6 May 05: Royal Albert Hall, Kensington Gore, Central London (England)

Eric Clapton Guest Appearance with Gary Brooker's Band du Lac – Benefit Concert in aid of HASTE (Heart and Stroke Trust Endeavour)
11 Jun 05: Wintershall Estate, Bramley, Guildford, Surrey (England)

Eric Clapton Guest Appearance with John Mayer– "Larry King Live: How You Can Help" Hurricane Katrina Telethon (CNN)
3 Sep 05: CNN Television Studios, Time Warner Center, Columbus Circle, New York, New York (United States) – live television broadcast on CNN, CNN International and CNN Radio

Cream – 2005 New York City Reunion Concerts
24 Oct 05: Madison Square Garden, New York City, New York (United States)
25 Oct 05: Madison Square Garden, New York City, New York (United States)
26 Oct 05: Madison Square Garden, New York City, New York (United States)

Eric Clapton – "Today" Television Show (NBC-TV)
18 Nov 05: NBC Television Studio 1A, Rockefeller Plaza, New York City, New York (United States) – live television broadcast

Eric Clapton & Friends – New Year's Eve Dance (Private Event)
31 Dec 05: Woking, Surrey (England)

Eric Clapton & His Band – 2006 / 2007 World Tour (Europe – Leg 1)
5 May 06: La Palestre, Le Cannet (France)
8 May 06: Scottish Exhibition and Conference Centre (SECC), Glasgow (Scotland)
9 May 06: Manchester Evening News Arena, Manchester (England)
11 May 06: National Exhibition Centre, Birmingham (England)
12 May 06: Hallam FM Arena, Sheffield (England)
14 May 06: National Ice Centre, Nottingham Arena, Nottingham (England)
16 May 06: Royal Albert Hall, Kensington Gore, Central London (England)
17 May 06: Royal Albert Hall, Kensington Gore, Central London (England)
19 May 06: Royal Albert Hall, Kensington Gore, Central London (England)

Eric Clapton Guest Appearance with Gary Brooker's Band du Lac – "Highclere Rocks" Countryside Alliance Benefit Concert
20 May 06: Highclere Castle, Highclere Park, Newbury, Berkshire (England)

Eric Clapton & His Band – 2006 / 2007 World Tour (Europe – Leg 1) cont'd
22 May 06: Royal Albert Hall, Kensington Gore, Central London (England)
23 May 06: Royal Albert Hall, Kensington Gore, Central London (England)
25 May 06: Royal Albert Hall, Kensington Gore, Central London (England)
26 May 06: Royal Albert Hall, Kensington Gore, Central London (England)
26 May 06: Bercy, Paris (France)
29 May 06: Zenith Arena, Lille (France)
31 May 06: Sports Paleis, Antwerp (Belgium)
1 Jun 06: Ahoy Halle, Rotterdam (Netherlands)
3 Jun 06: Festhalle, Frankfurt (Germany)
4 Jun 06: Schleyer-Halle, Stuttgargt (Germany)

6 Jun 06: Leipzig Arena, Leipzig (Germany)
7 Jun 06: Berlin Wuhlheide, Berlin (Germany)

Eric Clapton & His Band – "2006 Hampton Court Palace Festival"
9 Jun 06: Hampton Court Palace, East Molesey, Surrey (England)
10 Jun 06: Hampton Court Palace, East Molesey, Surrey (England)

Eric Clapton & His Band – 2006 / 2007 World Tour (Europe – Leg 2)
7 Jul 06: Piazza Napoleone, Lucca (Italy) – live radio broadcast in Italy
8 Jul 06: Umbria Jazz Festival, Perugia (Italy)
10 Jul 06: Arena di Verona, Verona (Italy)

Eric Clapton & His Band – "Moon & Stars Festival"
11 Jul 06: Piazza Grande, Locarno, Ticino (Switzerland)

Eric Clapton & His Band – 2006 / 2007 World Tour (Europe – Leg 2)
13 Jul 06: Cologne Arena, Cologne (Germany)
14 Jul 06: Westfalenhalle, Dortmund (Germany)
16 Jul 06: Wiener Stadthalle, Vienna (Austria)
18 Jul 06: Sportarena, Budapest (Hungary)
20 Jul 06: Sazka Arena, Prague (Czech Republic)
22 Jul 06: Olympiahalle, Munich (Germany)
23 Jul 06: SAP Arena, Mannheim (Germany)
25 Jul 06: Colorline Arena, Hamburg (Germany)
26 Jul 06: Augustenborg Slotspark, Augustenborg (Denmark)
28 Jul 06: Spektrum, Oslo (Norway)
29 Jul 06: Globen, Stockholm (Sweden)
31 Jul 06: Hartwall Arena, Helsinki (Finland)
3 Aug 06: Red Square, Moscow (Russia) – cancelled as the promoter's permit was withdrawn by city and state authorities

Eric Clapton Guest Appearance with Jimmie Vaughan (support for Bob Dylan)
13 Aug 06: Cooper Stadium, Columbus, Ohio (United States)

Eric Clapton & His Band – 2006 / 2007 World Tour (North America – Leg 1)
16 Sep 06: Xcel Energy Center, Minneapolis, Minnesota (United States)
18 Sep 06: Scottrade Center, St. Louis, Missouri (United States)
20 Sep 06: United Center, Chicago, Illinois (United States)
21 Sep 06: Van Andel Arena, Grand Rapids, Michigan (United States)
23 Sep 06: The Palace of Auburn Hills, Auburn Hills, Michigan (United States) postponed due to illness until 5 Apr 07
24 Sep 06: Air Canada Center, Toronto, Ontario (Canada)
26 Sep 06: Scotiabank Place, Ottawa, Ontario (Canada)
28 Sep 06: Madison Square Garden, New York City, New York (United States)
29 Sep 06: Madison Square Garden, New York City, New York (United States)
30 Sep 06: Madison Square Garden, New York City, New York (United States)
3 Oct 06: Bank North Garden, Boston, Massachusetts (United States)
4 Oct 06: Bank North Garden, Boston, Massachusetts (United States)
6 Oct 06: Mohegan Sun Arena, Uncasville, Connecticut (United States)
7 Oct 06: Mohegan Sun Arena, Uncasville, Connecticut (United States)
9 Oct 06: Wachovia Center, Philadelphia, Pennsylvania (United States)
10 Oct 06: Verizon Center, Washington, District of Columbia (United States)
12 Oct 06: John Paul Jones Arena, Charlottesville, Virginia (United States)
14 Oct 06: Gwinnet Civic Center, Duluth, Georgia (United States)
15 Oct 06: RBC Center, Raleigh, North Carolina (United States)
17 Oct 06: Charlotte Bobcats Arena, Charlotte, North Carolina (United States)
18 Oct 06: Birmingham Jefferson Arena, Birmingham, Alabama (United States)
20 Oct 06: TD Waterhouse Center, Orlando, Florida (United States)
21 Oct 06: Veteran's Memorial Arena, Jacksonville, Florida (United States)
23 Oct 06: American Airlines Arena, Miami, Florida (United States)

Eric Clapton & His Band – 2006 / 2007 World Tour (Japan)
11 Nov 06: Osaka-Jo Hall, Osaka (Japan)
12 Nov 06: Osaka-Jo Hall, Osaka (Japan)
14 Nov 06: Osaka-Jo Hall, Osaka (Japan)
15 Nov 06: Osaka-Jo Hall, Osaka (Japan)
17 Nov 06: Rainbow Hall, Nagoya (Japan)
18 Nov 06: Rainbow Hall, Nagoya (Japan)
20 Nov 06: Nippon Budokan, Tokyo (Japan)
21 Nov 06: Nippon Budokan, Tokyo (Japan)
23 Nov 06: Nippon Budokan, Tokyo (Japan)
24 Nov 06: Nippon Budokan, Tokyo (Japan)
26 Nov 06: Sapporo Dome, Sapporo (Japan)
29 Nov 06: Nippon Budokan, Tokyo (Japan)
30 Nov 06: Nippon Budokan, Tokyo (Japan)
2 Dec 06: Saitama Super Arena, Saitama (Japan)
5 Dec 06: Nippon Budokan, Tokyo (Japan)
6 Dec 06: Nippon Budokan, Tokyo (Japan)
8 Dec 06: Nippon Budokan, Tokyo (Japan)
9 Dec 06: Nippon Budokan, Tokyo (Japan)

Eric Clapton Guest Appearance with Gary Brooker's No Stiletto Shoes – Benefit Concert for Local Charity
15 Dec 06: Chiddingfold Ex-Servicemen's Club, Woodside Road, Chiddingfold, Surrey (England)

Eric Clapton & Friends – New Year's Eve Dance (Private Event)
31 Dec 06: Woking, Surrey (England)

Eric Clapton & His Band – 2006 / 2007 World Tour (Far East)
13 Jan 07: Singapore Indoor Stadium, Kallang (Singapore)
15 Jan 07: Impact Arena, Muang Thong Thani, Bangkok (Thailand)
17 Jan 07: Asia World Arena, Hong Kong, Hong Kong S.A.R. (China)
20 Jan 07: Shanghai Grand Stage, Shanghai (China)
23 Jan 07: Olympic Gymnasium No. 1, Seoul (South Korea)

Eric Clapton & His Band – 2006 / 2007 World Tour (New Zealand / Australia)
27 Jan 07: Mission Estate Winery, Hawkes Bay (New Zealand)
29 Jan 07: Sydney Entertainment Centre, Sydney, New South Wales (Australia)
30 Jan 07: Sydney Entertainment Centre, Sydney, New South Wales (Australia)
1 Feb 07: Entertainment Centre, Sydney, New South Wales (Australia)
3 Feb 07: Rod Laver Arena, Melbourne, Victoria (Australia)
4 Feb 07: Rod Laver Arena, Melbourne, Victoria (Australia)
6 Feb 07: Brisbane Entertainment Centre, Brisbane, Queensland (Australia)
7 Feb 07: Brisbane Entertainment Centre, Brisbane, Queensland (Australia)
9 Feb 07: Adelaide Entertainment Centre, Adelaide, South Australia (Australia)
11 Feb 07: Member's Equity Stadium, Perth, Western Australia (Australia)

Eric Clapton & His Band – 2006 / 2007 World Tour (North America – Leg 3)
28 Feb 07: American Airlines Arena, Dallas, Texas (United States)
2 Mar 07: Toyota Center, Houston, Texas (United States)
3 Mar 07: SBC Center, San Antonio, Texas (United States) – guest appearance by Jimmie Vaughan
5 Mar 07: Ford Center, Oklahoma City, Oklahoma (United States)
7 Mar 07: Pepsi Center, Denver, Colorado (United States)
8 Mar 07: Delta Center, Salt Lake City, Utah (United States)
10 Mar 07: MGM Grand Garden Arena, Las Vegas, Nevada (United States)
11 Mar 07: U.S. Airways Center, Phoenix, Arizona (United States)
14 Mar 07: Staples Center, Los Angeles, California (United States)
15 Mar 07: iPay One Center, San Diego, California (United States) guest appearance by J.J. Cale
17 Mar 07: Honda Center, Anaheim, California (United States)
18 Mar 07: HP Pavilion, San Jose, California (United States)
20 Mar 07: Arco Arena, Sacramento, California (United States)
22 Mar 07: Key Arena, Seattle, Washington (United States)
23 Mar 07: General Motors Place, Vancouver, British Columbia (Canada)
25 Mar 07: Rexall Place, Edmonton, Alberta (Canada)
26 Mar 07: Pengrowth Saddledome, Calgary, Alberta (Canada)
28 Mar 07: MTS Centre, Winnipeg, Manitoba (Canada)
30 Mar 07: Fargo Dome, Fargo, North Dakota (United States)
31 Mar 07: Qwest Center, Omaha, Nebraska (United States)
2 Apr 07: Kemper Arena, Kansas City, Missouri (United States)
3 Apr 07: Mark of the Quad Cities, Moline, Illinois (United States)
5 Apr 07: The Palace of Auburn Hills, Detroit, Michigan (United States)
6 Apr 07: Jerome Schottenstein Center, Ohio State University, Columbus, Ohio (United States)

Eric Clapton Guest Appearance with Steve Winwood – "Countryside Rocks" Countryside Alliance Benefit Concert (The Country Channel Webcast)
19 May 07: Highclere Castle, Highclere Park, Newbury, Berkshire (England) live webcast

Eric Clapton Guest Appearance with John Mayer – "Good Morning America" Concert Series (ABC TV)
20 Jul 07: Bryant Park, Fifth Avenue & 42nd Street, New York City, New York (United States) – live television broadcast

"Eric Clapton's Crossroads Guitar Festival" (SBC Global Net Webcast)
28 Jul 07: Toyota Park, Bridgeville, Illinois (United States) – live webcast

Eric Clapton Guest Appearance with Jeff Beck
29 Nov 07: Ronnie Scott's, Frith Street, Soho, Central London (England)

Eric Clapton & Friends – New Year's Eve Dance (Private Event)
31 Dec 07: Woking, Surrey (England)

Eric Clapton & Steve Winwood – 2008 New York City Concerts
25 Feb 08: Madison Square Garden, New York City, New York (United States)
26 Feb 08: Madison Square Garden, New York City, New York (United States)
28 Feb 08: Madison Square Garden, New York City, New York (United States)

Eric Clapton Guest Appearance with Sheryl Crow at "SunFest"
30 Apr 08: Waterfront, Intercoastal Waterway, West Palm Beach, Florida (United States)

Eric Clapton & His Band – 2008 North American Tour
3 May 08: Ford Amphitheater, Tampa Bay, Florida (United States)
5 May 08: Seminole Hard Rock Hotel & Casino, Hollywood, Florida (United States)

Eric Clapton & His Band – Invitation-Only Concert (Private Event)
6 May 08: Amway Arena, Orlando, Florida (United States)

Eric Clapton & His Band – "Bunbury Cricket Club's Tribute to Sir Ian Botham"
8 May 08: The Great Room, Grosvenor House Hotel, Park Lane, Mayfair, Central London (England)

Eric Clapton & His Band – 2008 North American Tour cont'd
22 May 08: PNC Bank Arts Center, Holmdel, New Jersey (United States)

Eric Clapton & His Band – Invitation-Only Concert (Private Event)
24 May 08: Event Center, The Borgata, Atlantic City, New Jersey (United States)

Eric Clapton & His Band – 2008 North American Tour cont'd
25 May 08: Event Center, The Borgata, Atlantic City, New Jersey (United States)
27 May 08: Molson Amphitheater, Toronto, Ontario (Canada)
28 May 08: Bell Center, Montreal, Quebec (Canada)
30 May 08: Verizon Wireless Music Center, Noblesville, Indiana (United States)
31 May 08: Blossom Music Center, Cuyahoga Falls, Ohio (United States)
2 Jun 08: Mohegan Sun Arena, Uncasville, Connecticut (United States)
4 Jun 08: Comcast Center, Mansfield, Massachusetts (United States)
5 Jun 08: Nikon at Jones Beach Theater, Jones Beach State Park, Wantagh, New York (United States)

Eric Clapton Guest Appearance with Gary Brooker & Friends – Benefit Concert for Local Charity
14 Jun 08: Whithorn Farm, Haslemere Road, Brook, Godalming, Surrey (United Kingdom)

Eric Clapton & His Band – 2008 European Tour
20 Jun 08: The Marquee, Cork (Ireland)
21 Jun 08: Malahide Castle, Dublin (Ireland)
23 Jun 08: Trent FM Arena, Nottingham (England)

Eric Clapton & His Band – "Third Annual Hard Rock Calling Festival" (VH1)
28 Jun 08: Hyde Park, London (England) – EC headlines multi-act concert bill; guest appearances by Sheryl Crow, John Mayer and Robert Randolph during EC's set; pre-recorded for television broadcast in the U.K., U.S. and Japan

Eric Clapton & His Band – 2008 European Tour cont'd
29 Jun 08: Harewood House, Leeds (England)
6 Aug 08: The Koengen, Bergen (Norway)
8 Aug 08: Egilsholl Arena, Reykjavic (Iceland)

Eric Clapton & His Band – "Danmark's Smukkeste Festival"
10 Aug 08: Dyrehaven, Skanderborg (Denmark)

Eric Clapton & His Band – 2008 European Tour cont'd
12 Aug 08: Leipzig Arena, Leipzig (Germany)
14 Aug 08: Kosciuszko Square, Gdynia (Poland)
15 Aug 08: Waldbuhne, Berlin (Germany)
17 Aug 08: Konigsplatz, Munich (Germany)
19 Aug 08: Kurhaus Bowling Green, Wiesbasen (Germany)
20 Aug 08: Hallenstadion, Zürich (Switzerland) – guest appearance by Jakob Dylan

Eric Clapton & His Band – "Monte Carlo Sporting Summer Festival"
22 Aug 08: Salle des Etoiles, Le Sporting Monte Carlo, Monte Carlo (Principality of Monaco)
23 Aug 08: Salle des Etoiles, Le Sporting Monte Carlo, Monte Carlo (Principality of Monaco)

Eric Clapton & His Band – "Countryside Alliance Benefit Gala"
9 Sep 08: Floridita, Wardour Street, Soho, Central London (England)

Eric Clapton Guest Appearance with Gary Brooker's No Stiletto Shoes – Benefit Concert for Local Charity
22 Dec 08: Cranleigh Arts Centre, High Street, Cranleigh, Surrey (England)

Eric Clapton & Friends – New Year's Eve Dance (Private Event)
31 Dec 08: Woking, Surrey (England)

Eric Clapton & His Band – 2009 Japan Tour
12 Feb 09: Osaka-Jo Hall, Osaka (Japan)
13 Feb 09: Osaka-Jo Hall, Osaka (Japan)
15 Feb 09: Nippon Budokan, Tokyo (Japan)
18 Feb 09: Nippon Budokan, Tokyo (Japan)
19 Feb 09: Nippon Budokan, Tokyo (Japan)

Eric Clapton & Jeff Beck – 2009 "Together & Apart" Japan Concerts
21 Feb 09: Saitama Super Arena, Saitama (Japan)
22 Feb 09: Saitama Super Arena, Saitama (Japan)

Eric Clapton & His Band – 2009 Japan Tour cont'd
24 Feb 09: Nippon Budokan, Tokyo (Japan)
25 Feb 09: Nippon Budokan, Tokyo (Japan) – pre-recorded for television broadcast on 15 Mar in Japan (WOWOW)
27 Feb 09: Nippon Budokan, Tokyo (Japan)
28 Feb 09: Nippon Budokan, Tokyo (Japan)

Eric Clapton & His Band – 2009 New Zealand / Australia Tour
4 Mar 09: Vector Arena, Auckland (New Zealand)
7 Mar 09: Hope Estate Winery, Hunter Valley (Australia)
8 Mar 09: Entertainment Centre, Sydney, New South Wales (Australia)
10 Mar 09: Rod Laver Arena, Melbourne, Victoria (Australia)

Eric Clapton Guest Appearance with The Allman Brothers Band
19 Mar 09: Beacon Theater, Broadway, New York, New York (United States) live webcast on Moogis
20 Mar 09: Beacon Theater, Broadway, New York, New York (United States) live webcast on Moogis

Eric Clapton Guest Appearance with Joe Bonamassa
4 May 09: Royal Albert Hall, Kensington Gore, Central London (England)

Eric Clapton & His Band – Bunbury Cricket Club's Benefit Gala
9 May 09: The Great Room, Grosvenor House Hotel, Park Lane, Mayfair, Central London (England)

Eric Clapton & His Band – 2009 Ireland & U.K. Tour
11 May 09: The O2, North Wall Quay, Dublin (Ireland)
13 May 09: Liverpool Echo Arena, Liverpool, Merseyside (England)
14 May 09: Manchester Evening News Arena, Manchester (England)
16 May 09: Royal Albert Hall, Kensington Gore, Central London (England)
17 May 09: Royal Albert Hall, Kensington Gore, Central London (England)
19 May 09: Royal Albert Hall, Kensington Gore, Central London (England) 150th solo concert at the venue
20 May 09: Royal Albert Hall, Kensington Gore, Central London (England)
22 May 09: Royal Albert Hall, Kensington Gore, Central London (England)
23 May 09: Royal Albert Hall, Kensington Gore, Central London (England)
25 May 09: Royal Albert Hall, Kensington Gore, Central London (England)
26 May 09: Royal Albert Hall, Kensington Gore, Central London (England)
28 May 09: Royal Albert Hall, Kensington Gore, Central London (England)
29 May 09: Royal Albert Hall, Kensington Gore, Central London (England)
31 May 09: Royal Albert Hall, Kensington Gore, Central London (England)

Eric Clapton & Steve Winwood – 2009 U.S. Tour
10 Jun 09: Izod Center, East Rutherford, New Jersey (United States)
12 Jun 09: Wachovia Center, Philadelphia, Pennsylvania (United States)
13 Jun 09: Verizon Center, Washington, District of Columbia (United States)
15 Jun 09: Value City Arena, Jerome Schottenstein Center, Ohio State University, Columbus, Ohio (United States)
17 Jun 09: United Center, Chicago, Illinois (United States) – guest appearance by Buddy Guy
18 Jun 09: Xcel Energy Center, St. Paul, Minnesota (United States)
20 Jun 09: Qwest Center, Omaha, Nebraska (United States)
21 Jun 09: Pepsi Center, Denver, Colorado (United States)
23 Jun 09: American Airlines Arena, Dallas, Texas (United States)
24 Jun 09: Toyota Center, Houston, Texas (United States)
26 Jun 09: Jobing.com Arena, Glendale, Arizona (United States)
27 Jun 09: MGM Grand Garden Arena, Las Vegas, Nevada (United States)
29 Jun 09: Oracle Arena, Oakland, California (United States)
30 Jun 09: Hollywood Bowl, Los Angeles, California (United States)

Eric Clapton Guest Appearance with Bruce Hornsby – "Jay Leno Show" (NBC TV)
17 Sep 09: NBC Studios, Studio 11, West Alameda Avenue, Burbank, California (United States) – pre-recorded for same day television broadcast (Season 1, Show #4)

Eric Clapton Guest Appearance with Smokey Robinson – "Later ... with Jools Holland" (BBC 2 TV)
20 Oct 09: BBC Television Centre, White City, West London (England) live television broadcast; also pre-recorded for extended re-broadcast

Eric Clapton Guest Appearance – "25th Anniversary Rock & Roll Hall of Fame Concerts" Night 2
30 Oct 09: Madison Square Garden, New York City, New York (United States)
cancelled due to illness

Eric Clapton – "Children Action Benefit Gala"
23 Nov 09: Bâtiment des Forces Motrices, Geneva (Switzerland)
solo acoustic performance

Eric Clapton & Friends – New Year's Eve Dance (Private Event)
31 Dec 09: Woking, Surrey (England)

Eric Clapton & Jeff Beck – 2010 "Together & Apart" Tour
13 Feb 10: The O2, Drawdock Road, North Greenwich, East London (England)
14 Feb 10: The O2, Drawdock Road, North Greenwich, East London (England)

Eric Clapton Guest Appearance with The Plastic Ono Band – "We Are Plastic Ono Band: Yoko Ono's 75th Birthday Concert"
16 Feb 10: BAM Howard Gilman Opera House, Peter J. Sharp Building, Lafayette Avenue, Brooklyn, New York City, New York (United States)

Eric Clapton & Jeff Beck – 2010 "Together & Apart" Tour cont'd
18 Feb 10: Madison Square Garden, New York City, New York (United States)
19 Feb 10: Madison Square Garden, New York City, New York (United States)
21 Feb 10: Air Canada Center, Toronto, Ontario (Canada)
22 Feb 10: Bell Center, Montreal, Quebec (Canada)

Eric Clapton & His Band – 2010 U.S. Tour (Leg 1)
25 Feb 10: Mellon Arena, Pittsburgh, Pennsylvania (United States)
27 Feb 10: Sommet Center, Nashville, Tennessee (United States)
guest appearance by Vince Gill
28 Feb 10: Birmingham Jefferson Civic Center, Birmingham, Alabama (United States)
2 Mar 10: BOK Center, Tulsa, Oklahoma (United States)
3 Mar 10: Sprint Center, Kansas City, Missouri (United States)
5 Mar 10: FedEx Forum, Memphis, Tennessee (United States)
6 Mar 10: New Orleans Arena, New Orleans, Louisiana (United States)
8 Mar 10: RBC Center, Raleigh, North Carolina (United States)
9 Mar 10: The Arena at Gwinnett Center, Atlanta, Georgia (United States)
11 Mar 10: Bank Atlantic Center, Sunrise, Florida (United States)
13 Mar 10: Amway Arena, Orlando, Florida (United States)

Eric Clapton & Steve Winwood – 2010 European Tour
18 May 10: LG Arena, National Exhibition Centre, Birmingham (England)
20 May 10: Wembley Arena, Wembley, Northwest London (England)
21 May 10: Wembley Arena, Wembley, Northwest London (England)
23 May 10: Sportpaleis, Antwerp (Belgium)
25 May 10: Palais Omnisports de Bercy, Paris (France)
26 May 10: St. Jakobshalle, Basel (Switzerland)
28 May 10: ISS Dome, Düsseldorf (Germany)
29 May 10: GelreDome Stadium, Arnhem (Netherlands)
31 May 10: Malmö Arena, Malmö (Sweden)
2 Jun 10: O2 World, Berlin (Germany)
3 Jun 10: Colorline Arena, Hamburg (Germany)
5 Jun 10: Konigsplatz, Munich (Germany)
7 Jun 10: Stadthalle, Vienna (Austria)
9 Jun 10: Belgrade Arena, Belgrade (Serbia)
11 Jun 10: Rugby Park, Bucharest (Romania)
13 Jun 10: Turkcell Kurucesme Arena, Istanbul (Turkey)
venue changed from Santral Istanbul

"Eric Clapton's Crossroads Guitar Festival"
26 Jun 10: Toyota Park, Bridgeview, Illinois (United States)

Eric Clapton & His Band – "Summerfest"
28 Jun 10: Marcus Ampitheater, Henry Maier Festival Park, Milwaukee, Wisconsin (United States)

Eric Clapton & His Band – 2010 U.S. Tour (Leg 2)
30 Jun 10: Riverbend Music Center, Cincinnati, Ohio (United States)
2 Jul 10: Verizon Wireless Music Center, Indianapolis, Indiana (United States)
3 Jul 10: DTE Energy Music Theater, Clarkston, Michigan (United States)

Eric Clapton Guest Appearance – "The Clinton Foundation Benefit Gala"
23 Oct 10: The Cathedral Church of Saint John The Divine, Amsterdam Avenue, New York City, New York (United States)

Eric Clapton Guest Appearance – "The Prince's Trust Rock Gala 2010" (Sky 3D TV and DirecTV)
17 Nov 10: Royal Albert Hall, Kensington Gore, Central London (England)
pre-recorded for television broadcast on 19 Dec in the U.K. and 25 Dec in the U.S.

Eric Clapton & Friends – New Year's Eve Dance (Private Event)
31 Dec 10: Woking, Surrey (England)

Eric Clapton Guest Appearance with Paul Jones & Friends – Benefit Concert for Local Charity
13 Jan 11: Cranleigh Arts Centre, High Street, Cranleigh, Surrey (England)

Eric Clapton & His Band – 2011 U.A.E Date
11 Feb 11: Yas Arena, Abu Dhabi (United Arab Emirates)

Eric Clapton & His Band – 2011 Far East Tour
14 Feb 11: Singapore Indoor Stadium, Kallang (Singapore)
16 Feb 11: Impact Arena, Bangkok (Thailand)
18 Feb 11: Asia World Arena, Hong Kong, Hong Kong S.A.R. (China)
20 Feb 11: Olympic Gym #1, Seoul (South Korea)

Eric Clapton & His Band – 2011 North American Tour
25 Feb 11: Rogers Arena, Vancouver, British Columbia (Canada)
26 Feb 11: Key Arena, Seattle, Washington (United States)
28 Feb 11: Rose Garden Arena, Portland, Oregon (United States)
2 Mar 11: HP Pavilion, San Jose, California (United States)
3 Mar 11: ARCO Arena, Sacramento, California (United States)
5 Mar 11: MGM Grand Garden Arena, Las Vegas, Nevada (United States)
6 Mar 11: Valley View Casino Center, San Diego, California (United States)
8 Mar 11: Gibson Amphitheater at Universal CityWalk, Universal City, California (United States)
9 Mar 11: Gibson Amphitheater at Universal CityWalk, Universal City, California (United States)

Eric Clapton & Wynton Marsalis – "Play The Blues: Jazz at Lincoln Center Benefit Gala"
7 Apr 11: Rose Theater, Time Warner Center, New York City, New York (United States)

Eric Clapton & Wynton Marsalis – "Play The Blues" DVD Filming and Recording
8 Apr 11: Rose Theater, Time Warner Center, New York, New York (United States)
9 Apr 11: Rose Theater, Time Warner Center, New York, New York (United States)

Eric Clapton & His Band – Bunbury Cricket Club's Benefit Gala
7 May 11: The Great Room, Grosvenor House Hotel, Park Lane, Mayfair, Central London (England)

Eric Clapton & His Band – 2011 Ireland & U.K. Tour
9 May 11: The O2, North Wall Quay, Dublin (Ireland)
10 May 11: Odyssey Arena, Queen's Quay, Belfast (Northern Ireland)
12 May 11: Scottish Exhibition & Conference Centre, Glasgow (Scotland)
14 May 11: Cardiff International Arena, Cardiff (Wales)
15 May 11: Cardiff International Arena, Cardiff (Wales)
17 May 11: Royal Albert Hall, Kensington Gore, Central London (England)
18 May 11: Royal Albert Hall, Kensington Gore, Central London (England)
20 May 11: Royal Albert Hall, Kensington Gore, Central London (England)
21 May 11: Royal Albert Hall, Kensington Gore, Central London (England)
23 May 11: Royal Albert Hall, Kensington Gore, Central London (England)
24 May 11: Royal Albert Hall, Kensington Gore, Central London (England)
26 May 11: Royal Albert Hall, Kensington Gore, Central London (England)
27 May 11: Royal Albert Hall, Kensington Gore, Central London (England)

Eric Clapton & Steve Winwood – 2011 London Dates
29 May 11: Royal Albert Hall, Kensington Gore, Central London (England)
30 May 11: Royal Albert Hall, Kensington Gore, Central London (England)
1 Jun 11: Royal Albert Hall, Kensington Gore, Central London (England)

Eric Clapton Guest Appearance with Gary Brooker's Band du Lac – Benefit Concert in aid of HASTE (Heart and Stroke Trust Endeavour)
4 Jun 11: Wintershall Estate, Bramley, Guildford, Surrey (England)

Eric Clapton & His Band – 2011 Scandinavian Tour
6 Jun 11: Hartwall Arena, Helsinki (Finland)
8 Jun 11: Ericsson Globe, Stockholm (Sweden)
9 Jun 11: Norwegian Wood Festival, Oslo (Norway)
11 Jun 11: Jyske Bank Boxen, Herning (Denmark)

Eric Clapton Guest Appearance with Pino Daniele – "Benefit Concert for Open Onlus"
24 Jun 11: Stadio di Cava De' Tirreni, Cava De' Tirreni (Italy)

Eric Clapton & His Band – 2011 South American Tour
6 Oct 11: Centro de Eventos Fiergs, Porto Alegre (Brazil)
9 Oct 11: HSBC Arena, Rio de Janeiro (Brazil)
9 Oct 11: HSBC Arena, Rio de Janeiro (Brazil)
10 Oct 11: HSBC Arena, Rio de Janeiro (Brazil)

12 Oct 11: Morumbi Stadium, São Paulo (Brazil)
12 Oct 11: Morumbi Stadium, São Paulo (Brazil)
14 Oct 11: River Plate Stadium, Buenos Aires (Argentina)
16 Oct 11: Movistar Arena, Santiago (Chile)

Eric Clapton & Steve Winwood – 2011 Japan Tour
17 Nov 11: Hokkaido Prefectural Sports Center, Sapporo (Japan)
19 Nov 11: Yokohama Arena, Yokohama (Japan)
21 Nov 11: Osaka-Jo Hall, Osaka (Japan)
22 Nov 11: Osaka-Jo Hall, Osaka (Japan)
24 Nov 11: Marine Messe, Fukuoka (Japan)
26 Nov 11: Green Arena, Hiroshima (Japan)
28 Nov 11: Ishikawa Sports Center, Kanazawa (Japan)
30 Nov 11: Japan Gaishihoru, Nagoya (Japan)
2 Dec 11: Nippon Budokan, Tokyo (Japan)
3 Dec 11: Nippon Budokan, Tokyo (Japan)
6 Dec 11: Nippon Budokan, Tokyo (Japan)
7 Dec 11: Nippon Budokan, Tokyo (Japan)
10 Dec 11: Nippon Budokan, Tokyo (Japan)

**Eric Clapton & His Band – "Duke of Edinburgh's Award
& Outward Bound Trust Appeal"**
15 Dec 11: Buckingham Palace, Central London (England) – acoustic performance

Eric Clapton & Friends – New Year's Eve Dance (Private Event)
31 Dec 11: Woking, Surrey (England)

**Eric Clapton Guest Appearance – "Howlin' For Hubert: Jazz Foundation
of America Benefit Concert"**
24 Feb 12: Apollo Theater, West 125th Street, New York City, New York
(United States)

Six-String Stories features nearly 300 pieces from Eric Clapton's collection, which were sold across the 1999 – 2011 Crossroads auctions and are brought together here for the very first time.

**Eric Clapton's Guitars
In Aid of the Crossroads Centre**
24 June 99: Christie's, New York

**Crossroads Guitar Auction
Eric Clapton and Friends for the Crossroads Centre**
24 June 04: Christie's, New York

**The Eric Clapton Sale of Guitars and Amps
In Aid of the Crossroads Centre**
9 Mar 11: Bonhams, New York

Six-String Stories presents a 'family tree', making connections between Clapton's instruments and amps, and places them in the chronology of his career within this 50-year gigography.

Since 1998, Crossroads Centre has aimed to provide an effective, supportive and premier treatment experience for those suffering with, and affected by, addiction. Through the use of evidence-based interventions, including multifaceted assessment and individualised treatment planning, we address the psychological, physical and spiritual aspects of recovery. Our multidisciplinary treatment team includes an American Board-certified addiction psychiatrist; Masters level and certified addiction counsellors; a nutritionist; experienced physicians and registered nurses. Members of the treatment team work collaboratively to individualise programme services to meet the needs of each client.

Residential care may be the initial phase of our relationship with clients and families, but our support does not end there. We provide a full continuum of care, which can also include our transitional living and case management services at The Sanctuary in Delray Beach, Florida. Our main objective is to work with clients to develop a successful plan that will help them sustain their recovery well into the future.

Crossroads Centre offers a tranquil, private treatment environment in a unique setting on the southern shores of Antigua. The beautiful Caribbean island, with its year-round sunshine, cool tropical breezes and crystal blue waters, is the perfect place for individuals and families to begin the healing process, away from the distractions of everyday life. While Antigua offers a remote location, it is still easily reachable with several non-stop flights from major cities. Moderately priced, Crossroads Centre is a private, non-profit facility that is affordable as well as accessible. Proceeds from fundraising efforts, such as Eric Clapton's *Six-String Stories*, go directly towards client scholarships for those who are otherwise unable to afford treatment.

Central to our philosophy is the belief that people and families have the capacity to achieve recovery and an improvement in their quality of life. We continue to hold steadfastly to the belief that recovery is not only possible – it is forever life-changing.

'I am happy to report that I'm celebrating eight years of continuous sobriety. Upon reflecting on the journey so far, the greatest thing that has come from my recovery is the ability to maintain a peaceful, loving attitude and remain aware of the feelings of others. This is a significant change in my outlook on life. Instead of living in a fearful, unhappy and secretive way, I am comfortable in my life and know that if I keep things simple and honest then there is true freedom. It is easy to face the things that life offers from day-to-day, without the desire to dismiss what emerges. Thank you all at Crossroads, for introducing me to the first steps of recovery. I truly put my faith in you from the moment Ashley, the nurse, checked me in. When I arrived I knew I was safe and you helped sort out the confusion and pain brought on by my disease.' Jeffrey, 2011.

Genesis Publishers, Nicholas Roylance and Catherine Roylance, join Eric Clapton at the opening of the Brian Roylance Renewal Centre Crossroads, Antigua February 2008

BRIAN ROYLANCE
RENEWAL CENTRE

The publishers would like to thank everyone for their hard work and dedication to this book.

Firstly to Bonhams and Christie's, for kindly allowing us to use the lot photographs and information from the three Crossroads Guitar auctions.

Chris Gill for providing the background text to each lot featured in the book and Linda Wnek for Eric Clapton's touring history.

We are grateful to the following individuals for their important contribution:

Dick Boak and all at Martin Guitar Company; Nigel Carroll; Kristan Crossley, Peter Standish and all at Warner Music Group; Michael Doyle and all at Guitar Center Inc; Michael Eaton; Tony Edser and all at Where's Eric; Jasen Emmons and all at MoPOP, Seattle, WA; Liz Hale; Lisa S. Johnson; Kim Martin; Cecil Offley; Marc Roberty; Saiichi Sugiyama; Dominique Tarlé; Brad Iolinski; Wallace & Hodgson; Scooter Weintraub; Larry Yelen.

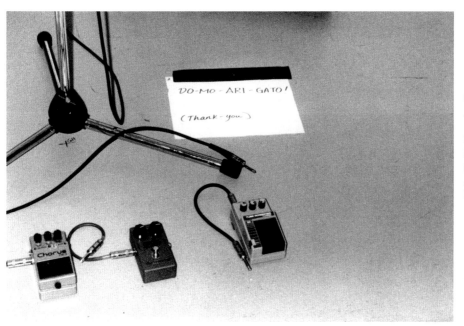

We would also like to thank the Genesis *Six-String Stories* team:

Uchenna Achebe, Francesca Balgobind, Katy Baker, Rona Elliot, Bruce Hopkins, Megan Lily Large, Sally Millard, Nicky Page, Alexandra Rigby-Wild, Marguerite Rooke, Rosie Strandberg and James Tribe.

And finally, to Eric Clapton for making this book possible.

All reasonable effort has been made to identify and contact the copyright holders of the images and artwork printed in this publication. Any omissions are inadvertent.

Lot images from the 1999 and 2004 auctions are Copyright © Christie's Images 1999/2004, reproduced by kind permission of Christie's.

Lot images from the 2011 auctions are Copyright © Bonhams, reproduced by kind permission of Bonhams.

Photographs of 'Fender "Blackie" Stratocaster' (Pages 122-131) and '1964 Gibson ES-335TDC' (Pages 26-37) are courtesy of Guitar Center Inc, California, USA.

Photographs of 'Brownie' (Pages 72-80) are courtesy of EMP Museum, Seattle, WA.

Black and white guitar imagery courtesy of Lisa S. Johnson. Lisa has been photographing significant guitars since 1996. In 1999, working with Virginia Lohle of the Star File Photo Agency, she was inspired to photograph the first collection of Eric's guitars being auctioned by Christie's in New York, proceeds from which benefited the Crossroads Centre. Her work may be seen at www.108rockstarguitars.com.

Photographers
Copyright © Walt Disney Television / ABC Photo Archives / Getty Images
Page 114
Copyright © Alex Agor / Camera Press
Page 138
Copyright © Gene Ambo / Retna Ltd / Corbis Images
Page 326
Copyright © Alexis Andrews
Page 205
Copyright © Alpha Press
Pages 269, 275
Copyright © Jørgen Angel
Page 82
Copyright © Moriyasu Aono
Pages 233, 249, 251, 261
Copyright © David Appleby
Page 179
Copyright © Bill Armstrong / Cache Agency
Page 53
Copyright © Martyn Atkins
Page 20
Copyright © David Bailey / Rolling Stone Magazine
Page 193
Copyright © Sir Peter Blake
Pages 218, 223
Copyright © Adrian Boot / Urban Image
Page 139
Copyright © Barry Brecheisen / Wire Image / Getty Images
Page 326 (x2)
Copyright © Linda Chapman
Page 185
Copyright © George Chin
Page 333
Copyright © Timothy Clary / AFP / Getty Images
Page 326
Copyright © Danny Clinch
Pages 334-335
Copyright © Paul Cox
Pages 235, 281, 285
Copyright © Andre Csillag / Rex Features
Page 162
Copyright © Dan Cuny
Pages 97, 120
Copyright © Dalle
Pages 82, 121 (x3), 180, 191, 197, 232, 307, 326
Copyright © Jeff Daly / PictureGroup / EMPICS Entertainment
Page 180 (x2)
Copyright © Delilah Films, Inc
Page 12
Copyright © Carl Dunn
Page 113
Copyright © Jack English
Pages 54, 96, 271
Copyright © Barry Feinstein Photography Inc.
Pages 80, 82
Copyright © Karl Ferris
Page 61
Copyright © Barry Fisch
Page 167
Copyright © Jeremy Fletcher / Redferns / Getty Images
Page 43
Copyright © Betsy Fowler
Page 53
Copyright © Akihiko Fukui
Page 143
Copyright © Jill Furmanovsky
Pages 39, 169, 316, 319 (x2), 321, 322-323

Copyright © 1974 David Gahr / Getty Images
Page 116
Copyright © Claude Gassian
Page 141
Copyright © Rob Grabowski / Retna Ltd / Corbis Images
Page 326
Copyright © Bob Gruen
Page 153
Copyright © Koh Hasebe
Page 145
Copyright © Richard Haughton
Page 189
Copyright © Dezo Hoffmann / Rex Features
Page 51
Copyright © Zak Hussein / PA Archive / Press Association Images
Page 180
Copyright © Mick Hutson / Redferns / Getty Images
Page 119
Copyright © Lisa S. Johnson
Pages 11, 49, 51, 60, 64, 100, 102 (x3), 103, 104, 110, 136, 142, 144, 154, 155, 158, 159, 162, 164, 165, 172, 178, 192, 199, 204, 210 (x2), 212, 213, 217, 220, 239, 244, 247, 248, 251, 254, 256, 262, 264, 276, 277, 300, 302
Copyright © Guido Karp
Page 271
Copyright © Tasos Katopodis / Stringer / 2007 Getty Images
Page 326 (x3)
Copyright © Robert Knight Archive / Redferns / Getty Images
Pages 83, 326
Copyright © Peter Kramer / Getty Images
Page 329
Copyright © Brad LeMee
Pages 65, 308
Copyright © Robert Matheu
Page 32
Copyright © Kevin Mazur
Page 33
Copyright © Kevin Mazur / Wire Image / Getty Images
Page 326
Copyright © Tom McGuinness
Page 24
Copyright © Tom McPhillips / Atomic Design, Inc
Page 327
Copyright © Bob Minkin / Cache Agency
Pages 182-183
Copyright © Mirrorpix
Page 155
Copyright © Kimiko Mitsui
Page 220
Copyright © Toru Moriyama
Page 301
Copyright © Music Man / Ernie Ball
Page 147
Copyright © Paul Natkin
Pages 160, 180 (x2)
Copyright © NBCU Photo Bank NBCUniversal / Getty Images
Page 253
Copyright © Terry O'Neill
Pages 68, 214, 230, 336
Copyright © Pace / Stringer / Getty Images
Page 28
Copyright © Don Paulsen / Reprise Records
Page 279

Copyright © Roger Pearce
Page 11
Copyright © John Peck
Pages 236, 237
Copyright © Jan Persson
Pages 55, 59, 67, 120, 121
Copyright © Barry Plummer
Pages 121, 148, 180
Copyright © Neal Preston
Pages 81, 83, 118, 120, 129, 187
Copyright © Chuck Pulin
Pages 165, 246, 279
Copyright © Michael Putland / Getty Images
Page 136
Copyright © Rancurl / Dalle
Page 63
Copyright © Brian Rasic / Rex Features
Pages 17, 211
Copyright © Reprise / Duck Records
Page 174
Copyright © Marc Roberty Collection
Page 50
Copyright © Amalie R Rothschild
Pages 74, 82-83
Copyright © Brian Roylance / Genesis Publications Ltd
Pages 2, 181, 192, 195, 205, 218, 219, 221, 223, 225, 226-227, 229, 295, 300
Copyright © Mike Sawin
Pages 205, 224
Copyright © Ken Settle
Page 180
Copyright © Gene Shaw
Page 305
Copyright © Lord Snowdon / Camera Press London
Page 85
Copyright © St. Blues Guitar Workshop, Memphis
Page 161
Copyright © Koo Stark / Camera Press London
Page 101
Copyright © Peter Still / Redferns / Getty Images
Page 152, 201
Copyright © Saiichi Sugiyama / Reprise Records
Pages 284, 311
Copyright © Dominique Tarlé
Page 15, 45, 62
Copyright © Minoru Tsubota
Page 248
Copyright © Chris Walter / Photofeatures
Page 124
Copyright © Warner Music Group
Page 245
Copyright © Barrie Wentzell
Pages 29, 58, 82 (x3), 83, 89, 93, 111, 121 (x3), 125, 135
Copyright © Martina Weselowski
Page 325
Copyright © Bob Whitaker
Page 31
Copyright © Val Wilmer / Cache Agency
Page 47
Copyright © Shinichiro Yoshino
Pages 207, 324
Copyright © Richard Young
Pages 291, 293, 294
Copyright © Michael Zagaris
Pages 120 (x4), 121, 126, 127, 132, 177
Copyright © Neil Zlozower
Pages 106, 259

Our new text from Eric Clapton is accompanied by quotes from
the following sources:

Altham, K. 'Eric Clapton: Another Crossroad', *Fusion* magazine (1970)
Charone, B. 'Eric Clapton: Any Objections?', *Creem* magazine (1977)
Charone, B. 'Eric Clapton: Farther On Up The Road', *Sounds* magazine (1976)
Charone, B. 'Eric Clapton: Please Take This Badge Off Of Me', *Crawdaddy!* magazine (1975)
Clapton, E. 'Eric Clapton Online Chat', *AOL* (2000)
Clapton, E. *Eric Clapton: The Autobiography*, Random House Group Ltd (2007)
Clapton, E. 'Introduction To The Stratocaster Chronicles' in: Wheeler, T.
The Stratocaster Chronicles (2004)
Clapton, E. *Journeyman* tour programme (1990)
Colletti, A. 'Amazing Grace', *Guitar World* magazine (1993)
Forte, D. 'Eric Clapton & J.J. Cale', *Vintage Guitar* magazine (2010)
Forte, D. 'The Interview – Eric Clapton', *Guitar Player* magazine (1986)
Forte, D. 'Tribute To Slowhand', *Guitar World* magazine (1989)
Forte, D. 'Out From Behind The Sun', *Guitar Player* magazine (1985)
Fox, D. 'Eric Clapton – Right Here, Right Now', *Guitar Player* magazine (2001)
Harrison, O. and Roylance, B. *Concert For George*, Genesis Publications Ltd (2004)
Grüner, G. 'Interview With Eric Clapton', *Stern* magazine (1998)
Guitar Center 'Eric Clapton', *Guitar Center* (2010)
Guitar Player magazine (1976)
Hail! Hail! Rock 'N' Roll! [Film], Directed by Taylor Hackford, Delilah Films (1986)
Henke, J. 'Eric Clapton: The Rolling Stone Interview', *Rolling Stone* magazine (1991)
Hrano, M. 'Reptile Interview', *Reptile* tour programme (2000)
Hutchinson, J. 'Eric Clapton: Farther Up The Road', *Musician* magazine (1982)
Keane, K. and Wallace, C. 'An Interview With Eric Clapton', *Christie's Crossroads Guitar Auction* catalogue (2004)
King, L. 'Interview With Eric Clapton', *Larry King Live* [TV], CNN (2007)
Kot, G. 'Exclusive: Eric Clapton Talks About His Passion For Chicago And Its Guitarists',
Chicago Tribune (2007)
Marten, N. *Guitarist* magazine (1987)
Marten, N. 'Would You Buy A Used Guitar From This Man?', *Guitarist* magazine (1999)
Mead, D. 'Eric Clapton: Time Pieces', *Guitar World* magazine (1994)
Melody Maker magazine (1963)
Nightingale, A. 'Conversation With Eric Clapton', *Eric Clapton And His Band And
Ronnie Lane's Slim Chance* tour programme (1976)
NPR 'Eric Clapton Looks Back At His Blues Roots', *NPR Music* (2007)
Pearce, R. 'ERIC CLAPTON: In The Beginning', *British Blues Review* (1988)
Pidgeon, J. *Eric Clapton*, Panther (1994)
Roberty, M. *Eric Clapton In His Own Words*, Omnibus Press (1993)
Roberty, M. *Eric Clapton – The New Visual Documentary* (1983)
Rolling Stone magazine (1968)
Sandall, R. 'Eric Clapton: The Solo Artist', *Q* magazine (1990)
Sharken, L. 'Eric Clapton: A Return To The Crossroads', *Vintage Guitar* magazine (2005)
Stuckey, F. *Guitar Player* magazine (1970)
Stuckey, F. *Guitar Player* magazine (1990)
Tolinski, B. and Steinblatt, H. 'From The Archive: Eric Clapton Discusses Songwriting And
The *Pilgrim* Album', *Guitar World* magazine (1998)
Uncut magazine (2004)
Warner Bros 'Clapton Discusses The Making Of His New Album *From The Cradle*' (1995)
Watson, T. 'Eric Clapton Turns 59', *Strat Collector* (2004)
Welch, C. 'Eric Clapton At The China Garden', *Melody Maker* magazine (1974)
Welch, C. 'Eric Clapton: Portrait Of The Artist As A Working Man', *Melody Maker*
magazine (1978)
Where's Eric!
Young Guitar magazine (1988)

Text from other contributors came from the following:
'Ivan The Terrible' *Guitar Player* magazine (1970)
'Claptones – The Tools Of A Journeyman's Trade', *Guitar World* magazine (1998)
Kay, M. 'The Zemaitis Touch – Conversations With A Very Colourful Guitar Maker',
Guitar World magazine (1982)
Percival, E. 'Interview With Tony Zemaitis', *International Musician* (1975)

Any omissions are inadvertent.